To Joanna & Daniel Rose
with great respect

From a proud father-in-Law
Abe Gellert
10/26/87

Feminine and Opposition Journalism in Old Regime France

Feminine and Opposition Journalism in Old Regime France

Le Journal des Dames

Nina Rattner Gelbart

UNIVERSITY OF CALIFORNIA PRESS

Berkeley   *Los Angeles*   *London*

University of California Press
Berkeley and Los Angeles, California

University of California Press, Ltd.
London, England

Library of Congress Cataloging-in-Publication Data

Gelbart, Nina Rattner.
Feminine and opposition journalism in old regime France.

Bibliography: p.
Includes index.
1. Journal des dames (Paris, France). 2. Women's periodicals, French—
History—18th century. 3. Press—France—History—
18th century. 4. Women—France—Social conditions. I. Title.
PN5189.P3J68 1987   074 86-7025
ISBN 0-520-05761-9 (alk. paper)

Printed in the United States of America
1 2 3 4 5 6 7 8 9

For Bill

Le succès du *Journal des Dames* nous fait triompher de nos *frivolites* qui avaient regardé ce périodique comme un petit ouvrage qui renfermerait seulement quelques bagatelles propres à les aider à tuer le temps. . . . Eh! c'est précisément ce que je veux éviter. . . . Laissez-nous écrire d'une manière qui soit digne de notre sexe; je l'aime, je suis jalouse d'en soutenir l'honneur et les droits. . . .

J'attends cette révolution avec impatience. Je m'efforcerai d'être une des premières à l'exciter.

> Mme de Beaumer,
> *Journal des Dames*, octobre 1761, mars 1762

La discussion des auteurs dramatiques contre les comédiens excite une fermentation générale.

La license d'écrire augmente journellement et l'on abuse de la douceur du nouveau gouvernement à tel point qu'il sera peut-être forcé d'employer toute l'inquisition de la fin du règne de Louis XV.

> *Mémoires secrets,* 19 avril 1775, 30 juillet 1776

Le public est malin. Il aime les méchancetés, mais il veut qu'on l'instruise.

> *Correspondance secrète,* 4 mai 1778

Un peuple qui veut s'instruire ne se contente pas de *La Gazette de France*.

> Pierre Manuel,
> *La Police de Paris dévoilée,* L'An II (1793)

Contents

Preface

When I first thumbed through the pages of the *Journal des Dames* many years ago, I realized that therein lay a tale. Its early issues were platitudinous and tame, but even though allegories, verses, and fluffy *pièces fugitives* continued to appear in later issues, the tone and content of the articles fluctuated wildly. Some were punctuated with bursts of ardent feminist rhetoric, others moved beyond the subject of womens' subordination to a more general defense of groups oppressed by the regime—Protestants, Freemasons, citizens desiring free public education, playwrights fighting for freedom of expression, overtaxed and hungry peasants. Messages were at times elliptical, communicated by implication and allusion. But there were also some frontal attacks on such hallowed institutions as the Académie française, the Comédie-Française, and official, state-protected newspapers like the government's *Gazette de France*. I had thought this kind of criticism was confined to furtively exchanged clandestine newsletters. Here, however, was a paper that dared to be bold and nevertheless passed through the channels of censorship. That a legitimate periodical published in Paris could voice opposition or *frondeur* sentiment intrigued me. And that such lively protest against a "despotic" government was destined for an audience of female readers I found astonishing. I realized that between the conservative, royally privileged official papers and the forbidden, underground *chroniques scandaleuses* lay a middle category of tolerated, permitted journalism that deserved a closer look.

Life had not been easy for the *Journal des Dames,* and the copy bore the marks of struggle. Some title pages were handsomely decorated about the border and printed on fine Dutch paper; others were brittle, dark, smudged, filled with typographical errors. Whole issues of the paper were missing, the narratives breaking off suddenly, leaving unfinished stories, reviews, serialized plays and articles meant to be continued the following month. Early issues sported colorful fictitious imprints, like the "Vallons de Tivoli"; others sold openly at addresses in Paris, sometimes from reputable *libraires*, but sometimes from former *colporteurs* "under the cloak" and occasionally from makeshift offices in the homes of the editors themselves. There were numerous *avis* to the readers apologizing for delays and begging their indulgence while the editors worked out problems with printers, censors, collaborators, or rival papers. The occasional publicity for goods and services ranged from ads for luxurious elixirs to notices about humble artisans. There was some consumer feedback in the form of letters to the editor, not a single fashion illustration, but a beautiful engraving of Benjamin Franklin's glass harmonica. Many issues had nothing to do with women and appeared to be using the feminine title as a smokescreen, the editors hoping perhaps to avoid serious scrutiny by the censors. These frequent and extreme alterations in mood, message, and even material, coupled with the mysterious lacunae in the twenty-year span of the collection, convinced me that a curious drama had taken place behind the scenes of the *Journal des Dames*. Who were its editors? What censors had permitted it, and to what strategies of propitiation had they responded? For what audience was this paper really intended?

To reconstruct its story, to find the pieces of the puzzle that would allow me to tie together the ideas in the paper with the people who thought, printed, censored, marketed, and read them, I had to venture beyond the journal's neatly bound volumes at the Bibliothèque de l'Arsenal. Only in musty archives would the tumultuous world of Old Regime journalism come to life, enabling me to weave the paper's insides and outsides into a coherent picture. Because the copy itself raised so many questions, I embarked on my adventure of "reading between the lines."

Parish records furnished the *états civils*—birth, marriage, and death information—on some of the more obscure editors. Correspondence between the journalists and their censors, the booktrade and police directors, their printers, and the syndics of the *librairie* were found in the manuscripts department of the Bibliothèque Nationale. Several of the *Journal des Dames*'s editors had brushes with the law, and information on them turned up in the Archives de la Bastille, housed at the Bibliothèque de l'Arsenal. Documents from the Musée Postal yielded information about problems with the paper's international distribution at times when editors neglected to provide sufficient funds, when foreign recipients refused to pay charges, or when war and shifting political allegiances made mailing to certain areas unwise. The archives of the Comédie-Française had rich dossiers on several of the journalists who also tried their hand at dramatic writing. Various publishing arrangements and some wonderful journalistic gossip in unpublished *nouvelles à la main* were found in cartons at the Bibliothèque Mazarine and at the Bibliothèque Historique de la Ville de Paris. Here too were marvelous maps of eighteenth-century Paris, which allowed me to conjure up mental pictures of streets and neighborhoods long gone, corners where my editors met their printers, gardens and lemonade stands where they gossiped and gathered news, markets where they shopped, alleys and private enclaves where they found lodgings or sought asylum.

The Archives de la Seine had bankruptcy records for some of the journal's publishers and the sketch of a testament for one of the editors, the full text of which has disappeared. Finally, the Archives Nationales yielded gold mines after weeks of digging: raids and seizures of the *Journal des Dames*'s offices orchestrated by the police, fat folders of *scellés* placed by police commissioners on the possessions of some of its editors and publishers at the time of their insolvency or death, and the private archives of several of the families involved. The Minutier Central, that part of the Archives Nationales that stores notarial documents, yielded transactions of meetings with angry subscribers and creditors, business contracts between the journal's various editors that helped assess the cost of such an enterprise, leases for offices and storerooms, wills, "successions," and "inventories after death" for several of the protagonists in the story. All of these documents provided invaluable information about their socioeconomic situations, business associates, family connections, lodgings, furnishings, wardrobes, life-styles (and death-styles!), and sometimes even the holdings of their personal libraries. This archival sleuthing proved to be the most enjoyable detective work I have ever done.

But it was more than fun. The fuller the picture became, the

more I realized that the *Journal des Dames*'s story had general value
as a case study of the press in the Old Regime. I had been attracted
to the paper initially by its feminine title, and three of its nine
successive editors did indeed turn out to be female. This unique
aspect of the paper—female journalists were extremely rare in the
eighteenth century—provided an extra bonus, a chance to examine the experiences of some unusually courageous women tackling
a career notoriously perilous even for men. But the more numerous male editors who worked on the *Journal des Dames* wrote also
for other periodicals. This paper seemed to have overlapping, reciprocal arrangements with a network of about ten others in Paris,
with provincial journals in Lyons and Bordeaux, and with French
papers published in London, The Hague, and Neuchâtel as well.
Its fate and theirs were inextricably intertwined. And not only
were there editorial connections. The teams of censors, publishers, ministers, gentlemen of the king's bedchamber, booktrade inspectors, and police spies involved with the *Journal des Dames* were
simultaneously supervising and harassing other journals. The
deeper I dug, the more frequently familiar names and patterns
resurfaced.

Here, then, was a paper both special and representative. Its
feminine theme obliged its editors to entertain views on "le beau
sexe" and to confront the question of what a widening reading
public would want. The women editors especially welcomed this
task, and here the *Journal des Dames* marks a particular *prise de
conscience* in the development of feminism during the eighteenth
century, shedding new light on women as writers, as subject matter, as audience. But the male editors also used the paper to prop-
agate their views on the greatness of Shakespeare and all things
English, the "despotism" of the Comédie-Française, the importance of provincial parlements, the grain famine and the floundering economy, the need to rekindle by reformed education an ethic
of public service and civic duty, the rights of journalists and playwrights to freedom of expression. At first they cloaked these serious articles in flowery tributes to the fair sex, but then little by
little they stopped bothering. The female journalists, who had
deliberately passed on their paper to men working for widespread
social and political change, urged them to treat such serious matters. Thus this journal grew to resemble many other increasingly
outspoken periodicals. A disapproving conservative editor, La

Harpe, acknowledged that it had come to typify these contentious papers by referring to it as *Le Journal "appelé" des Dames,* for he viewed it as unique in name only. This group of papers, which I have called the opposition or *frondeur* press, seemed to me worth examining in more detail, for it echoed the radical press of the Fronde and prefigured that of the Revolution.

There are of course many ways to present material of this kind. In offering the *Journal des Dames* as a case study and narrating its story episodically, I have departed from recent trends in eighteenth-century press history. Teams of French scholars in Paris, Strasbourg, Lyons, and Grenoble have put most of their efforts into thematic or quantitative studies. Some have enlisted the aid of the computer to examine themes in the press during certain years—1734, 1768, 1778. A group directed by Pierre Rétat has analyzed how a particular event, Damiens's attempt to assassinate Louis XV, was reported by different kinds of periodicals. Another approach, under the direction of Jean Sgard, has been the compilation of short biographical notices, published in the *Dictionnaire des journalistes* and its *suppléments* (four to date). A few monographs have appeared on important individual publishers and journalists, and the provincial press has received some attention. A book by Evelyne Sullerot, some articles, and an unpublished thesis have been devoted to surveying the feminine press, all papers "par ou pour les femmes." American scholars have studied various segments of the press, Robert Darnton and Robert S. Tate the underground news-sheets, Jack R. Censer, Jeremy D. Popkin, and Raymond F. Birn the extraterritorial French-language journals of Avignon, Leyden, and Bouillon. To my knowledge there are only a few books devoted to particular periodicals, and not one of them tells the complete story of a tacitly permitted paper published in Paris.

The *Journal des Dames,* unprotected by a royal privilege, represents a hitherto unexamined category of journalism, the tolerated paper appealing to an audience of marginal social status. The paper was merely permitted, and because permissions could be revoked, it was a vulnerable enterprise propelled and shaped by events, gaining and losing momentum at different historical junctures. To have dealt separately with its themes, its publishers, its audience, and the politics of its community of censors would have made incomprehensible its life rhythm and the ways in which it was altered, to use Norman Hampson's phrase, by both will and circumstance. I have therefore told its story chronologically and tried to situate the *Journal des Dames* within a broadening circle of contexts. Its content must first be linked with its material circumstances, its copy understood in relation to certain events taking place in its most immediate surroundings, the world of the press. It was affected, for example, by the birth, cost, and death of competitive journals, by the changeover from royalist to pro-parlement police censors, by the new booktrade laws of 1777, and by the advent of the first daily paper, the *Journal de Paris,* which sent shock waves—many of them fatal—through the whole network of existing weekly and monthly periodicals.

But to be fully appreciated, this picture must itself be seen against the political events taking place in the background, events indicative of the tensions and final crisis of the old order. A press so tied to the government was necessarily fragile. So, for example, we can only understand the conservative obsequiousness of the *Journal des Dames*'s first editor in connection with France's paranoia over Damiens's attempt on the life of Louis XV and her humiliating losses in the Seven Years' War. Gradually, after the Peace of Paris in 1763, the paper grew bolder. By the mid 1760s it was openly criticizing the elitist Académie française. Its suppression between 1769 and 1774—and the disappearance of many other journals as well—can be explained to a large extent by the repressiveness of Chancellor Maupeou's "triumvirate" for the world of letters. Only if we feel the exhilaration of 1774 that greeted the new young king, Louis XVI, his appointment of a reforming ministry, his recall of the exiled parlements, and the high level of tolerance for *frondeur* thought in certain aristocratic circles, can we understand why Louis-Sébastien Mercier, author of several proscribed books, became editor of the *Journal des Dames* in 1775 and used it to fight for press freedom. Within a few years, however, the liberal ministers were out, as were many permissive censors, and France toughened up for another war with England. Only if we consider her fear over this new confrontation in 1778 can we see why the *Journal des Dames* and its numerous associated papers were purged. And only when we realize that this new backlash of repression followed a period of relative leniency can we fully understand the rage and indignation of the dispossessed journalists, who gave up on legitimate press channels, fled France, scattered throughout England, Switzerland, and Holland, and churned out seditious libels from the diaspora.

A fascinating cast of characters worked for and against the *Journal des Dames.* Most of all I enjoyed getting to know them and the milieu in which they operated, a milieu that combined idealism and cynicism, public spirit and self-interest. Journalism was no career for the lily-livered. The paper cost some of its editors their health and reputation; it cost two of them their lives, if we are to believe contemporary accounts of how depression over journalistic failures could lead rapidly to death. Other editors, toughened by the experience, went on to challenge authority in new ways. Their original motivations for undertaking journalism were as varied as their personalities; some wished to print their own poems rejected elsewhere, some to make war, some to make peace, some (incredibly!) to make money, but most ended up pleading causes and trying to sway public opinion. The female editors had different motives still; for them the paper was an end in itself. Quite apart from what they wrote in it, the very act of taking on a career as a journalist was a drastic, unorthodox social statement that broke all the rules. But whatever their sex, the *frondeur* editors had panache: Mme de Beaumer racing around Europe in a worn black habit trying to beat swords into plowshares; Mercier fist-fighting in the lobby of the Comédie-Française in defense of his rights, then standing up "like a Roman" to the police chief; Dorat, in debt a staggering 60,000 livres over the paper, dying dolled up in wig and lace in the multiple arms of his totally devoted mistresses, refusing the sacraments.

The *Journal des Dames,* now forgotten, aroused strong feelings in its day. This book tries to show why it mattered.

Throughout my work I have been helped and encouraged by many people. Keith Michael Baker has been a steady source of guidance. Jack R. Censer, Raymond F. Birn, Joseph Klaits, Jeremy D. Popkin, Roger Hahn, Darline Gay Levy, Jonathan Dewald, Carolyn Merchant, Margaret C. Jacob, and Robert Darnton have

allowed me to bend their ears, listened attentively, offered suggestions on all or parts of the manuscript, and of course inspired me
through their own scholarly production. A full-year fellowship
from the National Endowment for the Humanities was a welcome
vote of confidence, allowing me to spend 1982–83 in Paris pursuing my research. While in France, I enjoyed talks with Daniel
Roche, Jean Sgard, Anne-Marie Chouillet, and a group of press
historians nicknamed the "Dominicaux." I was also helped by numerous librarians and archivists who showed warm and genuine
interest in this project, and by the friendship and generous table
of Ida and Sydney Leach. Back in California, deans James England
and David Danelski of Occidental College were generous with
both moral and financial support. A fellow historian, Candy
Waltz, looked over the entire book with a keen critical eye. Debo-
rah Holland Penley did a fine job of preparing the manuscript. My
editors at the University of California Press, Sheila Levine, Rose
Vekony, and Betsey Scheiner, gave useful suggestions and unfailing encouragement. Lieselotte Hofmann prepared the index. To
all of them I am grateful. For any infelicities remaining, I alone
am accountable.

My greatest source of strength has been my family—my supportive parents and parents-in-law; my son Matthew and daughter Eva, who tolerated my distracted state for years, only occasionally (and gently) teasing me about my egg that never seemed
to hatch; and my husband, Bill, who took over all duties when I
time-traveled backward through obscure documents into another
century. To him, for everything, I dedicate this book.

Introduction

JOURNALISM, FEMINISM, AND THE *FRONDEUR*
TRADITION

The *Journal des Dames,* a permitted monthly periodical, had deceptively innocuous beginnings. Conceived in 1759 by its male founder as a "rien délicieux" to amuse society ladies at their toilette, it did not remain a trivial bagatelle for long. Its title soon attracted maverick editors of marginal social status. It was taken over first by aggressively feminist women and then by insubordinate male *frondeurs* with bourgeois and even popular sympathies, the best known of whom was Louis-Sébastien Mercier. In their hands the paper became increasingly oppositional. Before the government purged and finally snuffed out the *Journal des Dames,* it had passed through the hands of nine persevering editors, six men and three women. It had been delayed, interrupted, doctored by the royal censors ("denatured," as the editors said), sued by another paper—the state-approved *Mercure de France*—confiscated, counterfeited, plagiarized, trailed, raided, seized, and suspended twice, but it repeatedly bounced back and only succumbed with its final suppression in 1778. Its life spanned, and was affected by, a number of acute pre-Revolutionary crises in religion and politics. Fifteen *libraires*, ten royal censors, and five police and booktrade directors were also involved working for and

Throughout this book I have intentionally referred to the female editors as "Mme" and to the male editors by family name only, because the women were determined to call attention to their sex and to the uniqueness of their role as *éditrices*.

1

against the paper during its stormy twenty years. Both its longevity and the drama of its story make it a rich laboratory specimen for studying the styles, purposes, and perils of Old Regime journalism. The vicissitudes of this paper also shed light on the kinds of tensions that riddled society and culture in late eighteenth-century France, the limits erratically imposed upon the expression of those tensions as the regime moved toward disintegration, and the ensuing resentment that ultimately contributed to the formation of a revolutionary mentality.[1]

The *Journal des Dames* was the first sustained effort to produce a French newspaper expressly for women. There had been a number of earlier attempts by journalists to reach this new audience, but they terminated after only a few issues. Although we can guess what direction some of them may have taken, it is difficult to conclude anything certain from such ephemeral publications.[2] The *Journal des Dames,* on the other hand, lasted two decades, a more than respectable lifetime for a tolerated paper in the Old Regime. Nevertheless, as it circulated for most of its years without the protection of a royal privilege, its existence was tumultuous, marked by numerous alterations of design and purpose and by constant turnover in editors and fare. This suggests that the paper was the locus of particular uneasiness on the part of its censors, its producers, and perhaps even its consumers once it ventured beyond its original docile and frivolous posture. In England the development of a press for women had progressed quite smoothly, and there were even several papers directed toward the more popular classes. The same was true in Germany, where female journalists abounded and feminist claims were voiced in numerous papers throughout the century.[3] The *Journal des Dames,* on the

1   The few other books on particular papers in the Old Regime concern different press categories and employ different approaches. Couperus, *Périodique français en Hollande,* deals with a short-lived Dutch paper operating outside French censorship. Feyel, *La Gazette à travers ses réimpressions,* and Moureau, *Mercure galant,* both deal with official, privileged, state-approved periodicals whose job it was to bolster authority or, as Moureau says, "to lend coherence and truth to royal ambition" ("Avant propos").

2   For two general surveys of periodicals by and for women, see Rimbault, "Presse féminine: Production," and Van Dijk, "Femmes et journaux." Both of these articles provide charts and lists enumerating even the ephemeral publications in this genre.

3   For comparative comments on the press in different European countries, see Van Dijk, "Femmes et journaux," 165, 177; Rimbault, "Presse féminine: Pro-

other hand, experienced every conceivable humiliation. Both the paper's scenario of disasters and its resilience attracted the attention of contemporaries, who marveled each time "the corpse stirred with new life" and "that it could be repeatedly reanimated after so many plummeting falls each of which seemed fatal."[4]

Like the proverbial cat, the *Journal des Dames* had nine lives, nine successive male and female editors drawn to its title for different reasons, who relaunched the enterprise after each catastrophe. The steady stream of editors, whose journalistic careers we will examine, testifies to the continuing allure and tenacity of their project. But the numerous attempts to dissolve or deactivate the paper, some by competitive journals and others by censors and police, reflect the discomfort of rival editors and government authorities over the exploitation of a female audience, a newly emerging group of impressionable readers neither well defined nor understood nor trusted, yet who were being offered increasingly contentious food for thought. Here was a paper that challenged entrenched institutions—the academies, the stage, the official state-protected press—in less and less tolerable ways, stretching acceptable protest to its very limit. The story of the *Journal des Dames* thus reveals much about feminist and antifeminist states of mind in France under the Old Regime and, more generally, about the tension between integrative and subversive modes of discourse concerning groups of marginal social and cultural status. And the paper's changing contents, strategies, and struggles, which tested the elasticity of French censorship, evince both the hitherto overlooked vitality and perseverance of the press and the complexity of the milieu in which journalists and censors operated under a crumbling monarchy.

The legitimate journalism of the Old Regime has generally been written off by historians as politically uninteresting. It was, after all, subject to rigorous scrutiny by royal censors, and no proper periodical was allowed to be launched without the express permission of the booktrade director, himself a chosen appointee

---

duction," 206–7; Adburgham, *Women in Print;* Botein, Censer, and Ritvo, "Periodical Press"; White, *Women's Magazines;* and Krull, *Das Wirken der Frau.*

4   See, for example, [Bachaumont], *Mémoires secrets* 16:294; 7:159; 10:35. See also *Journal (historique) de Verdun,* février 1774:132; *Avant coureur,* 1761:255; *Observateur littéraire* (1761) ii:354–57.

of the king as were all other royal ministers. Even though the literary underground (whose seditious manuscript news-sheets have been aptly elucidated by Robert Darnton's Grub Street studies) is now recognized to have been a veritable hotbed of pre-Revolutionary radicalism, the legitimate press continues to be dismissed by scholars as devoid of politically significant fare.[5] Darnton himself has never examined aboveboard periodical journalism, convinced that its growth was so "badly stunted." Papers, he argues, were restricted to nonpolitical subjects, could carry no news, and could print nothing offensive to Versailles. Because defamation was in principle rigorously excluded from legal periodicals, it is assumed they could not be responsive to the public appetite for exciting political controversy and therefore remained quite tame organs.[6]

But the journalistic scene of the Old Regime was rather complex, for there were several categories of legitimate journalism. It is essential to distinguish between them, because not all of them remained uncontroversial. Of course it cannot be disputed that some of the periodicals were unfailingly conservative. The official state-supported papers—the *Gazette de France,* the *Mercure de France,* and the *Journal des savants*—had been given exclusive royal privileges when the press originated in the seventeenth century, and they were authorized to cover, respectively, ceremonial events, literature, and scientific matters.[7] Théophraste Renaudot, the founder of the weekly *Gazette*, had been a protégé first of Richelieu, then of Mazarin. During the Fronde, a widespread, tenacious rebellion that despite its frivolous name (derived from a children's game of slingshot) had posed a serious threat to the monarchy from 1648 to 1653, Renaudot strove valiantly to defend absolutism in his paper. The tradition of loyalty and subservience to the king had continued after the Fronde in all three of the official journals and in two other quasi-official ones, the *Mémoires de Trévoux* and *La Clef du cabinet des princes,* which, although they did not appear to be organs of the state, were in fact used for the

---

5 Darnton, *Literary Underground* (especially "High Enlightenment and the Low Life," "Spy in Grub Street," and "Reading, Writing, and Publishing").

6 Ibid., especially 113, 143–44, 176–77, 203–4 on journalism.

7 For a general history of the origins of the French press, see Trénard, "Presse française." See also the classic works by Hatin, *Histoire du journal en France* and *Histoire politique et littéraire.*

Crown's purposes as "permanent auxiliaries" in the propaganda arsenal of the royal ministers.[8] Both court and booktrade kept a close protective eye on these periodicals, which joined the ranks of powerful, entrenched institutions bolstering the regime's authority. The profits from the *Gazette* and *Mercure,* for example, were used as literary pensions to support well-behaved writers, some of whom edited or contributed to these partisan journals and often even doubled as royal censors. This incestuous arrangement controlled the official papers and assured their continuing royalism.

How differently the forbidden and the official press dealt with material can be seen in their reportage of Damiens's attempt to assassinate Louis XV in 1757. We can better understand the two extremes of the journalistic spectrum by considering this illustration. Underground newsletters and the clandestine pro-parlement weekly of the Jansenists called the *Nouvelles ecclésiastiques* analyzed the shocking event in great detail and linked it with all other regicides in history in an attempt to marshal public opinion against authority's abuses. In this rendering, Damiens was no aberrant monster, but a man with legitimate political grievances whose act only illuminated the burning questions agitating the realm and the frustrations deep in the body of society that would surely erupt again and that augured ill for the monarchy. This forbidden discourse, far from dismissing the assassination attempt as an extraordinary accident, linked it with a historic tradition of rebellion against despotism and perpetuated its memory long after the event itself, laying bare the vices of the "gangrenous" administration, treating the incident as a revolutionary confrontation between monarchy and constitution, and dramatizing the need to alleviate the *misère du peuple*. According to this view, the king's oblivion to the needs of his subjects, and the corruption of the royal ministers, were responsible for Damiens's act. Thus the clandestine press, produced beyond the censors' reach but which police made every attempt to confiscate, gave a polemical, political interpretation to

---

8 See Klaits, *Printed Propaganda,* 35–57, 58–85. On the founder of the *Gazette,* see Solomon, *Public Welfare, Science, and Propaganda.* See also "Renaudot" and "Vendosme" in Sgard, *Dictionnaire des journalistes,* 312 and 367. Sgard's forthcoming *Dictionnaire des journaux* will have lengthy articles on the three original privileged papers. See also Birn, "*Journal des savants,*" and the works on the *Gazette* and *Mercure* mentioned in n. 1, above.

the event. From the perspective of the underground, Damiens had simply wished to reach out, to touch, to speak directly with his monarch and remind him of his duty to his people.

The official press, on the other hand, sought to comfort the king and calm the "fermentations" among the people with the reassurance that Damiens was an isolated phenomenon, a deranged, reprehensible subhuman creature. The *Gazette* and the *Mercure* dealt as little and as briefly with the incident as possible. These papers denied that Damiens had any political motives, or even that he had uttered any articulate words. In their coverage the criminal was amputated not only from his own words but from his history, his source. There was complete denial that this event had reasons, causes, links with the past, or implications for the future. It was reduced to the fanatical madness of a marginal, desperate individual. As the king himself commanded, there was to be a "law of silence" in the official press. Since words, in this view, constituted and influenced reality, to suppress discourse was to make the event nonexistent. Silence restored order and public tranquillity; the word was an infraction. The various edicts of silence issued by the king shifted public focus away from himself and onto the troublesome writings instead, divesting him of any responsibility for the general discontent and placing the blame for all agitation squarely on words, on books. Not only had Damiens to be eliminated, but so had language sympathetic to him. The *Gazette* reaffirmed absolutism and rehabilitated the king by euphemistically reporting the anguish of the people over their monarch's misfortune, and their unanimous cry of love, good wishes, and prosperity for the royal family. The *Mercure* expelled Damiens from history, turning his act into nothingness by avoiding its mention. This denial, this attempt to enforce national amnesia, hardly a solution to conflict, was typical of the official press. The Damiens episode was simply to be obliterated from memory.[9]

But between the *Gazette* on the one hand and the subversive underground news-sheets on the other, there flourished another category of periodical, which has never been systematically examined and to which the *Journal des Dames* belonged. This com-

9   See the excellent work on this subject by a team of researchers under the direction of Rétat, *L'Attentat de Damiens,* especially 30, 133, 155–95, 222–47, 337–47. This is probably the most interesting French comparative study on the press to date.

prised the numerous tolerated papers circulating with only tacit permission and whose status was as ambiguous as their lives were precarious. Such alternative papers had come into existence and been allowed to continue in print because the court had lost or abdicated control of France at several historic junctures. During such periods of disorder and decentralization, the periodicals with royal privileges had found it virtually impossible to enforce their exclusive monopolies. Marginal papers had made their first appearance during the Fronde, had diminished in number during the highly centralized and powerful reign of Louis XIV when surveillance and censorship were particularly intense, but had proliferated once again in the lenient, even lax atmosphere of the Regency. By the mid-1750s when our story begins, literally hundreds of permitted papers had come into being through the tacit acquiescence of the authorities, and although most had only an ephemeral existence and quickly expired, about fifty were still circulating.[10]

An examination of this large category of permitted, tolerated papers reveals great variety, vitality, and daring in publications long assumed to have been paralyzed. Caught as they were between two extremes—the official, privileged royalist press and the forbidden, furtively exchanged clandestine press that operated beyond the censors' grasp—the permitted papers went through all the legitimate channels of approval but their future was always uncertain, since their permission could be revoked at any moment, leaving them open to persecution and proscription. Not all these permitted papers were oppositional or *frondeur,* by any means. Many specialties and constituencies were represented in their own journals by the 1750s, and most of them were politically quite unadventurous. The Christian apologist Fréron's conservative *Année littéraire,* for example, had as its raison d'être to combat and undermine the philosophes. The latter had their own paper, the *Journal encyclopédique,* published in the nominally independent duchy of Bouillon, but although it made an attempt to keep philosophe thought alive during the *Encyclopédie*'s suppression, it was a quite moderate publication, often unappreciated by the very group it defended. The partisan Jesuit paper stood as a bulwark against any anti-Catholic or anti-establishment works. Medical doctors, agronomists, Physiocrats, musicians, and the military all

---

10   See Sgard and Gilot, *Inventaire de la presse,* 30–35.

had their papers. Most of these, published as they were on French soil, remained neutral or silent on matters of state and did not venture beyond the bounds of political decency.[11]

The same can be said of the majority of periodicals aimed at women, short-lived efforts that could hardly be called incendiary. Female audiences had been specifically targeted and courted by writers ever since the Renaissance, but we cannot assume that publications for women faithfully expressed their aspirations, pains, longings, or hopes. On the contrary, much of the literature destined for women was in fact by men, and therefore it propounded the theories and precepts of the dominant majority. The papers for women generally had to follow certain cultural rules, dictated by the social realities. Women were not free, and the literature meant for them served to reinforce their subordinate position by arguing that their charm lay specifically in their difference, their otherness, which automatically precluded equality. As Evelyne Sullerot has pointed out, papers for women by men thus tended to be conservative, based on both snobbism and futility, addressing their female readers as minors whose conduct was judged against standards of good or bad behavior imposed upon them by men or as invalids suffering from vapors and melancholia (diagnosed by doctors as the *maladie du siècle*), but never as human beings who defined themselves through activity and creativity. These male authors—"poètes pour dames" as they were typically called—filled their works with flattering gallantry and saw their function to be the distraction and amusement of a lower order of beings bored by satiety, restless from inactivity, and needing to be pleasantly soothed or even anesthetized.[12]

---

11   The *Année littéraire* is discussed quite thoroughly in Balcou, *Fréron contre les philosophes,* and in an unpublished *thèse* by Brun, *"L'Année littéraire."* On the conservatism of the *Journal encyclopédique,* see Birn, *Pierre Rousseau,* especially 170–79, 201–2. On the generally timid treatment of the *Encyclopédie* in the papers of the day, see Lough, "Contemporary French Periodicals." For brief discussions of the specialized periodicals, see Bellanger et al., *Histoire générale,* vol. 1; Hatin, *Histoire politique et littéraire;* Ledré, *Histoire de la presse;* and the forthcoming *Dictionnaire des journaux,* ed. Sgard.

12   On the manifestation in literature of the prevailing misogynistic view of women as meek, second-order creatures, see Sullerot, "Lectrices et interlocutrices," and Fauchery, *La Destinée féminine.* On the general timidity of works on women, see Abensour, *Femme et féminisme,* 355–428; Albistur and Armogathe, *Histoire du féminisme,* 368–72; Georges Ascoli, "Essai sur l'histoire."

Thus papers like the anonymous *Amusements du beau sexe* (1740) or *Amusements de la toilette* (1755) were conspicuously frivolous publications. So were the papers directed to women by conservatives like Fréron and Bastide, whose *Lettres de Mme la comtesse de . . . sur les écrits modernes* (1745) and *Nouvelles de la république des belles à Mme de ★★★* (1749), were decidedly chivalrous confections with no intention of treating anything serious. These male authors, in fact, assumed the literary guise of women because they believed readers to be particularly indulgent of anything produced by the second sex.[13] There had also been a few attempts to launch fashion magazines for women, whose exclusive focus on *modes* and *parures* only underlined the mindlessness of their audience.[14] Even those male authors who championed the female sex and argued for its superiority were still playing very much within the rules. They attracted a certain notoriety by stating a case contrary to common opinion, but theirs was a rhetorical game, an exercise in disputation. Panegyrics on women by men were common and socially innocuous, for the authors were defending a weak, subservient group that could not defend itself. They gallantly exercised their license to speak for women who were condemned to be mute, both by the social system and by women's acceptance of their own inferiority. Prevailing misogyny was so strong that it penetrated both sexes and served as justification for male usurpation of power. The condemnation of antifeminism by the very men benefiting from that usurpation guaranteed that the discourse remained purely speculative and abstract. This was mere ceremonial eloquence, piquant but not corrosive, filled with hyperbole but no commitment. The playful, exaggerated intent could best be seen in the fact that these men argued superiority rather than equality for women, in a variation of the age-old topos of "le monde à l'envers," a kind of misrule never taken seriously. Thus male feminists, served by the very dogmas they combatted, posed no threat to the existing order and did not instigate any serious contestation.[15]

13 Van Dijk, "Femmes et journaux," 175–76.
14 On fashion journals, see the unpublished *thèse* of Rimbault, "Presse féminine: Mode." See also Kleinert, *Die frühen Modejournale.*
15 See the very suggestive treatment of this subject in Angenot, *Champions des femmes.*

But the emergence of female journalists, the sudden voicing of views by people assumed to be mute, was a different matter altogether. As Elisabeth Badinter has shown, feminine ambition shocked the Old Regime, blurring sexual distinctions and threatening order.[16] Even here, however, we cannot assume that all papers written by women had feminist or even activist inspiration. We are hampered in our investigation by the paucity of information on the earliest female journalists, but we know that most of them, ambitious women but not foolhardy, avoided the double jeopardy of producing papers both by and for women, giving their journals neutral titles instead to make themselves less vulnerable. Thus a Mme du Noyer, a Huguenot émigrée in The Hague who seems to have had an aggressive personality, nevertheless called her publication *La Quintessence des nouvelles* (1711) and thus betrayed no interest in reaching out specifically to women. Mlle Barbier, editor of *Les Saisons littéraires* (1714), hid once again behind the neutrality of her title, as did Mme le Prince de Beaumont in her *Nouveau Magasin français* (1750). That Mlle Barbier had both feminist and populist inclinations can be seen in her correspondence with the Comédie-Française defending women's rights and in her play *Cornélie, mère des Gracques,* whose republican heroine she called "cette incomparable Romaine."[17] That Mme le Prince de Beaumont was considered a threat we learn from the file the police kept on her.[18] But these female editors' newspapers themselves remained fairly benign. Thus neither periodicals by men for women nor those by women for the general public had particularly controversial contents. Some anonymous papers for women during and after the Fronde, such as *La Spectatrice,* seem to have had female authors, but they never removed their literary disguises and revealed themselves. Only with the three female editors of the *Journal des Dames,* the first to proudly identify themselves as spokeswomen for their oppressed sex and crusaders for other social causes, in a paper "par et pour les

---

16 Badinter, *Emilie,* especially 7–38, 470–77.

17 See Chevalley, "Femmes auteurs-dramatiques."

18 Police Inspector d'Hémery's manuscript is alluded to briefly in Moureau, "Beaumont, Marie le Prince de (1711–1780)," in Chouillet and Moureau, *Suppléments* 3:1–2. See also the notice on Mme le Prince de Beaumont by Patricia Clancy in *Suppléments* 1:2.

dames," would the feminist aspect of the *frondeur* press show itself
most clearly.

We come now to the papers we have called *frondeur,* although
they have never been identified as a category before. These were
a subgroup of permitted journals that expressed opposition sentiment yet still managed to circulate and that can therefore teach
us a great deal about the regime and its internal enemies. These
papers were curious hybrids, combining the legitimacy of the protected papers with the challenging attitude of those produced outside the system of censorship. They were very much influenced,
for example, by the bold extraterritorial French-language papers
that had sprung up in Holland, England, Germany, and Switzerland, a lively journalistic diaspora created mostly by Huguenots
who had fled France at Louis XIV's revocation of the Edict of
Nantes.[19] An increasingly virulent criticism of French absolutism
and a pro-parlement slant could be found in such papers as the
Gazette d'Amsterdam, the *Gazette d'Utrecht,* and the *Gazette de
Leyde,* and even in the *Courrier d'Avignon,* published beyond
French borders in the papal enclave.[20] *Frondeur* papers incorpo-
rated these attitudes and yet managed to print them in France,
showing that the boundaries of Old Regime censorship could be
stretched surprisingly far at times. This press was able to transmit
contradictory, provocative signals, which were facilitated as opposition editors developed and deployed clever strategies for keeping their papers afloat.

Unlike the Grub Street pamphleteers who could say anything,
the *frondeur* journalists dealt daily with censors and therefore had
to navigate prudently, giving particular thought to the timing of
their copy. Certain subjects, neutral in some years, struck sensitive
nerves and were perceived as radical in different historical contexts. *Frondeur* editors, both male and female, thus learned how to
read and measure their moment, remaining silent during periods
of repressive censorship, propitiating uncooperative censors, cultivating and securing malleable, sympathetic ones—of which

19 See Sgard, *Inventaire de la presse,* 30, 33; Klaits, *Printed Propaganda,* 20–24,
38–39.
20 The volume of essays edited by Censer and Popkin, *Press and Politics,* includes articles on the *Courrier d'Avignon* and the *Gazette de Leyde.* See also the
discussion of foreign French papers in Rétat, *L'Attentat de Damiens.*

there were a surprising number—during more lenient periods. They chose neighborhoods like the *enclos du Temple* where they could live out of danger, selected distributors willing to take risks like the booksellers in the Palais Royal, communicated controversial messages and unorthodox attitudes to their readers even during difficult periods by allusion, innuendo, significant omission and repetition, and other elliptical means. Perhaps most interesting of all was the surprisingly high degree of tolerance for *frondeur* and even radical thought in certain aristocratic circles, indeed among royalty. The *Journal des Dames,* although many times suspended for its insubordination, circulated with the patronage and protection of some important blue bloods: the duchesse de Chevreuse, the princesse de Condé, the prince de Conti and the duc de Chartres. It was even presented at court to Louis XV in 1765, and although it was silenced and remained in eclipse throughout Chancellor Maupeou's royalist coup, during its last four years its title page boasted that Queen Marie Antoinette herself had accepted its dedication. Such a seemingly paradoxical situation merits more detailed analysis.

What we find, then, is a journalistic spectrum far fuller and more nuanced than has previously been recognized. Between the two extremes of the *Gazette* and the radical manuscript newssheets, and apart from the foreign papers smuggled into France in significant numbers, there surfaced on French soil itself a group of papers publishing much questionable material, which censors at relaxed times approved with impunity and at other, more sensitive moments struggled to squelch. These papers were not connected with the philosophes or the established Enlightenment; many of their editors, as we shall see, regarded the philosophes as adversaries, conservative traitors willing to keep their quarrels polite and secretly bent on preserving the status quo. The *frondeur* papers, on the other hand, meant to agitate, contest, and even overturn the existing order if necessary in their fight for an expansion of human freedom. Like the Fronde itself they combined both reformist and revolutionary tendencies. As Lloyd Moote has pointed out, the Fronde oscillated at all times between legitimacy and treason. Although it never realized its full revolutionary potential, it was a mixed opposition of uncanny duration and tenacity that claimed to be lawful even as it threatened to break France asunder. The "revolt of the judges," therefore, left an ambiguous legacy with deep, unresolved tensions, and the order that followed was in many respects only a facade.[21]

The papers we have called *frondeur* seem a recurring manifestation of the ambiguous legacy of the Fronde, combining integrative and subversive tendencies, working within the system by choosing the legitimate press but filling it with highly charged, potentially explosive material. Indeed, the word *frondeur* and the verb *fronder,* as they were used in the Old Regime, evolved from a quite specific definition to one that subsumed a broad spectrum of challenging attitudes. The meaning of *frondeurs* ranged in intensity from sympathizers with the parlements to impertinent individuals, prone to contradict, complain, and make noise within the system, to provoking, irreverent, unbridled critics, to seditious, revolutionary enemies of the existing order fighting for liberty at all costs. Voltaire meant by *frondeurs* people who denounced the government without measure. Chateaubriand had in mind those so oppressed by despotism that they became violent, implacable enemies of the court and the entire regime.[22]

The editors of the *frondeur* papers saw themselves as initiators of a healthy movement to use the press to shake things up, break old molds, invite contestation, and get the public thinking. What distinguished them from the radicals of Grub Street was their eagerness to try first for reform, to start, at least, within traditional institutions. Their choice of printed periodicals rather than manuscript pamphlets as the vehicle for their grievances shows a willingness to use established channels even as events led them to challenge with increasing assertiveness the legitimacy of the prevailing government. They were directly inspired by the Fronde, as can be seen in Mercier's frequent invocation of that "constitutional uprising" as the most inspiring moment in French history. Another editor, part of the network around the *Journal des Dames,* named his own periodical *Le Babillard* after an opposition paper by the same name that circulated during the Fronde.[23] These editors, it

---

21 Moote, *Revolt of the Judges,* 187–88, 280, 291, 355–76.
22 See *Trésor de la langue française,* vol. 8, s.vv. "Fronde," "Fronder," and "Frondeur." See also Robert's *Dictionnaire alphabétique et analogique de la langue française,* vol. 3, s.v. "Frondeur."
23 See Chapters 6 and 7, below.

should be stressed, were quite divided in their political approaches, some more strongly republican than others, but they all strove to remedy the regime's abuses by appealing to a broad public and by uniting popular and privileged opposition just as the Fronde had done. They were supported in their protest by lawyers and magistrates in parlement and by princes of the blood from the Condé and Conti families, the same aristocratic elites that had instigated the Fronde. For these journalists the law was an authority as high as, or higher than, the monarchy, and they supported the traditional remonstrances of parlement against arbitrary power, attacking royal ministers whose role they considered illegitimate yet all the while insisting on their loyalty to the king.

Most of the topics dealt with in their papers—the theater, the provinces, the academies, the English, even the woman question—were also dealt with in most other periodicals of the day. But the *frondeur* papers, whenever they had the opportunity, moved to the very brink of tolerable discourse and sometimes beyond it. Thus under the guise of perfectly acceptable, even common rubrics, their articles slowly shifted from the integrative to the subversive mode and became politically corrosive. Advocacy of *bienfaisance* and general charity toward the needy became support for the bandit Mandrin. Discussions of the Comédie-Française became propaganda for the new genre of bourgeois *drame* that, by depicting heroes from the lower classes, could inspire and lead the illiterate *peuple* out of ignorance and slavery. Articles on the provinces grew into rhapsodies depicting parlements throughout the realm as popular national tribunals, curbs on tyranny, and ramparts of public liberty. Admiration for all things English, from Shakespeare to constitutional rights, led to denunciations of France. References to protected newspapers turned into fulminations against censorship and demands for freedom of expression. And the discourse on women, a gallant literary tradition with a long history in France, now became a strident call for social action, a plea for women's rights that transcended feminism and spoke for persecuted Protestants, starving peasants, overworked *poissardes,* and the whole Third Estate, in short for all low-status groups oppressed by society. This *frondeur* alliance of feminism with other causes would continue well past the Revo-

14

lution. It is no accident that the great feminist and social activist Marguerite Durand, who launched a daily paper in 1897 that she used to fight for human rights and for a most notable defense of the falsely accused Dreyfus, named her paper quite simply *La Fronde*.[24]

Before going further, it will be useful to invoke some of Karl Mannheim's thoughts on the sociology of knowledge, the ways in which belief systems and idea-clusters function in a culture and accomplish social work. While Mannheim never applied his theory to feminism or to the French Old Regime, his formulations can elucidate any anthropological investigation of how views resonate and are used by different cultural groups. Mannheim employed idiosyncratic vocabulary to distinguish between two modes of ideas that are incongruous with the state of reality in which they occur. According to his formulation, such "situationally transcendent" ideas are "ideological" as long as they remain "socially impotent," but "utopian" when they "pass into conduct and tend to shatter, either partially or wholly," the existing order. Ideological thought may be challenging, even progressive and "well intentioned," but it remains integrated within the order of things, represents the values of the dominant culture, poses no threat, falls short of its professed intentions, and therefore has "no revolutionary possibilities." Alternative realities are merely considered and entertained, but never realized in these tolerable, even traditional forms of challenge. "Utopian" states of mind, on the other hand, translate into action and threaten to break the bonds of the existing order. Utopian thinking recognizes the dynamic, historically evolving character of reality and sees the present not as an absolute but as just one of the many possibilities. Since the present is recognized as being in the process of change, utopians strive to realize a better future. Far from integrating their ideas into the existing order, they mean to transform it and if necessary to raze and reconstruct it. Mannheim describes the dialectical relationship between utopia and the existing order. Every age allows to arise (in differently located social groups) those ideas and values in which are contained the unrealized and unfulfilled tendencies

24 For a brief discussion of Durand's newspaper, see Albistur, *Histoire du féminisme*, 368–72. See also Li, "Presse féministe."

15

and needs of that age. These are the explosive elements for bursting the limits of the established order. They hasten its disintegration. Ideas become action, beliefs dictate behavior, and the historical social situation is torn asunder.[25]

But as Mannheim points out, ideological and utopian varieties of an idea do not occur separately in historical process, and they are at first difficult to distinguish. Since they often coexist, it is only possible to tell them apart if we "participate in the feelings and motives of the parties struggling," that is, if we "enter into their world."[26] *Frondeur* journalism with its mixture of integrative and subversive tendencies, can only be understood by entering into the world of the people who produced, marketed, supported, and tried to thwart it. We must read between the lines of these papers—because the vigilance of censors often robbed the printed copy of the oppositional, even populist thrust it was meant to have—in order to find the reasons why *frondeur* thought grew less "ideological" and more "utopian," less theoretical and more activist, less containable within the system and more prone to contestation. We must watch the editors making the most of lenient periods, then straining within harsh limits intermittently imposed upon them as the regime struggled to secure its foundations, and finally being forced by the severe degree of repression into unacceptable forms of deviance. We must look at their writings, their personal and political associations, their social activity and the neighborhoods they frequented, their enemies, their total circumstance. To the extent that letters and other documents permit us to reassemble the pieces of their world, we can better understand their disaffection and why and how they were driven from a spirit of cooperative, integrative challenge into one of subversion, defection, and revolt.

Let us take a look now at the development of the opposition or *frondeur* press in historical perspective.

"We are in the habit," wrote the French historian Jacques Bainville sixty years ago, "of regarding the Fronde as a romantic and

---

25   Mannheim, *Ideology and Utopia,* especially 192–205 and 55–108.
26   Ibid., 196.

even a gallant episode because of the participation in it of so many women. It was, in reality, the revolutionary thrust of the seventeenth century."[27] Scholars of public opinion have long recognized the influence of the Fronde on the pre-Revolutionary imagination, one even labeling it the "veritable origin of 1789."[28] It is easy to see why the memory of that explosive rebellion against Queen Anne of Austria and Cardinal Mazarin would appeal to citizens hostile to church and state in the last decades of the eighteenth century. That "révolution manquée" had united princes of the blood, Jansenist magistrates, city mobs, and peasants in a brief but dramatic challenge to French absolutism. Not only was there an unprecedented blending of classes during this upheaval; Bainville reminds us that it involved women as well. For a fleeting moment, however varied their motivations, both sexes and all levels of French society had joined in a spectacular display of insubordination.[29]

During the Fronde, while the *Gazette* staunchly defended the Crown, a host of opposition papers sprang up, nineteen new ones appearing in 1649 alone.[30] Some of these, like the *Courrier français* and the *Journal de parlement,* which presented provocative constitutional arguments against absolutism, targeted bourgeois readers. Although these papers were challenging, they were fundamentally integrative, because their audience, however alienated temporarily, knew its destiny lay within the establishment. Other papers propagated popular radicalism, vilified monarch and minister, and were clearly subversive. One such *mazarinade* stated, "*Les grands* are powerful only as long as we carry them on our shoulders. We need only shake them to bring them face down"; another ventured, "The subject armed against his sovereign becomes his equal."[31] Cyrano de Bergerac's papers, among them *Le Gazetier désintéressé,* accused Mazarin of sodomy and of killing the

27 Bainville, *Histoire de la France* (Paris, 1924), 1:216.
28 See, for example, Aubertin, *Esprit public,* 16 and passim, and two works by Funck-Brentano, *Nouvellistes* and *Figaro et ses devanciers.*
29 Many books on the Fronde have emphasized the absence of any systematic or constructive program as the cause of its eventual fragmentation and collapse. Few deny, however, that this potentially significant crisis raised serious constitutional issues. For a summary of recent literature on the Fronde, see Keohane, *Philosophy and the State,* chap. 7.
30 See Sgard, *Inventaire de la presse,* 33.
31 Livois, *Histoire de la presse,* 31–32.

pope's nephews; they put proud language in the mouths of the people of the Third Estate who "remonstrated" that it was their industriousness that supported the whole nation. Cyrano, who wrote in the defense of women, certainly expected them to be among his readers.[32] Other papers were more explicitly directed at women, starred female interlocutors, and may even have been written by them. The *Gazette des Halles, Le Babillard,* and the *Gazette de la place Maubert* featured a certain "Dame Denise" and were aimed at a broader audience meant to include the lower classes and especially the fishwives, or *poissardes.* Just how literate this *petit peuple* was in the mid-seventeenth century is extremely questionable; probably such *gazettes* and *courriers* were intended to be recited aloud in the public markets, for many were written in a popular patois. In any case these seditious papers were low-priced and presented in an idiom of simple stereotypes to be accessible to unsophisticated readers and listeners of both sexes.[33]

The attempt by both mild and radical *frondeurs* to inform and rouse a wide public through the press, to broaden the realm of awareness and debate, and even to galvanize women into participation and protest, was very new. It sought to use the recently invented journalistic medium for political controversy and violated the traditional boundaries between the private and public spheres, between domestic economy and political life. Now fishwives could gossip about and pass judgment on the doings of princes. Noble women threw themselves into the fray as well. The wives of the magistrates in parlement, many raised on the nonconformist tenets of Jansenism, were well prepared to protest "despotic" ministerial whim.[34] Even highborn duchesses and princesses participated. Anne Marie Louise d'Orléans, *la grande mademoiselle* de Montpensier, used her amazonian stature and passionate oratory to inflame the masses. Like a second Joan of Arc, the new Maid of Orléans captured her city's heart. It is often argued that the Fronde had no overarching program, the actors no common cause, that the people were miserable and hungry and the

32 Mongrédien, *Cyrano,* 53–66.

33 Grand-Mesnil, *Mazarin,* especially 11–12, 49–66, 175–231. The author postulates a "presse populaire à grand tirage" (p. 185).

34 On the relationship between *frondeurs,* parlementaires, and Jansenists, see the works referred to in Keohane, *Philosophy and the State,* 216, and Van Kley, *Jansenists,* 21, 29, 45, 52, 57, 229–31.

nobles simply bent on recapturing feudal privileges. Indeed, it was doubtless these differences that split the uprising apart after a few years. But while it lasted, whether in popular *gazettes* or parlementary speeches, *frondeur* rhetoric evoked the memory of a republican past and promised, however vaguely, the recovery of lost liberties in a better future. Not until 1789 would male and female, capital and provinces, high and lowborn share such energies and hopes again.

The Fronde has been recognized by several historians as the dawn of French feminism, a feminism of action if not doctrine.[35] *Frondeuses,* and *frondeur* journalists, however divided in their political approaches, recognized the relatively new institution of the press as a means of swaying public opinion. They assumed women had the right to know, judge, and be involved in events, to support and participate in factions, and in general to challenge the established order. The dissidence of the Fronde manifested itself on many fronts, and in the years leading up to the revolt, male-dominated aristocratic culture had also been attacked in other areas besides journalism. Resentment of elite institutions and classical conventions could be seen in the theater as well, another arena in which women constituted a significant part of the audience and could influence the fate of plays, the fame of authors, even the dramatic trends.[36] As long as playwrights enjoyed the patronage of the powerful Richelieu, they obeyed the strict rules governing the stage. These rules ensured that plays would "teach things that preserve public order and work to hold the people in their duties." Corneille's plays, while depicting strong-willed, ambitious heroes, tried to preserve classical tragedy as an austere, dignified art form demanding intellectual effort from its public; they were therefore necessarily elitist.[37] Even Corneille's plays, however, with their independent, self-reliant heroines who seemed mistresses of themselves, have been seen by some as a "théâtre féministe" that greatly influenced the rebellious *frondeuses.*[38] And with Richelieu's death, conformity gave way to a

35 See in particular Abensour, *Histoire générale,* 147–59, and Payer, *Féminisme.*

36 Lough, *Paris Theatre Audiences,* especially 112–15, 155–62.

37 Couton, *Corneille,* 107–9.

38 Abensour, *Histoire générale,* 157, and Lough, *Paris Theatre Audiences,* 158–59.

new critical spirit and license in the theater. Plays attacked tyrannical kings, spoke of democratic elections, and advocated republican virtues. Cyrano's audacities were as great in the theater as in the press. Libertinage and impiety ran riot, and impure hybrid forms, such as melodrama, made their appearance.[39] One obscure Ogier had earlier attacked the sacred cows of classicism, the slavish imitation of Greek theater, the unrelieved gloom of tragedy, the forced and artificial constraints of traditional conventions, and had even urged that plays depict the true "conditions of people's lives."[40] Now, as the opposition gained momentum, a "vent de Fronde" blew through the theater, inciting subjects to audacity and ferocity by irreverently criticizing the government.[41]

That the Fronde spanned all ranks of society and spread throughout the provinces can be partially explained by the breadth of audience reached by both press and theater. Besides the revolt of parlements against the Crown and the betrayal of the royal princes, there were popular uprisings of significant proportions among marginal cultural groups. Highborn *frondeuses* aided and abetted the revolt of the lower classes in what one historian has called the first encounter between *grandes dames* and the populace.[42] The Ormée of Bordeaux, for example, a group of determined artisans, were against both the royal court and the parlement. Although they failed to produce a unified body of ideas on which to chart a future course, this largely illiterate group was inflamed by public readings from the opposition press. Their temporary but dramatic defeat of the ruling establishment demonstrates, according to a recent scholar, that during the Fronde "a high level of political maturity" was achieved by the lower classes.[43] It also shows that the Fronde decentralized France by creating provincial pockets of power that would deeply resent subsequent attempts by the capital to pull them back into line. The "révolution manquée" left wounds that festered, and the semblance of order re-

39 Couton, *Corneille*, 9–14; Mongrédien, *Cyrano*, 101, 141–44.
40 Lough, *Seventeenth-Century French Drama*, 101–3.
41 Couton, *Corneille*, 13–16.
42 Payer, *Féminisme*, 151, 159.
43 For a discussion of the most egalitarian "people's Fronde," see Westrich, *Ormée*, 134–41.

stored upon France by the Sun King masked discontent that would soon resurface.[44]

The Fronde was followed, not surprisingly, by a period of extremely repressive press censorship. Louis XIV, whose traumatic childhood memories of his narrow escape from the Paris mob were indelibly etched in his mind, kept tight reins on the press and used it very effectively for his own political propaganda. Very few new journals were launched, and the royal ministers filled the existing ones with planted stories to suit the court's purposes.[45] The Sun King also greatly diminished parlements' power of remonstrance, essentially eliminating it by insisting that laws be registered and made official before discussion. He thus reduced the opposition, both journalistic and political, to temporary impotence. During the Regency, however, the Crown's strict control began once more to break down. Many princes of the blood, frustrated younger brothers or cousins in the royal family who could never rule, had traditionally sided with the parlements in their attempts to limit the king's power. Condé, one of these royal cousins, had actually negotiated with Cromwell during the Fronde, promising to make Bordeaux a "people's republic" in exchange for English aid.[46] The coming to power of another such prince, the pro-parlement regent Philippe d'Orléans, during Louis XV's minority, meant again that royal authority would be undermined and the press more free.

New alternative papers began to proliferate after 1720 and grew increasingly difficult to control. The ranks of royal censors expanded to supervise the new writers and journalists, whose works needed to be read and approved before the right to print could be granted. But the generally relaxed atmosphere and a cavalier attitude on the regent's part allowed some improbable characters to obtain posts as censors, and they in turn approved some distinctly *frondeur* periodicals. A few men even doubled as censors and editors. F. D. Camusat, for example, was a rabid foe of the Jesuits with unabashedly republican sympathies, author of a feminist

---

44 Madelin, *Révolution manquée.*
45 See Klaits, *Printed Propaganda,* especially the chapter entitled "Censorship," where the suppression of inflammatory *gazettes* is discussed.
46 See Moote, *Revolt of the Judges,* 280, 291, and Knachel, *England and the Fronde.*

apology called *Les Vertus du beau sexe.* The regent died in 1723, and Camusat's periodical, the *Bibliothèque des livres nouveaux,* was soon suppressed "by superior orders" because the new man in power, Cardinal Fleury, regarded him as a public enemy for his Jansenism.[47] But although Camusat's own works were silenced, as royal censor he could still operate behind the scenes, and in 1728 he gave his approval to an anonymous newspaper called *La Spectatrice.*

The editor purported, as the title indicates, to be a woman, but we know nothing of this journalist's real identity. The paper itself was staunchly feminist and *frondeur,* calling for legal reforms, social change, and equality between sexes and the three estates. In one issue, "Si j'etais souveraine . . . ," the *Spectatrice* described a republican utopia run by a modest peasant woman whose instinctive thrift, practical wisdom, and natural organizational skills kept everything running smoothly. This *ménagère* appointed a senate of women and saw that everyone did that job in society for which he or she was best suited. There was no fanatical devotion to the state, but instead a harmonious relationship between civic-minded individuals and their community. "Those who would scorn such a woman shall be terribly disturbed by [the smoothness] of her government," since in the way of training for her job, "she had only good sense, firmness, and the experience of having run a household all her [previous] life."[48]

The plebeian family, the industrious, "naturally good" peasant unit, was thus the ideal building block of the state.[49] The author of *La Spectatrice* had no use for "philosophes with their grand airs," and she devoted herself instead to "simple subjects."[50] She aspired to write with the force and conviction of a man, to be a "controller" and "corrector" of an errant human race, to return it to the path of Roman austerity and public service.[51] Claiming to be self-taught, and nourished on Cicero, Cato, and Seneca, she craved involvement in affairs of state. In the corrupt, oppressive society

---

47 On Camusat, see Sgard, *Dictionnaire des journalistes,* 66–67, and Couperus, *L'Etude des périodiques,* 32–52.

48 *Recueil . . . de La Spectatrice,* 138–40.

49 Ibid., 44–45.

50 Ibid., 62.

51 Ibid., 37, 77–79.

of her own day, she saw her sex as a liability, marriage as a "miserable yoke of indignities," and "girlness" as a "disgrace." She therefore dressed in men's clothes until such time as her egalitarian vision could be realized and women could have rights as well as duties.[52] She may have been influenced by the reforming notions of Raoul Spifame, a bizarre *politique* of the sixteenth century who assumed the identity of Henri II and, in that utopian "If I were king" guise, mapped out a future world plan with both social and legal reforms. Spifame's visions later captured the fancy of at least one *Journal des Dames* editor, Louis-Sébastien Mercier, who would write a utopia called *L'An 2440* and talk of Spifame in both his newspaper and his famous (or infamous) *Tableau de Paris*.[53]

La Spectatrice was running on borrowed time. Camusat himself was a marked man. At least twice he sought refuge in Holland, but his own ideas were too strong even for the blood of Dutch publishers he approached.[54] Meanwhile the printer of *La Spectatrice* and at least one male "correspondant" were getting frightened. They sent notices to the journalist repeatedly, warning that her tone was too moralistic and severe.[55] Her future society, which replaced wealth, rich food, and high fashion with social mobility based on merit, good character, and public service, was not a vision with great buyer appeal, she was told. Printed notices to subscribers indicate that the paper was interrupted and delayed several times. The editor, undaunted, kept up her crusade to the end, vowing to "attack human turpitude" and force people to "read, talk, listen, and live" not just for amusement but to "perfect themselves."[56] Her ultimate faith in her audience was typical of the *frondeur* journalists who wrote with the conviction that the public, including common people and women, could learn, improve, and transcend its historical limitations. Unlike her "confrère," the journalist, Christian moralist, and self-professed misanthrope Marivaux, whose potentially feminist play *La Colonie* ended in total capitulation to the status quo and whose newspaper *Le Spec-*

52 Ibid., 25, 32, 83–98.
53 See Béclard, *Sébastien Mercier,* 591–92.
54 Couperus, *L'Etude des périodiques,* 37.
55 *Recueil . . . de La Spectatrice,* 257–58.
56 Ibid., 167.

tateur was fundamentally pessimistic, the author of *La Spectatrice* and her censor Camusat dreamed of a better future.[57]

But their blatant anticlericalism and their denunciations of the exisiting social order doomed them. *La Spectatrice* was stopped in 1729 after fifteen issues. Its anonymous editor was not heard from again, although her style, from masculine attire to belligerent rhetoric, would live on in Mme de Beaumer, an admirer of *poissarde* women and the first female editor of the *Journal des Dames,* and in the tough-talking, sword-sporting feminist leader of the Revolution Théroigne de Méricourt. Camusat, to avoid going hungry, was driven to editorial hackwork and clandestine "satires" and "infamies against respectable people."[58] Nor was he the only royal censor to lead a double life, working simultaneously within the system for reform and underground for revolution. The *Journal des Dames* would have several censors in the same mold, marginal men like Pidansat de Mairobert, who protected that newspaper while writing his own far more rabid manuscript news-sheets.

These alternating periods of journalistic leniency and repression, linked as they were to the relative weakness or strength of the Crown, accelerated in the last half of the eighteenth century. Recent research by Keith Michael Baker, Dale Van Kley, and William Doyle has ably shown the emergence after 1750 of a truly radical vocabulary and political climate. During the next two decades Jansenists, parlementaires, and the Orléans princes orchestrated the expulsion of the Jesuits and in so doing initiated the first sustained, concerted resistance to both clerical and royal authority. Jansenism functioned as a vehicle for political radicalism in much the same way as the later mesmerist phenomenon.[59] The Jansenists' clandestine *Nouvelles ecclésiastiques* inflamed public opinion against the "despotism" of church and royal ministers. The attack on the Jesuits and the denunciation of foreign papal influence engendered a rhetoric of intense patriotism. The parlements claimed to be protecting the nation against both ministerial whim and domination by a corrupt church. In the absence of the Estates General, the moribund representative body that had stopped meeting (and would not meet again until 1789), parlement de-

---

57 On Marivaux's pessimism, see Mason, "Women in Marivaux."
58 Couperus, *Etude des périodiques,* 40–41.
59 See Van Kley, *Jansenists,* 236, n. 18, and Darnton, *Mesmerism,* 36, 61.

clared itself "guardian of the fundamental laws of the realm."[60] It was unavoidable, in this atmosphere, that the *frondeur* press would reassert itself.

Malesherbes, director of the booktrade between 1750 and 1763, found the press in great disorder when he first assumed the position. Newspapers had proliferated at such a rate since the Regency that the exclusive privilege of the "official" *Gazette, Mercure,* and *Journal des savants* was now nothing more than a joke.[61] Malesherbes was in a tight spot. Friend of the philosophes, he disliked repression and had even written a *mémoire* that, although only published decades later, advocated freedom of the press.[62] On the other hand Malesherbes was a fervent monarchist, a friend of the Jesuits, a man who disliked "noise" and "fermentation," whose true feelings would come out in his defense of Louis XVI at the king's fateful trial.[63] How could he regain control of the press without incurring greater hostility against the regime?

Malesherbes's solution was to make official a new kind of publishing right, the *permission tacite,* and to use it to ratify or legitimize an already existing situation. Permissions gave authors the illusion of greater freedom. Permitted works were of course censored, but the censor's name did not appear on the printed approbation, and, thus protected by their anonymity, censors tended to permit more questionable material to get into print. On the other hand, unlike a privilege, which combined copyright and sales monopoly, permissions guaranteed nothing. They could be revoked on whim by the authorities, leaving authors with no legal redress.[64] The ambiguous results of Malesherbes's ambiguous measures can be best seen in the case of periodicals. The thirteen years of his directorship witnessed a journalistic explosion and the appearance of nearly two hundred new papers, one of which was the *Journal des Dames.* Most, however, were ephemeral, only one in

60 On the emergence of a revolutionary mentality after 1750, see Van Kley, *Damiens Affair;* Baker, "Ideological Origins"; Doyle, *Parlement of Bordeaux.*

61 On the breakdown of these privileges, see Birn, "*Journal des savants,*" 15–36.

62 Malesherbes, *Mémoires sur la librairie.*

63 See Jordan, *King's Trial,* 89, 118–30, 186, 191, 205–6, 235.

64 For a discussion of the various publishing rights, see Perrin, *Manuel de l'auteur;* Hermann-Mascard, *Censure des livres;* and Darnton, "Reading, Writing, and Publishing," especially 174–79, 186–87.

six lasting more than a few years, and some never getting beyond a prospectus or a first issue.[65]

The *Mercure,* the *Gazette,* and the *Journal des savants,* in a perpetual state of crisis due to the growing competition from alternative papers, could still, and did sporadically, exercise their exclusive rights to certain kinds of materials: theater reviews or military happenings or academic findings. That these official papers now had large deficits was a real concern.[66] Not only were they symbolic of central authority; the monarchy felt obliged to protect them because profits from their sale had traditionally been used to finance pensions for vigilant censors and royalist writers, thus encouraging loyalty to the regime. Such pensions were needed especially at that moment to support added surveillance of the wildly proliferating press. There were now more than 150 censors whose job it was to police the printed word and protect the regime from sedition. In spite of the alleged liberality of Malesherbes's *permissions tacites,* then, life was still precarious for censored newspapers, even those that remained relatively tame. Beaumarchais's hero described the situation as he explained his own journalistic failure in the *Marriage of Figaro:*

> As long as I do not speak in my paper of authority, religion, politics, morality, people in high places, privileged institutions, the Opera or other theaters, or partisans of received opinions, I can print everything freely under the watchful eye of two or three censors. Taking advantage of this sweet freedom and mindful to tread on no toes, I announce a *Journal inutile.* Whambang! One thousand poor hacks rise up against me, I am suppressed and once again out of a job.[67]

It is no accident that in the same play, by making common cause among his four heroines from the privileged Countess down to the plebeian Fancette, Beaumarchais protested the oppression of women. Feminism and the fight for press freedom were linked in this playwright's *frondeur* stance against the regime's abuses.[68]

65 See graphs and charts on the duration of periodicals in Sgard's *Inventaire de la presse,* 30–32.

66 The *Mercure* acquired only 160 new subscribers between 1763 and 1778. The *Gazette* had accumulated a 33,000-livre deficit by 1771. See Aimé-Azam, "Le Ministère des affaires étrangères." For more on the *Mercure*'s problems, see Chapter 4, below.

67 P. A. C. de Beaumarchais, *Le Mariage de Figaro,* act 5, sc. 3.

68 See Albistur, *Histoire du féminisme,* 204–5.

The *Journal des Dames,* begun by a conservative editor during the Malesherbes years, became increasingly *frondeur,* but since it had only a permission, it had to watch its step. Allegiance with the opposition could be communicated subtly to readers by poems filled with allusions, books recommended even if they could not be described in detail, the listing of patrons and protectors to whom the paper was dedicated, references to neighborhoods where it was distributed, and the kinds of plays it reviewed. From all these oblique signals readers could extract messages even though the paper also carried some conventional rhetoric favorable to the Crown. Such compromise with the booktrade authorities was necessary for survival during the 1760s, as parlement's remonstrances against the monarchy reached fever pitch and intensified royal paranoia.

Frondeur papers that were too sympathetic with the refractory provincial parlements during this period did not last long. *L'Iris de Guienne,* for example, a Bordeaux paper to which Mercier contributed in the early 1760s before taking over the *Journal des Dames,* tried to unite men and women, people and magistrates in a regional protest against the corruptions of an extravagant centralized monarchy. Its opening issue, filled with the words "citoyen," "république," "frugalité," "liberté," "vertu," "nation," "justice," "état," "bonheur des peuples" made obvious its republican inspiration.[69] Dedicated to eradicating provincial weakness, and featuring articles by parlementaires, women—it was strongly feminist—and several "Americans," *L'Iris* predicted that "the face of things will change, a revolution will come."[70] The Roman ideal of the family was again upheld as the "only basis for public order and law," and citizens of both sexes were urged to rise up against barbarous tyranny.[71]

L'Iris experienced problems from the start, the editor lamenting "the necessity of offering to the police only irreproachable material." The *poste* would not mail the paper, many daring articles had to be left out, and many subscribers were afraid to have their names openly associated with this journal.[72] The editor tried new strategies, but the intent was still obvious. One article on the

69 *Iris de Guienne,* janvier 1763:24–30.
70 Ibid., février:103–5.
71 Ibid., juillet:171, 192.
72 Ibid., février:75–76; avril:222; novembre:144.

beheading of England's Charles I, an event that had added fuel to the Fronde, did condemn the "excesses of sedition and revolt," but it still blamed the whole tragedy on the king's disregard for the law.[73] The paper was soon silenced, in spite of its dedication to the duc de Richelieu, governor of Bordeaux (and not to be confused with the seventeenth-century minister), which must have been a distasteful necessity for the editor in order to get into print at all. The decadent Richelieu, considered a haughty and imperious despot by the Bordeaux parlement, would later take great pleasure in dissolving that same parlement as part of the royalist coup perpetrated by Mme Du Barry, Chancellor Maupeou, and two other ministers, a coup known as the "triumvirate." "Here," wrote d'Argenson of the Bordeaux magistrates, "the parlement does not speak for its own rights and high prerogatives, but for the people, who tremble from misery and taxes."[74] That city's role in the Fronde was not forgotten, nor could its newspaper be permitted to print potentially mutinous material encouraging regional assertiveness and the formation of a provincial *ligue* against the Crown.

Malesherbes left the *librairie* in 1763, and his department was taken over by the police chief, Sartine. Until 1776, when a new director of the booktrade was appointed, men of letters felt with some justification that art was being treated as crime. Strong tensions developed between journalists bent on expressing themselves freely and censors tempted to let them, but instructed to scrutinize everything and held answerable to the chief of police. The powerful minister Choiseul, who secretly supported the parlements, afforded some protection to the *frondeur* cause until his disgrace in the late 1760s. To one observer it looked as if the forces of subversion were winning out. "Things have gotten to such a point," he wrote, "that the booktrade today is a commerce of frightful *brigandage* where license has no limits."[75] Certainly it looked that way to Choiseul's successor, the royalist chancellor Maupeou, who, fearing another Fronde, exiled the parlements, replaced them by docile magistrates, and imposed extremely repressive controls on the press until 1774.[76]

73   Ibid., août:272–73.
74   Doyle, *Parlement of Bordeaux*, 8.
75   Quoted in Shaw, *Problems and Policies*, 152.
76   See Chapters 4 and 5, below.

Only after the fall of Maupeou's triumvirate in 1774, the recall of the parlements, and the appointment of a new reforming ministry by young King Louis XVI, could blatantly *frondeur* journalism surface in France. The boundary between popular and elite opposition, between proscribed and permitted journalism, between Grub Street and the legitimate press became for a few years in the mid-1770s nearly indistinguishable.[77] Ideological lines began to blur, entrenched institutions no longer consistently protected their own, and the marginalization and alienation of dissidents from many camps allowed them to intermesh and make common cause. The *Journal des Dames* spearheaded a network of about ten other papers crusading vigorously for free expression through legitimate channels. Even Simon Linguet, no friend of the parlements, espoused many of the other causes of the *frondeurs* and joined his subversive *Journal de politique et de littérature* to their chorus of protest against oppression.[78] But the reforming ministry soon toppled, and in the late 1770s the opposition papers were purged by a government now determined to squelch internal rebellion and devote all its energies to the new war against France's enemy across the Channel, "le Neptune anglais." The *frondeurs* had been admirers of England since her "courageous" decapitation of her king. The *Journal des Dames* and its associated papers preferred Shakespeare to Corneille and Racine, considered Cromwell a patriot rather than a military usurper, and modeled their conceptions of the French parlements, "tribunals of the nation," on the English constitution. After the expropriation of their papers, when the *frondeur* journalists fled France, several of them chose England for their exile, meeting there other émigré journalists, like Brissot, and continuing their crusade in the diaspora.[79]

The *frondeur* papers, then, had several distinguishing characteristics, among them the assumptions that women and other marginal groups should be involved in the debate on serious matters

77 See Chapters 5 and 6, below. For a brief treatment of this phenomenon, see my "*Frondeur* Journalism in the 1770s."
78 See Chapter 6, below.
79 See Chapter 7, below.

and that the press, properly wielded, could be a catalyst in that debate. It comes as no surprise that the official privileged press disagreed with both premises, but so did the philosophes, the self-styled and reigning progressives of the day. The philosophes, as has been shown, were quite unadventurous in their feminism and regarded periodicals, especially those for women, as a lower form of literary life.[80] The articles in the *Encyclopédie* on *journal, gazette,* and related entries, written by Voltaire and Diderot, portrayed journalism as a bastard medium, worse still a parasitic one, dominated by writers incapable of creativity, who preyed upon the work of others. They contrasted present-day journalists, whom they called ignorant hacks, with the pristine example of Bayle, clear-eyed judge, master of all domains, dispenser of wisdom. Now, however, indecent and unscrupulous people wrote papers, and readers slavishly followed their twisted advice, believing whatever they were told. Grimm, whose *Correspondance littéraire* reached most of the princely courts of Europe, was ashamed of France's mania for journals and gave an official disclaimer in 1776 when *frondeur* journalism was at its height. "Journals have become an arena in which literature and authors are prostituted without shame for the amusement of the stupid and the spiteful."[81] Even Rousseau became witheringly scornful and snobbish on the subject of newspapers. No author who cared at all for his reputation or the purity of his art would go near a journal, "a flimsy work without worth or utility . . . whose contents teach nothing and serve only to flatter the vanity of women and fools." Papers were fit only for the provinces, for empty-headed females, for the scum of the earth, and editors were doomed to dishonor. "I regret to see men who should erect monuments content themselves with carrying blocks, and architects become manual laborers. . . . While they make papers for the streets, let us make useful books worthy of immortality."[82] Only in the last decades of the century, when the philosophes had "arrived" and fused with *les grands,* did

---

80   See Clinton, "*Femme et philosophe*"; Williams, "Politics of Feminism"; Zioutos, "Presse et l'*Encyclopédie*"; the articles "Femme," "Journal," "Journaliste," "Gazette," and "Gazetier," in the *Encyclopédie*.

81   Grimm et al., *Correspondance littéraire* 11:383 (novembre 1776).

82   *Correspondance complète de Jean-Jacques Rousseau* 3:116, letter from Rousseau to Jacob Vernes of 2 avril 1755.

they get deeply involved with the press. And then they used it as a defensive weapon, not to challenge but to prop the established order and protect it from upheaval. Voltaire's essential conservatism was clearly revealed in his view of the Fronde. During that "terrible" episode, as he saw it, parlement, "blind and ridiculous," had caused the ruin of the state, and the "people in their frenzy" had paid no attention "to the suffering of so many royal personages."[83]

This is doubtless one reason that *philosophie* played so little part in the *frondeur* press. Even *La Spectatrice* in the late 1720s had viewed philosophes as ivory-tower cowards, not men of action, and that perception continued. To be sure the philosophes became the enfants terribles of the 1750s and the early 1760s when their *Encyclopédie* was suppressed. But after that, as they were forgiven, wooed, and then systematically absorbed by the hallowed institutions of the regime, they were perceived by the *frondeurs* as yet another bastion of conservatism. Interestingly, the *frondeurs* did not distinguish between Fréron's *Année littéraire,* the official *Mercure,* and the philosophes' *Journal encyclopédique.* All pandered to the regime and conspired to keep the people in ignorance. These "pedants" and their "rancid rags of prejudice" failed to see the potential of periodicals as vehicles for social action, whose job it was to inform public opinion. How tame the philosophes had become can be seen in their takeover of the privileged government papers. La Harpe, with considerable help from d'Alembert, became editor of the state-protected *Mercure* in the 1770s, and Suard was entrusted with the *Gazette* by the keeper of the seals, Miromesnil.

After the 1770s the *frondeurs* were forever trying to dissociate themselves from privileged "journalistes, feuillistes, folliculaires."[84] They did not yet call themselves publicists, but their activism, their celebration of social utility, their assumptions of the

---

83 See Voltaire's *Le Siècle de Louis XIV* (1756), especially chap. 4.

84 For the mutual hostility of *frondeurs* and philosophes, see Chapters 6 and 7, below. Tate, *Petit de Bachaumont,* an otherwise excellent study of underground *nouvellistes,* is mistaken, I think, in treating *frondeurs* as a "philosophical sect." The differences between these two groups seem to me far more significant than their similarities. Enlightenment did not breed the subversive tendencies and popular sympathies that characterized the *frondeurs.*

public's right to know, and their *patriotisme* (by which they meant participatory citizenship), place them squarely in that category. Restif de la Bretonne, although an expert neologist, never coined a new term for the *frondeur* journalists, but he certainly recognized that they were "of a different *pâte* than the others," for they wished the people, their readers, to be more than "poor automata."[85] *Lumières* left these editors cold, but popularizing their ideas of justice seemed a most worthy activity. In attacking La Harpe's conservatism, Mercier used the verb "journaliser" to mean impotent verbalizing "without bringing to light a single new idea."[86] Events, not enlightenment, shaped the *frondeur* papers and gave them their vitality.

The philosophes, with the exception perhaps of Condorcet—who, significantly, became a journalist during the Revolution—had little use for the populace, as Harry Payne has shown.[87] With typical disdain d'Alembert referred to a play by Rutlidge, one of Mercier's journalistic colleagues, as worthy only of the rabble.[88] But contact with that audience appealed to the *frondeur* editors; they became aggressively plebeian at times, joining forces with like-minded lawyers who defended the rights of the Third Estate to a political voice, writing bourgeois and popular *drames* for the education of the illiterate *peuple,* even occasionally using the popular and phonetic orthography that had served the *poissard* papers during the Fronde. They warmed to the idea that their works, far more accessible than lofty treatises or lengthy novels, were reaching and teaching a broad audience, not only in bookstores but in reading rooms, cafés, cabarets, drink stands, public gardens, theaters, and fairs. People everywhere were reading or listening to readings from periodicals, at the Galeries du Louvre, the portes des Tuileries, the Palais Royal, the jardins de Luxembourg, the Hôtel de Soubise, the quai des Augustins, and on the newly planted promenades of the Boulevards.[89]

It would be wonderful to know who was reading these papers, but subscription lists for almost all Old Regime periodicals seem

---

85   Restif de la Bretonne, *Monsieur Nicolas* 6, part 9:3086–89, 3194.

86   See Mercier's letter to the *Journal de Paris,* 9 juin 1778:637.

87   Payne, *Philosophes.*

88   Voltaire, *Complete Works* 128:50–51, letter from d'Alembert to Voltaire of 23 novembre 1776.

89   Jèze, *Etat,* part 1:199–209; part 2:53–55.

to have gotten lost in the shuffle. On this sticky but intriguing problem we have to draw tentative conclusions from some circumstantial evidence. We can estimate that the *Journal des Dames* had between three hundred and a thousand subscribers. The associated *Journal des théâtres* was worth more money when it changed hands between editors and therefore may have had a still larger subscription list. The protected *Mercure* itself had only sixteen hundred subscribers, and the other official government papers complained of alarming attrition because readers were defecting to alternative periodicals in large numbers. And the *frondeurs* priced their papers low. The *Journal des Dames,* at 12 livres a year, cost half or less than half the price of the *Mercure,* the *Année littéraire,* and the *Journal encyclopédique,* but it was still expensive. Lodgings for a month at a Paris pension without food averaged about 15 livres, tuition for a child's boarding school about 30 livres a month, a meal at a restaurant anywhere from 4 sols to 2 livres. Subscribers to the *Journal des Dames* thus paid more for a single monthly issue than they would for a moderate dinner out, a night in a hotel, or a day's tuition.[90] Papers were not cheap.

Yet they were being read—or heard—and probably by far more people than actually bought them. Daniel Roche has shown that the habit of reading had grown steadily and had spread way beyond the educated elite, as seen by the impact of *brochures* in 1789.[91] We know there were many clubs, especially in the provinces, where people pooled their money in order to afford periodical subscriptions and developed the habit of discussion and involvement with the material these papers contained. One such group in Lyons subscribed to nineteen papers.[92] Jeremy D. Popkin's argument that even the revolutionary press reached only a restricted audience is a sobering corrective to those who would have Old Regime peasants and artisans reading.[93] Yet we must remember that reading in the eighteenth century was an activity intimately connected with life. As Darnton has shown in his work on Rousseau, readers often spoke words aloud, did much role playing, and were quick to apply the lessons in publications to

90   Ibid., part 2:31–40, 135.
91   Roche, *Peuple de Paris,* 214–25.
92   See Chapter 1, below.
93   Popkin, "Newspaper Press."

their own experience.[94] Subscribers to periodicals were responding to a fairly new medium, almost as if they were joining a club.[95]
These journals were not casual, disposable items like our newspapers today. They were printed only once or twice a month, and
their appearance was eagerly anticipated by subscribers. Marginalia appearing in many volumes show that they were spoken to,
argued with, pondered. And we know they were collected, presumably to be looked at again and again. Subscribers clamored
for complete sets. One editor of the *Journal des Dames* even gave
each year of his paper a *table raisonnée* showing all the different
rubrics treated. He performed this "laborious service," he explained, because readers had requested such a reference tool to
make the journal more "useful."[96] The enormous power editors
had over their public seems to be confirmed by the various guide-
books to Paris, nonpartisan publications that discussed periodicals
as a general genre without distinguishing between them. In 1760
Jèze's *Etat ou tableau de la ville de Paris* described journals as "a
branch of education along with schools, tutors, public courses,
lecture demonstrations, libraries, and academic meetings." The
public, "especially those who cannot or do not wish to think
deeply," appreciated journals for making difficult ideas accessible.
And frequently these papers would "excite curiosity in the initially
indifferent," whet their appetites, and spur them to think indepen-
dently. The *Bibliographie parisienne* of 1770 was "filled with equal
admiration for all journalists whose opinions were greatly respected by the public and who thus advanced the progress of humanity." Still in 1779 the *Dictionnaire historique de la ville de Paris et
de ses environs* reported that papers were greatly relished by their
readers and appreciated for "increasing, extending, and perfecting
knowledge. [The various journals] are different kinds of aids that
help to form reason, judgment, intelligence, taste, and manners."[97]

---

94   Darnton, "Readers Respond."

95   See Varin d'Ainvelle, *Presse en France*. For more general discussion of
how printed thoughts affected readers, see Eisenstein, "Conjectures About Printing."

96   See, for example, *Journal des Dames,* décembre 1765:"table."

97   See Jèze, *Etat,* 207–8; *Bibliographie parisienne,* viii–x; Hurtaut and Magny,
Dictionnaire historique 2:722, 3:664–74.

That women were reading the *frondeur* papers is clear from the number of them who contributed, but who they were is harder to say. They were probably not the ladies of Parisian high society. The privileged *précieuses,* in the business of using their salons to teach men of all ranks how to *vivre noblement,* were the antithesis of the *frondeuses.* As Carolyn Lougee has shown, salon ladies took commoners, provincials, bourgeois and made these men over with new behaviors fitting for high society.[98] But women associated with the *frondeur* movement were trying to do precisely the opposite. They wished to improve the lot of women so that they might possess more liberty and consequence; they had no interest in making or breaking the literary reputations of men. The more radical ones wished to equalize ranks, but downward for public service and active citizenship, not upward for celebrity in the extravagant society of court circles. Where *précieuses* shunned politics, *frondeuses* craved access to it. Where the promiscuous *précieuses* mocked the notion of romantic love, the female editors of the *Journal des Dames* upheld a bourgeois ethic of fidelity and a picture of unions based on affection, dignity, and mutual respect. They extolled motherhood as a claim on society but believed women should also play a public role. Their austerity and their notion of women in service to the state alienated the salon set. On the subject of feminism itself, *précieuses* almost missed the point. When the academician Thomas, an author much featured in the *Journal des Dames,* applauded independent and ambitious women in his separately published *Essai sur les femmes* of 1772, society women reacted with impatience to his severe message. Instead of confronting the issue, however, they criticized Thomas on niggling stylistic grounds. Mme d'Epinay, who dreaded the ascendancy of the dispossessed, told Grimm that Thomas's work was a "diatribe." Mlle de Lespinasse, also fiercely snobbish toward her inferiors, said that because Thomas was tediously erudite and never silly she would not take him as a lover. Mme Du Deffand, a famous but dependent woman who suffered terribly from melancholia and hated solitude so much that she kept her salon guests until dawn, felt intensely jealous of more self-reliant women and

98 On the *précieuses,* see Lougee, *Paradis des femmes,* especially 27–29, 53–55, 170, 212–14.

denounced the *Journal des Dames*.[99] There was here a mutual distrust. The paper repeatedly attacked the immorality and frivolity of the *précieuses*. The salon women, who played a graceful role in the patriarchal society of the Old Regime, had no interest in agitation, believed female journalists crass and unseemly for their virile pretensions, and gave their paper no support at all. The *précieuses* were fashionably integrated in society and thoroughly accustomed to playing by men's rules. As Badinter has pointed out, they did little more than provide a "lieu géométrique" in which men could meet, cherishing the delusion of participation in a gathering where in fact they functioned only as hostesses and intermediaries.[100] The *Journal des Dames,* because it advocated social conscience and a *féminisme d'action,* preached a position much closer to that of the *citoyennes* and *républicaines* of the Revolution, who defined liberty as the right to dignified political participation and to freedom of opinion and expression.[101]

The stated goal of most literary periodicals in the Enlightenment was both "to amuse and to instruct." In the case of the *Journal des Dames,* monthly octavo issues of 96 to 120 pages (see Appendix, plates 1–6), the amusing fare predominated in its opening and closing years, in 1759–61 when its *frondeur* tendencies were only latent, and in 1777–78 when they were muted and finally silenced. Poems, songs, ariettes, odes, stories, and word puzzles occupied most of the pages during those years. Such *pièces fugitives* (often defined as "poèmes et prose sans conséquence") continued throughout all the issues of the paper, a kind of necessary camouflage for which later feminist journalists felt considerable disdain,[102] but during its *frondeur* middle years, from 1761 to 1777, they were outweighed by increasingly serious instructional articles that took an activist stance. The proportions were then reversed, it could be said, between the "journalisme assis" of po-

99   Epinay, *Mémoires et Correspondance* 3:357; Charles Henry, ed. *Lettres inédites . . . de Julie de Lespinasse* (Geneva, 1971), 2:199; Du Deffand, *Correspondance* 2:393.
100   Badinter, *Emilie,* 15–17, 34–36.
101   See P.-M. Duhet, *Femmes et Révolution;* Levy, Applewhite, and Johnson, *Women in Revolutionary Paris.*
102   See, for example, the preamble to a paper emanating from one of the Revolutionary women's clubs, called *Le Véritable Ami de la reine, ou Journal des Dames,* part of which is quoted in Sullerot, *Histoire de la presse,* 50.

etry, fiction, and literary or musical commentary, and the "journalisme debout" of articles on causes inviting involvement. First the female editors, then the *frondeur* male editors filled the paper with discussions of significant issues, believing that women could be a particularly receptive and responsive audience for problems of injustice and oppression. They were far from practicing the "évacuation du réel" and linguistic reductionism so characteristic of the modern feminine press.[103]

The very fact that the *Journal des Dames* explicitly targeted and therefore validated an audience of marginal social status seemed to give it a momentum of its own. Originally designed to subdue, it inevitably provoked. In Mannheim's formulation, the overture to women had been meant to remain, like all "ideological" thinking, an unrealized good intention, a playfully entertained idea, a chivalrous, sporting gesture. One of the most interesting aspects of the paper's story is precisely the way in which it was sucked out of the hands of its unsuspecting founders and into the undertow of the pre-Revolution.

103   Dardigna, *Presse "féminine,"* especially 9–33, 72–107.

1

Feminine Journalism in the
Pre-Revolutionary Undertow

M. DE CAMPIGNEULLES TESTS THE WATERS (1759)

The *Journal des Dames* was begun by a man who had no idea what he was getting himself into. To Thorel de Campigneulles, a wealthy twenty-one year old from Lyons, the project seemed foolproof. Not that he cared any for the advancement of women; this paper was to be a demonstration of his devotion to his king. Precocious successes as a teenage novelist and membership in the learned societies of Villefranche, Caen, Angers, and Besançon had gone to his head. He would now take Paris by storm. A light, pleasant periodical, appropriately named for the fair sex, struck him as an ingenious idea. The authorities would love it. It could not possibly offend anybody and was precisely what his troubled country needed in 1759 to get people's minds off the facts that France was being trounced in her war against Frederick of Prussia and that Damiens had slashed at Louis XV with a knife. But Campigneulles knew nothing of the perils and ugliness of the capital's journalistic scene. He was in for a series of shocks that would send him reeling, because once he donned the journalist's hat, all the rules would change. The very same publishers, royal censors, and reviewers who had approved his novels would turn hostile. He had also failed to realize that the *question de la femme* was entangled with many other issues and would generate heated journalistic controversy. Readers whom he meant to flatter would find him ridiculous, and others whom he tried to instruct would be offended. He would scare fast, abandon the *Journal des Dames* after only four issues, and beat a hasty retreat back to the provinces. But it was too late; his reputation in the world of letters was ruined. Trying to please everyone had turned into a nightmare, and the literary critics did not suffer fools gladly.[1]

In the beginning, however, Campigneulles was the very picture of optimism. His short novels and a collection of essays had gone over well. Ignoring one critic's remark that *Le Temps perdu,* his first work, was an apt name for the hours wasted reading it, he focused instead on the reviewers who had encouraged his efforts. People bought his books in sufficient numbers to warrant second printings, new editions, even English and Dutch imitations.[2] Campigneulles had convinced publishers in Lyons, Geneva, Antwerp, and London of his talents. At nineteen, as part of a ritual followed by many aspiring writers, he had paid epistolary homage to the great Voltaire, who read a sample of his fledgling work and dictated to his secretary a vague but benevolent reply.[3] Several Paris papers had reviewed him favorably; one even praised profusely, acclaiming him among the brightest new stars on the literary scene.[4] And his triumph had already been crowned by membership in several provincial academies.

Intoxicated by the positive press, Campigneulles set out for Paris in 1758, ambitious and full of dreams. He had the means to choose any neighborhood he wished for his lodgings and decided upon the bustling but beautiful rue Saint Antoine, immediately

1   Charles-Claude Florent de Thorel de Campigneulles (1737–1809) has not been the subject of a biography. See Cioranescu, *Bibliographie de la littérature française* 3:1714. He is discussed briefly in Rustin, "'Suites' de *Candide.*" This article argues convincingly that many works attributed to Campigneulles in the Bibliothèque Nationale catalogue are not his.

2   For the negative remarks, see Fréron's *Année littéraire* (1756) vii:66. For the praise, see Campigneulles, *Anecdotes morales,* "Avis de l'éditeur," and *Censeur hebdomadaire* (1760) iv:303.

3   Campigneulles wrote to Voltaire on 20 October 1756: "Je suis très jeune, Monsieur, et l'ouvrage que j'ai l'honneur de vous envoyer en est, disent mes amis, beaucoup plus estimable. Leur jugement m'est suspect. Je crains presqu'autant les louanges que les satires. La mer sur laquelle je viens de m'embarquer imprudemment est fertile en naufrages. L'envie d'avoir des talents n'en donne pas. . . . Je pourrais aisément m'aveugler sur cet article important. Daignez, Monsieur, imposer des bornes à mon amour propre, en m'appréciant précisément ce que je vaux." Voltaire, *Complete Works* 130:159–60, letter D7032a. The answer, signed Wagnière, is on p. 160, letter D7055a.

4   See, for example, Abbé de la Porte's *Observateur littéraire* (1758) ii:236.

across from the Hôtel de Beauvais where the young Mozart would soon make such a sensation. This street was the official entry route into the city for royal processions from Versailles and for visiting dignitaries and celebrities, an ideal vantage point for an author who sought to secure his future by attracting wealthy, influential patrons and protectors.[5] Huge numbers of provincial writers flocked to the capital to be close to the center of power, hoping to be noticed by *le monde* and win a pensioned post of some kind. Perhaps Campigneulles aspired to become a reader or secretary in the royal household. For him the pension was of less importance than the label. He longed to ingratiate himself with the authorities so that his loyalty to the regime could be validated by an honorific title. Other journalists, although not many, had earned official functions by their pen. J. N. Moreau's royalist *Observateur hollandais* had led to his appointment as royal historiographer, and P. N. Bonamy, editor of the *Journal de Verdun,* had become one of the king's official librarians. Surely, if Campigneulles's paper contributed to bolstering the established order, he too would be deserving of one of these sinecures.

The *Journal des Dames* was to have its own unique angle. The new editor would prove his devotion to the state by writing something useless, something purely amusing and mindless, which would lull restless readers rather than teach them how to think. Like the bread and circuses of the Roman Empire, it would satisfy and numb, divert and subdue by providing an escape. Campigneulles disliked the utilitarian obsession of the philosophes. The very notion of making knowledge accessible, of spreading *lumières,* of changing the common way of thinking as the *Encyclopédie* aimed to do, frightened him profoundly. There were altogether too many scholarly publications bent on advancing knowledge and applying it in the name of progress. And popularizations of these ideas were even worse; now the littlest farmer believed he could transform the world. Focusing on techniques of industry and agriculture was no better than propagating materialistic systems of philosophy. Both had the same effect; they made

5 Campigneulles gave his address in the *Journal des Dames*. For descriptions of the rue Saint Antoine in this period, see Piganiol de la Force, *Description historique* 4:473. Mercier's *Tableau de Paris,* in which the street is mentioned often, refers to it always as "la belle rue Saint Antoine."

men vain and encouraged low-status social groups to think they had a say in the direction of things. Campigneulles believed that France would be in grave danger if commoners thought, read, and worried too much, fancying themselves able to find solutions to the world's woes. The ascendancy of the people would spell catastrophe. The government had just recently officially acknowledged the danger of the written word when the king was nearly assassinated by a subject who claimed to want to touch and converse with him. A law of silence had been imposed after Damiens's attack in 1757, and nearly all writing on any serious substantive question now came under scrutiny. The royal declaration, which was to be implemented by the booktrade and the police, threatened the author, printer, or seller of any book that might be understood to "attack religion, stir up discontent, undermine the government's authority, trouble the established order, or disturb tranquillity."[6] Broadly interpreted, that ruled out almost everything.

Thus Campigneulles had chosen a very troubled time to launch his project, a moment when printed words on almost any subject were construed to do damage, to undermine stability, and to encourage anarchy. Not only were past threats to the throne to be eliminated from the record; no matters of potential contention were to be broached at all. Laws of silence had been issued before by the monarchy when recalcitrant subjects seemed to have been inflamed by *mauvais propos*. Because absolutist discourse did not allow for the king to be at fault, the blame for unruliness and agitation traditionally fell not on royal policy, but on books. "It seemed to us," pronounced Louis XV in one such edict, "that it was above all important to prescribe absolute silence on questions that might disturb public tranquillity. . . . Desiring that all past troubles be sunk into oblivion, we have ordered that it shall be as if they never occurred." Claiming that silence is the most efficient means of stopping the course of a dangerous problem and the most capable of reestablishing order, the king, whose own life had been threatened and who sensed acute danger, this time demanded more than rigorous censorship, crowning his edict with the death

6 Bibliothèque Nationale, manuscrit français (henceforth BN ms. fr.) 22093, pièce 142. See also pièce 7 for another such edict of silence.

sentence for authors or bookdealers who defied it, "car tel est notre plaisir."[7] Had this edict been rigorously carried out, half the *libraires* in Paris would have been hanged.[8]

The *Journal des Dames* was designed to demonstrate Campigneulles's strict compliance with this royal declaration. As an antidote to the *Journal des savants*—he referred to them always as polar opposites[9]—it would contain nothing serious or even remotely profound. In the prospectus that Campigneulles circulated in 1758, he promised:

> Most papers today are filled with political, moral, or philosophical systems, or graceless dissertations laden with scrupulously researched citations. No room is left for delicious nothings, for the felicitous wisps of imagination . . . for nature, for joy and pleasure. Novels . . . are scorned by journalists . . . or analyzed to death. . . . An author who gladly leaves to others the glory of announcing useful discoveries to the scholarly world and displaying their vast erudition . . . will offer instead only the amusing. . . . Poetry, stories, plays, bits of history, everything agreeable or that even tries to be, will have a place here.

Turning now to the ladies of Paris society he requested their support for his plan. They, especially, should welcome an effort to amuse them, to round out their "circle of pleasure" and give them something suitable to fill their idle moments. That they had such moments of boredom was clear to Campigneulles. Why else would they fall prey to intellectual pretensions and embrace inappropriate pastimes like those ridiculed by Molière in his *Femmes savantes?* "You, fair sex, whom we regret to see struggling with the thorny problems of science, forever inaccessible to your vain curiosity, please gather instead the roses that our poets produce abundantly in their eagerness to please you." And not only would the *Journal des Dames* offer poems to women. It would also print

7   For more on the paranoia caused by Damiens's attack, see Rétat, *L'Attentat de Damiens,* "Censure," especially 156, 161.
8   This is the conservative estimate of Zephir in "Libraires et imprimeurs," 43.
9   See for example, Campigneulles, *Nouveaux essais,* 12:
> Obscure Zoîle, ennemi des talents
> Sans cesse en vain contre moi tu déclames
> On composait le *Journal des Savants*
> Il nous manquait un Journal pour les Dames.

anything written by them, delicate productions for which the patronizing Campigneulles claimed to have a "marked predilection." [10]

This, then, was to be his passport to success. He would win the eternal gratitude of women delighted to be rescued from their floundering in areas where they did not belong and could never hope to succeed. They would now be content and harmlessly busy. Posterity would thank him for having restored joy to an overserious age that had grown dangerously proud. Most important of all, his *Journal des Dames* would serve his country by helping to keep mental minors—women and the people—in eternal ignorance. He pointed out to Malesherbes, the director of the booktrade, the necessity of placating such potentially restless marginal groups in society: "If I am not mistaken, the government should do all it can to encourage authors who propose to entertain in an age where it is unsafe to teach *le peuple* how to think. I say *le peuple* because it understands nothing and makes miserable use of 'useful' discoveries." [11] Perhaps Campigneulles had stated his dim view of women's intellectual abilities a bit baldly—this was only a private letter—but he believed it was necessary to put women back in their place. His public statements in the *Journal des Dames* were sufficiently sugarcoated that he did not expect them to be insulting. He was, after all, offering to print ladies' "riens délicieux" every month to prevent them from being bored at their toilette and to give them an illusion of importance. No other journalist had ever created a paper for that purpose. And what if he had advertised his journal as a catchall for the frivolities rejected or disdained by more profound philosophical publications? He was a loyal subject who abhorred "fermentations." [12] Not for him the threat of the Bastille that hung over such enfants terribles as Helvétius, Diderot, and d'Alembert.

Campigneulles expected journalism to be a lark. His provincial hometown had spawned its own paper, *Les Affiches de Lyon,* a

10   *Prospectus pour le Journal des Dames,* in the Réserve des Imprimés of the Bibliothèque Nationale. It is identical to the "Avant propos" in the issue of January 1759.

11   BN ms. fr. 22134, fol. 164.

12   Barbier, *Journal historique,* talks repeatedly of the "fermentations" among the people caused by Damiens and by the *Encyclopédistes.* See especially vol. 4, beginning with descriptions of the year 1757, pp. 169–214.

decade earlier, for which there was a lively market. It had made a fortune for its editor, the *libraire* Aimé de la Roche, a practical man who conceived the *Affiches* to reflect and serve the everyday needs of a city fast becoming an economic and industrial center. The paper facilitated commercial exchanges, provided publicity for doctors, printers, governesses, and merchants, matched up people with jobs, services, and items they sought, and generally addressed the interests of a bourgeois readership. But there was hardly any literature in the *Affiches de Lyon*. Like several other provincial *affiches* granted permission around that time—in Toulouse, Normandy, Nantes, Bordeaux—it fell into a special category, answered local social and economic needs, and so posed no threat to the Paris periodicals. Aimé de la Roche's motto, "The useful must always predominate over the amusing," showed that his paper was antithetical to what Campigneulles had in mind. This was no place for a young man with literary ambition to get his journalistic formation. Yet there was a steady appetite in Lyons for the Paris papers, which were sold there and were available on loan from several *cabinets de lecture*. The *Affiches* carried numerous want ads from collectors of journals seeking missing issues and from parties interested in forming reading clubs to share subscription costs. One voracious fan of the press who followed with interest nineteen different newspapers placed the following invitation: "An individual *amateur du livre* would like to keep abreast of all that goes on in the republic of letters. Journals can best satisfy this need, but since it would cost me nearly 360 livres, including transport, to subscribe to them all, I seek fourteen other likeminded people who, by contributing one louis d'or each, can make possible our mutual procurement of these journals."[13] Campigneulles thus assumed he would be able to count on avid readers and even on helpful provincial distributors, for Aimé de la Roche and another Lyons bookdealer, Jean Deville, would advertise and sell his *Journal des Dames* from their shops.[14] With all these auspicious signs, what could go wrong?

Campigneulles's only contact in Paris was the publisher Michel Lambert, who was already selling his *Essais sur divers sujets* in his shop and whom the young author therefore naively took for an

13 *Affiches de Lyon,* 1759, no. 39.
14 See Gasc, "Naissance de la presse," especially 74.

ally. One of the most shrewd and enterprising Paris *libraires*—he would actually die rich instead of ruined, having managed the incredible feat of serving simultaneously as literary agent for the age's most famous archenemies, Voltaire and Fréron—Lambert held the exclusive publishing rights of a number of periodicals.[15] He was particularly proud of his greatest plum, the privilege on the venerable, century-old *Journal des savants,* which he now owned and because of which he was in very close touch with the powerful booktrade authorities. Theoretically, this arrangement gave Lambert a monopoly on all extracts of books and "nouvelles littéraires"; anyone wishing to publish a new literary journal had first to get permission from him. They had also to pay him a handsome compensatory sum for any economic losses the new competition might cause. A few papers had paid such high fees that they had virtually purchased a privilege of their own. Lambert had driven hard bargains in the past; often the terms he insisted on were crippling. The *Journal étranger,* begun in 1754, was originally granted the right to exist only on the condition that it include no announcements of new books at all and that it print extracts only from those books rejected as uninteresting by the *Journal des savants.*[16] Another paper, *Le Conciliateur,* was permitted only after promising Lambert a sliding fee that would increase with its popularity.[17] Fréron's *Année littéraire* paid Lambert over 5,000 livres each year for being allowed to circulate. Thus anything that threatened to interfere with the existing privileged paper was severely taxed. Some new journals that refused or failed to pay the agreed-upon sum, like the *Renommée littéraire,* were soon snuffed out entirely.[18]

It was not that the *Journal des savants* itself was especially lucrative. In fact, it had a fairly small and particular readership and was no longer considered a hot sale item.[19] But it was steady. And its privilege gave Lambert first rights on all would-be competitors, putting him in a position to judge the commercial potential of

15 On Lambert's financial situation, see Archives de la Seine, série DC⁶17, fol. 228r, and série DC¹⁰95, dossier 1305. Lambert's wealth and worth at his death are also discussed briefly in Zephir, "Libraires et imprimeurs," 112, 297.

16 See Smith, "Launching of the *Journal étranger,*" and BN ms fr. 22133, fols. 116–78.

17 BN ms. fr. 22135, fols. 134–54.

18 See [Bachaumont], *Mémoires secrets* 1:233 (11 avril 1763).

19 See Birn, "*Journal des savants,*" 15–36.

each newly proposed enterprise and to benefit from the revenues of those that succeeded. The laws governing periodical subscriptions stated that the *libraire* himself must guarantee the arrangement, assume full responsibility for collecting money and distributing copies, and be financially able to reimburse subscribers should the new journal be interrupted.[20] Publishers naturally hesitated to give such a vote of confidence to unknown journalists who had not proved their stamina, whose creative muse might run dry, or whose commitment might wane. The booktrade director therefore frequently balked at requests for subscription if the gamble seemed too great. Editors naturally preferred to sell their papers by subscription rather than by single issue, because the yearlong advance investment provided funds and a guaranteed, captive audience. Sometimes new editors even offered to put up the capital themselves. But either way subscription was a risk. Malesherbes's correspondence shows numerous cases where sanguine expectations on the part of editors and publishers ended in financial ruin. Potential newspapers were thus in a double bind. If they smacked of success they would be financially penalized for impinging on the rights of the *Journal des savants* and other protected papers. But if they appeared unpromising or too limited in appeal, Malesherbes would consider the financial gamble too great and would never let them get started in the first place.[21]

Campigneulles knew none of this when he buoyantly presented his *Journal des Dames* idea to Lambert. He visited him repeatedly to discuss his idea, at first puzzled, then irritated by Lambert's reluctance to let him purchase the rights necessary to start his own paper. Finally, when he threatened to have his newspaper published in Geneva instead, Lambert shot off a letter to Malesherbes. The aspiring editor seemed far more determined than the publisher had first thought. Lambert had no desire to create new competition for the *Journal des savants,* the *Année littéraire,* and the *Feuille nécessaire,* whose publishing rights he already controlled. Campigneulles was now "making a pest of himself," he explained

---

20 See Saugrain, *Code de la librairie;* Perrin, *Manuel de l'auteur.*

21 For Malesherbes's views on periodical subscriptions, see BN ms. fr. 22133–35. For an example of a bankruptcy of a periodical publisher, see the case of the *Journal étranger* at Archives de la Seine, Registre de faillite, série D4B⁶, carton 20, dossier 961.

to the booktrade director, and Lambert needed his superior's support so that, united, they could "discourage him altogether." The idea was to insist on prohibitive conditions: a payment of 1,000 livres each year for a minimum of three years paid up front and a refusal of subscription unless Campigneulles could put up a large additional sum. From the tone of Lambert's letter he clearly expected Malesherbes to share his disapproval of the *Journal des Dames,* and the director did concur that the paper should be denied a privilege and the right to sell by subscription.[22] But Malesherbes disliked the idea of the frustrated journalist publishing in Geneva and circulating his paper clandestinely in France. Not only would it be more difficult to control; why should another country get the profits if it proved successful? Malesherbes had suspended circulation of the *Journal encyclopédique* for economic, not political, reasons because it angered him that the editor, Pierre Rousseau, had abandoned his *patrie* for Bouillon, his paper now boosting a foreign treasury rather than that of France.[23] Malesherbes now answered Lambert without enthusiasm that he should put Campigneulles on hold for a few months with vague encouragement and that, if the young man still seemed bent on his project, he should let the paper have a go with a *permission tacite*.[24]

Malesherbes, however, was more resigned than supportive. He found periodicals a headache, admitting to one of the royal censors that he had at best "only the feeblest interest in them." Most of them were full of pettiness and quarrels, editors insulting each other in endless undignified exercise of the *loi du talion,* an eye for an eye. He personally never deigned to read them. For the authors themselves, "faiseurs de feuilles," he had only scorn.[25] He then promptly forgot the *Journal des Dames.* The delays caused by his indifference led Campigneulles to seek the intervention of an influential noble protectress, the duchesse de Chevreuse, for whom his father-in-law, a Lyons tax collector, performed some essential financial services. Insinuating rather unsubtly that she owed his

22 BN ms. fr. 22134, fol. 162.
23 See Birn, *Pierre Rousseau,* 200.
24 BN ms. fr. 22134, fol. 162. Malesherbes explained often in his correspondence with the chancellor Miromesnil that he preferred to grant *permissions tacites* rather than *privilèges,* because they could be easily revoked if necessary.
25 See Voltaire, *Complete Works,* letter D9126; BN ms. fr. 22157, fol. 159; Balcou, *Fréron contre les philosophes,* 96–98.

family a favor, he wrote her of his distress over all the obstacles placed in his path. After the procrastination of the printer, there had been more waiting before a suitable censor was found to examine the first issue. Now that the censor had approved the copy, Malesherbes was again holding him up "with all manner of different excuses." Campigneulles humbly requested the duchesse to alert Malesherbes to her support of the *Journal des Dames;* her protection, he was certain, would eliminate all further delays and allow the publication to proceed smoothly. And of course her favor would certainly redouble the zeal with which his father-in-law looked after the financial interests of her august family.[26]

This kind of noble intervention did not always bring about the desired results. The previous year another would-be journalist had attempted to launch *Le Courier de la nouveauté,* a periodical designed to inform society ladies of upcoming events and to provide names and addresses of hairdressers, wigmakers, cloth merchants, jewelers, florists, artists, and teachers. But because the privilege for all "annonces, affiches, et avis divers" was owned by the wealthy financier Le Bas de Courmont, whose interests in the *Gazette de France* and the *Affiches de Paris* prejudiced him against the proposed new journal, it was doomed. The duchesse de Bourbon was called upon to plead with Malesherbes on the journal's behalf. A heated exchange of letters followed, but the *Courier* never saw the light.[27] In 1760 Malesherbes would defy the dauphin, in 1761 the minister of foreign affairs. He was bothered when people of rank tried to influence his decisions, so it was not a simple matter of finding a patron or patroness with impeccable credentials.[28]

It could not be taken for granted, therefore, that the duchesse de Chevreuse would be able to help Campigneulles, but the note she sent to Malesherbes requesting that he expedite matters for the *Journal des Dames* did the trick in this case.[29] Perhaps Malesherbes had a special regard for the duchesse, herself very knowl-

26   BN ms. fr. 22134, fol. 165.
27   See especially BN ms. fr. 22134, fols. 142–54. The original arrangements on Le Bas de Courmont's privilege are in a carton of manuscripts at the Bibliothèque Historique de la Ville de Paris, cote provisoire 4012, fol. 65 (10).
28   See Birn, "*Journal des savants,*" 33.
29   BN ms. fr. 22134, fol. 165.

edgeable and interested in all the frontiers of literature and science, as her correspondence with the minister of the *maison du roi* and the holdings of her own personal library make clear.[30] In any case on 30 November 1758 the *Journal des Dames* received its ministerial go-ahead with a tacit permission.[31] We saw that Lambert had demanded at least 3,000 livres for having negotiated the printing rights, but the terms of the arrangement were not to Campigneulles's liking. A permission was far weaker than the privilege he had hoped to buy. Although purchased privileges did not have the same prestige as those granted by the state to the government-approved papers, they nonetheless gave editors financial security and legal protection against counterfeiters. Campigneulles's permission did none of that. And the paper would have to be sold by individual issue, a difficult situation for a beginning editor with no established following. Campigneulles had learned his first lesson and was no doubt put out by the government's failure to appreciate the contribution his journal was designed to make toward preserving the status quo. Earlier, as a provincial novelist, he had found it easy to deal with Lambert; but it seemed that now, as a Parisian journalist, he could expect only trouble from the press baron. The intransigence of the authorities had begun to alienate Campigneulles. To avoid his new antagonist Lambert, although he still had to pay him, Campigneulles arranged to have the *Journal des Dames* distributed through Léonard Cuissart, a less powerful and more accessible bookdealer nearby on the Right Bank, "au milieu du quai de Gèvres, à l'Ange Gardien," whose clientele, to judge from his stock, was probably somewhat marginal. Cuissart seemed genuinely interested in novelties and shared his *fonds* and *boutique* with a partner, Pierre Dufour, himself the author of light poems and skits. Cuissart, who made his money not on newspapers but on *almanachs,* was a few short blocks from Campigneulles's home on the rue Saint Antoine and probably far easier to deal with than Lambert. And Dufour, who had for years

30 See Archives Nationales, section ancienne, registres 0¹392, 0¹404, and 0¹406, which contain some of the numerous letters between them concerning the most recent books on art, literature, and botany. The duchesse de Chevreuse owned an impressive collection of books. See her "inventaire après décès," Archives Nationales, Minutier Central, XCII (847), 29 septembre 1782.

31 BN ms. fr. 21982, "Registre pour les permissions tacites," entry no. 886. See also BN ms. fr. 22161, fols. 1 and 11.

aroused the suspicions of the police and peddled prohibited pamphlets before settling down in a respectable bookstore, was no doubt sympathetic to literary novices being snubbed by the privileged authorities.[32]

But as Campigneulles had told the duchesse, there were also other problems. His new journalistic role had jaundiced his relationship with the censors too, good intentions and docile political conformity notwithstanding. There was no formal procedure for procuring a censor, but Malesherbes's correspondence shows that authors commonly requested a particular censor and that the booktrade director sometimes but not always honored such requests. These letters show too that editors often knew and socialized with their censors, which made for frequent conflicts of interest.[33] Malesherbes had several censors whom he favored for periodicals and whom he ordered to handle new journals when no particular request had been made by the editor. We do not know if Campigneulles asked for certain censors or not, but even the ones he knew from his previous printed works were behaving differently and disappointing him now. The *Journal des Dames* would be passed around and repeatedly refused, for the censors were even more reluctant than Lambert to bless new periodicals. As part of the regime's apparatus for policing thought, they were intimately linked both politically and administratively to the privileged, protected papers because their pensions were paid from these papers' profits. During Malesherbes's years as director of the booktrade, seventeen censors wrote for or received pensions from the *Journal des savants,* forty-one from the *Mercure de France.* In its determination to control opinion, the government had thus involved more than a third of its censors in the surveillance of the press, rewarding them for their vigilance with status and official

32   On Léonard Cuissart, see Archives de la Seine, DC⁶20, fol. 95v. The journals of the late 1750s and 1760s are full of publicity for *almanachs* chez Cuissart, such as *Les Fêtes de Comus, ou Recueil de chansons à boire; L'Ami de tout le monde en vaudeville; Almanach géographique et historique; Almanach des bêtes; Almanach du Parnasse,* etc. On his partner, Pierre Dufour, see Zephir, "Libraires et imprimeurs," 274. See also the police report on him discussed in Darnton, "Police Inspector," 166–67.

33   See, for example, the very interesting case of the *Journal de médicine,* BN ms. fr. 22134, fols. 201–15, and ms. fr. 22141, fols. 56–70. I am preparing a study of this periodical and the social message it propounded.

titles.[34] Malesherbes, once he permitted a new journal, was obliged to send it to a censor. But beyond this perfunctory procedure he felt no compunction and was even relieved if it continued to be refused. The censors, avid to protect their incomes, had already aborted many potential competitors. There was a long list of journalistic stillbirths. The *Journal des Dames* was just the newest threat to the papers that succored these censors, and they were determined to destroy it.

Coqueley de Chaussepierre, a particularly industrious censor, finally agreed to read Campigneulles's first two issues, but only reluctantly and on the condition that Malesherbes promise to find a replacement fast. Coqueley was already overloaded as censor of Fréron's *Année littéraire* and the abbé de la Porte's *Observateur littéraire,* and he was also one of the authors of the *Journal des savants.* He soon sent a note reminding Malesherbes that he was far too busy to continue reading the *Journal des Dames.*[35] He felt that the censoring of papers was becoming increasingly difficult and demanding. One solution, of course, would be to limit their number. Coqueley, who wrote frequently to Malesherbes and to Sartine, the director of police, and who considered himself their confidant, would prove to be a redoubtable adversary later as the *Journal des Dames* became increasingly *frondeur.* He was largely responsible for suppressing the paper in 1778. For now he simply dropped it and Malesherbes sent it next to the censor Gabriel Henri Gaillard, a devoted friend of Voltaire's. Gaillard should have had no objection to a publication for a female audience. He was himself the author of two books on rhetoric and poetry for *dames* and *demoiselles,* and he admired great women enough to have just

34 See Blangonnet, "Recherches sur les censeurs," 106–9. For the *Journal des savants*'s particular intolerance toward newly proposed periodicals, see BN ms. fr. 22042, fol. 171, "Mémoire sur les journaux." In this *mémoire* an anonymous censor, bent on protecting the *Journal des savants,* gave the kiss of death to the *Courrier qui dit tout, L'Année dramatique, Journal des récréations, Gazette poétique, Journal militaire,* and several other proposed papers.

35 BN ms. fr. 22134, fol. 166. See also BN ms. nouvelles acquisitions françaises (henceforth: nouv. acq. fr.) 3531, fol. 200. For Coqueley's involvement with the *Journal des savants,* see BN ms. nouv. acq. fr. 1180, d'Hémery's report, "L'Etat des journaux," mai 1765. That Coqueley was one of the busiest censors is confirmed by the tables in Blangonnet, "Recherches sur les censeurs," 149. Coqueley will be discussed at length in the last two chapters of this book, when he becomes a major protagonist in our story.

finished a biography of Marie de Bourgogne. But because he too was a pensioned author of the *Journal des savants,* he would not help Campigneulles in any way.[36]

The refusal of the third censor to cooperate and support him was the hardest blow of all for Campigneulles. It would devastate him. Philippe Bridard de La Garde, a former priest, had become Mme de Pompadour's personal librarian. He had been the censor of Campigneulles's earlier works and had approved his novels enthusiastically, even bothering to commend his politics and morality.[37] He had, in other words, absolutely nothing personal against the author. But this new project was another matter entirely. De La Garde was receiving a handsome 2,000-livre pension yearly from the *Mercure,* and he now perceived the *Journal des Dames* as a threat to his livelihood.[38] The *Mercure,* after all, saw itself as an entertaining paper that already fit in many ways Campigneulles's description of his "novelty." The original *Mercure galant* of the seventeenth century, although critics had called it "a step below zero" for doing so, had wooed and tried to amuse the ladies of high society.[39] Still oblivious to the fact that he was now regarded as unwelcome competition, Campigneulles had counted on the *Mercure* for support. Its former editor, Boissy, had published some of his poems, had passed on to him some kind words of praise from the great old man Fontenelle, and had encouraged him to think of the *Mercure* as his "cradle," as it had been for many others who went on to literary glory.[40] But Boissy had died, and the *Mercure's* new editor, Voltaire's protégé Marmontel, a philosophe who was already enjoying cooperating with the authorities, was not sufficiently sentimental to make good Boissy's promise of hospitality.

---

36 Gaillard had written *Rhétorique française à l'usage des demoiselles* (Paris, 1745) and *La Poésie française à l'usage des dames* (Paris, 1749).

37 BN ms. fr. 22143, fols. 93–95. De La Garde was a somewhat unusual censor in that he granted more *permissions tacites* than *privilèges* (thirty-seven out of forty-four according to Blangonnet's tables in "Recherches sur les censeurs," 153), an indication that he felt secure enough of his "in" at court to approve a disproportionate number of dubious works.

38 Marmontel, *Mémoires* 2:61 n. 1; 65. The terms of de La Garde's pension are in Marmontel's brevet for the *Mercure* privilege (27 avril 1758), Archives Nationales 0¹102, fols. 231–35.

39 See Moureau, *Mercure galant.*

40 Campigneulles reprinted his exchange with Boissy in his *Pièces fugitives,* 35–36.

Since Campigneulles had seen fit to compete in the role of editor, the *Mercure* would be a grave instead of a cradle. Marmontel, with the encouragement of Malesherbes and the censor de La Garde, resolved to safeguard the *Mercure's* exclusive privilege and put an end to the *Journal des Dames*. It was a simple matter of suffocation.

Campigneulles's prospectus had thus incurred the hostility of *libraires,* censors, and rival editors before the first issue of his paper even appeared. If we take his own word, he was already in a "deep melancholy" at this point.[41] Nothing had gone as planned. There had been no flock of grateful ladies knocking at his door. Instead, readers were angered by his proposed frivolity. He had been chastised for his flippant tone, which seemed to indicate that he failed to take his journalistic responsibilities sufficiently seriously. He was receiving articles far more meaty and controversial than the light poems he had solicited. Within months of his arrival in Paris, his confidence was shaken on every front.

Campigneulles's first issue of the *Journal des Dames,* which came out on 1 January 1759, showed him trying desperately to respond at once to all the conflicting pressures upon him. An anonymous self-appointed adviser had warned him to show more respect for his female readers, to be more serious, and to serve up worthwhile fare. Campigneulles printed the paternalistic letter, along with his diffident promise to adopt the advice immediately. He had taken it to mean that he should not eschew entirely subjects like the philosophes and the academies, which his conservative instinct had told him to leave out. Doubtless in response to the admonition, he played down feminine frivolity. He also printed articles, probably by contributors, that were far more controversial than he had wished. One such article, a review of Diderot's *Le Père de famille,* painted a glowing portrait of a sensitive, knowledgeable "mère accomplie" based on a bourgeois model. Here was a mother endowed with consummate prudence and great wisdom to teach her own children the most important things, to fortify them against excesses of imagination and against fear, to nurture their self-respect, and to steer them from pride, passions, and pleasures to a path of decency and honor. Another entry reviewed a work on mathematics that, it was argued, could

---

41 *Journal des Dames,* avril 1759:92.

render women's thinking more clear and precise. "In promising to review for you only amusing books," Campigneulles explained, "I did not entirely mean to exclude those in the arts and sciences that have something novel and singular to offer." Yet another article praised the Academy of Lyons for admitting the writer Mme Du Boccage, thus implicitly criticizing the Parisian academies that rigorously excluded women. One letter, from a woman who found female subordination indefensible, even scandalous, excoriated Rousseau for his misogyny. Wishing to "avenge her sex," she explained that her feminism was as strong as most men's patriotism: "So be it. I take credit for representing a rare point of view."[42] Pretty madrigals and parodies were sprinkled about, but the tone of the issue was far more combative than Campigneulles had originally intended. Yet he had no choice but to treat heavy and sober matters. His nameless critic had assigned himself unasked to the *Journal des Dames* and planned to stay on the case. Identifying himself only as a "member of the Arcades de Rome," he claimed to be old and experienced enough to prescribe a formula for responsible journalism. Campigneulles's proposed superficiality would never do. A paper must communicate "not just *words,* but *things.*" And a journalist must demonstrate "justice, precision, clarity, the ability to get straight to the heart of a matter . . . fine and subtle discernment. . . . I will keep watch," the letter concluded ominously, "to see if you are worthy of the job you have undertaken . . . and I will tell you frankly if you are not."[43]

Thus, ironically, the conservative Campigneulles's opening issue violated his own pledges. It was far too daring. He had meant only to tickle the vanity of ladies, to make them a gallant overture of the kind that male champions of the fair sex had offered them for centuries. He had hoped to assuage their feelings of futility, their "mal de la satiété," which he feared might turn into discontent, by encouraging their literary efforts. If they felt appreciated, Campigneulles believed they would quiet down. But he had certainly not expected to be treating serious matters in his paper. It was precisely that tendency in other papers that he had hoped to counteract. Obviously intimidated by his nameless adviser, he

---

42   Ibid., janvier 1759:30–31, 58–59, 66, 80.
43   Ibid., 89–91.

asked him to identify himself. He soon learned he was Jean-Charles de Relongue de la Louptière, a poet who had been encouraging literary ladies for years in the *Mercure* and the *Journal de Verdun* and was doubtless annoyed at himself for not having thought of a *Journal des Dames* first. He would become Campigneulles's successor and was already insinuating himself into the editor's seat. This was his first move. Because he already had proprietary designs on the paper, he tried to prevent Campigneulles from giving it a bad name. He contributed many poems of his own, held up the *Journal de Verdun* as an example of a respectable periodical, and generally hovered over Campigneulles in an attempt to upgrade the contents.[44] Louptière worried that the young man would fast become a laughingstock if he served up only mindless drivel and that he would drag the potentially interesting and successful paper down with him. Louptière failed to grasp the extent of Campigneulles's cowardice.

The events of January 1759, during which his first issue circulated, convinced Campigneulles more than ever that weighty matters were to be avoided completely. Telescoped into that month, according to Barbier's chronicle, were enough examples of government repression to make any author's blood run cold. *Monsieur le procureur général* was denouncing Helvétius's *De l'Esprit,* the *Encyclopédie,* and "six brochures that smacked of materialism," including an *Almanach des esprits forts* and Diderot's *Etrennes aux esprits forts.* Such titles had aroused suspicion before, since an *esprit fort* was synonymous with *libre penseur* or *frondeur.* Three years earlier Campigneulles himself had written a youthful *Cléon, ou Le Petit Maître esprit fort*—a title he had no doubt chosen to be fashionable—which had been examined doubly closely by censors both in Paris and Lyons.[45] Turning out to be totally innocuous, the work had been cleared for publication, but it now seemed to Campigneulles a most inauspicious moment to attract new attention to himself. His case might be reopened, and in the present climate every printed word could be construed as incriminating. He watched as many works were proscribed over and over, by the archbishop of Paris, by the committee of examiners at the Sor-

---

44 See especially *Journal des Dames,* mars 1759:55, 89.
45 BN ms. fr. 22143, fols. 93–95.

bonne's faculty of theology, and by several *jurisconsultes,* for "troubling, with their pernicious principles, religion, and the order of the state." Before January was over, the works had been "lacerated and burned" as a warning and "grand declaration against the philosophes of our century."[46] Campigneulles had been right from the start; he felt vindicated. The works of the philosophes, although they monopolized the limelight, were indeed dangerous. Too many people had been dazzled by their spell already. Campigneulles himself envied their power, their ability to attract attention, and the fact that they could inspire so many people to flirt with dangerous causes. But readers definitely needed a distracting alternative if the regime was to survive.

The remaining three issues of Campigneulles's monthly *Journal des Dames* reflected his renewed determination to stick with his original intention, maintain a light tone, steer clear of the philosophes, cooperate with the authorities, and keep women amused with trivia. He would not be thrown off course again. Military poems and anecdotes abounded. With young men so eager to fight for their country, gushed Campigneulles in flagrant contradiction of the facts, France was sure to emerge victorious from the (Seven Years') war.[47] Women, on the other hand, could best serve their *patrie* by avoiding involvement in anything serious and by contentedly producing poems. His prospectus had lamented that women occasionally got tangled in the "buissons d'épines" of the hard sciences, and this condescending attitude now echoed in a book review describing an imaginary land where "women aspired to be sages and that spoiled everything. They could not raise themselves to the level of the sciences, so science had to be brought down to them."[48] But the pursuit of poetry was different. Women's confections restored levity to life. They could, of course, never be judged by men's standards. But whatever women wrote would be automatically facile and lovely, imbued with a "je ne sais quoi" that would assure their pieces a place in the *Journal des Dames.*[49] Campigneulles denounced works that dealt too ponder-

---

46 Barbier, *Journal historique* 4:301–5.

47 See for example, *Journal des Dames,* avril 1759:62, "Le Citoyen."

48 *Journal des Dames,* février 1759:10. This is a review of Tiphaigne de la Roche's *Bigarrures philosophiques.*

49 *Journal des Dames,* mars 1759:63.

ously with the subject of women or made strong claims for their intelligence. He insisted that the female public, "bizarre" as it was, preferred to feel and intuit things rather than have them proven, and that it could countenance nothing heavy or ponderous. The *Bibliothèque des femmes,* a short-lived periodical that encouraged women to pursue science, even though they could never be geniuses, was denounced as worthless, indeed painful reading for women: "Such paradoxes get their hopes up only to dash them."[50] And the *Ami des femmes,* which stressed the importance of women as society's moral backbone, was criticized for being too distant, analytical, and austere for female readers, far from the fluffy fare they truly craved.[51]

Campigneulles's condemnation of the extremely successful *Ami des femmes* as too feminist deserves some comment, for it reveals the full extent of his conservatism. The author of the *Ami,* Joseph Boudier de Villemert, was a supporter of the established order whose work lauded women for their soothing, civilizing influence. Boudier had no interest in reconstructing society but advocated the moral transformation of women within the status quo. Like Campigneulles he discouraged women from attempting science and other "thorny problems" and from trying to emulate such exceptional females as Mme Dacier, the classics translator, or the physicist Mme Du Châtelet. Boudier, horrified by arguments for feminine equality, stressed the complementary differences between the sexes, the otherness, uniqueness, and separateness of women. Although he put the whole comparison in terms most

50 Ibid., février 1759:59–60. The *Bibliothèque des femmes, ouvrage moral, critique, et philosophique* (Amsterdam and Paris, 1759) apparently had two issues (see Georges Ascoli, "Essai sur l'histoire"). I have only been able to find the first, at the Bibliothèque de l'Arsenal. Its editor was one obscure Chateaugiron. Even though he argues that it was beyond the female character to match Euclid, Kepler, or Newton (p. 96), he was still far too feminist for Campigneulles's taste. The *Bibliothèque des femmes* systematically attacked the prejudice that denied women stimulating education, professions, and civic responsibilities and that placed so much importance on men's superior physical strength (p. 13). What if, mused the author, "dans la manufacture des cerveaux, les féminins, loin d'avoir été négligés, ont mérité des soins et une attention particulière?" (p. 11). This possibility would have been inconceivable to Campigneulles.

51 *Journal des Dames,* avril 1759:26. The author of the *Ami des femmes,* Boudier de Villemert, also edited a newspaper called the *Avant coureur,* in which he would soon return the compliment. On the *Ami des femmes,* see Williams, "Fate of French Feminism."

flattering to women—they were more delicate, refined, sensitive, and graceful, the yeast in the social dough, the peaceful influence that kept men from ferocity and barbarism—Boudier's intention was clearly conservative. His theory, his "scientific sexism," as a recent scholar has called it, was designed to stress the specificity of men, to discourage women from stepping into the sphere of virile activities, and to persuade them to be satisfied with their condition.[52] The hypocrisy of Boudier's panegyric on women's moral virtues—he devoted two very severe chapters in his *Ami* to attacking feminine extravagance and vanity—can be seen in the fact that he himself tried to start up a fashion magazine called *Le Courier de la mode, ou Journal du goût*.[53] This, then, was the man whom Campigneulles found too serious and heavy on the *question de la femme*. It was tantamount to admitting that he no longer wanted to deal with the question of women at all.

Campigneulles's strongest motivation now seemed to be avoiding *embastillement,* and he gave little thought to what this determination to remain innocuous, even trivial, would do to his literary reputation. The *Journal des Dames* carried out his promise to print pleasant things rejected elsewhere. Typical was a review of *La Bazoche,* a *brochure* from Avignon, which Campigneulles announced proudly would not even be mentioned in other journals. They would scorn it. "That entitles it to a place in ours. . . . Besides, even the most insipid works almost always have something amusing. In the thickest darkness a glimmer can usually be perceived. Pearls often take some finding."[54] But this broadcasting of low standards was doing the *Journal des Dames* irreparable harm. As a repository of rejects it became a self-parody, virtually inviting the ridicule it now received. By the third issue, that of March, Campigneulles was apologizing for the sloppiness of his former writings and judgments and pleading with male contributors to stop bombarding him with rubbish. To add insult to injury, he was expected to pay the postage for their miserable manuscripts. "The great number of bad pieces I am receiving from men, especially in the provinces, obliges me to discourage those readers who think too highly of themselves or not highly enough of my

52 See Angenot, *Champions des femmes,* especially 148.
53 See Rimbault, "Presse féminine: Production," 203.
54 *Journal des Dames,* janvier 1759:32.

paper."[55] Even some female readers, insulted that the paper dedicated to them had become something of a joke, were themselves mocking and disrespectful, sending either fulsome praise or smut. One gushed, "Don't you realize your project is marvelous!" and raved about having a captive audience for her poems, which no other editor, no self-respecting journal like the *Mercure,* would print.[56] In Campigneulles's last issue he was forced to print a story from an elderly nobleman's sexually frustrated young wife, who had finally contrived to install her lover in the château as a domestic. "You must print this," she teased, "for you have promised it suffices to be female to appear on your pages."[57] How had a puritanical *gaulois* like Campigneulles brought this upon himself? It had never occurred to him that his *Journal des Dames* might be offending the very audience he had aimed to placate and gratify.

Campigneulles's advertised timidity, his obsequious eagerness to please and play it safe, also made him a sitting duck for his enemies. "People who honor me with their suggestions," he had announced in his opening issue, "will be sure to find in me a great *fond de docilité.*"[58] The man obviously had no fight in him; now rival journalists and censors began their series of moves to snuff him out, knowing this job would be easy. Each month the *Journal des Dames* suffered a new amputation. The first issue had contained reviews of plays at the Comédie-Française and the Théâtre Italien. By the second issue Campigneulles announced that this rubric had been suppressed by the censors and editors of the protected journals. He was "startled that they should feel in the slightest threatened by my paper," but of course he would comply, "without a moment's hesitation," restricting himself in the future to discussing printed rather than performed plays.[59] To compensate for the loss of the theater review rubric, Campigneulles increased the portion of his journal devoted to miscellaneous *pièces fugitives.* They had occupied a third of his January issue; by the April issue, his fourth and last, they took up two-thirds of the pages. Although most of the contributors Campigneulles acknowledged

55 Ibid., mars 1759:"Avis," 4, 41.
56 Ibid., mars 1759:61–63.
57 Ibid., avril 1759:51.
58 Ibid., janvier 1759:91.
59 Ibid., février 1759:61.

were male, a few women had actually begun to send in poems by then, and the editor may have had a fleeting moment of satisfaction when it seemed his idea had finally caught on. But Marmontel and de La Garde, watching from the *Mercure,* chose this moment to deal the final blow. The *Mercure,* they reminded Campigneulles, had an exclusive privilege on *pièces fugitives.* He would no longer be able to print any.

Campigneulles's swan song appeared in his fourth and last issue of the *Journal des Dames.* The suppression of the *pièces fugitives* completely denatured his paper, forcing him to change its format entirely. Instead of serving up the work of others, he would need to "fill it from my own resources," a task "far beyond my abilities and absolutely contrary to my taste."[60] Without theater reviews and little poems, the paper would need to carry bold articles and confront substantive matters. This would force Campigneulles to deal with subjects that it had never been his intention to touch and that his conservative soul feared. In particular, he would need to look closely for the first time at his female audience, which was quite different from what he had anticipated and which frankly appalled him. His readers seemed to want to discuss serious matters. One woman had just sent him her translation of an English work on commerce, agriculture, and the liberty of the press.[61] Where were the meek, enchanting creatures he had envisaged? No, he had definitely not understood enough about the implications of a paper for women when he took on the *Journal des Dames.* Bent on furthering his own interests, he had given hardly any thought to whom he was addressing. He now begged women's forgiveness for ever having conceived the "singular folly," the "pretentious ambition" of attempting to satisfy and amuse them. "Moi, le journaliste des dames!" Describing himself as a country bumpkin who felt "ill at ease and tongue-tied" in the *cercles* of Paris society, he confessed a total inability to fathom the mysterious women of *le monde.* He simply wanted to amuse and soothe, but the whole experience had been traumatic. "My character has already suffered too much in this career," which he had undertaken "ni *propter famam,* ni moins encore *propter famem.*"[62] He had no choice now but to drop the whole affair.

60 Ibid., avril 1759:92.
61 Ibid., 3ff.
62 Ibid., 92.

With this sign-off, Campigneulles left Paris and feminine newspapers behind forever. In four short months he had somehow antagonized both men and women, publishers and censors, and he had apparently irritated Malesherbes. Since journalism was obviously not going to be his path to glory, Campigneulles immediately bought himself a noble title in the form of a financial office and henceforth signed himself "trésorier de France en la généralité de Lyon."[63] Campigneulles's father-in-law was a financier, and he must have already felt comfortable in that milieu. The particular post he purchased had been advertised for sale in Querlon's *Annonces, affiches, et avis divers* since August 1758. "It gives nobility and the *droit de committimus* [the right to represent oneself in certain high courts], brings in annually 2,920 livres 18 sols, and residence is not obligatory."[64] For Campigneulles, who still wished to indulge his taste for literature, this was ideal. He now had the honor and privilege he had wanted as well as a non-negligible steady income, and he was still free to travel between his various academies and to write again the kinds of light stories he had produced before his *Journal des Dames* fiasco.

First, though, he needed to undo the damage. He would of course continue to assure the authorities of his conservatism. But he had to remedy the awkward problem that men of letters no longer took him seriously. Winning their respect once more would require a new strategy, and Campigneulles, not confident that he could do it on his own, decided he would need the help of a big name. Perhaps he also felt safe and a bit bolder as an official trésorier de France. In any case, having spent considerable energy attacking *philosophie,* the indecisive young man now took the surprising and fateful step of seeking Voltaire's blessing as he had five years earlier when he had first begun to write. The patriarch of Ferney was, after all, nearly as powerful as the king. He could make or break the literary fortunes of newcomers. He was far less rabid than many of the philosophes; he even wrote light verse! Campigneulles would hitch his wagon to a star by editing a book

---

63 See, for example, his letter to Malesherbes dated 26 octobre 1760, BN ms. fr. 22134, fol. 164.

64 *Annonces, affiches, et avis divers,* 16 août 1758:129. Querlon, the editor of these familiarly called *Affiches de province,* will appear again later on in our story. For a brief discussion of a brief period of his journal, see Marion, "Dix ans des *Affiches.*"

of Voltaire's poems that he had culled during his editorship of the paper. The Lyons *libraire* Reguillat agreed to publish it.

The philosophes were furious about this project. Somehow Campigneulles had gathered together poems Voltaire considered unworthy of printing himself, to which the young upstart had no legitimate claim at all. Besides, he had made such a nauseating show of his political conformity and of his hostility to the *esprit nouveau*. He could not have it both ways and would have to be taught a lesson. It would be fun, the philosophes decided, to watch him squirm. The appearance of an anonymous, scandalously licentious *Suite de Candide* in early 1761 provided the perfect occasion. Voltaire disavowed it immediately and got his desired revenge as well by having Grimm attribute the work to Campigneulles.[65]

Campigneulles *agonistes* made an amazing spectacle. He groveled. He did somersaults of protest. Desperate to broadcast his denial of this malicious attribution and to do so through approved government channels, he wrote in an open letter to the *Mercure de France* that he had nothing whatever to do with *Candide, deuxième partie:*

> I want to disclaim this work definitively for the sake of all my
> virtuous, honorable friends, who surely would be puzzled if I
> remained silent. I pray fervently that they are thoroughly con-
> vinced that I have never written anything contrary to decency,
> to the principles of morality, and to true religion. . . . I abhor
> in the *Suite de Candide* the license, godlessness, and *philosophie*
> one finds on every page . . . and I beg you to make this letter
> public at once. . . . [Such an attribution] profoundly wounds
> both my heart and my soul.[66]

Campigneulles could have published this letter in the *Journal des Dames,* which had by now resumed under the direction of Louptière, but he must have believed the paper attracted the wrong kind of readers. The following month, when the *Journal encyclopédique* threw *Candide* back in Campigneulles's lap again, he stepped up his disclaimer with a fawning "Discours sur les gens de lettres"

65 Grimm et al., *Correspondance littéraire* 4:400 (mai 1761). See the discussion of this attribution in Rustin, "'Suites' de *Candide*," 1409–11.
66 *Mercure de France* (juillet 1761) i:99.

delivered at the Académie de Villefranche. All writers, he urged, should be "modest, submissive to the salutary brakes of religion, imbued with love and respect for the august house of our sovereign authority." Bending over backward to cleanse his own record, he argued that only a few government-authorized, official journals should exist, the implication being that marginally tolerated papers like the *Journal des Dames* must be abolished. Reiterating the conservative argument of his original letter to Malesherbes, he advocated stricter "examiners," a "tribunal of sovereign judges" to guarantee that nothing dangerous ever got into print for "le peuple" to read.[67] It is significant in this connection that Campigneulles later contributed articles from Lyons to the *Mercure de France,* endorsing the approved, protected paper.[68]

Because of all the furor over *Candide, deuxième partie,* Campigneulles had second thoughts about his edition of Voltaire. He may have wanted to stop it completely, but evidently it was too late. Instead, he inserted many of his own pieces into the volume. When the *Pièces fugitives de M. de Voltaire, de M. Desmahis, et de quelques autres auteurs* actually appeared in late 1761, it even contained the text of Campigneulles's Villefranche speech denouncing *philosophie.* This book was the final outrage, a total travesty in the minds of the philosophes. When they attacked this time, which they did immediately in an anonymous *Examen fugitif des Pièces fugitives,* they pulverized not only Campigneulles but his printer and every journalist who announced his work.

The *Examen* may have been written by Marmontel, who as editor of the *Mercure* would have welcomed an opportunity to blast rival journalists. Its author might even have been Voltaire himself: it described with bitter sarcasm the "joy of being anthologized by M. de Campigneulles,"[69] who had no talent, no taste, and no class; living in Lyons opulence, oblivious to the woes of the world, he seemed to think he could buy a reputation in literature just as he had bought his nobility.[70] Sickened by Campigneulles's cowardice and by his conceit that he could serve up the

---

67 Campigneulles, *Pièces fugitives,* 87–94.

68 See Chouillet and Moureau, *Suppléments* 3:18.

69 *Examen fugitif des Pièces fugitives. . . .* (Plaisance, 1761). See, in particular, "Lettre à l'imprimeur des *Feuilles hebdomadaires de Lyon,*" 64–86, especially 82.

70 Ibid., 51.

work of others, the author of the *Examen* traced the problem back to journalism and delivered a diatribe against it. "Huge quantities of works, worse than mediocre, assault the public every day because of the looseness of the press."[71] *Libraires* like Reguillat should be ashamed to print such miserable books, but journalists like Aimé de la Roche, who advertised them in his *Affiches de Lyon,* were guiltier still for spreading the poison, and the *Gazette d'Avignon* and the Paris *Feuille nécessaire* contributed further to the polluting of men's minds.[72] Ever since the *Journal des Dames* Campigneulles had fancied himself a master of miscellany. Because his own poems were so miserable—they distorted the original definition of *pièces fugitives* beyond recognition, necessitating a new one[73]—he pirated and mixed the work of great writers with his. The man had no sense of decency, no respect for the age's geniuses, and apparently none for the public either. His newspaper was proof and this latest anthology confirmation. Other readers echoed the sentiments of the anonymous author of this tirade. Grimm understood why Campigneulles's *Journal des Dames* had been a catastrophe. After seeing his latest offering, he declared the ex-journalist unworthy of even uttering Voltaire's name.[74]

So Campigneulles's attempt to rehabilitate himself had made matters worse. We saw that he had much earlier lost the respect of his female readers. As one of them would put it, he had affronted them by creating a frivolous, disparaging "bagatelle."[75] Now the philosophes thought him a worm, and their traditional adversaries, Fréron and Sabatier de Castres, disliked him too. Politically tamer than a lamb, Campigneulles had merely wished to

---

71   Ibid., iv.

72   Ibid., 65, 68. Campigneulles's *Journal des Dames* had done faithful publicity for Aimé de la Roche (for example, avril 1759:77). He doubtless felt obliged to reciprocate.

73   Ibid., 71–73. *Pièces fugitives* should be "fugitives commes ces beautés modestes, ou finement coquettes, qui fuient, qui se cachent à demi et qui échappent, pour se faire rechercher, poursuivre, saisir, et embrasser avec plus de plaisir," or "comme la mousse spiritueuse et divine du vin de champagne; ou comme les ondes fugitives d'un ruisseau bordé de fleurs, et dont le murmure est aussi doux que les plus beaux concerts." But instead Campigneulles's offerings are "fugitives comme les criminels qui fuient pour éviter l'ignominie, la brûlure et cetera, fugitives parce qu'elles semblent avoir honte de se montrer."

74   Grimm et al., *Correspondance littéraire* 4:400, 486 (novembre 1761).

75   See Chapter 3, below.

create a harmless, integrative "journal inutile" much like the one prescribed by Beaumarchais's *Figaro*.[76] But journalism had proved to be a fast and dirty game in which one had to take sides and fight. One could not even withdraw from the fray without scars, and trying to be inoffensive offended. A paper for women had proven to have still more problems, arousing unsavory, contentious responses among readers Campigneulles had thought passive. He had confessed in the end that journalism was a "demanding career," an "arduous obligation" that he had undertaken "on whim, rashly, without thinking things through."[77] He even wrote a transparently autobiographical tale about the humbling of a vain literary novice.[78] But such apologetic gestures failed to disarm his critics. Impulsiveness and stupidity were no excuse. The journalist Beffroy de Reigny, future friend of Robespierre and Camille Desmoulins, who would assume the name of Cousin Jacques in his own newspaper during the Revolution and who knew firsthand about editorial pressures, found Campigneulles pitiful and fatefully indecisive, "moitié figues, moitié raisins."[79] Sabatier called him simply a "disgrace to the world of letters."[80] Grimm considered his humility cloying and wished he had succumbed to a fleeting impulse to throw all Campigneulles's works into the fire.[81]

Campigneulles's journalistic failure, although extremely unpleasant for him, hurt only his ego and his literary future. He was still trésorier de France with plenty of food on his table and money in the bank. Some later editors of the *Journal des Dames* would be less lucky. They had more at stake, and when the paper failed to work for them, they went hungry and made noise. Several would be radicalized by the regime's intransigence toward their journalistic efforts. When the revived *Journal des Dames* became *frondeur* and incendiary in their hands, Campigneulles would shudder and quake at the monster he had inadvertently sired. When he had begun the paper, the philosophes represented the most daring group on the intellectual scene, and he himself had been badly hurt

76 See Introduction, above.
77 *Journal des Dames,* avril 1759:92.
78 See "Ce n'était pas cela," in Campigneulles's *Anecdotes morales.*
79 Beffroy de Reigny, *Dictionnaire néologique* 2:485.
80 Sabatier de Castres, *Trois Siècles* 1:"Campigneulles."
81 Grimm et al., *Correspondance littéraire* 5:296; 7:102.

by playing on their coattails. Within a few years, however, the *Journal des Dames* would be denouncing the philosophes as conservatives and even reactionaries, men who preached progress but in fact were committed to and dependent upon the regime's entrenched institutions and whose *Encyclopédie* had done nothing to advance the cause of women.[82] Privately Campigneulles regretted ever having had the idea of a feminine periodical. Publicly he hid his paternity.[83] Expert at antagonizing everyone, this timid man would survive the Revolution, which he detested, because he had by then finally learned how to keep quiet. A lifelong defender of monarchical principles, Campigneulles had at first been completely oblivious to his newspaper's explosive potential. He had seen journalism as a means to please and subdue, not inform and agitate, as a palliative for restless groups in society, an anesthetic diversion whose function was entirely integrative. We saw that he linked women with the people, second-order beings who needed to be kept in check, even kept in darkness. He did not want an exchange with his audience, had no intention of diagnosing its social situation, and shunned the notion of becoming its spokesman. In just four months, however, he had discovered that simply inviting the participation of women in his paper opened a dialogue that threatened to challenge dominant presuppositions and evoke unorthodox responses. In the next chapter we shall see how the disruptive tendencies of the discourse on women frightened a second male editor, one considerably more feminist at the outset than was the *Journal des Dames*'s founder.

82 See Chapters 3, 4, and 6, below.

83 Only once, in 1765 when its then editor Mme de Maisonneuve presented the *Journal des Dames* to the king and became a *pensionnaire du roi,* did Campigneulles try to cash in on his role as founder. In 1774 when another female editor, Mme de Montanclos, protégée of Marie Antoinette, had just relaunched the paper after a five-year suspension, Campigneulles contributed a poem, but this time he signed himself only as a "subscriber." When *frondeurs* like Mme de Beaumer and Louis-Sébastien Mercier were in charge (1762–63 and 1775–76), Campigneulles wanted nothing to do with the paper.

2

Chivalric Journalism Gets a Social
Conscience

M. DE LA LOUPTIÈRE AND THE *PARTERRE* (1761)

Jean-Charles Relongue de la Louptière needed a wealthy wife; he was looking for an intelligent one in the bargain. Descended from the *noblesse d'épée* of Languedoc, the aspiring poet had a château and a coat of arms, but no money. He was struggling on a rente of 600 livres a year when ten times that was considered necessary to live "correctement" in Paris.[1] The ideal spouse had not yet come his way, however, and once past his thirtieth birthday, Louptière began to pursue his matrimonial search more urgently. For years he had been sending pastoral verses to the *Mercure* and the *Journal de Verdun* that drew enthusiastic responses from female readers. Some of these admirers began to seek Louptière's advice on their own poetry, and he had gradually become a self-styled agent for timid yet talented ladies, submitting their poems to the journals along with his own.[2] As his fan club grew, it dawned on him that

1 According to his obituary by Imbert (*Mercure de France,* décembre 1784:179–82), Louptière was born in Champagne in 1724 and died there sixty years later. For other biographical information, see Babeau, "La Louptière"; Balloffet, "Monsieur Pezant." See p. 126 of this last article for Louptière's financial situation in 1757, just before he took on the *Journal des Dames.* The estimate of 6,000 livres as a minimum for living "properly" was made by Turgot in 1750. See Blangonnet, "Recherches sur les censeurs," 116.

2 Louptière first published poems in the *Mercure* in 1749. By 1755 he was already sending poems by his female admirers to the *Journal de Verdun,* such as the following, printed in the November issue:

> Pourquoi loin de tes yeux, illustre la Louptière
> Le sort a-t-il placé le berceau de mes jours?

among his followers he might find one sufficiently endowed to marry. But his attempt to woo them, which began in earnest in 1755, was hampered by his having nothing but charm to offer. Repeated rebuffs taught him that he needed to enhance his own status and fortune before he could be considered an attractive suitor. To achieve these ends, he got himself accepted to several learned academies, first Châlons-sur-Marne, then Villefranche, and finally the Arcades de Rome. And he became editor of the *Journal des Dames*. What more gallant homage could he pay to the fair sex? This would prove to potential fathers-in-law that he was a success in the world of letters and that his intentions were completely honorable.

That the *Journal des Dames* was something of a mating game for Louptière can be seen from his previous techniques of courtship. The literary flirtations he undertook were for him potential marriages. When, for example, a certain "Bergère Annette" sent him poems for correction in 1755 and again the following year, accompanied by flattering letters and a description of herself, Louptière saw in her a talented writer but also a possible future wife. Determined to discover her true identity, he traced the postmark on her correspondence to a town near Villefranche and wrote to the mayor, furnishing the hints he had gleaned from the letters and requesting help in learning "the name of the studious miss and of her château."[3] When she proved to be from one of the oldest, most distinguished families in the realm, the enterprising poet, unabashed, next asked his informer the financial worth of the young lady's father, the number of other sisters and brothers in the family, and the customs in Beaujolais dictating the fraction of inheritance received by daughters. The answers evidently delighted him. He seemed ready to move there and marry the poetess sight unseen—he had inquired of her looks but said her age was unimportant!—yet he restrained himself in a letter of introduction to her father, claiming to have "feelings of a completely

---

Ta muse ingénieuse, agréable et légère,
L'eût rendu florissant et fameux pour toujours.

3   This remarkable exchange of letters was saved by the mayor of Villefranche, M. Pezant, in the archives of its academy. Sworn to secrecy at the time, he never made them public, but they were discovered and quoted at length by Balloffet, "Monsieur Pezant," 1928:192.

platonic kind" for the gifted "Annette."[4] She, delighted by the attentions of this "first favorite of Apollo" and by his detective skills in tracking her down, invited him to pay her a visit. The father, however, was unimpressed with the prospect of a journalist son-in-law. He warned Louptière of the "dangers" of splashing the family's real name in all the "petites gazettes," of "exposing his daughter to the public." The "assembled counsel" of the family put a quick stop to the budding romance; there would be no més-alliance for Mlle de Monspey, owner of the lands of Charantay, daughter of the comte de Vallières.[5] The young woman never married; she retired to a nunnery, but Louptière continued his quest. Another poetess, the marquise de Chênelette, a much older widow, was the next to refuse his chivalrous literary overtures.[6] Throughout 1759 and 1760 he undertook similar courtships in Normandy and Champagne without success.[7]

The time had obviously come for the hungry bachelor to make something of himself, to capitalize on the role he was already play-ing as impresario for female writers, to finally reap the fruits of his labors. The *Journal des Dames* seemed the obvious place to continue his activities. Impatient to take it over, he had latched onto Campigneulles from the time he first read his prospectus, watching his activities with proprietary zeal, contributing numer-ous poems and articles, and intimidating the already beleaguered founder with his own superior maturity and expertise. Louptière, after all, had had a journalistic apprenticeship as a contributor to other papers, and he considered himself entitled to a journal of his own. Relations between the two men appeared cordial on the sur-face—Campigneulles recommended his successor positively to Malesherbes, and Louptière praised his predecessor when he first took over[8]—but the young man had been outmaneuvered. The *Journal de Verdun,* which had for years harbored and humored Louptière's growing fan club, announced his new editorial role at

4   Ibid., 1929:109.
5   Ibid., 114–20.
6   Ibid., 126.
7   See *Journal (historique) de Verdun,* mars 1759:213, mai 1759:373–75, août 1759:117–18, and décembre 1760:450–54.
8   Bibliothèque Nationale, manuscrit français (henceforth BN ms. fr.) 22134, fol. 164, and *Journal des Dames,* avril 1761: "Avant propos."

the *Journal des Dames* as "legitimately his by right of conquest."[9]

Two years elapsed between Campigneulles's last issue and Louptière's first, probably because the new editor could not afford to buy the rights to the *Journal des Dames*. At times Louptière could barely buy food. He never gave an address in Paris, saying instead he could be reached through his *libraire,* and he seems to have been too poor to rent permanent lodgings. But he maintained his dignity in spite of his indigence. Mercier, a later editor of the *Journal des Dames,* described in his *Tableau de Paris* an encounter with Louptière at a lemonade stand. Mercier offered to buy the "gentle poet" a dinner, knowing he could scarcely afford coffee and bread a few times a week. "No, thank you," Louptière replied with a smile, "I ate yesterday."[10] The gracious manner that moved Mercier charmed many others besides and must have helped Louptière find financial backing for his newspaper. When his revamped *Journal des Dames* finally appeared in April 1761, it was dedicated to the princesse de Gallitzin, the wealthy wife of the Russian ambassador, who may have provided the necessary funds. This noble lady was perhaps even privy and sympathetic to Louptière's secret motives and his desperate need to demonstrate that he had "arrived." In any case, she generously lent her name to his journalistic enterprise. And it may have been she who added a feather to his cap by arranging his membership in the Académie des Arcades de Rome.[11]

Louptière had meanwhile also been busy negotiating improved terms and a loftier status for his paper. Besides its noble dedication, it now had a look of prosperity. Filigreed borders decorated the title page, it was printed on high-quality white paper, and there were engraved pages of songs with musical accompaniment. The *Journal des Dames* still had only a tacit permission rather than

9 *Journal de Verdun,* juin 1761:430–34. This and other favorable reviews of his revamped *Journal des Dames* were proudly reprinted by Louptière years later in his *Poésies et oeuvres diverses* 2:73ff.

10 Mercier, *Tableau de Paris* 11:45.

11 The princesse de Gallitzin, whose husband became fast friends with Diderot, was known in the world of letters primarily for translations and had a reputation for grace and kindness. The *Journal des Dames* continued to be dedicated to her until December 1761 when she died, and at just that point the paper's serious troubles began. See Louptière's "Dédicace," avril 1761, and her eulogy, janvier 1762:59ff.

a privilege[12] but Louptière had arranged for subscriptions where Campigneulles had failed, by convincing a new publisher that his project was commercially viable. The journal, now distributed "chez Quillau," cost 12 livres for the whole year, or 24 sols a month, making it advantageous to subscribe. Jacques-François Quillau was one of the first Paris bookdealers to set up a public *cabinet de lecture,* where readers could browse, drink refreshments, and familiarize themselves with the latest literary "nouveautés." They could also, for a nominal fee, receive a catalogue and borrow books and journals for home use.[13] Since Quillau, in his own words, "prided himself on knowing and selling only works with a wide appeal," his endorsement of the *Journal des Dames* was a vote of confidence and a coup for Louptière.[14]

Nothing was going to stand in his way now. When the censor de La Garde, still faithfully protecting his beloved *Mercure,* again refused the *Journal des Dames* as he had under Campigneulles, Louptière wrote a strong letter to Malesherbes protesting what he considered trumped-up and "chimerical" charges against him. He reminded the booktrade director that he already had a considerable female following and argued the importance of satisfying "different classes of readers," whose tastes, he believed, he had successfully ascertained. His journal would enrich, not hurt, the French press, if he could simply be allowed to carry out his "sacred intentions" unfettered.[15] Malesherbes may have liked Louptière's directness or his idea of tapping a new set of consumers; we saw that he disapproved of authors relying on intervention by patrons and protectors and that he was eager to boost the French economy by exploiting the market of readers as completely as possible. In any case, the next censor to whom the *Journal des Dames* was sent approved it and allowed it to appear smoothly for the six months of Louptière's editorial tenure. This censor, François Marin,

12   BN ms. fr. 21992, fol. 14, no. 94.
13   Lottin, *Catalogue alphabétique,* mentions the warm reception given Quillau's *cabinet* by the public (p. 145). For details of the *cabinet* itself, see BN ms. fr. 22108, fols. 223–25.
14   Quillau's catalogue, or *Magasin littéraire,* was still offering the *Journal des Dames* in 1766. See BN ms. fr. 22085, fol. 52. Quillau was very successful. His family would later become printers of the lucrative daily *Journal de Paris.* See his testament at Archives de Paris, DC¹⁰422, dossier 311.
15   BN ms. fr. 22134, fol. 163.

would soon be catapulted to power, first as *censeur de la police* in 1762, then as *secrétaire général de la librairie* in 1763, and in these capacities would cause great trouble for later editors of the *Journal des Dames* when it entered its *frondeur* stage. Right now, however, in 1761, Marin was new on the job, not yet bound to one of the privileged papers, and he did not see Louptière's project as any threat at all.[16]

The first issue of Louptière's *Journal des Dames* showed his eagerness to broaden his search for female talent. Of course he advertised only his professional interest in advancing the work of literary ladies, but we know that he had other motives as well. In the *Journal de Verdun* his letters, songs, and poems had successfully galvanized many women writers into activity. Just recently he had begged a Julie de la Croix to shed her nom de plume and had tracked down a Mlle Brohon to a convent where he had persuaded her to continue her writing.[17] A certain "Bergère des Alpes" had sent a *musette* with sufficient merit to whet Louptière's editorial (and matrimonial) appetite.[18] He seemed confident that such women, and many yet unknown to him, would welcome his *Journal des Dames*. Louptière warmed to the idea of speaking for a mute, undeservedly scorned group in society and saw his own paper as license to pursue this chivalrous task with renewed zeal. By offering women a journal of their own, he boasted, he could now guarantee their immortality, their eternal glory. In an earlier letter to a potential father-in-law, he had praised the daughter's poems and spoken of his eagerness to "favor and nurture newborn reputations." He was seeking her out, asking her to state her true name, so she could be appropriately honored. "I am rendering a service to the republic of letters," he explained, "and I willingly sacrifice my own precious time to this cause." But he confided to a friend that his motives were far more personal and romantic.

16 Marin appears repeatedly in Voltaire's correspondence and in the Anisson-Duperron collection of manuscripts on the *librairie*, BN ms. fr. 22061–193 and BN ms. nouvelles acquisitions françaises (henceforth nouv. acq. fr.) 1180–83, 3344–46. He was the butt of Beaumarchais's *mémoires* in 1773–74, after which he fell from grace. For an overview of his life by an author eager to rehabilitate him, see Ricard, *Victime de Beaumarchais*. More will be said about Marin in the chapters that follow.
17 *Journal de Verdun,* mars 1759:213; mai 1759:374–75.
18 Ibid., décembre 1760:450–54.

"The greatest joy for a man of letters would be to find in the companion of his days also a colleague in his studies."[19] Now in the *Journal des Dames* he was expanding the horizons of his quest, and his eagerness to encourage women writers was fueled by his desire to find one for himself. *Femmes de lettres* were invited by the new editor, not just from Paris and provincial cities but from every remote corner of the countryside, "even the obscure ones living in their châteaus. Women throughout the world have natural rights to the *Journal des Dames*. Not a single remarkable word of theirs will escape me."[20]

The reaction of the rival journalists was mixed. Two of the crustiest competitors, de la Porte and Fréron, accepted Louptière's *Journal des Dames,* feeling they had nothing to lose. They had, after all, seen Campigneulles fail, and the new editor probably would too. Before starting his *Année littéraire,* Fréron had written a periodical under a female pseudonym, *Lettres de Mme la comtesse de . . . sur les écrits modernes,* but had not found his audience particularly receptive to or indulgent of the feminine slant. It seemed folly to count on an exclusively female public. These editors regarded Louptière's paper as a harmless but ultimately doomed experiment. Even the *Journal de Verdun,* from which Louptière's admirers would now defect, encouraged his going off on his own, obviously feeling it could comfortably endorse the *Journal des Dames* without seriously jeopardizing its own market.[21] The *Observateur littéraire* quoted Louptière's opening issue, praised his ability to evoke responses from his female readers, and patronizingly wished him luck.[22] Fréron, who considered women capricious and had little hope for Louptière's gamble but was curious to see what would happen, wrote in the *Année littéraire:* "It is for women to decide the fate of this periodical composed for their sake. If M. de la Louptière can win their blessing, he shall be well compensated for his work."[23] Grimm cast his vote with the naysayers but was much more blunt; he too felt certain the *Journal des*

---

19 Balloffet, "Monsieur Pezant."
20 *Journal des Dames,* avril 1761:"Avant propos."
21 The *Journal de Verdun* carried Louptière's prospectus in January 1761 (pp. 60–64) and gave extracts from his first issue in June 1761 (pp. 430–34).
22 *Observateur littéraire* 2:354–57.
23 *Année littéraire* (1761) iii:47.

Dames would have no "buyers" and would soon expire, sinking forever into obscurity. "I pity with all my heart women who entrust their productions to Louptière . . . if they have any hope of being remembered by posterity."[24]

Other editors, however, seemed seriously concerned that the *Journal des Dames* would be a success. The *Mercure* felt threatened, perhaps because 10 percent of its subscribers were female and its editors considered that a substantial fraction. It had previously regarded itself as satisfying the needs of a diverse reading public, and already had a reputation of catering to "le beau sexe."[25] With only sixteen hundred names on its subscription list, the *Mercure* did not want to lose any. D'Aquin's *Censeur hebdomadaire* also eyed the *Journal des Dames* with suspicion. D'Aquin himself shared Louptière's eagerness to encourage women in their intellectual pursuits. His paper even rejoiced over the admission of a female astronomer as an honorary associate of the Académie de Béziers.[26] Like the *Journal des Dames,* the *Censeur hebdomadaire* was only a permitted, not a protected paper. Its editors had recently fought among themselves, its finances were particularly precarious at this point, and its prognosis was bad.[27] At 18 livres a year it was one-third more expensive than its newest rival. D'Aquin therefore sought to strengthen his position by discrediting Louptière, accusing him of talking down to his readers and panning the new *Journal des Dames* as an "insubstantial frivolity," an "insipid bagatelle," disrespectful of the very social group it meant to please. He and Louptière exchanged accusations in their respective papers.[28] They obviously felt they had an audience worth fighting over, although their sense of its needs and desires was neither clear nor well defined.

---

24 Grimm et al., *Correspondance littéraire* 4:400.

25 When Daniel Mornet discovered how many female subscribers the *Mercure* had in 1763, he appears not to have known of the *Journal des Dames* and was prompted to conclude: "Le *Mercure* était le journal des femmes et cela a son importance si l'on songe à ce qu'il donnait des choses très sérieuses, infiniment plus sérieuses que nos modernes *magasines* à succès." See his "Sur l'intérêt historique."

26 *Censeur hebdomadaire* (1761) v:11.

27 [Bachaumont], *Mémoires secrets* 1:38 (8 février 1762), reported that d'Aquin's paper had been diminishing in length and circulation and predicted that it would not last long.

28 *Censeur hebdomadaire* (1761) ii:216–19, 391; *Journal des Dames,* juin 1761:217; *Censeur hebdomadaire* (1761) iii:54–56.

Most of the journalists of the day realized the existence of a female reading public, but because of the pervasively misogynistic views of the dominant aristocratic culture their attitude toward it was generally negative. They blamed women for forcing men to lower their literary standards. They argued that since women, like commoners, were mostly unschooled and naturally muddle-headed, they should not aspire to understand serious matters, yet pretension and curiosity drove them to try to follow events in the world of letters. This then made necessary a drastic simplification and, inevitably, a falsification of all substantive articles in the newspapers. This superficiality had now spread to male subscribers in the upper classes, and even though the journalists were glad that more people were reading and buying, they mourned the loss of discriminating taste and intellectual purity that had prevailed in the days of Bayle and appeared threatened by the encroaching influence from below. Complaints of this kind were numerous, the finger of accusation always pointed at "lectrices" and at "the people," both groups of marginal social status. The *Journal étranger* had been constrained to lighten its tone to appeal to a broader audience, its editor explained, "because everyone, even women, seems to want to read these days." Articles with "depth, abstraction, or erudition would be distasteful to our frivolous readers, who unfortunately are in the majority."[29] The *Religion vengée* echoed this concern,[30] and the *Ephémérides du citoyen* excused itself for simplifying sophisticated material:

> The multitudes are incapable of studying and learning; they want to skim and know things without effort. . . . French women have for years gone pale at the sight of a real book; this malady is contagious and has now affected men as well. This is not the only *délicatesse* of this kind that has been communicated by one sex to the other. Hence we need *brochures* and papers [to satisfy the tastes] of our century.[31]

The *Nécrologe des hommes célèbres* argued that those women who would buy a *Journal des Dames* were looking only for trivial gossip.[32] The *Avant coureur* predicted that Louptière was seriously

---

29 See Smith, "Launching of the *Journal étranger*."
30 See the prospectus for *La Religion vengée,* BN ms. fr. 22137, fols. 111–12.
31 Quoted in the *Journal des Dames,* décembre 1765:70.
32 *Nécrologe des hommes célèbres,* 1769:248–49.

overestimating women. His expectations both for their own literary creativity and for their interest in serious things were unrealistic. He would end up having to fill the *Journal des Dames* himself—this critic strongly suspected that the prolific Louptière had wanted to do that all along—because women could not create anything of quality or substance. "He will soon run dry," came the dire forecast, "for no paper will sustain the interest of the female readers whom he has principally in mind."[33]

Louptière appeared undaunted by these prophets of doom. It seemed to him unfair that women were discouraged from cultivating their talents and then blamed for their apparent ignorance. He became in fact more determined than ever to champion literary women in the face of their negative press in other "feuilles" and continued to insist on the uniqueness of his, setting it up as an alternative to more traditional institutions. Whereas most books, plays, even ordinary conversations excluded *femmes de lettres,* he would give them the recognition and publicity they deserved. The first three issues of his *Journal des Dames* were unusually aggressive in their claims for women writers, arguing repeatedly that they should be accepted in learned academies, that "their lack of emulation is the sole cause of their slow progress."[34] He pointed out that in the last century such women as Mlles de Scudéry and Deshoulières had won academic prize competitions and that a Mlle de Bermann's essay on virtue had just been awarded the prize for eloquence by the Académie de Nancy. Such examples, although lamentably few, should persuade women that "blushing from writing . . . thinking . . . enlightening one's century [is wrong] . . . that one's forehead is not blemished, only enhanced, by a crown of laurels."[35] These early issues featured the works of contemporary female writers. The first, that of April 1761, devoted over thirty pages to the works of one Mme de Beaumer, a fascinating character who soon became Louptière's successor and about whom more will be said later.[36] In the May issue he dealt with the writings of Mme de Puisieux, mistress of Diderot—the

---

33   *Avant coureur,* 1761:255.

34   *Journal des Dames,* avril 1761:"Avant propos," viii.

35   Ibid., avril 1761:57. In another issue (juin 1761:250ff.) Louptière published the eighteen-year-old Mlle de Bermann's essay in its entirety.

36   Ibid., avril 1761:11–43.

police's favorite "bad boy"—and a declared enemy of the immorality of *précieuses*.[37] Mme de Puisieux had just finished a book defending women's intellectual abilities and civic virtues. "If talent, erudition, philosophy, and other titles of superiority are crimes for a woman," concluded Louptière, then this author "is more guilty than ever."[38] He provided a list of twenty-two "dames" and fifteen "demoiselles" whose literary productions deserved attention. The purpose of the list, the editor explained, was both to make these authors aware of their solemn obligation to a public eager for more and to display for passive but potential female writers the inspiring "literary riches of their sex."[39] The Académie des Arcades de Rome had been formed by Queen Christina of Sweden and had always admitted women.[40] The princesse de Gallitzin, Mme Du Boccage, and Mme Du Châtelet were among its members. If only the academies of France would learn to do the same!

Louptière maintained this aggressive tone throughout April, May, and June. More than any other male journalist he argued for the literary rights of women and meant to build their self-confidence. For them he put his own career on the line. Campigneulles had simply wanted to keep women busy and out of trouble, but Louptière genuinely admired and respected women with intellectual gifts and fancied himself their defending knight. His "parenthèses lyriques," which he inserted throughout the *Journal des Dames* as a flattering running commentary, seemed to please his readers greatly.[41] His list of female contributors grew. Earlier admirers were joined by Mesdames Estienne, Bourette ("la Muse Limonadière"), Bénoit, Vermont de Trecigny, Mesdemoiselles d'Ales du Corbet, de la Guesnerie, la vicomtesse de Vienne. Other women submitted their works cryptonymously or signed them "une savante allemande."[42] This high level of reader participation was a response to Louptière's insistence that his paper was to be an open dialogue. He had priced the *Journal des*

37 See Darnton, "Police Inspector," 183–87, especially 186.
38 *Journal des Dames,* mai 1761:105.
39 Ibid., avril 1761:49–54.
40 Ibid., "Dédicace."
41 See, for example, ibid., mai 1761:107.
42 See, for example, ibid., avril 1761:81, 84.

Dames far lower than many of the other literary journals to make it accessible to more people.[43] And just as he pledged to welcome his readers' suggestions, he was confident that they would be ready listeners for what he had to say.

To what kind of woman was Louptière really speaking? Certainly not to the ladies of Parisian high society, for he preached an austere morality antithetical to courtly ways. He seems to have been targeting less sophisticated provincial women. The ads he carried were sometimes for items being sold in little provincial towns near the capital like Etampes. No promiscuity or vanity for his readers. Like *La Spectatrice,* he warned of the dangerous "tourbillons de la ville" and waxed rhapsodic over the joy of breathing "l'air des vertus champêtres."[44] The *Journal des Dames,* he promised, would be decent always, so that "daughters and mothers could read it together without blushing."[45] A long article attacked "les bourgeoises du bon ton" who spent all their time at their toilette so busy aping corrupt aristocrats that they had entirely lost sight of their proper values. Relations between the sexes should be based on friendship and respect, not glamour and money. Natural, open, informal social intercourse should replace fashionable galas and pomp.[46] Women, argued Louptière, should cultivate their inner resources and care less about their external charms. In a review of Graville's *L'Ami des filles* he quoted a knowing heroine who complained: "My admirers maintain a humiliating silence concerning my mind. . . . I would rather be uglier than Sappho and have her talents."[47] Another new book, Gaudet's *Les Nouvelles Femmes,* described healthy relationships based on character and

43 Only the *Journal de Verdun* was lower, at 8 livres 8 sols a year. The *Feuille nécessaire* and the *Annales typographiques* cost 12 livres, the same as the *Journal des Dames.* The others were all more expensive: *Trévoux* (12 livres, 16 sols); *Observateur littéraire* (15 livres); *Savants* (16 livres, 14 sols); *Censeur hebdomadaire* (18 livres); *Journal étranger, Mercure, Conservateur,* and *Année littéraire* (24 livres); and the *Journal encyclopédique* (above 30 livres). These figures, for 1761, come from Jèze, *Etat,* 199–209.

44 *Journal des Dames,* avril 1761:85, juin 1761:266. See also the numerous poems on the beauties of his Champagne, "more lovely than any fairy tale," reprinted in his *Poésies et oeuvres diverses.*

45 *Journal des Dames,* avril 1761:"Avant propos."

46 Ibid., septembre 1761:234–47, "Remonstrances aux bourgeoises du bon ton par un complaisant révolté."

47 Ibid., mai 1761:110.

intelligence rather than external charms. "[Women] should look for solid qualities, personal merit, a righteous heart, a straightforward manner, less passion and more sense, fewer declarations and more integrity."[48] Louptière hoped to restore spontaneity and affection to male-female relationships and thought this only possible if women abandoned their affectations and faced their real feelings. With less attention to their looks and more to their minds, they could become true companions.

But Louptière was sending a mixed message. He made strong claims for women's intellectual abilities, yet he was a social conservative. Those people who had to struggle in the world did not interest him, and equality between the sexes never entered his mind. He had no particularly advanced ideas on female education, no ideas on that subject at all in fact. His ideal woman was naturally brilliant; it did not appear to worry him that most women were taught nothing of substance, and his *Journal des Dames* carried no articles on pedagogical theory. His only comment on Rousseau's *Nouvelle Héloïse* was that it was full of contradictions.[49] "Bergère Annette," a poetess whom he pursued arduously and described in his private correspondence, was just what he thought a suitable companion should be. She was, first, "de condition." "This illustrious girl was *born* with a taste for books, a love for poetry and music. . . . A young person who has *received from nature* . . . such rare talents . . . must be appreciated for her merits. There is no risk of confusing her with the crowd."[50] "You are," he told her, "far superior to the common of your sex."[51] She was gentle and shy, having discreetly hidden her true identity. Although Louptière hoped to coax such women out of their timidity and teach them not to be ashamed of their gifts, it was their purity and modesty that attracted him. This had been the rule with his earlier followers at the *Journal de Verdun*. Many of the women whose anonymity he had tried to penetrate persisted in their secrecy, which only intrigued him further. "My rest, my happiness, and my tranquillity," one told him, "depend on my name remain-

48 Ibid., juin 1761:210–15.
49 Ibid., avril 1761:86.
50 Balloffet, "Monsieur Pezant," 1928:letter of 16 avril 1756. The emphasis in the quotation is mine.
51 Ibid., 1929:110.

ing undiscovered."[52] To be a knight in shining armor for these intelligent but retiring damsels who lacked self-confidence, accepted their subordination, and needed consolation and a boost seemed to Louptière a worthy and gallant undertaking. And because he had defended a group that rarely defended itself, much of his rhetoric was only ceremonial. Louptière, like so many champions of the female sex before him, had counted on the stability of the social order and never meant his discourse to transgress beyond the accepted limits of female panegyrics. His crusade depended, in short, on a system in which antifeminism was a fact.

But now that he was editing a *Journal des Dames,* he was reaching a wider audience, and as he began to listen to the feedback from his readers, he did not altogether like what he heard. Not all of his buyers fitted his picture of bright yet refined and socially correct ladies waiting to be discovered in their châteaus. He had spoken so boldly about women's rights to intellectual recognition, their need to be encouraged in their literary productivity, precisely because he pictured them blushing at the very thought. The word "rougir" comes up frequently in Louptière's overtures to women writers, for he expected them to be reserved. But after a few months as editor, he began to pick up a different tone from his audience. The *avant propos* of his opening issue, and *avis* in most of the subsequent ones, had invited his readers to express their candid reactions to the paper and to send suggestions for changes they might want him to make, and Louptière seems to have received and listened carefully to many responses. Some women, it seemed, were interpreting his arguments for literary liberty as something more, as a call to action, as an invitation to bring about social change as well. Far from blushing, they were fairly bursting with discontent and resentment. Instead of poems, these contributors sent long, disgruntled letters, explaining that they were considered misfits in their towns. And these women were not as "naturally enlightened," as refined and knowledgeable, as Louptière had imagined. He was, for example, startled (and doubtless appalled!) to discover how few of them could read the music of his original songs. In response to the complaints of the many who

52 *Journal de Verdun,* mai 1759:373–74. See ibid., août 1759:117–18 for another demure reply.

could not, he promised in July to "adjust to their level." All his future lyrics would be written to universally familiar melodies.[53]

One must of course be cautious when dealing with so-called letters to the editor, because there is no way to establish beyond a doubt that they were genuine and because many editors generated them in-house to suit their needs. In the case of Louptière, however, the letters he printed marred so badly the image he wished to create that there is no reason to suspect he fabricated them, and indeed it seems more likely he suppressed the most unorthodox ones. Even so, many of Louptière's readers portrayed themselves as socially unacceptable. Because of their interest in intellectual things, they were resented and ostracized by the more tradition-ally feminine members of their sex. Some even warned Louptière of the dangers of becoming a pied piper or an official spokesman for the likes of them. Not only had other women turned against them, but most men found them obnoxious as well. One woman told of a secret society to which she belonged, whose members met daily to discuss serious matters both literary and political. They spent no time on their toilette and had become the objects of ridicule for caring so little about their "parure." Devoted to the life of the mind, they exchanged their philosophical reflections even over meals, argued about new books, and presented works of their own. But they needed to maintain total secrecy on their doings, since the world was so incapable of understanding or even tolerating them.[54] Another correspondent bemoaned the paucity of men with sufficient inner strength to appreciate truly indepen-dent women. Was Louptière really willing to fight for the social changes that went hand in hand with intellectual liberation? Did he realize what a dangerous campaign this would be? Was he aware that "the salt he sprinkled would sting"? These women, as usual, begged to remain anonymous, but now, instead of taking the whole burden upon themselves, they blamed the world for forc-ing them to feel embarrassed about their intelligence. In their let-ters frustration turned to anger. "I live in a country," concluded one of them, "where the title of *savante* is almost an infamy."[55]

---

53 *Journal des Dames,* juillet 1761:88.
54 Ibid., août 1761:180.
55 Ibid., juin 1761:271–77.

Slowly it got through to Louptière that he was playing with fire. It seemed one could not fight for intellectual recognition without taking on a bigger battle. Louptière, in a casual mixture of metaphors, had himself unwittingly acknowledged that it was hard to draw the line. His *Journal des Dames,* he had said in his first issue, was to be filled entirely with the writings of women, "literary heroines, amazons, who will admit no writings by men among theirs. What gentleness there will be in the honey made purely from these queen bees."[56] The belligerent image had crept into Louptière's venture in spite of himself, but he had never meant to be a leader of amazons. Yet working on the *Journal des Dames* had brought him into contact with women totally different from those he had encountered before. Some were strange, fiercely independent creatures who could write nice poems but who had much else brewing under the surface. There was Mme de Beaumer, for instance, who had brought herself to his attention as soon as she saw his prospectus. He had featured her work in his first issue. But there were things about her that frightened him. He liked the morality and piety of her verse and of her mythological allegories that taught "lessons of the fragility of love." But her political writings, such as her *Dialogue entre Charles XII, roi de Suède, et Mandrin, contrebandier* were "unbecomingly daring," and her proposed *Lettres de Magdelon Friquet,* featuring a low-class *poissarde* heroine, could not be written within the bounds of decency.[57] No, Mme de Beaumer was not at all the type of woman he had hoped to meet and marry, and yet she was watching his *Journal des Dames* with the same predatory interest that Louptière himself had had for Campigneulles's. Association with her and with others like her was the last thing he needed; it would scare off rather than attract the fathers of young ladies "de condition." Clearly, Louptière would have to get out.

The *Journal des Dames* was fast becoming a liability. Unlike Campigneulles, however, Louptière kept his head. Before leaving, which he would do with his usual grace, he was determined to have his brief journalistic experience pay off in some way. The original intention had been to enhance his reputation and thus his

56 Ibid., avril 1761:57.
57 Ibid., avril 1761:33–35, 43.

82

eligibility, both as suitor and literary aspirant. Since feminine journalism had backfired, attracting a nonconformist audience quite different from the one he had banked on, Louptière would have to flaunt instead his academic membership. A good part of his last issue was devoted to a history of the Académie des Arcades de Rome, which, since it had had the perspicacity to elect him, was definitely in need of some publicity. The Arcades had begun to have a negative press, even in Italy. Louptière would now become its fervent apologist and public relations man in France.[58]

The Arcades (or Arcadie), he explained, had been inspired by Queen Christina of Sweden who had surrounded herself in Rome with artists, poets, and scientists of the highest quality and impeccable taste. After her death these scholars formed the Académie des Arcades, each taking the name of an ancient Greek shepherd in an attempt to recapture the simplicity of an earlier world. The first assembly took place in 1690. Democratic and international, it accepted both sexes, all fields, and all ranks, "scholars in any domain, as long as they excel." Louptière went into great detail on the history, function, statutes, and activities of Arcadie and its criteria for membership. Each member was allotted a parcel of Italian countryside for private contemplation, but they met together for fruitful exchanges seven times a year. Only the cream of the cream, he said, were admitted into the society of these virtuous shepherds and shepherdesses, "composed of the greatest geniuses of the universe."[59]

Louptière's defense of this institution, however, was fighting the tide. By the mid-1700s Arcadie had begun to grant membership so liberally that it had turned into an object of scorn. And its whole raison d'être was being attacked as retrograde, even comically so. Few took seriously any longer its pastoral golden-age aspirations or the possibility of recapturing lost innocence, and Arcadie had come to symbolize obliviousness to the problems of

---

58 The Académie des Arcades de Rome admitted numerous figures of the French Enlightenment. A greal deal had been written on its history in Latin and Italian, but Louptière's is the first and only history of it in French that I have seen. In 1756, according to Louptière, a M. Gortscher wrote one in English, but I have found no trace of it. Moulinas, in his *Imprimerie, librairie, et presse,* mentions a "tribut académique" in verse by a certain abbé Dufour, but it was apparently not historical.

59 *Journal des Dames,* septembre 1761:267–83.

contemporary life. Criticism of Arcadie was common in the Italian press of the late 1750s. The Venetian journalist Gaspare Gozzi, editor of the *Gazzetta veneta,* mocked his own wife, the Arcadian poetess Luisa Bergalli, who had ruined him by her pindaric administration of their household of five children, reducing them to dependence on whatever he could earn by his pen. Giuseppe Baretti, in letters on his travels in England, had poked fun at the bucolic frolic of the Arcadians, who he argued had no right to compare themselves with serious academicians busy exploring science and pursuing truth. His newspaper, the *Frusta letteraria,* and Beccaria's *Il Caffè,* modeled on the English *Spectator* and dedicated to enlightenment and reform, would soon add their voices to others discrediting Arcadie's irrelevant grandiloquence.[60]

Similar writings against antiquated values had begun appearing in France. Their argument was social as well as literary. Abbé Galiani (a Neapolitan) and Abbé Coyer had been trying to coax the landed but impoverished aristocracy into business and money-making and out of their nostalgic pining for a past that was forever gone. Coyer's *La Noblesse commerçante* of 1756 was based on the premise that fortune, not birth, was fast becoming the principal social criterion. Coyer's argument had been countered by the chevalier d'Arc's *La Noblesse militaire,* demanding that the aristocracy of the sword hang on to the Spartan values of simplicity and honor and that the old society of orders not yield to one of classes.[61] Louptière was strongly partial to this classical tradition and would gladly have turned back the clock. His *Journal des Dames* had been filled with admonitions that his was an overly sophisticated and corrupt century and that his contemporaries could learn far more valuable lessons from virtuous Sparta than from rich, proud, "enlightened" Athens.[62] Louptière was alto-

---

60   Very little has been written in recent years on the Académie des Arcades de Rome. Paget, *Studies on the Eighteenth Century,* devotes a chapter to it, and it is mentioned in Bédarida and Hazard, *L'Influence française en Italie.* The *Dictionary of Italian Literature* has an article by Gustavo Costa on Arcadia (pp. 17–19), as do several of the Italian literary encyclopedias. Some links between Arcadie and Freemasonry are suggested in Lelièvre, "Trio de francs-maçons," 372. See also Hauvette, "Arcadie et métastase" and "Le Mouvement Scientifique au XVIIIe siècle," in *Littérature italienne,* 322–57.

61   On the shifting of social and financial values in this period, "une société en pleine mutation," see Durand, *Fermiers généraux,* especially 183–94, 213–16.

62   See, for example, *Journal des Dames,* juin 1761:252.

gether prepared to admit the necessity of money; his *Journal des Dames,* on one level, was an elaborate attempt to find some. But the honor of devoted service to his *patrie* mattered far more. He was, as he liked to point out, an "ancien mousquetaire et officier des armées du Roi." The last issue of his paper, with its long article on Arcadie, was his final chance to state clearly where his loyalties lay, to advertise what kind of man he was, and to reverse the damage done by having inadvertently encouraged in his readers disturbing, unorthodox ideas.

For Louptière, Arcadie represented everything that was pure in style, and he never abandoned his propaganda in its behalf. He had brandished his membership in that academy on the title page of each issue of his *Journal des Dames.* These pages also bore the fictitious imprint "aux Vallons de Tivoli," probably the area awarded to him upon his election to Arcadie, whose grottos, waterfalls, ruined aqueducts and temples appear in the paintings of Hubert Robert. In 1774 Louptière would still be playing French host to new Arcadians, sending poems to the *Journal des Dames,* welcoming the latest members.[63] By then Arcadie had become a farce and a profanation. Most of its regular meetings had ceased, and the "crowning" of the great actress-poetess Morelli by the discredited academy in 1775 led to her harassment and lampooning. But Louptière continued to claim that it was a beacon of virtue and taste; Sabatier de Castres would admire his unabashed devotion to the ancients and to the values of a lost world.[64]

The *Journal des Dames* had failed Louptière on many counts. It had not procured him a wife—he would not find one until 1765—and it had blemished, not polished, his image. The journalistic public had turned out to include some unsavory customers, and he felt them pulling him down. He sensed a pulse he did not like among his anonymous readers and resented them for having misconstrued his chivalrous efforts in their behalf and for transforming his innocent paper into a forum for transgressive, socially dis-

---

63 Ibid., mai 1774:20, 43–45, and octobre 1774:247. Obscure journalists often flaunted their Arcadian credentials, especially when they lacked any others. One Mme d'Ormoy, for example, editor of the short-lived *Journal de monsieur,* wanted her readers to know that Arcadie had crowned her and allotted to her "les campagnes paladiennes" (*Journal de monsieur,* avril 1779:126). D'Ormoy was a conservative, not a feminist; her paper was addressed to courtly circles, dedicated to the king's brother, and not directed at a female audience at all.

64 Sabatier de Castres, *Trois Siècles* 3:"La Louptière."

ruptive reflections. He would later tell the writer Mme Guibert of the hazards of sitting on a "literary tribunal." He was relieved to be a private citizen again, to have given up his role as "judge" and been released from his regular engagement with the public.[65] Furthermore, the *Journal des Dames* seems not to have been a financial success. Mme de Beaumer, to whom Louptière sold it, was in even more desperate straits than he and could afford no large investment. Since she managed somehow to pay for it, the business could not have been worth much. About that Grimm had been right. Finally, the paper had not secured Louptière's literary reputation. Far from it. He would have to collect and reprint his own poems repeatedly—in 1765, 1768–69, and 1774—to avoid falling into complete obscurity even before his death. But these anthologies did not help either. Grimm greeted them with his customary snobbery and even took a swipe at Louptière's portrait at the head of his *Poésies et oeuvres diverses*. The man actually *looked* as dull as his writings were insipid! Only provincials would tolerate such a bore.[66]

Louptière left the *Journal des Dames* six issues and six months after taking it on, because he had a sense of self-preservation. As a result of his experience on the paper, he now had serious doubts about the wisdom of pushing for the advancement of women; he retreated from his earlier stance, and his future writings would stress feminine beauty rather than intelligence.[67] This tendency had been latent in his *Journal des Dames,* which even in its more feminist issues had carried advertisements for perfume, jewelry boxes, decorated fabrics, artificial flowers, rouge, and beauty creams.[68] He became a great admirer of Rousseau, even naming his son Jean-Jacques, and appears to have embraced his views on women, views that had been strongly criticized by an early *Journal des Dames* reader who thought she and other women should have

65 *Journal des Dames,* mars 1764:76.
66 Grimm et al., *Correspondance littéraire* 8:160.
67 See the *Journal des Dames,* septembre 1762:254, where Louptière sent a poem advising a young girl not to trouble her pretty head with the essays of Montaigne; and ibid., mars 1764:76, where he explained to Mme Guibert: "l'attrait de la vie champêtre et d'une philosophie un peu Epicurienne m'a fait abdiquer la fonction d'Arbitre des Ecrits de votre sexe pour reprendre celle d'Esclave de ses beaux yeux."
68 See the sections on fashion and toilette at the end of each issue.

social and political functions, public roles in which they could take pride, as had the Vestal Virgins of Rome.[69] A basically kind man, Louptière had found the ugliness Grimm and d'Aquin printed against him distasteful, and there had almost surely been other insulting words that his pride prevented him from making public. Meanwhile, each issue of this thankless journal was burning up what little money he had; half a year in the capital had been more than enough and the rigors of recurring periodical deadlines were wearing him down. And women like Mme de Beaumer, pressuring him from behind the scenes, eager to stir and agitate, were making him nervous. Another of his most frequent contributors, Charlotte Bourette, who called herself "la Muse Limonadière," owned a soft drink stand on the rue des Petits Champs, the sort of place where commoners gathered to exchange songs, gossip, and news. Police Inspector d'Hémery kept a file on her and watched her establishment.[70] Louptière wanted no such associations.

But that was not what he told his public. In print he stressed the positive, wanting to walk away with his head held high. Unlike his predecessor, he made no confessions or apologies. His sign-off was brief, gallant, and dignified. He explained first that his *Journal des Dames,* an enormous success, now had an English imitation, which he regarded as the sincerest form of flattery and a confirmation of his enterprise's timeliness and popularity.[71] "This [triumph] gave me the idea of transmitting my occupation to a woman. By chance I came upon Mme de Beaumer. Readers will notice immediately that the next volume is of her making. Everything that we [men] have done for the emulation of women is but the dawn of the days that will shine for them under *savantes journalistes,* who alone can properly fulfill the delicate function of appraising the writings of their sex."[72]

Sarcasm was not Louptière's style, but the double entendre of

---

69   *Journal des Dames,* mars 1759:80.

70   See Darnton, "Police Inspector," 154.

71   England had many women's magazines during this period, but only two were begun around Louptière's retirement date of 1761. He may have been referring to the *Ladies' Magazine, or Polite Companion for the Fair Sex* (London, 1760–63) or to the *Ladies' Museum By the Author of the Female Quixote* (Charlotte Lennox) (London, 1760, 1761). Both are listed in the British Museum catalogue.

72   *Journal des Dames,* septembre 1761:"Avertissement," 283.

this farewell is unmistakable. He had washed his hands of the whole affair and was no longer responsible for the *Journal des Dames's* fortunes. Considering Mme de Beaumer's *frondeur* inclinations offensive, he would surely have preferred to leave the paper in other hands. There must have been no takers. The next best thing to do was to remind her pointedly that her function was "delicate" and limited to editing, in the hopes that she would confine herself to "appraising the writings of her sex" and refrain from propagating her own views on reforming the world. Mme de Beaumer seemed ominously like his angry anonymous correspondents, and he would leave them to each other. What they would do together remained to be seen, but he would rather watch it from afar.

The role of *journaliste des femmes* had only damaged Louptière, as it had his predecessor. Both had encountered problems with publishers, censors, critics, and readers. Their gallant but conservative impulse had led them against their will toward contestation and polemical postures neither could embrace. Louptière retired to Champagne to escape guilt by association, married unhappily, and sank from sight. In 1774, he applied for a pension on the *Mercure.* He did this in the form of a poem that he sent to the *Journal des Dames,* whose then-editor, Mme de Montanclos, was a protégée of the young queen, Marie Antoinette. Because it looked finally as if his journalistic offspring had gotten back on a proper track and might find favor, this seemed the right moment to claim his paternity. Flattering the finance minister and the new king, Louis XVI, Louptière reminded them that he had early sung the praises of "les Grâces."[73] No pension was granted. Instead Louptière's request was widely ridiculed. "The verbose L——," went one such mockery, "solicits a pension for having bored the public. If every other equally pathetic poet asked the same and we had to accord them, all the revenues in the land would not suffice."[74] Louptière, who had once hoped to be remembered and

---

73 Ibid., septembre 1774:112ff. Louptière wrote to the new editor: "Comme la vertu aime à sourire à la beauté, je dépose la Requête que je présente à M. le Duc de la Vrillière, dans le Temple des Grâces; votre journal mérite ce titre, et je vois déjà le ministre dont je réclame, accueillir ma supplique, ne fût-ce que pour applaudir à la voie que j'ai prise pour la lui faire parvenir."

74 *I. K. L., Essai dramatique,* 16.

rewarded for the uniqueness of his *Journal des Dames,* had been forgotten in his own lifetime. His *bergères* had done little to redeem him. He would die destitute in a drafty château, leaving nothing to his greedy, bickering sisters and estranged wife but a parchment genealogy attesting to his blue blood.[75]

The fundamentally patrician Louptière was as dismayed as his predecessor at the *frondeur* turn his paper would take in the hands of other editors. Both men had found after just a few months that they could not control their journalistic offspring. This paradoxical situation, however, was the result of the ambiguous tendencies built into the attitude toward women shared by nearly all male champions of the female sex, an attitude with elements of both integration and subversion.[76] These two men had taken a risk but had done so out of self-interest rather than utopian zeal. They had hoped to capitalize on the plight of a discontented social group by giving it a measure of recognition and a large dose of flattery. To further their own careers, they thus took a stance contrary to common opinion and to dominant cultural presuppositions. The defense of women in the *Journal des Dames* was to be a rhetorical exercise; neither editor had dreamed that his paper might become an instrument of combat. Yet both men, by basing their business on a pledge to recognize feminine talent in a newly created forum, an alternative institution, were toying with an idea that had distinct transgressive potential and could undermine their own legitimacy. Even in its tamest manifestation, the simple acknowledgment that women as a group had been mistreated by society had disruptive implications.

Furthermore, by devoting themselves to a female audience, these two editors compromised their own reputations to an extent that they had probably not anticipated. They were interested in the literary creations of women as commodities for their paper, not as revelations of the anxieties, hopes, and fears of an oppressed group. Yet they had provided an opening for dialogue with women readers, and it was inevitable that many of these readers

75　"Procès-verbal de levée des scellés dressé le 11 juin 1784," Archives Judicaires de l'Aube, no. 1455. The full text is in Babeau, "La Louptière."

76　See the general discussion in Angenot, *Champions des femmes,* "Elements de Conclusion," 151–72. This attitude has already been discussed at length in my Introduction.

would reveal feelings and frustrations that the editors were neither interested in nor prepared to deal with. The timidity of their polemics thus disappointed their female readers. But their male colleagues disdained them as well, for becoming the *poètes des dames* seemed an admisson of their own limitations as writers. It was generally assumed, in the misogynistic culture of the Old Regime, that any author who addressed an exclusively female audience was an inferior writer, one who rehashed and repeated after others to distract mental minors, one who could really not create but only recreate (in both senses).[77] The two male editors of the *Journal des Dames,* although they had brought it upon themselves, obviously resented the mockery of their male colleagues in addition to the abuse from the female readers they defended. Many of their readers, it seemed, would bite the very hand that fed them. Thus what turned out to be a doubly thankless editorial experience for Campigneulles and Louptière appears to have reinforced their basic conservatism and antifeminism. They were visibly disturbed by the confused yet intense contestations and high emotional charge generated by their paper against their wishes, but even more by the fact that they ended feeling exploited by the very group they had planned to exploit.

Both male editors had stressed the uniqueness of their paper in an effort to emphasize the separateness, the otherness, of women. Rather than draw them into serious matters, the intention was to set them apart and remind them continually that they, by their natural charm and lightness, had something special and different to offer. "The *Journal des Dames,*" Louptière had said, "has nothing in common with any other paper."[78] Through all the flattery ran a strong patronizing tone. Campigneulles, who claimed to find women's writing "enchanting," insisted that it could never be judged by men's standards, and the same condescending indulgence permeated Louptière's complimentary commentary. His paper was to be "reading for the toilette," and he asked that he be permitted his bursts of praise, even when they interrupted his reviews and extracts, for the productions of women moved him to

77 See Sullerot, "Lectrices et Interlocutrices."
78 *Journal des Dames,* avril 1761:vi.

the point where such spontaneous rhapsodies could not be controlled.[79] The most either man had meant to do was turn women
from dissipation and encourage them in their literary pursuits,
which both saw as a harmless channel for feminine energies. Campigneulles had announced that he meant his paper to dispel the
"insufferable boredom" that marred women's lives, and both
he and Louptière received a few letters from female readers
confirming that for some of them literary exercise did indeed alleviate the "pain" of their condition.[80] It has been suggested that
the period between Louis XIV's death and Rousseau's glorification
of domesticity was a particularly trying time for many women.
They were freer than under the autocratic Sun King and not yet
restricted by the ideal of motherhood, but most women, unable
to organize their time and take advantage of the opportunities,
floundered instead without a sense of definition, feeling futile and
meaningless.[81] The male editors of the *Journal des Dames* had a
vague sense of this phenomenon and felt threatened by the widespread restlessness of women, most of whose children were either
at wet nurses, convents, or *collèges,* who had no access to politics
or to important public roles, and who truly had nothing to fill the
void in their lives. The editors had proposed female participation
in their paper to allay this terrible emptiness and boredom, but for
the more outspoken women in their audience this was not a satisfactory or sufficient solution.

The male editors of the *Journal des Dames* had never advocated
that women play a public role, but their suggestion that women
contribute to the paper appears to have encouraged some to think
that they could become journalists themselves. Louptière had said
he wished women to fill the pages of his journal, but he had certainly not foreseen that they would want to take it over as spokeswomen for their own oppressed constituency. The list he printed
of nearly forty female authors, designed to encourage them and
others to submit poems and small pieces to his paper, had an effect
that exceeded his expectations and distorted his intentions. A few
were so inspired by Louptière's enumeration of literarily active

79   See, for example, ibid., mai 1761:107.
80   Ibid., avril 1761:84.
81   See Badinter, *Emilie,* 29–34. See also the same author's *L'Amour en Plus.*

women that they sought the editorship of the paper, eager to take on the responsibility for guiding the whole female public. This unanticipated reaction forced the male editors to measure the risks that liberating female writers could cause for them, to realize that literary recognition for women had socially disruptive possibilities, and ultimately to abandon their championing of an oppressed group that might upset the established order. Louptière's treatment of Mme de Beaumer illustrates his predicament. At first he featured her light pieces in his paper, welcoming her as one of his newly discovered female talents. As we saw, he then went on record as disapproving of some of her other works, whose excessive boldness and subversive potential he condemned. But that gained both the author and her dialogue on Mandrin a certain notoriety. She grew more determined to take over the editorship of the paper, and Louptière, realizing that only by leaving things in uncensured oblivion or silence would they remain inert, stopped his journalistic career after just six months. He wanted no association with the corrosive writings or outrageous actions of such *frondeur* women, who wished to turn the speculative game of female advancement from theory into practice, thus realizing the danger inherent all along in feminist discourse.

We can assume that both male editors would have left out of their papers the most flagrantly radical submissions they received. That they nonetheless printed controversial pieces—feminist attacks on Rousseau, a review of Diderot's republican *drame Le Père de famille* (which would be performed in four provincial cities before being allowed on the Parisian stage),[82] letters from ambitious, rebellious women who refused to accept the limitations placed arbitrarily by patriarchal society on their sex, thoughts on the liberty of the press in England—suggests that the directors of the *Journal des Dames* received some even stronger stuff. In the case of Mme de Beaumer we know Louptière left out her deviant writings, those that ventured beyond tolerable limits. Both editors, unwittingly, had tapped a raw nerve. They had offered to speak for the mute, to defend those who could not defend themselves. They had counted on being served by the very prejudices they attacked and assumed they could continue to benefit from the

82 See Lough, *Paris Theatre Audiences*, 266.

usurpation of female recognition that they themselves denounced. But when women began to defend themselves, to call for protest and action, to identify with causes of major social significance, this broke all the rules of traditional discourse on the woman question. Women fighting for their own rights through a periodical violated all comfortable assumptions and caught male editors, censors, police inspectors, and even readers off guard. The phenomenon of female journalists speaking through a feminine paper to female readers was unprecedented. Never before had women taken on this task, but now three successive female editors did so. From October 1761 when Louptière retired, until 1775 when Mercier took over, the *Journal des Dames* would bear the name of a female editor on its title page. The mute suddenly had decided to speak.

In the next chapters we shall see how the three female *journalistes des femmes* would continue to attack frivolity and dissipation, but now they would try to show by their own example that women in a public role could still be virtuous. The very notion of ambitious females was shocking, of course.[83] By becoming journalists they had undertaken to compete in an almost exclusively male profession, and this high risk in itself was a measure of their ambition. In the beginning they felt no guilt at their own audacity. All three wanted power, more power than could be achieved by the publication of isolated books. Journalists were far less solitary than novelists, for they had a dialogue, an exchange, with their audience. These three women wanted an ongoing, direct relationship with their public, witnesses to their influence, listeners for their views. They were determined to affect, impress, persuade, even to change the course of events. Theirs was more than a doctrinal feminism; it was a *féminisme d'action* of the *frondeuse* variety, with a direct impact on reality. They practiced little autocensure. Their language itself reflected their boisterous assertiveness. The first female editor would call for a feminist "revolution," the second would claim to speak to and for "all people," the third would vow to "break conventions." These ambitious women were not satisfied with present conditions. Although many of the women whom they addressed were bored and melancholic, they them-

---

83   See Badinter, *Emilie,* 25.

selves had goals and strove to achieve them. Ambition, as Badinter has pointed out, was a strong antidote to existential emptiness and anguish.[84] The three female editors functioned on the premise that passion made great things happen, that intensity of feeling and commitment to a cause could change and improve the quality of life.

Ambition in the Old Regime meant defiance, refusal to accept one's assigned place. Absolutist ideology demanded a rigorous social hierarchy with respect to nature, power, and God, allowing for no mobility. Those who sought to better their position tended to be regarded as suspect, recalcitrant, unbridled, excessive; women who did so were more suspicious still. Such women also appeared denatured for they challenged the distinction between the sexes. Their behavior flew in the face of accepted feminine frivolity, but it also defied the specificity of man. Operating on the truly feminist premise first articulated by the Cartesian Poullain de la Barre that the mind has no sex, the female editors of the *Journal des Dames* insisted on the complete intellectual equality of men and women. The first and most radical of them went beyond that to dress and behave like a man as well, which made her threatening to contemporaries of both genders. Her refusal to accept the limits assigned to her sex led her to rebel against the high-society women of the theater *loges* and to identify instead with the largely bourgeois and plebeian *parterre*.[85] In the next chapter we shall see how the authorities reacted to the strident hyperbole and bizarre behavior of Mme de Beaumer, a woman with truly Promethean ambitions who wished to reach the "entire universe" with her plea for the liberation of the oppressed.

84 Ibid., 7–19.
85 On the different social significance of the *loges* and the *parterre*, see Lough, *Paris Theatre Audiences*, 187–228, 270. See also his *Writer and Public*, 258–274.

3

An *Editrice* Hides in the *Frondeur* Temple

MME DE BEAUMER, THE PRINCE DE CONTI, AND THE

DUTCH CONNECTION (1761–1763)

"Mme de Beaumer," wrote the censor Marin to Malesherbes in February 1763, "*authoress* of the *Journal des Dames* that was so cruelly abandoned by me, rejected by M. Gibert to whom I so generously gave it, and finally accepted by M. Rousselet, has appeared this morning in my chambers, a large hat on her head, a long sword at her side, her chest (where there is nothing) and her behind (where there is not much) covered by a long culotte, and the rest of her body in a worn, narrow black habit. Interrogated about the disguise, she replied that since she now runs her paper alone relying only upon herself, she dresses thus for reasons of economy and to be admitted to the all-male *parterre* of the theater to judge and review the latest play for 20 sous." Marin continued the letter in frustration, for since she had no endowments, he could not tease her that the "freshness of her features, the vivacity of her eyes, the gentle curves of her stomach, and the smoothness of her legs . . . would betray her." Mme de Beaumer, who surely must have been aware of Marin's sneering, would have come to see him only for a pressing reason. But the letter was designed to alert the booktrade director to her latest eccentricity and mentioned nothing about the substantive matter she had wanted to discuss. Obviously put out and threatened by her defiance, Marin said only that he wished she would "change her ideas."[1] She had no business doing a man's job.

Because there was so little precedent in France for dealing with female journalists and none at all for women addressing a feminine public through their own paper, the tendency was not to take Mme de Beaumer seriously at first, to wish her away, to invalidate her effort. But the men with whom she dealt found both her principles and her manners reprehensible. Malesherbes and Sartine, the inspector of police, would not grant her appointments; a string of censors refused her; and Marin, the only censor she successfully cornered, was led by the failure of his usual techniques with women to resent and ridicule her. Then, as her rhetoric grew more bombastic and her posture more petulant, the reigning elites and the authorities tried to scratch her from the record by denial and silence. Grimm spread the word around that nobody of either sex read her paper,[2] and the yearly *Etat de Paris,* which provided a comprehensive list of newspapers in the capital and whose author, Jèze, lived with Malesherbes as his secretary, never mentioned the existence of Mme de Beaumer's *Journal des Dames.*[3]

This was an elaborate attempt to obscure the fact that her paper was politically upsetting to the authorities, that the censors doctored it for months, and that Malesherbes even temporarily suspended it in the spring of 1762, only allowing it to resume under a substitute male editor. That the first female *journaliste des femmes* particularly discomfited Malesherbes can be easily understood by a look at her writing before the crackdown. For Mme de Beaumer was prime Bastille material. A vehement champion of women's abilities and even more belligerent than *La Spectatrice,* she was also a crusader for the rights of the poor, for social justice, religious toleration, Freemasonry, republican liberty, and international peace. Far more passionate than logical, she never defined these terms rigorously but repeated them provocatively in both her public and private writings. Unlike Campigneulles and Louptière,

---

1 Bibliothèque Nationale, manuscrit français (henceforth BN ms. fr.) 22135, fol. 90, "Lettre de Marin à Malesherbes l'informant du projet de Mme du Beaumer, 'directrice' du *Journal des Dames,* d'aller au théâtre sous un habit masculin."

2 Grimm et al., *Correspondance littéraire* 5:76.

3 Jèze, *Etat,* 199–209. Jèze's work was published every year in the early 1760s until the author left Paris.

whose journalism had been born of self-interest, Mme de Beaumer had a calling far beyond her personal needs. She wanted
sweeping and speedy changes in government and society. Firebrand, utopian zealot, and something of a desperado, she meant
to set the process in motion herself. Her *Journal des Dames,* quite
simply, was meant to change the world. And this of course could
not be permitted.

About Mme de Beaumer's life very little is known. She allegedly claimed to be distantly related to the maréchal de Belle-Isle,
and one document describes her as a vicomtesse,[4] but even her
own contemporaries had difficulty learning any biographical details. People who tried to reconstruct her career were frustrated;
one biographer seems to have suspected that traces of her journalistic activities had been deliberately expunged from official records. She merited a brief entry in the abbé de la Porte's *Histoire
littéraire des femmes françaises:* after stating that she lacked fortune,
beauty, or grace, the abbé pointed out that in the absence of any
documents on her civil status, he could say nothing even about
her birth or marriage. He mentioned only that she had strong ties
to Holland, traveling there often and dying there obscurely in
1766.[5] Almost surely she was a Huguenot. This would explain
why the legal details of her life in France were never recorded;
Protestants preferred to baptise their children and marry clandestinely rather than be branded "illegitimate" by the official Catholic
church.[6] It would also explain the intensity of her commitment
not only to women but to underdogs in general, her hatred of
Richelieu ("the destroyer of La Rochelle"),[7] the dedication of her
Journal des Dames to the Protestant Condé branch of royal cousins,
her residence in Paris with the Huguenot Jaucourt family for over
a year during which she shuttled back and forth to Holland (a
Protestant republic), and finally her choice as successor of Mme
de Maisonneuve, who used the journal to seek justice in the Calas
affair.

Mme de Beaumer's radical sympathies had surfaced before she

---

4   BN ms. fr. 22085, p. 2.
5   La Porte, *Histoire littéraire* 4:525. Abensour, *Femme et féminisme,* 310,
praises Mme de Beaumer's poetry but comments again on her extreme obscurity.
6   See Stewart, "Huguenots Under Louis XV," especially 61.
7   See for example, *Journal des Dames,* septembre 1762:268.

took over the *Journal des Dames*. By comparing some earlier works of hers that somehow slipped by the censors with her newspaper, which was watched much more closely, we can measure how her journalistic copy was bent and altered under government pressure. She may have been the author of the cryptonymous *Lettres curieuses, instructives, et amusantes,* an unsuccessful periodical launched in The Hague in 1759 designed to show that women were no longer content to "flirt, sew, and spin." The *Journal des Dames* later attributed the work to Mme le Prince de Beaumont instead, but the author was identified on the title page simply as Mme de Beau★, and the opening statements of the first issue had the belligerent tone of Mme de Beaumer's later writings. If she was indeed the author of this declaration of war against the French booktrade authorities, she would have had good reason to hide the fact when she later began to publish in France. "In order to publish these letters," the French author had explained about their appearance in Holland, "I was forced to resort to a foreign land . . . to that happy country where truth, supported by her sister freedom, enjoys the inestimable privilege of making its voice heard without having to fear those infamous spies so numerous [in France] . . . that detestable brood of informers that, to our country's shame, have begun to swarm lately."[8] The *Lettres curieuses,* Mme de Beau★ explained, were also available at bookdealers Luchtmans in Leyden, Beman in Rotterdam, Spruyt in Utrecht, van den Kleboom in Breda, Bartinkhof in Groningen, and Gillissen in Middleburg. Exactly the same booksellers were advertised two years later as Dutch distributors of Mme de Beaumer's *Journal des Dames,* so she must have considered them kindred spirits and maintained contacts with them. But no doubt to minimize the damage of having denounced the French royal censors and police, she never claimed the *Lettres curieuses* for her own.

---

8 *Lettres curieuses, instructives, et amusantes, ou Correspondance historique, galante, critique, morale, philosophique, et littéraire entre une dame de Paris et une dame de province; contenant un grand nombre d'histoires, d'anecdotes, et d'aventures aussi variées que curieuses et intéressantes, publiées par Mme de Beau★ à la Haye chez Isaac Beauregard,* 1759:iv–vii. This periodical is mentioned, without any inquiry into its authorship, in Hatin, *Gazettes de Hollande,* 204. Although Hatin cites the author as Mme de Beau, the journal itself says Mme de Beau★ on the title page. An asterisk in a cryptonym usually indicated a missing syllable. For a fascinating discussion of this quasi-anonymous device, see Quérard, *Supercheries littéraires.*

Mme de Beaumer's diatribe suggests that she or someone close to her might have clashed with censors and booktrade authorities in some now lost episode. We know that she was friendly with Aublet de Maubuy, whose work on the history of women, *La Vie des femmes illustres,* supported her newspaper and in turn received favorable reviews in it. Aublet had spent more than a year in the Bastille in the early 1750s for writing and distributing *libelles* concerning the Jansenist protest against church and crown. Inspector d'Hémery, acting on orders from the king, had traced him to a room on rue de la Coutellerie, where the police seized, among other things, *Le Parlement vengé, ou L'Impertinence jésuitique punie.* Interrogation and captivity in the Bastille nearly drove Aublet mad, and in his thirteenth month of confinement the police extracted from him a promise to behave.[9] Released from prison but exiled to his lands in Sens, Aublet kept his word to avoid *frondeur* causes. Only much later, in the late 1770s when he supported Mercier and condemned the "martyring" of dramatic authors by the "despotic" Comédie-Française, would he allow himself a new burst of protest. But the intervening years found him broken and cowed, and it may have been to her friend Aublet's persecution by the authorities that Mme de Beaumer now alluded.

Despite her misgivings about the dangers of speaking openly in France, she published her *Oeuvres mêlées* there the following year. This collection of allegories, dialogues, and poems, although full of incendiary ideas, was sufficiently cloaked in mythological metaphor to get by the busy censor Marin,[10] a fact that would later cause him considerable embarrassment. The work received some critical acclaim. One reviewer, Jean Goulin, a Freemason, self-styled republican, and himself the author of an egalitarian utopia, praised Mme de Beaumer in the *Mémoires de Trévoux,* saying she deserved the gratitude of humanity for her "wise morality . . . and her beautiful way of writing." Goulin, who no doubt recognized a Masonic strain in the *Oeuvres mêlées,* was also an editor of the *Annales typographiques* and would later

9   On Aublet's pursuit and arrest, see Archives de la Bastille, MS 11794, fols. 73, 83, 96, 98, 112, 144, 156, 187, 196; MS 11807, fol. 282.

10   For Marin's permission to print the *Oeuvres mêlées,* see BN ms. fr. 21994, fol. 57, no. 416. The work bore the fictitious imprint "à Liège," but it was really distributed in Paris, chez Cuissart.

give Mme de Beaumer's *Journal des Dames* a positive press there as well.[11]

The *Oeuvres mêlées* have become quite rare today; they exist only in mutilated form, *brochures* separated from each other, with several parts missing. This fact attracted the attention of a recent scholar, J. Rustin, who decoded one of the "true stories" in the *Oeuvres mêlées* and explained how it became embarrassing to the French authorities. It was a section called "Caprices de la fortune," in which Mme de Beaumer, using changed names, sought to vindicate a young Dutch bourgeoise friend who had been seduced, married but then abandoned by a German prince, and left with a baby girl. The courts of Holland had ruled in favor of the young mother, but the father's family refused her financial support and she had been reduced to living in a miserable hut, a victim of the ruthless, the wealthy, and the powerful.

What Mme de Beaumer had failed to mention in this flagrantly partisan rendition of the story, designed to make the heroine the very picture of virtue, was that the real-life young mother had later taken another lover and given birth to an illegitimate son in Brussels. The truth came out, however, and the scandal broke in Holland in late 1760, shortly after Mme de Beaumer's *Oeuvres mêlées* appeared in print. The court in The Hague reversed its earlier position and in November 1761 freed the German prince of any financial obligation to his daughter. Another ruling in December 1762 declared the woman, one Benjamine Gertrude Kaiser, "wanton, immoral," and "without honor" and banished her from Holland. In early 1763 Kaiser, now fallen from grace, sought refuge in Paris at the Hôtel de Soubise. Mme de Beaumer's story, originally designed to arouse sympathy for her, was now attracting unwelcome attention.[12] Marin, who had even allowed Louptière to reprint the "Caprices de la fortune" in his *Journal des Dames,* had regarded it as nothing other than a simple tale of star-

---

11   *Mémoires pour servir à l'histoire des sciences et des beaux-arts (Mémoires de Trévoux),* avril 1760:939–41. See also *Annales typographiques,* 1762:545. On Goulin, see Sgard, *Dictionnaire des journalistes,* 178–79.
12   This fascinating piece of detective work can be found in Rustin, "Roman et destin." Rustin's interest is the eighteenth-century passion for "histoires véritables," especially those that could be "decoded."

crossed lovers.[13] Now severely compromised by the identification of its protagonists and the political and diplomatic ramifications of their affair, he doubtless helped to liquidate the remaining copies of the *Oeuvres mêlées*. At this point, the resentful Marin became Mme de Beaumer's nemesis and remained so for the rest of her career.

Other parts of the *Oeuvres mêlées* would also have displeased Marin profoundly if he had read them closely, but he apparently never looked beyond the mythological regalia and pagan imagery to the powerful messages they contained. Mme de Beaumer, like Jurieu before her and Court de Gébelin after her, made full allegorical use of myth in the French Protestant tradition to moralize against vain ambition, social inequality, corrupt law tribunals, religious persecution, against the evils of war, conquest, riches, and false grandeur.[14] She put forth a pacific, stoic philosophy—she, like the Huguenot *Encyclopédiste* Jaucourt in whose brother's house she lived for years, was a great admirer of Seneca and forgave the great Roman his suicide—preaching the ideal of public service, brotherhood, and commitment. She stressed the importance of industry and energy in manual as well as intellectual labor and espoused the Masonic ideal of a worldwide "nation spirituelle" in which moral virtue was more significant than any particular theology and in which secular scientific progress was an article of faith.[15] Her feminism led her still further. Only female rulers, she argued, were truly humane. Queen Christina of Sweden (Thincrèse in the dialogue "Le Triomphe de la fausse gloire") was one

13   See *Journal des Dames,* avril 1761:35. Louptière had underlined the story's factual base: "A philosophical reader will discern that the events reported here belong more to history than to fiction. This is a recent anecdote in which Mme de Beaumer merely changed the names. The heroine, still young, is a respectable friend of hers whose merit attracted the author's interest."

14   The most complete copy of the *Oeuvres mêlées* that I have found is at the Bibliothèque Historique de la Ville de Paris, 21061, nos. 4 and 5. It includes "Dialogue entre Charles XII, roi de Suède, et Mandrin, contrebandier"; "Le Triomphe de la fausse gloire"; "La Mort des héros"; "Le Temple de la fortune"; and "Ode tirée du cantique que Moïse et les Israélites chantèrent . . . au passage de la Mer Rouge." Mme de Beaumer advertised another, "Les Effets de la jalousie dans les infortunes d'Agathe et d'Hector," but it seems to have been lost.

15   On paganism and the Protestant use of myth in this period, see Frank Manuel, *Eighteenth Century Confronts the Gods,* 29–33, 186–96, and 245–57. Mme

of the few monarchs to understand that "rulers must surrender their own liberty," that they are justified only if their subjects thrive and prosper, that "the scepter is never to decorate the one who holds it." Under Thincrèse commerce flourished, and law, arts, and sciences soared to new heights. But her successor, Gustave (Vegatus in the tale), was power-hungry like all male rulers, not content with the limits of his own country, seduced by stories of the military exploits of Caesar and Pompey, thirsty for empire, determined to plunder and rule the world, "drunk for false glory and bloody war."[16]

The "Dialogue entre Charles XII, roi de Suède, et Mandrin, contrebandier" in the *Oeuvres* showed Mme de Beaumer at her most *frondeur*. Mandrin was a famous bandit who in 1755 had been burned alive before a sympathetic and admiring crowd of ten thousand, after successfully eluding massive deployments of police for years. This Robin Hood, a brigand with enormous panache, would become the hero of a vast pamphlet literature, a mythic symbol of revolution. Mme de Beaumer's dialogue, which cast Mandrin as an inverse king, showed her resentment of royalty, irreverence toward social hierarchy, suspicion of police, disgust with depraved judges, and frank admiration of the insurrectionary bandit who had fought vice, outwitted the corrupt tax farmers, and defended the weak and needy. In the dialogue, set as a conversation between the dead shades of the interlocutors, the haughty monarch scorned Mandrin as a "crook from the vilest blood of the populace," but the fair judge of the underworld, Minos, saw his greatness of character and treated subject and king as equals. Mandrin's courage, cleverness, and generosity had won

de Beaumer's thoughts closely resemble those found in Court de Gebelin's *Le Monde primitif*, a nine-volume work sent to subscribers between 1773 and 1782. An active Mason, Court de Gebelin (often called "le restaurateur du protestantisme en France") had been trying to start up a Protestant periodical since 1752. He came to Paris to pursue his project in the early 1760s and may have known Mme de Beaumer. See Chouillet and Moureau, *Suppléments* 2:47–52. For the thoughts of another Huguenot whom Mme de Beaumer surely knew since she lived for at least two years in his brother's house, see Morris, *Chevalier de Jaucourt*.

16   Mme de Beaumer, *Oeuvres mêlées*, "Le Triomphe de la fausse gloire," 31–38.

him the admiration of millions, whereas King Charles, born into a life of luxury, had squandered his subjects' automatic obedience and devotion by waging wanton war and by abusing his power. Charles had been dazzled by stories of Alexander the Great into emulating his insatiable need to plunder and subdue. Military historians, wrote the pacifist Mme de Beaumer, "commit a crime by glamorizing conquest." They should tell the truth about carnage and pillaging, about suffering and the sheer waste of human life. Then there would be no war, no warring nations. But instead, historians wrote propaganda, depicting military heroes as gods, stirring up hatred, perpetuating the appetite for power. "If Mandrin had been Charles XII," she mused, this enemy of oppression would have spread wealth evenly among his people and brought peace to a unified world.[17] This sensitivity to the *misère du peuple,* crushed by the excessive taxes needed to finance unpopular and unnecessary foreign wars, had been one of the hallmarks of radical protest literature throughout the Fronde.[18] Mandrin as a literary subject was of course forbidden by the booktrade authorities, and rigorously so since Damiens's attack on the king, for the two criminals had analogous grievances against the regime. Seen in this context Mme de Beaumer's defense of Mandrin was extraordinarily daring.[19]

Having paid homage to Mandrin, a man of the people, Mme de Beaumer took her next inspiration from a *poissarde,* a woman of the people, and submitted a proposal for a newspaper to be called *Lettres de Magdelon Friquet.* Because the censor de La Garde refused it in February 1761 and Malesherbes would not deign to explain why, we can only guess what it contained.[20] Almost certainly it was modeled on the *Gazette des Halles* that circulated during the Fronde. Magdelon Friquet was a fictional "type," a character in the plays of the *genre poissard,* a low-class, marginal, indigenous French theater form similar to the Italian *Commedia*

17   Ibid., 1–26, especially 14–20. On the significance of Mandrin for the Revolution, see L. S. Gordon, "Thème de Mandrin."

18   See Introduction, above, and Grand-Mesnil, *Mazarin,* 66–69, 275.

19   See Rétat, *L'Attentat de Damiens,* especially 155, 195.

20   BN ms. nouvelles acquisitions françaises (henceforth nouv. acq. fr.) 3346, fols. 311–15.

dell' Arte. It showed the manners, customs, and traditions of inhabitants of the popular quarters—fishwives, pickpockets, re-
cruiters, oyster sellers, bakerboys, rag pickers, ferrymen, and the
ubiquitous porters called "forts des Halles." Filled with uproarious
slang, these plays were often vehicles for social and political propaganda. Their gutsy but good-hearted protagonists, male and female rascals with agile wits and sharp tongues, upset the staid
literary critics, who denounced the *poissard* plays for depicting the
vulgar and "la basse nature."[21]

Since these comedies of democratic types, although often performed, were rarely printed, we have no specifics about Magdelon
Friquet as a character. The plays in which she was featured seem
not to have survived. We do know, however, that L. A. Dorvigny,
the author of *Magdelon Friquet et Colin Tampon,* also wrote the
revolutionary *La Démonseigneurisation,* and that A. L. Beaunoir,
the author of *Magdelon Friquet et Monsieur Vacarmini,* also wrote
Les Amours de Colombine and *Le Diable à la cave* and was censured
by the ecclesiastical authorities.[22] Louptière, as we saw, had
warned in his *Journal des Dames* that Mme de Beaumer's proposed
heroine could not be treated within the bounds of decency. That
this character, part of a forgotten lore, was either a radical strum-
pet or a strong-arm fishwoman can be deduced from the popularity of her name as a Revolutionary pseudonym. In 1789 a "Magdelon Friquet" penned a pamphlet called *Grande et Horrible
Conspiration des demoiselles du Palais Royal contre les droits de
l'homme.* This was followed by *Avis important d'une dame des Halles
(Magdelon Friquet) pour la diminution des vivres* in 1792. Such tracts
mixed sex with revolution, and Mme de Beaumer's proposed
manuscript was probably a similar mixture of feminism and popular radicalism. The censor de La Garde, who refused it, was quite
liberal, on record for dispensing many permissions for dubious
works, so his outright rejection of her manuscript suggests that it
must have been explosive.[23] It confirms Mme de Beaumer's pen-

21   For a general discussion, see Moore, *"Genre poissard."*
22   See Manne and Ménétrier, *Galerie historique des comédiens,* 56; the same
authors' *Galerie historique des acteurs français,* 14; Brenner, *Bibliographical List of
Plays.*
23   For de La Garde's censorship activities, see Blangonnet, "Recherches sur
les censeurs," 153. See also Chapter 1, above, n. 37.

chant for dangerous, even radical ideas, and her strong identification with the lower classes.

This was the situation when she pressured Louptière into selling her the *Journal des Dames*. If she was ever to make her message known, now that the censors seemed bent on keeping her quiet, she would have to be let in the back door of an enterprise that was already launched, had access to a wide audience, and—although it had been challenged by protected papers like the *Mercure*—had so far aroused no political suspicion. She counted on the fact that censors were not watching Louptière too carefully. And for a few months, from October to December 1761, Mme de Beaumer got away with it. Her first three issues of the paper made an unfettered display of her feminist, Masonic, cosmopolitan, and egalitarian sympathies. But there was an urgent tone to her extravagant rhetoric, matched only by the magnitude of her dream. She had much to do and little time to do it. One censor, de La Garde, already mistrusted her, and she expected to be muzzled soon again. She needed to show nothing less than that the subjugation of women was a universal tragedy, that mutual respect between the sexes would lead to the same between social classes and eventually between nations, that a revolution in *moeurs* would thus result in social harmony and international peace. Even if only briefly, she now had listeners, and the censors were not monitoring the paper yet. Making the most of the opportunity, her approach was frontal, demanding, aggressive. The time had come to begin her crusade.

"The honor of the French nation is intimately linked to the continuation of the *Journal des Dames*. . . . Let no one think this statement singular, ridiculous, or absurd. . . . Be silent, all critics, and know that this is a woman addressing you!" With these strident words Mme de Beaumer launched her campaign to vindicate women's rights and to persuade the world that her newspaper was of profound and far-reaching importance. "My only merit is to know the full worth of my sex. . . . How I would rejoice to rid the whole earth of the injurious notion [that we are inferior] still held by some barbarians among our citizens who have difficulty acknowledging that we can think and write." An invitation was extended to women from the provinces and throughout Europe to send their works to the *Journal des Dames,* where they could set in motion a true international exchange of ideas. Beyond these outside contributions, Mme de Beaumer promised to provide articles that would exemplify the glory and potentialities of women past and present, thus inspiring confidence and restoring dignity. She would of course amuse, but her primary goal was to instruct. Utility was an obsession for her. Montesquieu and Racine should be as much a part of a woman's life as ribbons and other accoutrements of toilette. Science too would be included in the journal, for stripped of its "pedantic charlatanism" it could be understood by women as well as men. Encouraged by the response of Louptière's audience and by his unusual list of active female writers, Mme de Beaumer was sure that her female readers were ready for more intellectual challenge. She held high hopes for her public, and even though she would be demanding of her readers, she communicated to them her respect. After all, the success of her ambitious venture depended on them, "my first judges, my true protectresses."[24]

Stressing that women should take courage and strength from having their own paper and an editor of their own sex, Mme de Beaumer argued that beauty is fleeting but wisdom lasting, that women must take advantage of their opportunities to advise and influence men, but that to do so they must abandon vain frivolities, throwing themselves instead into vigorous study, improving their characters as they honed their minds. Mme de Beaumer denounced the dissipation of the *précieuses,* holding up instead a puritanical bourgeois ethic.[25] Unfashionably, she sang the praises of marriage and sexual fidelity, called for new standards of behavior, and extolled relationships based on equality, companionship, and trust. "Let it be firmly *resolved,*" she declared, "that women will henceforth be enlightened and intelligent." Their talents, art, and genius will hold men in thriving unions, whereas relationships based on superficial attraction wilt like cut flowers. If women become as knowledgeable as men, Mme de Beaumer proposed, "if we educate ourselves, men will recognize that we are not only useful but indispensable." It is sad but true that "we are physically weaker . . . that war and peace are made without us." But wisdom

24 *Journal des Dames,* octobre 1761:"Avant propos," i, iv.
25 Ibid., 57.

in counsel could make women powerful nevertheless. They must demonstrate their solidarity, their readiness to take on the "occupations of citizens." By cultivating their minds, she urged her readers, they could form and shape the character of their families, instruct them in all matters, become the very backbone of society, and bring about world harmony. To succeed, however, women must get rid of mirrors and look instead within themselves. Their friends should be frank and critical, their partners not vain flatterers or empty-headed seducers but men of virtue and substance. They must avoid those men "in the depth of whose souls we are only playthings" and seek out instead the steady and civic-minded, like themselves. Only then would relationships between individuals be based on strong, durable foundations and only then would the same be possible between nations. Like the feminist who had written to Campigneulles protesting Rousseau's misogyny and lamenting the rareness of her own attitude, Mme de Beaumer fervently wished there were more women writers so that their impact on society could be profound. She hoped her *Journal des Dames* would bring this about. "Courage, women, no more timidity. Let us prove that we can think, speak, study, and criticize as well as [men]. . . . I await this revolution with impatience. I will do my utmost to be one of the first to precipitate it." [26]

Mme de Beaumer's bombastic entrance upon the journalistic scene occasioned instant ridicule, which only reinforced her determination to continue fighting for long overdue reforms. Male readers mocked her seriousness of purpose and ethic of decency, expecting her to falter, yield to their advice, and, as she said derisively, be "métamorphosée en Elégante." Because she was not pretty and did not seek to please men in the usual manner, she knew she had caused feelings of resentment, and her critics now sought to confuse and paralyze her with discordant "advice." She announced in her second issue that she would ignore these detractors. "I will henceforth close my ears to you, *messieurs les critiques.* We women think under our coiffures as well as you do under your wigs. We are as capable of reasoning as you are. In fact, you lose your reason over us every day." [27] Mme de Beaumer would con-

26 Ibid., 78–80.
27 Ibid., novembre 1761:103–5.

tinue to rail against conceited dandies bent on perpetuating flirtatious, superficial relations between the sexes. It was they who stood in the way of her mission's first step, the nurturing of feminine self-respect. "Women everywhere must scorn these useless encumbrances. Disdain is the only answer they deserve."[28] Determined to ignore them, she pursued her campaign.

To demonstrate the greatness of women at all levels of society Mme de Beaumer filled her issues of the *Journal des Dames* with *éloges* of great women who had distinguished themselves both intellectually and politically. She made a point of praising Princess Anne of The Hague, daughter of King George II of England, which gave her a chance to recommend the Orangeist cause and republican Holland, where she herself spent so much time.[29] Nearly every issue of her paper carried at least one *éloge,* meant to demonstrate that throughout history women had distinguished themselves not only in every branch of learning but also in public and even military roles and had carried out their duties with glorious dignity. Marie de Gournay, Mlle Descartes and Mme Du Châtelet, staunch feminists, had rivaled the greatest philosophers and scientists; Christina of Sweden was an exemplary ruler, Mesdames de Sévigné, Deshoulières, and de La Fayette had excelled in literature. But Mme de Beaumer did not confine herself to *éloges* of the privileged, wealthy, and powerful. Less illustrious women were just as worthy of attention. She argued that any woman could understand practical subjects perfectly. Panning a new book, *Les Journées physiques,* an attempt to popularize physics for female readers based on Fontenelle's classic model, she strenuously objected to the author's sugary style. Science was "the most useful of the arts," and women needed serious instruction, not watered-down drivel.[30] She pointed out Mmes Dacier, Du Boccage and Du Châtelet as examples of women whose great intellectual accomplishments showed clearly that their sex did not need to be patronized. The repeated inclusion of Mme Du Châtelet in these lists shows that Mme de Beaumer did not feel threatened by a member of her sex considered by most other women to be too "virile" and egotistical.[31] The editor herself reviewed books

28 Ibid., août 1762:192. Also septembre 1762:passim.
29 Ibid., décembre 1761:244ff.
30 Ibid., 199.
31 See Badinter, *Emilie,* 473–77 and passim.

on a wide range of subjects. She traced the roots of a novel by Tiphaigne de la Roche to the occult Rosicrucian tradition and displayed her familiarity with his freethinking, *libertin* predecessors, among them Cyrano de Bergerac, whose significance in the Fronde we have already seen, and the "comte de Gabalis."[32] Far more useful, however, was a book called *Le Gentilhomme cultivateur,* because it advocated practical activity for the aristocracy and because it dealt with agriculture, which had an importance and a value for humanity that women could recognize as well as men.[33]

But Mme de Beaumer's greatest enthusiasm was reserved for obscure female artists, merchants, artisans, and musicians from the lower classes. This abundance of capable, talented women, everywhere and too numerous to name, seemed to confirm all her arguments. Industrious and motivated from within, women succeeded at all tasks even without recognition and honor; with some well-deserved encouragement these commoners would rise to ever greater challenges, providing the world with the energy it now lacked. The senseless war had put Europe to soul-searching. It had dragged on for years, proving only that the "civilized" eighteenth century was as barbaric as any other despotic age. *Esprit* alone was worthless. What people needed was a revival of commitment and *chaleur,* the kind that had led the Romans to work virtuously for their society. What good were philosophical systems? Maupertuis was brilliant, but his ideas could not be applied to better the world; Rousseau was negative, seemingly determined to spew "paradoxes," put humans "back on all fours," and alienate both men and women from their quest for improvement. The only useful thing men had done lately, and Mme de Beaumer considered it a "phenomenon," was to propose that the poor get the same justice as the rich, but so far the proposal had come to nothing and would doubtless remain in the safe realm of idle speculation.[34]

The editor strongly preferred practice to theory and was im-

---

32 *Journal des Dames,* novembre 1761:105. *Le Comte de Gabalis, ou Entretiens sur les sciences secrètes* was written in 1670 by the irreverent anticlerical abbé de Monfaucon de Villars, an advocate of toleration and liberty and a great favorite of Bayle's. His ideas, often reprinted in the Enlightenment, included some very akin to Mme de Beaumer's. See *Biographie universelle* 43:435.

33 *Journal des Dames,* novembre 1761:123.

34 Ibid., octobre 1761:62–63 and 50–52, "Sur l'institution des avocats et procureurs des pauvres."

patient to replace ivory tower philosophies, no matter how well intentioned, with industry and public service. Mme de Beaumer had the Huguenot penchant for productive, even frenetic activity. She called commerce the "motor nerve of all great legislation."[35] But unlike the *Encyclopédie*'s glorification of the useful arts, Mme de Beaumer's stressed the crucial economic role played by women. Looking about she saw large numbers of creative yet modest women busy at tasks, a ready energetic force within society waiting to be tapped and challenged. She provided notices about female painters, shopowners, science illustrators, engravers, miniaturists, naturalists, sculptors, rugmakers, clockmakers, lens-grinders, collectors, taxidermists, weavers, chemists, singers. Some of them had already begun to make their mark upon the world. A Mme de Moutiers had drawn for the famous biologist Réaumur, a Mlle Biheron, who molded artificial anatomical parts out of wax, had actually won praise from the Académie des Sciences. Such steady, self-reliant, productive women—they were not the exception but the rule—proved themselves the equals of men. Mme de Beaumer invoked their example in her answers to letters sent by melancholic readers searching for advice. The editor was an activist and saw goals as powerful antidotes to the prevailing acceptance by women of their own inferiority. If all women would throw themselves into useful, constructive activity, the precedent for self-respect would be established. And this was the essential first step in her "revolution."[36]

Mme de Beaumer's views were reflected in a poem written to her by the poet and Mason Baculard d'Arnaud, "Couplets à Mme ** sur l'Air des francs-maçons," which she printed in the December issue of *Journal des Dames*. The poet was the orator at two Masonic lodges, one at the Hôtel de Soisson, the other called the Loge de la Cité. Most of the members of these fraternities were merchants, bourgeois whose sympathies were devoutly Jansenist and who believed deeply in the solidity and value of the family. Baculard d'Arnaud now brought to Mme de Baumer's paper his support for fidelity and wisdom with all their Masonic over-

35   Ibid., février 1762:180.
36   Ibid., octobre 1761:78–79, 92–96; novembre 1761:190–92; décembre 1761:254–65, 281–84; janvier 1762:95–96; février 1762:201–3; avril 1762:106–7; mai 1762:202–3; juin 1762:283–88.

tones.[37] A well-stocked mind and a busy life compensated for the passage of beauty and youth, and lasting companionship filled the future with promise, not fear. Had Circe used Mme de Beaumer's vanquishing tone instead of relying on her feminine wiles, Ulysses would surely have stayed with her. Knowledge combined with virtue, maturity, and perspective were the gifts of eternal Minerva, the best tools for dealing with life.[38]

In general, Mme de Beaumer espoused the ideals of Masonry. She may have been a Mason herself. In The Hague, where she spent much time, at least one coeducational lodge had existed since 1751. Many of its members were actresses at the Théâtre Français in Holland, and the *Journal des Dames* carried a letter from one such actress about her youth in La Rochelle. The paucity of nobles in this Huguenot refuge gave the wives of *négociants* unprecedented power, and the letter described with obvious relish the inversion of the traditional social order.[39]

But whether a Mason herself or not, Mme de Beaumer embraced the Masonic vision of universality more vigorously and more literally than most other journalists of her day. She reserved her highest praise for people with "l'esprit de l'univers."[40] Convinced that her message applied to all people in all places, she advertised a list of eighty-one booksellers in as many cities throughout France, Germany, Switzerland, Holland, Spain, Italy, Portugal, Russia, Sweden, and England where the *Journal des Dames* was for sale. Published at the beginning of the December 1761 issue, her third, and filling several pages, such fanfare could not fail to catch the eye and make its point. No other paper had anything like it. And in an additional effort to show her journal's popularity, Mme de Beaumer cautioned her readers to avoid coun-

37 On Baculard d'Arnaud, see Chevallier, *Histoire de la franc-maçonnerie* 1:65–68; Inklar, *Baculard d'Arnaud.* On the commitment of Masonry to marriage and sexual fidelity, see Jacob, *The Radical Enlightenment,* 206–8.

38 *Journal des Dames,* décembre 1761:276. For other Masonic poems on this theme, see, for example, *Recueil de chansons de la très vénérable confrérie des franc-maçons,* 38, 80, 105.

39 Jacob, "Freemasonry, Women, Paradox." The "Lettre de Mlle ★, actrice au Théâtre Français de ———," is in the *Journal des Dames,* avril 1762:62–76, an issue published while Mme de Beaumer lived in self-imposed exile in The Hague.

40 *Journal des Dames,* janvier 1762:62.

terfeit versions, "to accept only those papers bearing her signature."[41]

The list of international distributors was a sham, a publicity stunt and a grandiose hyperbolic gesture that cannot be taken at face value as a recent historian of the press has done.[42] Copies of the paper may indeed have been sent by the overeager editor to some of these bookdealers, but not in response to any real demand, for Mme de Beaumer mistook her own fiction for fact in her desire to make it come true. Her desperate financial situation, which she would soon reveal to Malesherbes, showed there were no takers for these international mailings. In her determination to impress her readers she had misled herself into imagining and reaching out to a market that did not exist. The *Mercure,* considered to have an unusually broad circulation, reached only forty-six cities, mostly in the French provinces. There was, according to contemporaries, little call for even the best-known Paris periodicals outside of France. "In foreign countries," wrote the well-traveled Chevalier d'Eon in 1763, "we do not find the same love

41   Mme de Beaumer's list of cities grew gradually over several months. In the October 1761 issue, the *Journal des Dames* was said to be available at particular bookdealers in Versailles, Poitiers, Nice, Nancy, Le Mans, Frankfurt, Brussels, The Hague, Amsterdam, Utrecht, Leyden, Rotterdam, Breda, Groningen, Liège, Bern, Geneva, and Lausanne. In November, Lyons and Rouen were added, both Protestant strongholds and centers of trade in forbidden books from across the border. In December the list was much longer, its order rearranged, and some of the bookdealers had changed (for example, Utrecht [chez Spruyt] now read Utrecht [chez Croon]). December added to the above list specific shops in Angers, Arras, Aix, Alençon, Amiens, Besançon, Bordeaux, Bayonne, Caen, Dieppe, Douai, Limoges, Lille, Grenoble, Dijon, Toulon, Marseilles, Metz, Montpellier, Montauban, Nantes, Nîmes, Orléans, Pau, Reims, Rennes, La Rochelle, Saint-Malo, Troyes, Strasbourg, Châlons-sur-Marne, Frankfurt an der Oder, Frankfurt am Main, Middleburg, Antwerp, Avignon, Barcelona, Berlin, Cadiz, Cologne, Dresden, Florence, Fribourg, Hamburg, Leipzig, Lisbon, London, Madrid, Mannheim, Milan, Mons, Naples, Parma, Placentia, Ratisbon, Rome, Stockholm, Turin, Venice, Saint Petersburg. Mme de Beaumer's signature and the notice about counterfeiting appeared in her first issue, *Journal des Dames,* octobre 1761:96, and was repeated in every subsequent one.

42   See Rimbault, "Presse féminine: Production." Page 215 provides a map of the *Journal des Dames*'s distribution under Mme de Beaumer and uses her list as proof that the feminine press was "broadly international." But the list disappeared completely after three months, and subsequent editors of the paper only claimed to sell to a few cities beyond Paris (for example, Lille and Strasbourg under Dorat in 1777). The conclusions drawn by Rimbault are thus misleading. The list was merely Mme de Beaumer's political dream.

and enthusiasm for periodicals that prevails in Paris. I know from the best London bookdealers that they will not handle any of our papers, not even the venerable *Journal des savants.*"[43] D'Aquin, who thought Mme de Beaumer's predecessors were imbeciles, teased in his *Censeur hebdomadaire* that she seemed to have suddenly achieved worldwide fame while they had gone unnoticed, that one woman could obviously do what two men could not.[44] Still, the list in the *Journal des Dames* seemed to awaken the slumbering authorities, who suddenly took action against Mme de Beaumer. Although we have no record of their precise charges against her, there was plenty here to disturb them and convince them that the editor needed disciplining. She was allegedly doing business with France's enemies, London and Berlin, and even with Saint Petersburg at a time when Russia, in a sudden turnaround at the czarina's death, had just joined forces with Frederick of Prussia against France. She conspicuously left out the Hapsburg cities with which France was allied. Mme de Beaumer had been against war from the start, but she now seemed to be broadcasting her hostility to the Austrian alliance so dear to Choiseul. Her list was tantamount to treason.

Mme de Beaumer's daring up to this point can be partially explained by her residence in the sheltered "enclos du Temple," the home address she gave in her first issues of the *Journal des Dames,* one of the *lieux privilégiés* of Paris where the court's police could not penetrate, and therefore something of a refuge for outlaws. The Temple, a walled enclave in the Marais housing about four thousand souls, was presided over by Louis-François de Bourbon, prince de Conti, a cousin of the king, head of the chevaliers de Malte, grand prieur de France. Although a prince of the blood, Mme de Beaumer's protector Conti was a *frondeur* leader, freethinker, *libertin,* and active Mason who attracted within the walls of his haven numerous skeptics, Protestants, Jansenists, and fugitives. Conti strongly supported the parlements against the Crown. He hid Rousseau in the Temple at several junctures, harbored secret presses for the Jansenists' clandestine *Nouvelles ecclé-*

---

43   The chevalier d'Eon to the duc de Praslin, the minister of foreign affairs (31 mai 1763), quoted in Hatin, *Histoire politique et littéraire* 3:98. For the *Mercure's* forty-six cities, see *Mercure* (janvier 1762) ii:"Avis."

44   *Censeur hebdomadaire* (1761) iv:175.

siastiques and for the *Courrier d'Avignon,* allowed the selling and possibly the copying of libelous *nouvelles à la main.* At this precise moment, with the help of the Temple bailiff Le Paige, Conti was busy orchestrating the ouster of the Jesuits from France.[45] "His love of independence," wrote a contemporary about Conti, "displeased the government with which he often fought. At the Temple he lived freely, far from the intrigues of the court where he ceased making appearances; . . . he liked to descend from the lofty rank where an accident of birth had placed him."[46] Within the close quarters of the Temple's walls, the high and the low did indeed rub shoulders. Next to the several grand *hôtels* ran narrow streets lined with crowded barracks, tiny studios, and workshops full of artisans. In the many little courts merchants ran a lively market. The cafés were filled with a mixture of workers and people of rank. But the Temple was best known as a refuge for insolvent debtors. Furnished rooms were sublet to people who needed a place to stay while they restored order to their affairs. For 5 livres and a few sous they could request a *permission de séjour* of three months, during which creditors could not harass them. If this proved to be insufficient time to solve their financial problems, the *séjour* was generally renewed. The Temple was a world unto itself. "Here one lived under one's own laws. . . . It was like being in a foreign country yet in the heart of one's own land."[47] "It is good," wrote Louis-Sébastien Mercier, biographer of Paris and a subsequent editor of the *Journal des Dames,* "that there should be in a city a sanctuary for victims of the agitations and vicissitudes of human life; here people and art have a kind of liberty too often fettered and denied them elsewhere."[48]

Certainly Mme de Beaumer qualified on a number of counts as needful of asylum. Her refusal to take a retiring posture had an-

45   See Barillet, *Recherches historiques sur le Temple,* especially 46–47. On Conti's harboring of Jansenist presses, see BN ms. fr. 22093, fols. 421, 384. See also Funck-Brentano, *Figaro et ses devanciers,* 155, 288. On Conti's sheltering of Rousseau, see for example, [Bachaumont], *Mémoires secrets* 2:275 (18 décembre 1765). On Conti's involvement with the expulsion of the Jesuits, see Van Kley, *Jansenists,* 60–71.
46   Barillet, *Recherches historiques sur le Temple,* 194–95.
47   Ibid., 123–24. See also *Provincial à Paris,* vol. "Quartier du Temple," part 2, pp. 155–56.
48   Mercier, *Tableau de Paris,* ed. Desnoiresterres, 306.

tagonized the male authorities with whom she was forced to deal. Her politics were sufficiently at variance with French foreign and domestic policy to make staying out of reach prudent. Her letters from this period reveal that she had incurred debts of 9,000 livres for the *Journal des Dames*—perhaps simply buying the paper from Louptière had necessitated her seeking refuge there—but in the Temple she was safely protected from her creditors, for as Mercier explained, "here the sheriff's exploits become null and void, arrest warrants expire on the threshold."[49] In this teeming, colorful microcosm, Mme de Beaumer could mingle inconspicuously with the crowds, and she obviously felt comfortable. Nearly every issue of her paper carried poems by the Temple's resident poet, the anticlerical abbé Mangenot, and publicity for Temple artisans and merchants whom she described with admiring affection.[50] She had chosen the safest place in Paris from which to launch her crusade.

But even in the Temple, where her person was out of danger, Mme de Beaumer could not escape the threat that her *Journal des Dames* would be silenced, once it and she were perceived as political liabilities. Her printer, after all, was not within the walls. Sometime in December 1761 she must have been dealt a harsh warning, because the January issue of her paper was drastically transformed. Since she was a woman, she was handled more gently than the journalist François Chévrier, whose profile was quite similar to hers. He too wrote a hymn to Mandrin, urged peace, frequented Masonic circles in The Hague, and claimed to have a worldwide network of followers. Both his *Gazetin de Bruxelles* and *Le Colporteur* were silenced now and a lettre de cachet was issued by Choiseul, who upon learning Chévrier had escaped to Holland demanded his extradition. The police spy sent to trail him described him as a "bad subject . . . declared enemy of his *patrie,* in cahoots with the *frondeurs* of Paris."[51] Much the same could have

49   Ibid., p. 305.
50   See, for example, *Journal des Dames,* octobre 1761:94; novembre 1761:190, ads for Mme Martin and Mme Ravysi.
51   On Chévrier's claims to universality, see BN ms. fr. 22085, p. 160, quoted in Funck-Brentano, *Figaro et ses devanciers,* 49. See, in the same work by Funck-Brentano, pp. 241–55. The chevalier de Rutlidge, who would later be involved with Mercier's *Journal des Dames,* would also be compared to the reprobate Chévrier. See Chapter 6, below.

been said for Mme de Beaumer. She would be made to show respect for the king if she wished to stay in print.

The *Nouveau Journal des Dames,* which appeared in January 1762, showed that Mme de Beaumer's censors had struck a hard bargain. She was permitted to continue her feminist campaign, but her copy during the next three months was intensely patriotic and royalist. The authorities seem to have felt that her bombastic rhetoric in defense of her sex was subversive only when combined with republicanism and claims for universality. Severed from these other causes her feminism lost its power in their eyes. They therefore allowed it as long as Mme de Beaumer would demonstrate her willingness to be a good subject. She had even been persuaded to write a *Histoire militaire, ou Celle des régiments de France dédiée à son altesse Monseigneur le maréchal prince de Soubise.* She announced in the January issue her project to "immortalize the deeds of those who gave their lives for the king, the *patrie . . .* the state."[52] The prospectus for this work, hot off the press, was sent to Malesherbes with a letter soliciting his good will.[53] The same prospectus then appeared in the March issue of the *Journal des Dames.* France must win the war, Mme de Beaumer now argued, for the glory of King Louis XV, "the love, the delight, the father of his people, and the veneration of all the earth." There followed effusive, indeed fulsome praise for acts of bravery and valor. French soldiers must be as brave as Achilles, as wise as Nestor, as prudent as Ulysses. Mme de Beaumer explained that writing the *Histoire militaire* was difficult for her, since the cause of women interested her far more than male heroism in battle. But she would sacrifice all for the immediate needs of her *patrie.*[54]

We know from Mme de Beaumer's *Oeuvres mêlées* that she found military history totally abhorrent. Yet now she compromised her standards and capitulated to the booktrade authorities. Did she feel that drastic measures were necessary to keep her newspaper going and to maintain her lifeline with her readers? Another English and Dutch sympathizer with subversive tenden-

---

52 *Journal des Dames,* janvier 1762:58.
53 BN ms. fr. 22085, fol. 57.
54 *Journal des Dames,* mars 1762:289ff. "Prospectus pour *l'Histoire militaire,*" 2–9. For a brief discussion of Malesherbes's insistence that subjects demonstrate affection for their ruler, see Kelly, "Political Thought of Malesherbes."

cies, the abbé Raynal, had just been plied into service for France, "commissioned by government orders" to write an *Ecole militaire* which the *Mercure* applauded for "using the lives of great warriors to inspire and animate the young to defend our *patrie*."[55] For Raynal's willingness to be tamed he had even been rewarded with a 3,000-livre pension.[56] Mme de Beaumer needed money sorely and must have thought her gesture of propitiation foolproof. In an extra nod for approval, she even dedicated her *Histoire militaire* to Soubise, the king's closest friend and Mme de Pompadour's favorite general, against whom public opinion had turned because the well-liked General de Broglie had been exiled for France's humiliating defeats while Soubise continued to enjoy royal favor.[57] Grimm, pointing out the similarities between Raynal's work and Mme de Beaumer's, implied that too many such efforts could backfire. All these military panegyrics seemed almost impertinent when France's soldiers were performing no heroic deeds.[58]

During these months, Mme de Beaumer's feminism was permitted to continue, a probable consequence of her concessions to the authorities. Her *Journal des Dames* praised the novels of Marie-Anne Roumier Robert—a woman who admired the lowly and virtuous more than the highborn and whose industrious activity as a writer saved her from the *maladie à la mode*[59]—welcomed letters from readers who supported her efforts to make this the "siècle des dames,"[60] and adopted the suggestion of one subscriber who urged her to reclaim the French language from the men who had ravished it. "The career you pursue puts you in the unique

55 *Mercure,* juillet 1762:66.
56 [Bachaumont], *Mémoires secrets* 1:69 (7 avril 1762).
57 Soubise's friendship with Louis XV earned him the nickname "l'ami du coeur du roi." He dined at all the *soupers des cabinets* and was fast friends with Mme de Pompadour. On the military plane, however, his exploits were less successful. His worst disgrace was the Battle of Rossbach in 1757, where he could easily have defeated Frederick of Prussia but failed because of last-minute strategic blunders. He and de Broglie were also outmaneuvered at Wittinghausen (July 1761), for which defeat de Broglie was exiled by Pompadour to his *terres* (February 1762) at just the moment Mme de Beaumer chose to dedicate her work to Soubise. For the extreme unpopularity of this move, see the mocking songs about Soubise in [Bachaumont], *Mémoires secrets* 1:48–49, 57, 62–63 (20 février, 15 and 28 mars 1762).
58 Grimm et al., *Correspondance littéraire* 5:76.
59 *Journal des Dames,* janvier 1762:31–34.
60 Ibid., février 1762:195–97.

position and gives you the right to use and make acceptable the feminized form of *author* and *editor*. . . . It is in fact a dishonor for women that such words are not in common parlance . . . since they have shown in literature that they can equal and surpass men." Delighted to accept the innovation of her sympathetic neologist, Mme de Beaumer henceforth referred to herself as *autrice* or *éditrice,* "since this question concerns the prerogatives of my sex, whose rights I uphold."[61] Mme de Beaumer continued to brandish her journalistic career as proof that women could do even the hardest jobs. To those who had expected the *Journal des Dames* to be a mindless time killer, a triviality, she protested, "that is precisely what I am determined to avoid!" She portrayed herself as teacher, guide, and *porte-parole.* "I love my sex; I am determined to support and to vindicate its honor and its rights."[62] She would show that women could be great historians and journalists. "We are daring enough to try and courageous enough to persevere in careers." The very use of the term *autrice* she knew would offend "puristic and caustic" males who, "jealous of our glory," could never admit women capable of independent thought. It was even rumored that a man was ghostwriting her own *Journal des Dames.* This made her furious; she was no mere *prête-nom.* "I am not and have never been the *dame* of any man; when one speaks of productions *under my name* one should realize that they are completely my own."[63]

Taking advantage of the protection afforded by her new royalist guise, which seemed at least temporarily to make her feminism less threatening to the authorities, Mme de Beaumer used the prospectus for the *Histoire militaire* to state her strongest claims for female equality. Insisting that the mind has no sex, that there is no such thing as male or female genius, she made a concerted attack on both women who relied on the help of men and male writers who pretended to be female. Honesty was necessary in literary as well as personal relationships; it must be frankly admitted, without any of these games, that women could write as well as men. And the public must learn to accept that; instead of being conde-

61   Ibid., 126–31.
62   Ibid., mars 1762:"Avant propos," 223–25.
63   Ibid., "Prospectus" following 289, especially 6–7.

scendingly solicitous of female writers, readers must be educated to expect their works to be as serious as any others. Mme de Beaumer referred with disdain to "the Mlle Bernard of M. de Fontenelle, the Mlle Barbier of M. l'abbé Pellegrin, the Mlle de la Vigne of M. Desforges-Maillard, and the comtesse de ★ ★ of M. Fréron," famous cases in which male journalists had tricked the public into believing they were women and had therefore won a more indulgent reception for their writings. She anticipated that her own journalistic effort, more virile and aggressive than any previous paper by a woman, would be attributed after her death to a man. She therefore announced that the *Journal des Dames* was entirely her own, refusing to be denied credit for her bravery by present and future "enemies of our sex."[64] Mme de Beaumer had also begun to stress that feminism had a strong historical precedent. She was indeed the first outspoken female journalist, but women in other fields had been speaking up for centuries. The cause of women must therefore be seen not as an exceptional, passing fashion; feminism had a solid past and was now gaining the momentum to sustain it in the future.[65] This linking of the *Journal des Dames* with a historical tradition had the same subversive tendencies as the linking of Damiens's assassination attempt with earlier regicides. It made it virtually impossible to dismiss these protests as isolated and therefore insignificant events.[66]

As part of her bargain with the censors, Mme de Beaumer had evidently agreed to suppress her claims to universality. The many-page list of eighty-one cities that had opened her first few issues now had disappeared entirely. No longer in demand throughout the world, the paper advertised that it was for sale simply in Paris. In exchange for this sacrifice, Mme de Beaumer allowed herself a number of splenetic outbursts even in the royalist articles that had been forced upon her. Along with several reviews of books on patriotism in which Louis was compared to Clovis, both of whom were "not tyrannical but fatherly," came a blistering attack on male dandies who refused to fulfill their military obligations:

64   Ibid., 7. On Desforges-Maillard, see Chouillet and Moureau, *Suppléments* 3:32–38.
65   *Journal des Dames,* février 1762:204 and mars 1762:244.
66   See Introduction, above.

What sweet revenge it would be, gentlemen, if today, like the ancient Amazons, we could force you to spin and braid, you the *frivolites* especially, in love with yourselves like Narcissus, who spend your time on fashions and powder and how best to place your handkerchief. . . . You are more effeminate than even the coquettes whom you seek to please. Since Heaven gave you strength, do not degrade it. *Use* it to serve your king and *patrie,* become good "compatriotes," go to battle, face and kill our enemies, subdue them under the feet of the monarch of France. He deserves to be the ruler of the universe.[67]

In another article praising the daughter of Soubise, the editor stressed that her true "grandeur" lay not in her noble birth but in her *bienfaisance,* her giving of money to the poor and unfortunate and her support of needy artisans who wished to work and live in dignity.[68]

But despite her concessions, Mme de Beaumer was clearly under a great deal of strain, and her negotiations with the censors must have continued to be stormy. She had never written her promised *Histoire militaire.* Her paper was several times delayed and as the issues appeared she had to apologize to her readers for lateness.[69] Her printer Quillau now turned uncooperative—he was known to favor conformist *bons livres* of the kind the relatively tame *Journal des Dames* had been under Louptière—and Mme de Beaumer was obliged to withdraw her registers from him.[70] But up to this point, at least bits of her message had been getting out, and paying lip service to the king seemed to be buying her some time. Then in March 1762 while they were examining her April issue, the censors suspended her paper entirely. Marin had just been promoted to *censeur de la police,* and even though he had gotten her to toe the line, he simply did not trust her. She was indeed speaking glowingly of the king and of the *patrie* in her paper now, but the praise seemed insincere, not reverential. The censor no doubt held against Mme de Beaumer his own earlier careless-

---

67 *Journal des Dames,* mars 1762:225–26.
68 Ibid., janvier 1762:86–90.
69 Ibid., 204.
70 On Quillau, see Zephir, "Libraires et imprimeurs," 324. In the *Journal des Dames* of mars 1762, Mme de Beaumer asked her readers to settle their accounts with Quillau and deal directly with her in future.

ness in having approved her *Oeuvres mêlées,* whose section on Mandrin would have been refused by even the most lenient of his colleagues.[71] Although Marin never stated precisely the reason for the suspension of the *Journal des Dames,* Mme de Beaumer's repeated protests that she did indeed respect her superiors suggests that the general charge against her had been insubordination.

With communications severed completely between her and her readers, Mme de Beaumer became frantic, and this quickly diminished her effectiveness. A series of letters she wrote to the authorities when she learned of the *Journal des Dames*'s suspension show her running around in circles of fury and panic. On 16 March she wrote to Malesherbes that she had been twice to see him the previous day but in vain. She needed absolutely to know of what crime she was being accused. Referring to the ways in which she had already capitulated, she claimed she had "always rendered [the authorities] their due." Her paper was now deeply in debt, and she was looking for a loan of 9,000 livres. Her new subscriptions were due (Louptière had revived the journal exactly one year before), she was being forced to find a new printer and to fire an uncooperative employee. Now, as if this were not enough, Malesherbes chose her most vulnerable moment to suspend the *Journal des Dames,* broke all appointments with her, and refused to divulge his reasons. "Why are you punishing me?" she cried, "for I have followed all your rules, and I am far too unfortunate to withstand much prejudice." If only she could afford a *privilège* she would not be vulnerable to such victimization. "I almost believe that some evil genie has biased you against me. I know the goodness of your heart, which makes the injury I suffer at your orders all the more painful." She begged for a new censor, M. Piquet, described herself as "eaten up by gout," and blamed Malesherbes for reducing her to ruin when all she wanted was to pursue a career. Why did he not have the decency to meet with her? "I certainly do not deserve your cruelty in my sad situation,

---

71 The censor de La Garde, for example, whose liberalism we have already discussed, nonetheless denied permissions to works dealing with Mandrin. On his refusal of a tragedy called *La Mort de Mandrin,* see Rétat, *L'Attentat de Damiens,* 155.

my lot is so unhappy, the fatality that pursues me is without example."[72]

Christophe Piquet, the censor Mme de Beaumer requested, was one of the most active readers of manuscripts and was reputed to be liberal. Where most censors reviewed a few dozen works during the years of Malesherbes's directorship of the booktrade, Piquet reviewed nearly three hundred and did not scrutinize things too carefully. In February 1761 he had helped prepare a Swiss edition of Rousseau's *Nouvelle Héloïse* and had allowed many passages against religious intolerance and social injustice to go unexpurgated.[73] He would doubtless have allowed Mme de Beaumer greater liberty, but Malesherbes did not want to facilitate that. Quite the contrary.

Two days later, because she received no response, Mme de Beaumer wrote again to Malesherbes, telling him her subscribers were losing patience. She had followed his earlier suggestion that she try to settle the matter with Sartine, the chief of police, but Sartine, claiming to have "nothing to say," had refused to discuss serious issues with her.[74] She was trying desperately to figure out in her own mind what had gone wrong. Perhaps a satire she had advertised from Lyons had offended? Perhaps she should have gotten permission before printing the prospectus for her *Histoire militaire?*[75] She begged again for the new censor Piquet, said she had already prepared a substitute for the suspended issue, and threatened to leave France forever if Malesherbes continued to sabotage her efforts and conceal the charges against her.[76] Malesherbes, who probably disliked the thought of her publishing in a "freer foreign country," responded to her threat by finally answering her but told her to address herself in future only to Marin, "who will make all

72 BN ms. fr. 22151, fol. 75.
73 On Piquet's activities, see Blangonnet, "Recherches sur les censeurs," 200–215. Of the 283 works he censored, nearly half were given *permissions,* indicating they were too dubious to receive a *privilège* but that Piquet still thought they should be read.
74 BN ms. fr. 22151, fol. 71.
75 Ibid., fols. 74, 76. A prospectus was the accepted way of advertising a coming work. Usually three hundred were printed, and they needed to be approved by a censor. See Perrin, *Manuel de l'auteur,* 27.
76 BN ms. fr. 22151, fol. 72.

the necessary arrangements,"[77] presumably to assign some substitute editor to the *Journal des Dames* whom the authorities would find more acceptable. Marin by now regarded Mme de Beaumer as "offensive to public morality" and told Malesherbes that she and her followers were of an "uncommon rashness, a singular indiscretion."[78] He too preferred to wear her down than deal with her directly. A final wild and fragmented note, scribbled by Mme de Beaumer on an envelope, begged Marin to spare her the painful and vain legwork and be civil enough to grant her an audience. "My trips to see you are useless . . . my gout excruciating. . . . I suffer deeply from your injustice. I am exhausted from running. . . . I beg you to finish this matter."[79] Worn and broken, she now really did leave for Holland, under the cloud of a still unspecified crime.

Before her departure, however, Mme de Beaumer had found a young man named Du Rozoi to take over the *Journal des Dames,* under whose direction Marin allowed it to resume. Marin may have reasoned that if the *éditrice* still had a paper going in Paris, however whitewashed, she might not start up another fiercer one in exile. Perhaps her willingness to agree to the authorities' substitute upset the prince de Conti; in any case she was now no longer under his protection. The April issue of the paper, which still had Mme de Beaumer's name on it, gave a new Paris address for her "chez M. le comte de Jaucourt, rue Mêlée près la porte Saint Martin."[80] Houses on the rue Mêlée, just a few blocks from the Temple, ran along the city ramparts and backed onto "les boulevards," the wide, newly popular, tree-lined promenades at the outer edge of Paris. Here courtisans and countesses walked alongside clowns, street acrobats, merchants, and thieves in a crowded, colorful, and continuous spectacle. This neighborhood, open to all estates, allowed high and lowborn to mingle and gape at each

77 Ibid., fol. 76.
78 See Ricard, *Victime de Beaumarchais,* 52.
79 BN ms. fr. 22151, fol. 73.
80 This was the address given for Mme de Beaumer in the *Journal des Dames* from April 1762 to April 1763, when she gave up the paper. In 1792 another feminist and republican, Mary Wollstonecraft, would live on the rue Mêlée and watch from her window as Louis XVI was wheeled by on the way from his prison in the Temple to his trial.

other and was probably much to Mme de Beaumer's liking. It was, like some of the gardens, a place where people gathered to read gazettes and journals as they sipped their *limonade*.

Mme de Beaumer's new protector, a Huguenot nobleman with numerous relatives in Holland, was a direct descendant of Philippe de Plessis-Mornay, the probable author of *Vindiciae contra tyrannos,* one of the most radical political treatises of the sixteenth century, proclaiming violent opposition to absolutism. Although much tamer than his ancestor, Comte Pierre de Jaucourt was active in his own right helping French Protestants fight for their civil liberties.[81] He was *premier gentilhomme* of the king's Protestant cousin Louis Joseph de Bourbon, prince de Condé, and the *Journal des Dames* was suddenly dedicated to Condé's daughter. How strenuously Jaucourt helped Mme de Beaumer is not clear. His main home, called the "Hôtel des Huguenots," was located on the rue de Grenelle in the prestigious faubourg Saint Germain. While Mme de Beaumer probably visited there—in February her paper started carrying notices for female artisans on the rue de Grenelle—she was not housed in the primary residence. Jaucourt was undoubtedly sympathetic to her cause. His younger brother, the *Encyclopédiste* Chevalier de Jaucourt, was one of the most radical and outspoken male critics of women's historic subordination, as can be seen in his article "Femme" in the *Encyclopédie.*[82] The elder Jaucourt seemed willing to provide a base for Mme de Beaumer's travels and correspondence between Paris and Holland. By giving her a secretary, facilitating her Dutch connections, and putting a roof over her head, Jaucourt did more than anyone else was willing to do for Mme de Beaumer, but he could not force the booktrade authorities to deal directly with her. And as long as they refused to see her, there was no point in her staying in Paris.

Pierre Barnabé Farmain Du Rozoi was nineteen years old and extremely ambitious. His politics were antithetical to Mme de Beaumer's; he would spend his life in the service of the monarchy.

81 On Pierre de Jaucourt, see the introduction to *Correspondance du comte de Jaucourt;* see also Jacob, *Radical Enlightenment,* 226–27.

82 Jaucourt's was the most feminist of the four articles on "femme" in the *Encyclopédie.* For a brief discussion of them, see Abensour, *Femme et féminisme,* 365–77; Albistur and Armogathe, *Histoire du féminisme,* 189–193; Dock, "The Encyclopedists' woman"; and Williams, "Politics of Feminism," especially 338–39.

He had probably volunteered to help her with her advertised *Histoire militaire,* for which his interest, unlike hers, was genuine. Later, under the protection first of Choiseul, then of Vergennes, he would edit a *Journal militaire* for the Ministry of Foreign Affairs in a labor of patriotic love. During the Revolution his passionately royalist *Gazette de Paris* would round up hostages willing to exchange their lives for the emprisoned and condemned Louis XVI.[83] Now, when he took over the *Journal des Dames* in April 1762, he already demonstrated his ability to charm the powerful. Immediately the suspended paper was allowed to resume publication under a new censor, Rousselet. Du Rozoi had won the support of Mme de Pompadour and proudly announced that the duchesse de Choiseul herself had become a subscriber.[84] Obviously he was doing something right.

What Du Rozoi did was to lighten the tone of the paper by filling it with his own poems, stories, and plays. He was thrilled at the chance to further his own literary career and completely eschewed political matters. Mme de Beaumer continued to send articles, which he grudgingly printed, but the prevailing tone of his *Journal des Dames* was antifeminist, fashionably risqué, even slightly bawdy, and her message was effectively drowned out. Much more attuned to the mood at court than to wholesome bourgeois values, Du Rozoi dealt with the "woman question" in a totally integrative, traditional manner. He stressed the delicacy of the female temperament and the fickleness of women but clearly appreciated their beauty and grace. Vanity and flirtation were for him the essence of the feminine character. Serious work did not become women, original invention was beyond them. Several articles were devoted to female infirmities in an effort to underscore the natural weakness of women and their need to be coddled and pampered. Marriage was portrayed as a state of imprisonment that stifled and ultimately killed love.[85]

Du Rozoi may have kept the *Journal des Dames* going, but he

83 On Du Rozoi, see Sgard, *Dictionnaire des journalistes,* 328–29, and Marc Martin, *Origines de la presse militaire,* 38–44 and passim. The only detailed account of his life is filled with serious inaccuracies. See, with caution, Estrée, "Farmin de Rozoi" [*sic*].

84 *Journal des Dames,* juillet 1762:69.

85 See, for example, ibid., avril 1762:53; juillet 1762:27, 33–38; septembre 1762:260; octobre 1762:143; novembre 1762:230.

alienated most of Mme de Beaumer's former subscribers with his mockery and license. Although no record survives of the arrangement between them, Mme de Beaumer appears to have lent rather than sold him the paper. She did not take him on as an official partner but had turned things over to him informally and temporarily to keep her paper alive and maintain communication open for her eventual return. Some of her most loyal subscribers stayed with the paper, but they were deeply offended by a story of a woman unable to choose between two lovers, who settled for caressing one while the other caressed her. Du Rozoi was forced to print an apology but did nothing to change his tune.[86] His conceit led him to compare himself favorably with the great writers of all time, a habit for which he was never forgiven.[87] D'Aquin's *Censeur hebdomadaire* expressed astonishment that this tasteless young fop was being allowed to make a travesty out of the *Journal des Dames*. Du Rozoi had apparently even circulated a mock prospectus ridiculing excessive claims for women in the burlesque style of Molière's *précieuses,* and he had chosen a new *libraire* for the paper, Charles Pouilly, who had a reputation for selling steamy fare.[88] Mme de Beaumer would later have to disavow most of these issues, which were published either "without [her] seeing them" or "against [her] will."[89]

Meanwhile from April 1762 to the end of the year, she was licking her wounds in Holland and rekindling her courage to brave the forces in Paris one more time. The few articles she sent to Du Rozoi showed her fortifying her feminist faith and gathering evidence that women were on the brink of an intellectual and social

---

86   Ibid., décembre 1762:285, 279.

87   The consensus of Du Rozoi's literary colleagues, even such diverse ones as Grimm, Bachaumont, Voltaire, Sabatier de Castres, and Restif de la Bretonne, was that he was one of the worst and most boastful writers the world had ever seen.

88   *Censeur hebdomadaire,* 5 juillet 1762:224; 12 juillet 1762:table; 415, 259. For Du Rozoi nothing was sacred except himself. "Quoique très jeune Ecrivain," wrote d'Aquin, "sans expérience, sans génie, ce M. Du Rozoi a passé toutes les bornes prescrites à la Médiocrité du Talent. Il tranche en Pédagogue, il juge en Souverain. D'un côté il mutile les statues des hommes les plus célèbres de l'antiquité, de l'autre il égratigne nos plus illustres modernes" (p. 419). "Le beau livre à présenter aux Dames! N'est-ce pas là manquer de respect à la plus aimable partie du genre humain?" (p. 415).

89   *Journal des Dames,* mars 1763:306–7.

breakthrough, that academies in Padua, Amiens, and Pau favored admitting female members, that reticence was now seen as unhealthy for women.[90] Feminine modesty, Mme de Beaumer declared with new conviction, was a contraband virtue; women must speak openly about themselves.[91] She may even have gone to England to visit the spirited Lady Wortley Montagu just before she died there in August 1762, because that very month Mme de Beaumer sent to the *Journal des Dames* the great Englishwoman's reminiscences on smallpox inoculation, marriage, and the place of women in society.[92] In general she took advantage of this sejour to meet with women friends whose countries were at war with France.[93] And Mme de Beaumer began to pave the way for her return to Paris with an elaborate attempt to secure financial backing from the wealthy financier Pierre Durey d'Arnoncourt, whose splendid mansion on the rue de Vendôme backed onto the Temple and to whom she now referred as "my dear neighbor." An article she sent from Holland to the November 1762 *Journal des Dames* praised him as a "great protector of the arts."[94] How much this gentleman helped Mme de Beaumer is not clear. At his death his library was found to contain no trace of her paper but many issues of the *Moniteur français,* whose royalist author J. N. Moreau also wrote the *Observateur hollandais,* a bitterly Anglophobic periodical printed tacitly by the French government during the Seven Years' War. D'Arnoncourt may have been moved enough by Mme de Beaumer's flattery (and by her printing of his "brilliant" essay on icecubes in her journal!) to humor her briefly, but given his taste for newspapers by the government's hired pen Moreau, he could not have approved her politics.

Shortly after the end of the war, in early 1763, Mme de Beaumer slipped back to Paris. She knew she was a marked woman,

90 Ibid., novembre 1762:190, janvier 1763:94.
91 Ibid., septembre 1762:287.
92 Ibid., août 1762:161–80.
93 See, for example, the letter from one of her English friends in the *Journal des Dames,* février 1763:171.
94 *Journal des Dames,* novembre 1762:181. On Durey d'Arnoncourt (Mme de Beaumer calls him M. d'Harnoncourt), see Durand, *Fermiers généraux,* 170, 238, 453, 470, 523, 562–66. The d'Arnoncourt mansion on rue de Vendôme is discussed in François Martin, "L'Habitat parisien." On the *Moniteur français,* see Sgard, *Dictionnaire des journalistes,* 283–84.

but Du Rozoi's issues, however offensive to her, were rolling along smoothly and she hoped to insinuate herself back into command at the *Journal des Dames* before anyone noticed. The copy she submitted was once again a dizzying blend of contestation and propitiation. Knowing she would still need to deal with Marin, she buttered him up with gushing praise for his *Lettre sur un projet intéressant pour l'humanité* and for "the charming character, the sensitive soul of this amiable and estimable author . . . a man who never loses sight of those whom blind fortune has injured." She sang the greatness of "Condé, Soubise, and the Bourbon name . . . all written on the Book of Destiny."[95] But other articles were shrill and pugnacious. On the death of Desmahis, whose entry "Femme" in the *Encyclopédie*—one of four articles on the subject—was antithetical to Jaucourt's feminist entry and upset Mme de Beaumer with its gallant niceties born of pity, she branded him an "enemy" and wrote that his death detracted nothing from his reputation nor had his life added to it. She celebrated the Peace of Paris, although its terms were humiliating, even disgraceful for France, and showed inappropriate admiration for Frederick of Prussia. She would use her paper to crush any "esprit de parti" that might renew hostilities between nations. And Mme de Beaumer repeated her claims that the women's revolution was gripping the entire world. Women everywhere were "laborieuses et estimables." Her *Journal des Dames* was an international affair, essential for posterity, for the very survival of humanity. "The universe is my domain; I want to sweep the horizon! My journal is widely known in every country of the world where the French language is spoken! . . . Men everywhere are being forced to recognize that Nature made the two sexes equal."[96]

Rousselet, Du Rozoi's censor, was completely baffled by Mme de Beaumer. He had never dealt with her before. Marin wrote to Malesherbes that Rousselet did not know what to do with "the Beaumer woman." Some of her copy was fine, other parts were ambiguous, still others were entirely unacceptable. How was he to handle the surprise return to the scene of "the *authoress* (as she

95 *Journal des Dames,* janvier 1763:45–51; avril 1763:61.
96 Ibid., janvier 1763:63, 39, 67; mars 1763:196–200.

styles herself!)"?[97] Marin himself was in no mood to be tolerant of the unpredictable *journaliste des femmes* or to bother sorting out the mixture of integrative and subversive messages she served up. In early March Marin was put in the Bastille for carelessly letting by four lines in a play that seemed insulting to the king. The playwright, Dorat, who would become the last editor of the *Journal des Dames* and had already contributed a few poems to it, implied a similarity between the indolent Louis XV and the earlier *rois fainéants* by portraying a monarch "relaxing in purple" while his ministers did all the work.[98] So even as *censeur de la police* Marin was not beyond being disciplined by his superiors. His twenty-four hours in the Bastille convinced him he would need to be stricter in future. One of his first steps in this toughened frame of mind was to break Mme de Beaumer once and for all. He evidently told her that her paper could continue only as a fashion magazine, knowing full well she could not stomach female vanity.

In March the *Journal des Dames* carried the announcement that it would henceforth appear twice a month, feature color engravings of women's costumes and coiffures, and cost 36 livres a year rather than the present 12 livres.[99] Subscribers had not flocked to Mme de Beaumer, and the women for whom she fought so hard found her too extreme. Since they seemed more willing to spend on "frivolities and gambling" than on her journal in its "useful" form, perhaps an amusing illustrated periodical would indeed suit them better.[100]

But Mme de Beaumer could not go through with it. Such a paper would have violated all the principles she held dear. This was not compromise but complete betrayal. She was now being asked to undermine her campaign to strengthen women's intellect, creativity, and character. Painful as it must have been, she probably realized that a fashion magazine would indeed be more successful, but she could not be the one to do it. Besides, she was

---

97   BN ms. fr. 22135, fol. 92.
98   [Bachaumont], *Mémoires secrets* 1:210 (6 mars 1763). Marin's twenty-four hours in the Bastille are discussed at length in Voltaire's correspondence of March 1763.
99   *Journal des Dames,* mars 1763:204–5.
100   Ibid., mars 1763:206, 306–7, and avril 1763:95.

bankrupt and ill. The best thing she could do for her cause was to back out of the picture, for Marin's and Malesherbes's personal aversion to her had jaundiced their view of her paper. They had even turned her new printer, Valleyre, against her. He had come to say that "superior orders" prevented him from continuing to print her notice that the paper was for sale from her home. Private distribution of journals from an author's residence was against the booktrade laws, but Mme de Beaumer, along with numerous other journalists, had been permitted to do it for nineteen months and there had been no sudden change in the regulations. Clearly her militant feminism had been self-defeating. In bed with fever and gout, she delivered to Malesherbes a final bilious diatribe against publishers and printers as government pawns, only the latest villains in a never-ending saga of social abuse and political oppression. Why must authors, disseminators of truth, hold the beggar's pan while *libraires* feasted on oysters? "I know their monopolies; that is why I have decided to renounce my paper. It is pathetic to work like poor wretches [*misérables*] only to be ruined in the end."[101]

Although thwarted, Mme de Beaumer had a last revenge. She managed to find as her successor a woman sufficiently connected in *le monde* to win the booktrade authorities' blessing, yet daring enough to lend her name to the increasingly *frondeur* fare of her male collaborators. Under Mme de Maisonneuve, the *Journal des Dames* would enjoy several stable, successful years, and later accounts of the paper commonly gave her the credit for making it a thriving enterprise.[102] This was in marked contrast to Mme de Beaumer's experience. She personally had not come close to taking the world by storm, and she died a few years later in Holland apparently without ever writing anything more. Perhaps in her dreams her paper was "known throughout the universe," yet according to Bachaumont, Du Rozoi's treachery had cost her all but seven subscribers.[103] Nevertheless she had set certain precedents and put forth a new conception of the journalist's role. Unlike

101   BN ms. fr. 22135, fol. 91, "Lettres de Mme de Beaumer à Malesherbes qu'elle cède le *Journal des Dames* à Maisonneuve" (30 mai 1763).

102   See, for example, *Bibliographie parisienne,* 10; Hurtaut and Magny, *Dictionnaire historique* 3:669.

103   [Bachaumont], *Mémoires secrets* 16:294 (31 décembre 1765).

Campigneulles, who had conceived the *Journal des Dames* as a tranquilizer, Mme de Beaumer wanted it to deal with serious issues, to stir people, to generate action. She wanted to reach an audience both socially and geographically broad. She instinctively sensed the power of the press to mold public opinion. Papers could do more than amuse or convey bits of information. They could sway emotions, transform beliefs into behavior, change theories into reality. They could, potentially, reform the world. Furthermore women could and would play "un rôle frappant sur la terre," as political leaders, as workers, as citizens, and as journalists.[104]

But because frontal, sustained attacks on the regime were impossible in a permitted, legitimate paper, Mme de Beaumer had been forced to settle for getting fragments of her message into print. She had initiated a technique of jousting with the censors while she placated them. Alternately demanding and diffident, bold and respectful, she had repeatedly thrown them off their guard and managed to communicate her *frondeur* ideas elliptically if not bluntly. Her last issue, for example, directed her female readers away from gossip about novels and fashion and toward the works of Lenglet Du Fresnoy, whose histories, she said, would teach them solid lessons. She did not mention that the author of these recommended histories had been trailed by the police for years because his works were "full of very strong things about families in power." Here then was Mme de Beaumer urging her public to read works by a parlementary *frondeur,* whom the authorities privately described as "a dangerous man who would overthrow a kingdom."[105] This had been the pattern of her strategy all along. Sometimes she appeared scattered, sometimes organized and assertive, sometimes dangerous. She reviewed plays and art exhibits, dealt with printers, hired and fired workers, attended concerts, researched the activities of women in her neighborhoods, dispatched mailings, traveled widely, courted financiers, marshals, princes of the blood. Even in her angriest letter to Malesherbes, she pointed out that she was an extremely busy woman

104   *Journal des Dames,* fevrier 1762:186.
105   Ibid., avril 1763:25–26. On Lenglet Du Fresnoy's police record, see Darnton, "Police Inspector," 177–78.

whose time was taken up with numerous duties related to her career. Completely inexperienced in business matters, she of course made serious mistakes. By the end her finances were in a shambles. But despite all the obstacles thrown in her path, she was not easily discouraged. And her persistence paid off. Although the paper was tampered with and, as we saw, even temporarily suspended, it had not been entirely suppressed. Mme de Beaumer had paid dearly for it, but the channels of communication remained open. She would have been pleased that her successors managed to circumvent the censors and keep the enterprise alive for another fifteen years.

Finally, Mme de Beaumer had linked the cause of women's emancipation to much broader social and political issues and especially to freedom of expression. She had early denounced the Comédie for refusing to perform *drames,* had stated that the law was as high an authority as the king, and had protested the injustice of existing law codes toward women and other oppressed groups.[106] Her paper fought for reform on all fronts—she had even used the word "révolution"—and its title, although leading many readers to expect a light confection, would henceforth be a smokescreen for criticism of the regime's most cherished institutions. Both Campigneulles and Mme de Beaumer had argued that their paper was essential to France, but for antithetical reasons. As we saw, the male founder had conceived it as a stabilizing force to keep potentially restless marginal groups entertained and ignorant. Mme de Beaumer wished to forge an alliance between those very groups and saw her paper as an instrument of combat for their liberation. No country could be healthy, she believed, as long as the majority of its citizens were oppressed. This first female editor initiated serious contestation in a paper meant to be a mere frivolity, and never again would the *Journal des Dames* be benign.

106 See *Journal des Dames,* octobre 1761:59; février 1762:195; mars 1762:223, 251; mars 1763:75.

4

From Success at Versailles to Provincial *Patriotisme*

MME DE MAISONNEUVE AND THE JANSENIST MATHON DE LA COUR (1763–1769)

Catherine Michelle de Maisonneuve's life, on the surface, reads like the success story of a socially ambitious woman. Her testament shows she was married for a time to a member of the tax farmers' corporation and died with sufficient funds and possessions to make necessary a detailed will. Her brother was a valet in the king's wardrobe and the recipient of numerous royal favors.[1] These connections in both court and financial circles helped her to climb from the tiny cul-de-sac Bertaud, a dead-end alley off the rue Beaubourg in the once elegant but faded *quartier* of Saint Avoye where we first find her living, through a series of moves, to a final house of her own on the prestigious rue Saint Honoré, "vis-a-vis l'Oratoire."[2] A residence in the Palais Royal neighborhood was a clear mark of having "arrived." Dominated by the Opéra, the Louvre, and magnificent newer mansions of the financial nobility, this was the "heart of the city," where tastes and trends were born before radiating out to Saint Germain, the Ile

---

1 A sketch of Mme de Maisonneuve's testament is in a *registre de décès* at the Archives de la Seine, DC⁶256, fol. 64v. The entire document, which may have told us more about her, was supposedly deposited with the notary Lenoir but is missing from his dossier at the Minutier Central.

2 These successive addresses are given in *Journal des Dames,* mai-juin-juillet 1763, mars 1764, and novembre 1764.

Saint Louis, and last of all the sleepy Marais. Of Mme de Maisonneuve's first area Mercier would write: "Here one finds a Louis
XIII atmosphere . . . not misery, but the accumulation of old prejudices. . . . Lovely ladies, relegated by some fatal star to this sad
neighborhood, receive no other company than old soldiers and
old lawyers, all most proper and correct." The Palais Royal district, on the other hand, throbbed with life and doings of great
importance. "There, insolent Swiss butlers inevitably answer that
Madame . . . is not available." Fashions, coiffures, but also political news were made in this *capitale de Paris*.[3] On the rue Saint
Honoré itself Mme de Tencin and Mme de Geoffrin had held their
salons, where Mme de Pompadour, the daughter of a financier,
had received her *formation*.

Why, then, would Mme de Maisonneuve, gliding smoothly up
in the world, have wished to have anything to do with Mme de
Beaumer's discredited *Journal des Dames?* At first, quite simply,
because she was bored. Life had treated her gently, she had none
of her predecessor's axes to grind, yet she could not tolerate the
emptiness of an idle, rich existence. Financial circles were not
known for their advanced attitudes toward the education of
females. Mme d'Epinay, author of books on female pedagogy,
claimed to have been allowed to read only ancient history and
devotional literature as a child, to have received no tutoring in
subjects that truly interested her, but instead strict, joyless lessons
in heraldry and music. So intellectually thirsty was she that upon
her marriage she proceeded to devour her husband's library. Mme

---

3   On the atmosphere of the different *quartiers,* see Hurtaut and Magny, *Dictionnaire historique* 4:186–97. For an excellent discussion of the migrations of
Paris's social-climbing financiers, whose pattern Mme de Maisonneuve followed
exactly, see Durand, *Fermiers généraux,* especially his chapter "L'Espace quotidien," 445–503, 645. The quotations from Mercier's *Tableau de Paris* are in Durand, 453–54. Mme de Maisonneuve was in an ideal position to benefit reciprocally from both her brother's and her husband's perquisites. The latter, a *commis
au ferme* (whose name—Joubert—she never assumed) could have been greatly
helped by association with the royal household. See Durand, 87, 118. A delightful song described the scenario of success (p. 233):

On voyait des commis
mis
Comme des princes
Après être venus
nus
De leurs provinces.

de Maisonneuve felt much of this same frustration, as revealed in a piece she wrote for the first issue of her *Journal des Dames,* a dialogue between two young girls. One of them, who wished only to dance, sing, and play the clavecin, was furious with her mother's progressive pedagogical philosophy. "She wants to make a *boy* out of me," Victoire complained to Sophie, "and would have me learn everything my brother is taught." Victoire wished she might be sent to a convent for society girls and vowed to dispatch any daughters she might have to one. Sophie, on the other hand, envied her friend's opportunity and greatly admired her own father whose learning made him resourceful and self-reliant; he could spend eight hours a day in his study and never know boredom. She admired those women in history who against formidable odds had educated and distinguished themselves. It was to them and not the empty-headed dancers that the world would one day give preference.[4] Mme de Maisonneuve may not have seen herself shuttling between France and Holland in a worn black suit trying to precipitate a feminist revolution as Mme de Beaumer had done, but she felt stifled in an atmosphere that required no more of her than a smile, a beautiful gown, and the kind of gracious hostessing described by an admirer to whom she had once most delicately served pears.[5]

So Mme de Maisonneuve, considerably less self-satisfied than appeared on the surface, decided to spice up her life with a challenge. Not only would she take over the *Journal des Dames,* now immobilized by the authorities, but she would make of it a great success, precisely by avoiding earlier mistakes. Unhampered by Mme de Beaumer's fierce independence and suspicion of male helpers, the new editor welcomed whatever assistance was forthcoming. Whereas Mme de Beaumer, defiantly self-reliant, had sought the support and applause of men only in extremis,[6] Mme de Maisonneuve saw an association with *hommes de lettres* as a necessity from the beginning, not because she was incapable, but simply because she was new at the game and wished to avoid the

---

4 *Journal des Dames,* mai-juin-juillet 1763:21–36. Mme d'Epinay's similar frustrations are discussed in her autobiography, Roth, *Pseudo-Mémoires de Mme d'Epinay* 1:239.
5 *Journal des Dames,* janvier 1764:31.
6 Ibid., mars 1763:"Nouveau Prospectus."

pitfalls of inexperience. But if she had no previous literary record, she could contribute her name, money, protection, and social station to the enterprise. In exchange she invited writers interested in the advancement of women to give her guidance and good material to print. This was to be a healthy, symbiotic relationship. Mme de Maisonneuve did not want martyrdom but success, and had chosen a propitious moment to make her journalistic debut. Her brother seems to have been rewarded frequently by the *maison du roi,* or king's household, with extra pensions, favors, and vacations in foreign lands, and this royal generosity peaked just when she took on the *Journal des Dames.*[7] Of the paper's nine editors Mme de Maisonneuve had the best sense of timing, and capitalizing on her brother's good fortune, she now became another beneficiary of monarchical largesse. By June 1765 she had the personal honor of presenting her journal to the king at Versailles, under the protection of Choiseul, Soubise, and other smiling powers, and by the end of that year, she herself became a *pensionnaire du roi,* receiving 1,000 livres annually for a poem honoring Louis XV in the fiftieth year of his reign.[8] Mme de Maisonneuve would advance the cause of women by riding with, not against, the tide.

Her astonishing resuscitation of the moribund paper was itself a feat worthy of admiration and analysis. How exactly was it accomplished? But even more interestingly, Mme de Maisonneuve remained the *prête-nom* of the *Journal des Dames* for four years after its fleeting moment of glory, watching, apparently unperturbed, while her male collaborators used it to press for the *frondeur* cause. Did she surprise herself by protecting their more daring exploits, by fulfilling so faithfully her pledge to be "useful as well as amusing?" Or had this been part of her original promise to Mme de Beaumer?

'7   See Archives Nationales, F⁴1940 d and F⁴1941 g for some pensions awarded Jean-Baptiste de Maisonneuve in 1758 and 1759, and 0¹108, fol. 162, "Brevet lui permettant d'aller en Espagne et d'y rester six mois" (22 avril 1764).

8   The *Journal des Dames* of May 1765, which appeared two months late, announced on p. 119 that the newspaper's April issue had been presented at court on Friday, 21 June. The December 1765 issue printed on the title page that Mme de Maisonneuve was now a *pensionnaire du roi.* The poem for which she was awarded this pension appeared in the July 1765 *Journal des Dames* (pp. 5–6) and was reprinted in the *Journal encyclopédique* (1765) iii:117–18, and in the *Alamanach des muses,* 1766:97–98.

That the two women had met to discuss such things we know from a letter sent to Malesherbes, announcing the turnover of the paper, and from an agreement showing that Mme de Maisonneuve paid 3,000 livres in cash for its rights.[9] Clearly, for the *Journal des Dames* to survive, a fresh start would have to be made, and Mme de Beaumer must have realized her successor would need to be as polished and trusted as she was gruff and suspect. A true crusader, Mme de Beaumer had been unwilling to repudiate the principles of a lifetime by producing a fashion magazine as Marin had insisted, but she had been ready to bow out of the enterprise if it could continue in a worthwhile form. It was thus probably by mutual agreement that Mme de Maisonneuve made a public break with her predecessor, since her harsh words appear in an issue they produced jointly. Openly disdaining Mme de Beaumer as "cette dame," refusing her the compliments traditional at such editorial junctures, hastening to state that her predecessor's political views and business ineptitude had long filled her with "tacit disgust," Mme de Maisonneuve wiped the slate clean.[10] Documents reveal that Malesherbes approved her for the job of continuing the paper, more precisely that she had both his "advice" and "consent," so her strenuous efforts to dissociate herself from Mme de Beaumer's radical bunglings and abrasive behavior evidently paid off.[11] It may even have been by design that the issue the two women produced jointly announced the return of Du Rozoi, whom the government approved, as a helper on Mme de Maisonneuve's paper and that the new editor's third issue carried an insipid pastoral love poem by her predecessor, "Couplets especially sent to Mme de M. by Mme de B."[12] Completely contrary in spirit to anything else Mme de Beaumer had ever written and much more the sort of thing proper ladies were expected to produce, "Un Rien, un rien" may have been a deflecting tactic to erase the memory of the paper's stormy past, the first female editor's final self-effacement

9 Bibliothèque Nationale, manuscrit français (henceforth BN ms. fr.) 22135, fol. 91, and BN ms. fr. 22085, fol. 10.

10 *Journal des Dames,* avril 1763:"Avertissement," 6. Although the May issue was Mme de Maisonneuve's first, she had already printed a few notices, like this one, the previous month.

11 BN ms. fr. 22085, fol. 10, "Mme de Maisonneuve s'en chargea après en avoir pris l'avis et agrément de mr de Malzerbe" [*sic*]. The transfer is then referred to as a "rétrocession" (reassignment, reconveyance).

12 *Journal des Dames,* avril 1763:93ff. and novembre 1763:103.

for the sake of the *Journal des Dames*'s future. Olympe de Gouges, a future journalist and feminist of the Revolution, would comment that in the Old Regime aggressive women who lacked or refused to exploit beauty and charm were branded to have a "bizarre character" and a "rare philosophy" and "deemed to be crazy."[13] That had certainly been the fate of Mme de Beaumer, and her successor wished fervently to avoid it.

In spite of all these maneuvers, however, Mme de Maisonneuve's first months as editor were difficult, a true test of her mettle, as she would remind her readers later. Mme de Beaumer's troubled negotiations with the booktrade authorities over her last few issues had seriously delayed their publication, so the new director had to catch up by subsuming the months of May through October in two rushed volumes in order to be on schedule again by the end of the year. These two issues were uninspired and disorderly, scattered with pastorals and stories of animals, restaurants, flowers, and Dijon mustard, because Mme de Maisonneuve had not yet had a chance to recruit quality collaborators. By way of apology for these opening issues, which she would look back on as "feeble," she suggested that subscribers pay for their year of the paper only after reading and judging her worthy. She wanted their satisfaction, not their charity, and so took it upon herself to announce that until she earned their respect she would continue to send the *Journal des Dames* to former subscribers as well as new readers who expressed interest, "but it is no longer a matter of paying in advance for the future."[14] This brought a knee-jerk reflex from the postal directors, whose system was based on the convention that recipients of mail usually paid the postage. Mme de Maisonneuve's offer freed them of that obligation, but the sender herself appeared to have no intention of paying for the paper's mailings either. Thus it looked as if the postal officials were expected to carry packets of the journal without any commitment to pay at either end. They had already been badly burned by Mme de Beaumer's erratic mailings to *libraires* in her imaginary worldwide network of followers who had neither ordered nor paid for

13   See de Gouges, "Les Droits de la femme," in Levy, Applewhite, and Johnson, *Women in Revolutionary Paris*, especially 93.
14   *Journal des Dames*, avril 1763:96.

her paper. The *Journal des Dames* was in fact still carrying notices that readers and bookdealers everywhere had failed to settle their accounts with her.[15] Now another woman showed the same dangerous proclivities. The time had come for the postal directors to crack down. The flamboyant free offer made by Mme de Maisonneuve in her first issue was immediately rescinded "upon [their] insistence" and replaced by a prudent practical policy in her second, to the effect that subscribers pay in advance "as for all other journals."[16] And in her third, that of November 1763, she announced some new, extremely severe restraints that the postal authorities had placed upon her, obliging her to guarantee the cost of mailings before they occurred. Considering the general instability of the newspaper's finances under its first three editors, the post office could hardly be blamed.

Exasperated by the unprofessional conduct of Mme de Beaumer, whose debts made it impossible for her to reimburse them, burdened often with manuscripts submitted to the *Journal des Dames* for which neither sender nor recipient would pay the postage, the Farmers General of the Post Office spelled out the following strict rules to Mme de Maisonneuve, hoping to recover some of the money owed them. She would need to prepay every copy she sent, and there would be no reduced rates for packets of several sent together, as other papers enjoyed. There were a series of other regulations about material submitted to the journal going straight to the dead letter office [*rebut*] unless prepaid by the sender and about the *poste* receiving a fraction of each subscription price. But some of the stipulations went beyond financial concerns and cast the *poste* in a policing role. Mme de Beaumer may have been more dangerous than anyone realized and may have been sending clandestine *nouvelles,* manuscript *notes à l'épingle* inside her bound volumes, because now there was repeated insistence that the *Journal des Dames* be sent *sous bande,* securely wrapped, "with no other

15   See, for example, *Journal des Dames,* décembre 1763:119. In février 1764:120, Mme de Maisonneuve announced that since these pleas had been unsuccessful she would discontinue them. The issue of March 1764 carried the last such "Avis pour messieurs les anciens abonnés au *Journal des Dames* qui doivent à Mme de Beaumer, et à messieurs les libraires chargés de le débiter qui ne lui ont pas rendu leurs comptes."
16   *Journal des Dames,* août-septembre-octobre 1763:120.

papers slipped in." Finally, the intendant and each and every general administrator of the *poste* were to receive gratis copies of the monthly issues to examine. Such free copies to the mailman went in 1763 to thirty officials—the grand master, two general supervisors, two secretaries, a treasurer, four visiting supervisors, eight departmental administrators, three cashiers, and nine bureau chiefs in charge of distribution. If Mme de Maisonneuve deviated in any way from these rules—not that it was likely with thirty pairs of eyes watching—the *Journal des Dames* would be suspended. "This subscription," the document concluded ominously, "will last only as long as it pleases the gentlemen of the postal firm to grant it."[17]

Part of Mme de Maisonneuve's initial job, then, was convincing the *poste* that she was above suspicion, and this she seems to have done reasonably fast. It helped that she had plentiful resources to pay their required charges. Although a M. Laurent, postal inspector, kept a close eye on her paper through 1765 as a notice in each issued explained, he was gradually converted from adversary to watchdog and finally to benefactor. By December of that year the *poste* was facilitating mailings of the *Journal des Dames* to subscribers in Germany, Belgium, and Holland. At the end of 1766 it offered a special rate for the paper sent jointly with the *Almanach des muses*. The following year it made possible coupled discount mailings with yet another periodical, the *Nécrologe des hommes célèbres*.[18]
What, then, was the secret of Mme de Maisonneuve's success? How did she charm the very people Mme de Beaumer had antagonized? How did she gather hundreds of subscribers where her predecessor had scared them away? How did she manage to attract the attention of the publisher Panckoucke, who possessed the best

17 "Extrait de la soumission que MM. les fermiers généraux des postes ont fait souscrire à Mme de Maisonneuve," *Journal des Dames*, novembre 1763:117. The list of postal officials in the higher administration comes from the *Almanach royal* for 1763. For the tax reduction benefits enjoyed by other periodicals, see *Registres des délibérations des administrateurs de la ferme générale des Postes*. See vol. 2, "Règlement pour les modérations de port que l'administration accorde aux auteurs, libraires, et imprimeurs des publications périodiques."

18 *Journal des Dames*, octobre 1766:103. For an excellent discussion of the ways the *poste* could assist in periodical diffusion and distribution, see Moulinas, *Imprimerie, librairie, et presse*, 379ff. See also Vaillé, *Histoire générale des postes*, vol. 5 (6) (1691–1789). Unfortunately, Vaillé's promised volume on the *poste* and the *presse* never appeared.

nose for successful enterprises of any *libraire* of his time and who featured the *Journal des Dames* centrally in his shop near the Comédie-Française from October 1764 until December 1765?

Mme de Maisonneuve, doubtless through her brother, knew what was fashionable at court, knew how to strike just the right balance of spice and respectability. She shared certain feminist beliefs with her predecessor, or she would never have gotten involved with the *Journal des Dames* at all. Her will shows, for example, that she kept her maiden name and identified strongly with female family members. But more important to her than bludgeoning readers with ideas they were unready to accept was proving to the world that a woman could succeed at journalism. She therefore maintained a confident but measured tone. She claimed in her first issue that women, given proper encouragement, could rival such male writers, scientists, artists, and rulers as Homer, Virgil, Horace, Milton, Descartes, Voltaire, Alexander, and Rubens.[19] Laziness and boredom, she wrote, were damning for women, whereas intellectual activity could save them from feelings of worthlessness and futility.[20] To believe, as most men still did, that feminine virtue and brilliance were mutually exclusive, was a backward attitude similar to the turn of mind that had twelfth-century warriors convinced a brave man should not be able to sign his name.[21] Mme de Maisonneuve continued the *éloges* of famous women and published a long list of female writers far more detailed than Louptière's of two years before—stressing interestingly that many of these women were Protestant—arguing that this was "the best refutation one can give of the prejudice that denies women the right to cultivate their minds."[22] Her paper, whose advertised purpose was "to speak only of women," would show that men were not the sole dispensers of celebrity. They had their academies, but women had their *Journal des Dames,* which by stretching their minds and encouraging their own creativity and ambition would "engender that noble pride that makes people

19 *Journal des Dames,* mai-juin-juillet 1763:"Nouveau Prospectus," 7, 9.
20 Ibid., août-septembre–octobre 1763:93.
21 Ibid., janvier 1764:106; octobre 1765:9.
22 Ibid., juin 1764:33–45. This list, impressively long and detailed, stressed works by Protestant women or on the subject of Protestantism, in connection with the fashionable subject of religious toleration.

capable of accomplishing great things."[23] Plenty of scholarly subjects were included, articles on the decadence of the Carolingians, the smallpox inoculation controversy, Egyptian laws, the annexing of Brittany, the physical systems of Newton and Descartes.[24] "Experience proves," protested Mme de Maisonneuve against Rousseau, "that women can learn, reflect, meditate, think profoundly; that they can read fruitfully, that they can equal men. . . . There is no real difference between the two sexes. . . . Thousands upon thousands of examples contradict the partisans of a modern philosophe who argues that our mental faculties were not equally distributed."[25] She would not let her paper become a satire of her sex by treating only frivolities.[26]

But Mme de Maisonneuve pushed this kind of argument only as long as she met with no resistance. She had no desire to ruffle feathers, to go beyond the stylish limits of protest or, if such a tone would jeopardize her enterprise, to sound truly outraged. She generally confined her points to the intellectual potential of her sex, suggesting nothing at all about social upheaval, and she tried to maintain a cool, controlled attitude. Mme de Beaumer, in claiming to speak for a public, was actually seeking one; in her zeal she had refused to face the fact that broad-based support for her feminism was not there. Mme de Maisonneuve, in contrast, tried to assess her audience realistically. Fairly quickly she became persuaded that most women were not about to be prodded from their lethargy, that they were perhaps best left there, and that she had already come on a bit too strong. She therefore stated unequivocally that women were not fit for politics.[27] She now wrote of the need to condense and simplify information for most of her female readers "because we cannot tax or overload our memories if we wish them to store what we put in them."[28] By her fifth issue she already made it a point to address not only intellectual women but also the pious and those "less occupied with study," who would rather read about "amusing novelties."[29] One such woman

23 Ibid., décembre 1763:113 and octobre 1764:46.
24 See mai-décembre 1763, mars 1764, and mai 1764.
25 Ibid., mai-juin-juillet 1763:"Nouveau Prospectus."
26 Ibid., juillet 1764:53n.
27 Ibid., juin 1764:10.
28 Ibid., mai-juin-juillet 1763:35.
29 Ibid., janvier 1764:106.

wrote her an irate letter in which she took offense at Mme de Maisonneuve's "monstrous" claims. "You absolutely insist, Madame, on imposing laws upon us. Why does our laziness bother you so? Don't you know that women, in general, do not *like* to write, except for a rare moment now and then. We are actually not very good at it. . . . Our conversation, on the other hand, can be gay and delightful, and men like that. To claim distinction in literature is to step out of our sphere. Knowledge and wisdom are the provinces of men. Let us not presume to eliminate their advantage."[30]

Male readers, many of whom were acquainted with Mme de Maisonneuve's previous demure lifestyle, were still more insistent that she abandon her professional pretentions and resume a more conventionally ladylike role. A Marquis de ★★★ was totally taken aback when she chose to moralize rather than spout flowery poems.[31] Marmontel, to whom she had written for help with a translation of the Greek satirist Lucian, whose style she felt sure women could emulate, replied with patronizing surprise that such a subject could interest her. "The very title of your newspaper would seem to exclude from it such difficult discussions, and the answer you request demands details that very few women can comprehend."[32] Mme de Maisonneuve graciously resigned herself to the seeming ubiquity of this attitude and abandoned a stance her reader found too polemical. To demonstrate her fairness and openmindedness, she even printed an antifeminist epigram to prove her "objectivity."[33] The preaching of doctrinal feminism itself disappeared from the *Journal des Dames,* and she chose instead to emphasize how successfully she, a woman, had resurrected the "disparaged work." Wishing above all to please, to succeed, and to triumph in her career, Mme de Maisonneuve disarmed her male

30 Ibid., février 1764:99.
31 Ibid., avril 1764:75.
32 Ibid., février 1765:46.
33 Ibid., juillet 1764:60.
> Qu'on ne me définisse une femme
> Ce mélange piquant de défauts et d'appas
> En Turquie elles n'ont pas d'âme;
> Elles l'ont double en nos climats.

"On m'a envoyé cette épigramme pour mon journal," wrote Mme de Maisonneuve in a footnote, "et je l'y place sans difficulté. Quoiqu'il en soit, des femmes, on conviendra du moins que je suis assez impartiale."

adversaries by pointing out how much men of letters had helped her. For her this was no disgraceful capitulation. The very essence of her cleverness, she now said, reverting to an argument with which men would feel comfortable since it stressed the differences between the sexes, had been to recognize the ways in which she and they could complement each other, could work together to produce something both entertaining and informative. Was that not the goal of any serious journalist? By early 1765 she believed she and her colleagues had found the magic mix. She had not published a prospectus, regarding such "empty promises" as the worst "charlatanism of literature," but she now allowed herself a bit of boasting in an *avertissement* marking her seventeenth issue, a copy of which she sent to Sartine, head of both the booktrade and the police ever since Malesherbes's retirement in October 1763. She hoped her paper could "distract him from the heavy duties with which he was so preoccupied." [34] She now announced triumphantly to the world that a woman had achieved journalistic stardom. "To continue an esteemed work, keep the public's approval, follow in the successful footsteps of a predecessor, is difficult enough. But to revive a discredited work, to make readers . . . give it a second chance, to overcome prejudices against it, this is far more daring. Everyone should be grateful that a woman undertook the reanimation [of the *Journal des Dames*] without having succumbed to the many discouraging obstacles." [35] She wanted due credit for a job well done, which would necessarily reflect glory upon all her sex.

Mme de Maisonneuve was not determined to fight any further. The motto on her title page read "If uniformity is the mother of boredom, then variety must be the mother of pleasure," which showed clearly that her cast of mind was less belligerent than her predecessor's. Had feminism been marketable, she would have stuck with it, but it seemed to fall on deaf ears. Some female readers, surely, felt unfairly treated by society. These were the ones who had frightened Louptière away with their smoldering anger and who had urged Mme de Beaumer to call herself *éditrice*. But most were scared by the dirty world into which the feminists

34 BN ms. fr. 22085, fol. 7. The letter to Sartine is dated 24 February 1765 and was accompanied by the January 1765 *avertissement* of the paper.
35 Ibid., janvier 1765:"Avertissement," 4.

tried to thrust them, and there certainly was no general sense of solidarity among them. Even those women who succeeded in gaining some literary recognition eschewed the advancement of their sex as a major focus of their writings or as a cause célèbre, and they did not think of themselves as members of a group mistreated by society. Mme Guibert, a friend of Mme de Maisonneuve and also a *pensionnaire du roi,* who for a few months had center stage in the *Journal des Dames,* had just published her *Poésies et oeuvres diverses.* Despite Grimm's quip that they "did not run the risk of becoming classics," Mme Guibert's works were nonetheless quite popular. But they were not strongly or consistently feminist. She praised women's administrative and teaching skills but implied that they were not always trustworthy and threw in a "tragédie contre les femmes" called *La Coquette corrigée.* Too heavy a dose of challenge or bile, she knew, would frighten away readers. This ambivalent message continued in her *Pensées détachées,* in which Mme Guibert extolled the "brilliant" Mme Du Boccage and even defied men to prove that the mind had a sex, but then picked up the very gauntlet she had thrown down. "There are women who despise the way men think about us, who attack their reasoning, but I am not among them. I esteem men; they have more intellectual power and solidity than we do, and where is the woman who would deny, after reasoning it out, that we are only the second beings of humanity?"[36] Such autocensure, such embarrassment at their own audacities, was typical of the work of many female writers of the day. Others never addressed serious issues in the first place. Marie-Anne Roumier Robert, a much-published and successful novelist reviewed often in the *Journal des Dames* and whom Mme de Maisonneuve also evidently knew personally, summed up the indifference of her *contemporaines* to feminist issues and her own reason for avoiding them: "I am always astonished that women have not yet banded together, formed a separate league, with an eye to avenging themselves against male injustice. May I live long enough to see them make such profitable

---

36 See her *Pensées détachées,* 50, 52, 84, and 89. Mme Guibert's poems were featured in nearly every issue of Mme de Maisonneuve's *Journal des Dames* and in the companion *Almanach des muses* for 1766–69. Her *Poésies et oeuvres diverses* were favorably reviewed, and some of her poems were set to music by Mathon (see his "Table pour le *Journal des Dames* de 1765," for example, mars 1765:46, "Chansonnette").

use of their minds. But up until now, they have been too coquettish and dissipated to concern themselves seriously with the interests of their sex."[37] Mme Roumier Robert never helped the *Journal des Dames,* although her novels were rapturously received and reviewed by all three of its female editors. She seemed ready to resign herself to the limitations of her audience as long as they bought her writings. Thus the attitude of these *femmes de lettres* was curiously symptomatic of the apathy they themselves diagnosed and lamented.

Feminism, then, was not writ large in Mme de Maisonneuve's very successful *Journal des Dames,* and it was not from other women authors that she got her support. When she called for assistance, a large number of minor but prolific male writers rushed to rescue the damsel in distress. Mathon de la Cour, a handsome, polite young Lyonnais recently arrived in Paris and already homesick, was to become her contractual partner. They seemed ideally suited to work together. Mathon, who had entered the Parisian literary scene in September 1763 with a series of *Lettres à Mme* ★★★ *sur les peintures,* found the capital cold and intimidating. He yearned for a more personal involvement, because "in spite of the wonderful theater and the thrill of seeing up close some famous men, I felt that my soul would fall irretrievably into numbness from which nothing would save it." Writing his little essays on art criticism had helped, but he still found Parisians haughty, motivated by self-interest, incapable (in such a "tourbillon immense") of knowing each other well enough to truly *care,* and he missed his unpretentious friends in the provinces.[38] Mathon would demonstrate by his lifelong involvement with journalism that he considered periodicals a useful and worthwhile manner of communicating with the public. He stayed for five years with the *Journal des Dames* and the *Almanach des muses* and later edited a *Citoyen français,* a *Journal de musique,* and for almost a decade the *Journal de Lyon.* Mme de Maisonneuve, by giving him his first journalistic

---

37   This quotation is from Marie-Anne Roumier Robert's *Voyage de Milord Ceton dans les sept planètes* (The Hague and Paris, 1765–66), discussed in Abensour, *Femme et féminisme,* 429. For reviews of her works in the *Journal des Dames,* see, for example, janvier 1762:31–35 and août-septembre-octobre 1763:93–100.

38   Mathon de la Cour, *Lettres à Mme* ★★★, letter no. 1, pp. 5–6, dated 8 septembre 1763.

opportunity, thus opened up for him a career and a medium to which he would devote much of his future attention and energy. He was truly grateful.

She, for her part, was delighted to find a young man with good looks and good manners, obviously knowledgeable in the field of art history, with a pleasant writing style, and clearly sympathetic to women. His letters on the Louvre paintings, which appeared weekly in September 1763 just as Mme de Maisonneuve prepared her second issue of the *Journal des Dames,* raved about the canvases of Mme Vien, the wife of a member of the Academy of Painting who had herself won membership in 1757, and cheered that "the despicable and barbarous prejudice that denies women all knowledge and talent has not infected the Académie royale de peinture." This academy had admitted a few women since its founding in the seventeenth century, and even though their membership was honorary—they could not attend classes, teach, hold office, or compete for prizes—Mathon stressed the fact that the very admission of women was a triumph for their sex. He not only praised the female artists in the academy but spoke of the exhibition of their work at the salons as inspiration for female spectators, "who now begin to believe that ignorance is not a merit or a duty. . . . Your sex should no longer be condemned by frivolity. . . . Learn the sciences . . . study the marvels of nature. . . . Cultivate belles lettres and the arts."[39] Mathon went on to compliment the instinctive good judgment of female museum-goers whose comments he listened to as he wandered through the crowds. They had little confidence, but their intuitive reactions were fresh and true, invariably more sound than those of the pompous "demi-savants" pontificating in front of each tableau.[40] There was already, by Mathon's third letter, some indication that Mme de Pompadour was smiling upon his efforts, for he now referred to her as an "illustrious benefactress of art and literature

39 Mathon's first two *Lettres* were published separately on 8 and 22 September with no printer's name. Then the *libraires* Desprez and Duchesne put out the five letters together. This quotation is from letter no. 3 in this second edition, pp. 51–52. For a brief discussion of women in the Académie royale de peinture, see Harris and Nochlin, *Women Artists,* 34–45.

40 Mathon, *Lettres à Mme ★★★,* letter no. 4, pp. 88–90, dated 30 septembre 1763.

to whom we can never show enough gratitude."[41] The painter Van Loo, apparently devastated by Mathon's and Mme de Pompadour's critical remarks about his painting *Les Grâces,* actually burned the canvas out of shame.[42] By all appearances Mathon had a future in society, and Mme de Maisonneuve was pleased to recruit him for her *Journal des Dames* when he presented himself, immediately reprinting his remarks about Mme Vien in her second issue of the paper. The match had been made. They proceeded to fill their pages with a mix that appealed to readers and authorities alike.

Mathon also brought with him his brother-in-law Le Mierre, Dorat, Baculard d'Arnaud, Sautreau de Marsy, Meusnier de Querlon, and Blin de Sainmore, a small band of young poets and playwrights vaguely intrigued by the *question de la femme* but mostly eager to get some publicity and advance their own careers. This seemed the ideal opportunity. Mme de Maisonneuve willingly paid for the printing, paper, engraving, binding, leather coverings, and even such luxurious "extras" as decorative foldout pages of music, choreographed dance patterns, and one magnificent illustration of Franklin's glass harmonica. Such engraved pages, seven of which appeared between July 1764 and July 1765, were prohibitively expensive, and most periodicals had none of them, but Mme de Maisonneuve wished to do her share to make the *Journal des Dames* attractive.[43] The writers, for their part, provided entertaining articles and verses, at first on the topics their patroness suggested would go over well at court. So much did they enjoy working together that they spilled over into another publication and began the yearly *Almanach des muses,* a collection of poetry that first appeared in 1765 and became one of the most lucrative periodicals in the second half of the eighteenth century.[44]

41 Ibid., letter no. 3, p. 71, dated 23 septembre 1763.
42 [Bachaumont], *Mémoires secrets* 2:260 (11 novembre 1765).
43 Contemporaries joked about the astronomical cost of such decorations. "Si la fantaisie de se faire imprimer avec ce luxe d'estampes et de vignettes dure à nos jeunes poètes," warned Grimm, "ils s'y ruineront, ou leur libraire sera banqueroute." See *Correspondance littéraire* 4:491.
44 Although the *Almanach des muses* often had a bad press, its scope and success were astonishing. See Lachèvre, *Bibliographie sommaire,* especially the introduction. For examples of disparaging remarks about this anthology, see [Bachaumont], *Mémoires secrets* 16:241; Grimm et al., *Correspondance littéraire* 4:433; 7:224; 8:446; Barbier and Des Essart, *Nouvelle Bibliothèque* 2:377; Beffroy de Reigny, *Dictionnaire néologique* 1:96.

Nearly all the poems they wrote for the *Journal des Dames* served double duty in the annual *Almanach des muses*. This, clearly, was a very happy arrangement.

Delighted with these developments, the young writers got into the habit of slapping themselves and one another on the back at every opportunity. In his first *Almanach des muses,* Mathon made an incestuous plug: "The *Journal des Dames* is a periodical that contributed greatly to the present collection. This newspaper, since it came into the hands of Mme de Maisonneuve, has emerged with great luster from the obscurity to which it previously seemed condemned."[45] Mathon, of course, advertised in the reverse direction as well. In the November 1764 issue of the *Journal des Dames* he announced the forthcoming *Almanach des muses:*

> I hasten, with pleasure, to announce an *almanach* as well conceived and tastefully executed as this one; it must not be confused with all the other short-lived *almanachs* whose fleeting utility ceases on the last day of the year or with those in which one can look up the exact name of princes one never knew existed. The *Almanach des muses* will be a literary pleasure forever. It is a collection of the best *pièces fugitives* that have appeared during the year. The poems of Dorat, Blin de Sainmore, Le Mierre, Querlon, Saint Peravi, etc. have most embellished this first volume. The editor has included critical notes on every page. These notes are, for the most part, true, judicious, and fair. I strongly exhort the editor of this anthology to renew it every year, and I am persuaded that this enterprise will achieve ever greater degrees of perfection.[46]

Meusnier de Querlon, a frequent contributor and self-styled "tributary" to Mathon's team and himself the editor of the *Annonces, affiches, et avis divers,* also called the *Affiches de province,* gave the *Journal des Dames* two rave reviews in his own newspaper.

---

45   *Almanach des muses,* 1765:"Avertissement." In the 1766 volume of *Almanach des muses,* 98, Mathon gave yet another plug: "*Le Journal des Dames* s'est fait remarquer depuis les derniers mois de 1764, par un choix agréable de pièces fugitives et une impartialité soutenue dans les extraits des livres nouveaux." The *Almanach des muses,* vols. 1767 and 1768, continued to advertise the *Journal des Dames.* Conversely, the latter carried promotional notices for the former in September 1766 (pp. 93–94), October 1766 (p. 103, with the announcement that by adding 30 sols to the *Journal des Dames* subscription, the *Almanach des muses* could be had as well, thanks to the generosity of the *poste*), and January 1767 (pp. 73ff.).

46   *Journal des Dames,* novembre 1764:116–17.

"Under the name of Mme de Maisonneuve," he wrote approvingly, "this journal is now in truly capable hands, which becomes more and more obvious. . . . Its form and content are constantly improving."[47] Blin de Sainmore, not content to supply numerous poems to Mathon's newspaper, sent laudatory letters to the editor as well. "How wonderfully surprising," he gushed, "that the *Journal des Dames,* hitherto swamped by dull poems from lovers without talent to mistresses without charm, is now the respository of our best poets' productions."[48] Campigneulles, the founder of the *Journal des Dames,* who had previously maintained a low profile but who knew Mathon personally from their native Lyons, now wrote hoping to cash in on all the praise, and Louptière, in his bucolic retreat, now piped up that he followed the newspaper's progress with pride.[49] The self-congratulatory spiral knew no bounds. "We undertake," wrote Mathon, "to reject with unfailing severity those cold, flat poems and stories that inundate editors from all sides. We do not want our great writers to blush at the works we publish beside theirs. We will always strive to conserve true taste."[50] And after Mme de Maisonneuve's audience with the king it seemed to the staff altogether appropriate to regard the *Journal des Dames* as the proper forum for the "nation's greatest writers." Royal favor, boasted the editor, would surely now inspire them all to send in their masterpieces.[51]

For over two years Mme de Maisonneuve and Mathon de la Cour worked successfully together. Their *Journal des Dames* was far more pro-philosophe than it had been before or would be again. In 1763 the philosophes found new favor, and the editor, ever watchful for fashionable trends at court, banked on rumors that the suspended *Encyclopédie* would resume soon, as its volumes of illustrated plates already had. Voltaire's protégé Marmontel was

---

47 *Annonces, affiches, et avis divers,* 1766:194; see also ibid., 1764:146.
48 *Journal des Dames,* août 1765:34.
49 Campigneulles's poem appeared in the issue of February 1764, "Vers au sujet du *Journal des Dames* que compose aujourd'hui Mme de Maisonneuve, et dont M de ★★★ a été l'inventeur." For Louptière's remarks, see mars 1764:76.
50 *Journal des Dames,* janvier, 1765:7.
51 Ibid., mai 1765:119. This invitation "aux meilleurs écrivains de la nation" stressed the importance of the king's approval: "Ce motif doit sans doute suffire pour animer leur zèle. La récompense la plus glorieuse pour les Français est de mériter les regards de leur Maître."

not only elected to the Académie française that year but had presented his *Poétiques* to the king at court. Now that the Seven Years' War was over, there was a thaw in the official attitude toward these former enfants terribles, enough to allow their infiltration into several entrenched institutions of the regime. Choiseul adored them. Even the Calas affair and the issue of religious toleration became things about which philosophes and monarchs could converse and begin to agree. Frederick of Prussia and Voltaire, Catherine of Russia and Diderot, Louis XV and Marmontel—such odd couplings signalled a rapprochement between royalty and the *esprit nouveau*. Mme de Maisonneuve's *Journal des Dames* immediately reflected this fusion of the Enlightenment and the establishment, the alliance of philosophes with *les grands*. Her third issue, that of November 1763, praised the king's goodness, her fourth carried Voltaire's "Requête au roi pour la veuve Calas."[52] Throughout 1764 and 1765 the paper lauded Catherine's support of the philosophes, carried lengthy extracts of their works, featured Marmontel's *Contes moraux* on toleration and d'Alembert's educational proposals. As soon as Calas's posthumous exoneration was official in March 1765, Mme de Maisonneuve's next issue devoted fifteen pages to the great clemency of France's enlightened king.[53] Both monarchs and philosophes appreciated her efforts. Catherine of Russia sent her a golden snuff box.[54] Louis XV made her a *pensionnaire du roi*. The *Journal encyclopédique,* in acknowledgment of her services for its cause, reprinted Mme de Maisonneuve's poem to the king.[55]

But the editors knew not to push this cosmopolitan *philosophie* and toleration too far. Choiseul, still smarting from the humiliations of the war, hated the English, wished fervently for a revival of French patriotism, and was secretly supporting the parlements in their constitutional struggle against the centralized power of the Crown. The recent suppression of the too-worldly Jesuits, in which Choiseul had been instrumental, was to be the first step in revitalizing the nation, and the *Journal des Dames* strongly supported the idea that fresh kinds of schooling and training could

52 Ibid., novembre 1763:68 and décembre 1763:10.
53 Ibid., avril 1765:71–86.
54 Ibid., 5–6.
55 See n. 8 in this chapter.

produce zealous, passionately patriotic citizens. Mathon's friend Sautreau de Marsy, a great admirer of Rousseau's *Emile,* who would later write his annals of the Revolution under Robespierre's direction, contributed a series of letters proposing a new system of national education based on ideas from Sparta and republican Rome, a system that would simplify studies and make them available to all citizens without distinction of rank. This training, short enough so that artisans and "citizens without fortune" would still have time each day to teach their children a trade, was to be based on French history, stories of great national heroes, exercise, music, and practical skills, all in proper doses to stir the heart, make the body robust, fortify the person to deal bravely with the vicissitudes of life and inspire total devotion to the *patrie.* A "Maison d'éducation" proposed by the philosophe's friend Bastide, based on principles of d'Alembert, was criticized as being elitist, too cerebral, and effete. Rousseau, on the other hand, had correctly realized that men must be toughened for adversity if they wished to be truly free. National pride and feelings of worth, even superiority, were essential; toleration and objectivity carried too far could be profoundly dangerous and lead to a paralysis of will, an inability to act effectively. "Only passions produce great deeds," argued Sautreau. "Wisdom is cold, but feelings are alive." The Greeks knew better than anyone how to nurture loyal citizens by involving them in affairs of state. French education must be remodeled along these lines so all would be civic-minded from youth. Patriotism was "a sacred fire, so nearly snuffed out, but so easy to rekindle." Civilization with all its refinements threatened to rarify mankind to the point of incapacity. Fanaticism was indeed terrible, as was superstition, but overintellectualizing had to be checked. "All men are not made to be reasoning philosophers, but all are made to be active citizens." [56]

The successful *Journal des Dames* thus reflected all the fashionable and sometimes inconsistent currents of the day. There was something for everyone. Without taking sides, it supported Voltaire and Rousseau, the Crown and the *patriotes,* the Protestants

56 Sautreau's articles on education appeared in the *Journal des Dames,* septembre 1764:29–35, février 1765:56–65, mars 1765:32–38, and avril 1765:41–46. Bastide's Maison d'éducation received attention also in [Bachaumont], *Mémoires secrets* 2:104–5, 108.

and the establishment. All this diplomacy was sugar-coated with *pièces fugitives*, music articles, theater reviews, and even a tasteful smattering of feminism. To enhance further this delicious confection, the editors heaped praise on Marin, more powerful than ever since being chosen by Sartine as *secrétaire générale de la librairie* upon Malesherbes's retirement in October 1763. Mme de Maisonneuve had flattered Marin from her very first issue, and when his plays were printed in 1765 the *Journal des Dames* extolled not only the "ingeniousness" of his dramatic writing but his own critical judgments of his work. Marin was indeed "at every instant an honest soul, a sensitive heart, and a true man of letters."[57] According to the gossipy Collé, Marin's plays were bad enough to be booed and hissed in performance, yet many periodicals in 1765 greased his palm with compliments.[58] The *Journal des Dames* outdid them all, and Marin was not insensitive to flattery. He and everyone else seemed to be smiling on the paper now. It was enjoyable but piquant, light yet concerned with worthy causes. The finished product was polished and not threatening in the slightest. "The author," wrote one genuinely enthusiastic male fan, "has combined in her paper all the natural graces of her sex with the force and tone of ours. It is as if a man were thinking it and a woman writing it."[59] Bachaumont predicted immediately after Mme de Maisonneuve's audience with the king that the paper's popularity would soar, and by late 1765 people were indeed scrambling to snatch up copies.[60] The canny Panckoucke, now in charge of its distribution, had meanwhile seen to it that buyers could not procure single issues without subscribing.[61]

Just when everything looked glorious for the *Journal des Dames* and precisely because it was quite the rage, the state-protected *Mercure* and the *Journal des savants* registered a complaint with Sar-

57   See the *Journal des Dames,* novembre 1763:75, mai 1765:88–103, and juin 1765:58.

58   See Collé, *Journal historique inédit,* 244–48. See Bachaumont's similar point in *Mémoires secrets* 16:254 (15 mars 1765).

59   Mannory, *Plaidoyers et mémoires* 16:xvi.

60   [Bachaumont], *Mémoires secrets* 16:274, 294; BN ms. fr. 22085, fol. 9.

61   When Panckoucke took over the *Journal des Dames*'s distribution in October 1764, he had immediately tightened the purse strings. An *avis* in the December issue stated that henceforth there would only be printed the same number of copies as there were paid subscribers. A later notice by the *libraire* Edme confirms that issues for 1765 became collectors' items (see BN ms. fr. 22085, fol. 9).

tine and filed a lawsuit against Mme de Maisonneuve and Mathon "to curtail the progress of [their] paper and . . . to limit the amount and kind of material they could treat."[62] The honeymoon was suddenly over.

After harassing Campigneulles in 1759, the *Mercure* had left the *Journal des Dames* alone. Its years under Mme de Beaumer were troubled enough without any interference from the privileged papers, but now it seemed truly to be flourishing. The *Mercure* found this particularly irksome because its own fortunes had taken a downward turn and its profits were no longer sufficient to pay its promised pensions. Throughout 1761 and 1762 numerous letters from the court to special clerks appointed to the *Mercure*'s "recovery" indicate that the crisis at the protected paper was already causing royal embarrassment. The new editor La Place, who took over from Marmontel in late 1762, was admonished by the king's Conseil des dépêches, and at one point Louis XV himself demanded to look at the *Mercure*'s budget records and list of subscribers in order to understand what had gone wrong with its "confection."[63] Bachaumont, one of the paper's many detractors, carried a running commentary on the blandness and mediocrity of La Place's "detestable" *Mercure* beginning with his takeover in late 1762. La Place had managed to evoke and enforce the *Mercure*'s century-old exclusive privilege in order to destroy such permitted, alternative papers as the *Négociant* and the *Renommée littéraire,* and he was now after the *Avant coureur* and especially the *Journal des Dames,* which he perceived as his most threatening rival. He boasted that he had more subscribers each day, but to prove it he published a list purported by his enemies to be padded with the names of many dead people. The *Mercure,* concluded Bachau-

62 [Bachaumont], *Mémoires secrets* 16:294, and BN ms. fr. 22085, fol. 10.

63 These letters about the *Mercure*'s difficulties can be found at the Archives Nationales, Registres des dépêches series 0¹. In July 1761 attempts were already being made to "rehausser le produit s'il est possible, ce qui semble beaucoup dépendre des mesures qui seront prises pour sa confection" (0¹403, no. 841). The letters of 1762 can be found in 0¹404, no. 60 and no. 557 (to Lutton, "commis au recouvrement du *Mercure*") and nos. 559, 662, and 1189 (to the editor La Place). See also 0¹400, nos. 490–91 and 0¹403, nos. 28–29, where efforts are openly discussed to suppress the rival newspapers, for example, "on travaille plutôt à parvenir à la suppression de quelques ouvrages périodiques qu'à en augmenter le nombre qui font tomber le *Mercure.*"

mont, covered itself with ridicule by claiming to occupy the sole attention of the state, when in fact it could only keep its readers by starving them, eliminating all the competition and leaving nothing else to satisfy their appetite for journals.[64]

Since La Place believed there was sufficient audience overlap with the *Journal des Dames* to warrant legal action against it, his lists of subscribers may be suggestive of the general contours of Mme de Maisonneuve's readership as well. The *Mercure* had 660 subscribers in Paris, 900 in the provinces and 40 in foreign countries. Of the 650 whose names and social positions were given, about a third were nobles and ecclesiastics, a tenth were *magistrats* and *avocats au parlement,* and the rest were bourgeois *fonctionnaires d'état,* members of the liberal professions, and *commerçants.*[65] Without an equivalent list, we have no way of knowing the exact distribution of the *Journal des Dames,* but evidence indicates a geographical and social range at least as wide. Campigneulles, Mathon, and Louptière had recruited subscribers from the areas around Lyons and Champagne, and most of the numerous letters to the editor came from the provinces. Although it was not selling "throughout the world" as Mme de Beaumer had dreamed, the *Journal des Dames* was reaching at least some subscribers in Belgium, Holland, and Germany.[66] It carried announcements of new books and academic doings from many foreign countries. The services and courses offered in its pages show that it had penetrated far beyond the nobility to reach a more practical-minded readership. Next to the ads for lectures in geography, history, modern languages, and physics, designed primarily for ladies of leisure, were notices for tutors, teachers, boarding and day schools, engravers, binders, musicians, accountants. Later the *Journal des Dames* would show specific concern for the petite bourgeoisie, even advertising free training in commerce for those who could not pay tuition, and Sautreau was already addressing him-

64 [Bachaumont], *Mémoires secrets* 16:175–76, 178, 180–81, 183, 191, 196, 200–201, 205, 294.
65 For an analysis of La Place's list, see Mornet, "Sur l'intérêt historique." For further discussions of the *Mercure*'s audience see Zioutos, "Presse et l'*Encyclopédie*." See also the map showing cities of distribution in Roche, *Siècle des lumières* 2:590.
66 *Journal des Dames,* mai 1765:"Avis."

self to the education of artisans and other "citoyens sans for-tune."[67] The *Journal des Dames* was a further threat to the *Mercure* because at 12 livres a year its subscription was only half the price of the protected paper. And although we do not know how many, it was rapidly acquiring subscribers. Long after its prime Mathon still boasted that he had three hundred faithful followers, and his collaborator Dorat, when he became editor of the *Journal des Dames* in 1777, counted on one thousand subscribers, an overly sanguine expectation as it turned out but one probably based on some now-lost information in the journal's track record. The ac-tual number probably fluctuated between seven and eight hun-dred, a quite respectable circulation for the day.[68]

December 1765 was a turning point for the *Journal des Dames*. Mme de Maisonneuve, who felt she had quadrupled its value and piloted the paper to its moment of glory and who wanted to avoid the messiness of the *Mercure*'s suit, now turned the business com-pletely over to Mathon. She had earlier relinquished many of her editorial duties to him but suddenly claimed that "her health no longer permitted the quality and punctuality that His Majesty and the public deserved."[69] She insisted, however, that her name re-main on the title page as author until her death, that Mathon pay her a proprietor's pension of 600 livres each year for a twenty-year total of 12,000 livres, which would be hereditary, and finally that she and only she "have the right to present the *Journal des Dames* to all the crowned heads of Europe."[70] Her paper's success was such that it had even inspired a Dutch imitation, the *Bibliothèque des Dames*.[71] Panckoucke, sensing correctly that the *Journal des*

67 Nearly every issue of the *Journal des Dames* carried ads for services. See especially the last pages, octobre and décembre 1764, avril and octobre 1765, avril and novembre 1766, and mai 1767; février 1775:266–68; and avril 1775:131.

68 [Bachaumont], *Mémoires secrets* 16:294–95 and 10:32.

69 *Journal des Dames,* janvier 1765:4–8; avril 1767:81; BN ms. fr. 22085, fol. 10.

70 BN ms. fr. 22085, fol. 10.

71 *La Bibliothèque des Dames, ou Choix de pièces nouvelles, instructives, et amu-santes en prose et en vers* (Amsterdam, 1764). Twenty-five issues of this *Bibliothèque des Dames* circulated in Holland during 1764, seemingly modeled on Mme de Maisonneuve's newspaper. There were several attacks against Rousseau's attitude on women, one of which ended with the blunt declaration, "Je crois que ceci suffit pour fermer la bouche à ceux qui nous reprochent injustement une faiblesse à laquelle ils nous ont eux-même condamnés" (part 2, p. 213). Female authors were praised, and the work of six women artists was analyzed, all of whom had

Dames's fortunes had peaked, also abandoned it. Doubtless struck by the power of the protected *Mercure* to wreak havoc with smaller, merely permitted papers, Panckoucke would return to periodical publishing in the mid-1770s, as we will see, but this time on the government's side. Ironically, as publisher of the *Mercure* in 1778, he would eliminate forever the *Journal des Dames*. For now, he simply dropped the paper, leaving Mathon to refashion it as best he could since the *Mercure*'s newly enforced privilege had deprived him of poetry and theater reviews. When Campigneulles faced the same situation six years earlier, he had given up the fight. Stripped of light *pièces fugitives* he had not wanted to fill his paper with articles on serious matters. But Mathon, made of sterner stuff, welcomed the chance to use the paper in a new way. He chose now to distribute the *Journal des Dames* "chez Durand," a family of daring *libraires* considered by the police inspector d'Hémery "one of the most sly and suspect of the booktrade."[72] Still hiding behind Mme de Maisonneuve's name for as long as he could get away with it, he would abandon frivolity and press for reform. The *Mercure*'s intervention had merely precipitated a change that had been brewing in his mind. Mathon de la Cour, after all, came from a family of Jansenist magistrate *patriotes* in Lyons. He could play the debonair courtly Parisian only so long.[73]

A close look at Mathon's writings indicates that he had hoped to make a useful contribution to revitalizing his nation and that devoting himself exclusively to life's artistic and cultural pleasures

---

gained recognition from the Académie royale de peinture (part 1, p. 95). Women's heroic actions, their courage in pain and death, and tales of the prowess of Amazons were scattered throughout (part 2, pp. 193–206, 214, 217, 233). The articles on "l'éducation du beau sexe" were, however, far less feminist. The object, it seems, was ultimately to please and serve others, to impress in the minds and hearts of women "les connaissances et les sentiments prêts à former des épouses qui fassent le bonheur de leurs époux, des mères capables d'élever leurs enfants, et des femmes qui soient l'ornement de la société encore plus par leurs vertus que par leurs talents et leurs grâces" (part 1, p. 65). See the discussion of this in Gay, *Bibliographie des ouvrages* 1:389. I have found no evidence, however, to support Gay's claim that Fanny de Beauharnais and Dorat were the authors of this work.

72 Zephir, "Libraires et imprimeurs," 275.

73 For the scant biographical information on Mathon, see "Mathon de la Cour," *Archives . . . du Rhône,* 300–305, and occasional references to him and his father in Trénard, *Lyon,* especially 1:127, 137–39, 177, 216–17, 226, 246, 282, and Vallas, *Musique à l'Académie de Lyon,* 175, 178–80, 189, 193–200, 227.

caused him some guilt. Even his early pamphlets on the paintings exhibited at the Louvre salon had *frondeur* tendencies, arguing that Rococo mannerism or art for art's sake made men soft, that instead art should stretch and inspire, turn away from the shallowness and conformity of vain portraiture and back to the classical depiction of ancient heroism, patriotic virtue, and civic devotion, all characteristics embodied by the parlements. In terms that would be echoed twenty years later in the radical art criticism of Gorsas and the praise for David in Carmontelle's pamphlet *Le Frondeur,* Mathon argued that art should be virile, should serve the state, "make Frenchmen long to surpass themselves," and "excite veritable enthusiasm." Art, in short, should be experienced in political terms.[74] At one point Mathon almost left Paris to undertake law studies, as he explained in his poem "Les Adieux" in the *Journal des Dames.* The author, "destiné à la magistrature," bid farewell to spectacles, concerts, light books, musical instruments, scientific and mathematical diversions, dinners, salons, and dances, to devote himself to "the most austere studies . . . to serve his fellow citizens . . . to be useful." Ashamed at his own hesitation, at feeling torn between delights and duties, he threw himself into his "destined career" and with "zeal, honor, virtue, and ardor," dedicated his life to his *patrie.*[75] Whether or not Mathon actually did undertake legal studies, he was increasingly drawn to the solemn issues of liberty and justice. As the climate became more stormy between the Crown and the provincial parlements after 1765, Mathon's true loyalties began to emerge. For Mme de Maisonneuve he had maintained a certain levity and sense of humor, but the *Mercure* had stripped him of camouflage, and his serious articles in the *Journal des Dames* now stood naked and unadorned. The game was up.

For other reasons, too, Mathon was ready to take risks. Despite his auspicious beginnings, he had failed to make it in society. The newspaper had done great things for his protectress but nothing at all for him, and he was being rebuffed by Parisian snobbery. He had competed each year, unsuccessfully, in the essay prize com-

---

74 Mathon, *Lettres à Mme* ★★★, 91–93. For a discussion of the threat posed by David's paintings and the "enthousiasme" they provoked, see Crowe, "Oath of the Horatii," especially 428–33, and 457.

75 *Journal des Dames,* juin 1764:16–17.

petitions of the Académie française. His art criticism, welcomed the first year as a promising novelty, had now come under attack. Bachaumont, himself an expert on art, found Mathon's judgments inappropriately harsh given his lack of experience. "His daring assertions are unpardonable for a man with no rank in either literature or art."[76] Grimm had a heyday with the *Almanach des muses*. The collection, he said, was pitiful, full of poems by illiterate rascals that even La Place's awful *Mercure* would never consider printing. The *fatras* was bad enough, but Mathon's critical notes were "without fail of a rare stupidity." Grimm was scandalized that people had mistaken Mathon's art essays for the work of Diderot, who was known to be writing on the same subject. "This is like attributing a cheap sketch to Michelangelo or Tintoretto." The sarcastic baron went on to mock the fact that a person with pretensions of improving mankind could produce something as worthless as a bad poetry anthology. Perhaps it included rubbish because the director was frightened of making enemies and therefore accepted everything indiscriminately? "But how could he imagine that he could exercise in this world the important and glorious function of editor of the *Almanach des muses* without exposure to envy and human injustice? One is never useful to humanity without great cost. . . . There is such enormous distance between an editor of the *Almanach des muses* and an ordinary man."[77]

This barrage of ridicule inclined Mathon more and more toward Rousseau's negative attitude about the elite of the capital. We saw that Sautreau's articles had already drawn on many ideas from *Emile,* but now Mathon himself turned against the disdainful philosophes, who for all their brilliance somehow lacked soul, and he became a strong partisan of the persecuted Genevan outcast and of his republican ideals. He may even have met Rousseau when the fugitive returned to France in 1767 and traveled through Lyons on his way to Paris, because that year Mathon wrote an essay on Lycurgus analyzing "why the great republic of the Lacedaemonians lost its taste for liberty." This work, large sections of which were reprinted in the *Journal des Dames,* underlined the wonders

76 [Bachaumont], *Mémoires secrets* 2:260 (11 novembre 1765). Compare these with the earlier favorable comments in 16:188 (15 octobre 1763).
77 Grimm et al., *Correspondance littéraire* 4:433, 473; 7:224–25; 8:445–46.

of Spartan education and its similarities with the ideas in *Emile* and advocated that women turn from *luxe* and pretension to the serious business of raising their children, "the most glorious works a good woman can produce."[78] Mathon praised the natural equality and harmonious life of "nobles sauvages" at every opportunity and devoted many sympathetic articles in the *Journal des Dames* to Rousseau's persecution and defense.[79]

Increasingly suspicious of the capital, partial to the provinces, and concerned for the *bien publique* of the whole nation, Mathon preached the *frondeur* principle of developing regional confidence, self-esteem, and strength. Later, in a work praising the political ideas of Montesquieu, Mably, Rousseau, and Franklin, he would write with fervor on the importance of provincial power to prevent the unhealthy domination of France by its corrupt center, and he came to regard Paris as "a monstrous vampire that sucks, saps, and devours the rest of the state."[80] This aversion to the Paris brain drain eventually drew him back to Lyons, but his work on the *Journal des Dames* was not yet done. The authorities would not allow him to print political news, he explained to his readers, but he resolved to make the paper useful in other ways. He would portray contemporary mores for posterity. Women, he said often, needed their own historian, someone who would treat them seriously. His paper would be a social document of great value, a catalogue of his times. Even if he could not report current events, he was determined to treat issues. Mathon was not set on dealing exclusively or even at all with the subject of women in his paper, but he was in a certain sense more feminist than other male champions of the female sex, for he implicitly assumed that his female audience would want to read about the same subjects as men. He had already announced in January 1765 that the *Journal des Dames* would add to its treatment of books, plays, and poems new rubrics dealing with science, mechanical inventions, manufacture and industry, and phenomena of nature. Now he showed a new

78 Mathon, *Par quelles causes,* 5–6, 57–59. Large parts of this work were reprinted in the *Journal des Dames,* août and septembre 1767.

79 *Journal des Dames,* septembre 1766, janvier and juillet 1767 (see especially 87–93), and janvier 1768.

80 Mathon, *Discours sur les meilleurs moyens,* "Avertissement" and 13–14, 46–50, 53, 55. In spite of his republican leanings, Mathon could never bring himself to denounce kingship; he was guillotined for insufficient radicalism in November 1793.

resolution to include issues of social and political consequence. Various government *arrêts* had recently forbidden discussion of religious matters in the press, and a royal declaration of 1764 had imposed a silence on such inflammatory financial issues as the liberalization of the grain trade or the fiscal policies of the government, but none of this was going to stop Mathon now.[81]

Articles and comments on the forbidden subject of finances appeared on and off in the *Journal des Dames,* but at first Mathon seemed reluctant to state his position unequivocally. His "Réflexions sur le commerce, le luxe, et l'industrie" praised "le Grand Colbert" and spoke of the need to regulate the proportion of exports and imports, but it also drew on Dutch and English examples to show that a natural "equilibrium" was ideal for trade and that economies could flourish if allowed to arrive at a proper "balance."[82] In other articles and allusions to questions of population and exportation his ideas came out more clearly. When Laverdy—a frugal, hardworking parlementaire and Jansenist who with Conti and Conti's bailiff Le Paige had orchestrated the Jesuits' expulsion—became controller general of finance, Mathon welcomed his efforts to curb court extravagance and paid him a verse tribute in the *Journal des Dames.*[83] Money, he believed, should be used throughout the realm for public works, medical care, and philanthropic projects. He knew and fell under the influence of Benjamin Franklin and the physiocratic "friends of man," extolling their new paper, the *Ephémérides du citoyen, ou Chronique de l'esprit national* for its service to the *bien publique,* for its open criticism of flaws in existing society.[84] The abnormal frosts of the 1760s had ruined crops and vineyards; by 1768 there was a widespread grain famine that put most of the population into a panic, while a few rich speculators who had been hoarding grain now

81 *Journal des Dames,* decembre 1765:"Table générale," and janvier 1766:2–3, "Avertissement." For the *arrêts* against discussion of finances and religion, see Bellanger et al., *Histoire générale* 1:161.

82 *Journal des Dames,* juin 1765:31–33.

83 Ibid., mai 1764:3. The magistrate Laverdy's appointment to this high financial post showed that the Crown recognized, as it had during the Fronde, that the parlements were a force to be reckoned with. For Laverdy's *frondeur* involvement with Conti and Le Paige, see Van Kley, *Jansenists,* 42, 52, 85, 128, 133–36, 231.

84 *Journal des Dames,* décembre 1765:69 and the issues of janvier, mai, juin, and juillet 1766.

took it out of storage and exported it for indecently high profit. The peasants starved, but the prince de Soubise spent 200,000 livres entertaining the king for a day. It was to the inequities of this situation that the Physiocrats, with Mathon's total support, addressed themselves. Already evident in the *Journal des Dames,* Mathon's admiration for Turgot would come out clearly later in his work on France's finances, designed to advocate the open disclosure of royal fiscal policy for judgment by public opinion and to "reanimate in the soul of all citizens that passion for *la chose publique* that inspires great efforts, directs them properly, and makes all sacrifices worthwhile."[85]

Franklin's influence on Mathon had many dimensions. A beautiful foldout picture of Franklin's glass harmonica was the only illustration in the fifty volumes of the *Journal des Dames*. Mathon would write a *Testament de M. Fortuné Ricard* in 1784, about the importance of economizing. Even Grimm admired the "public utility" of Mathon's hymn to frugality, and it was well enough written to have been attributed often to Franklin himself.[86] The American's friendship with the journalists of the *Ephémérides,* men like Nicolas Baudeau, Pierre Du Pont de Nemours, and François Quesnay, whose political persuasions were as much to Mathon's liking as their economic views, renewed his faith in newspapers as proper vehicles for contestation.[87] Franklin himself would later contribute eloquent propaganda for the American "insurgents" to several French journals, which Mathon echoed in his *Journal de Lyon*. Franklin and Mathon also shared a love for science and inventions. Mathon's father was a mathematician in the Académie de Lyon, and the *Journal des Dames* was filled with reports of academic lectures and demonstrations, descriptions of wondrous wheeled and electrical contraptions, articles on such musical instruments as Franklin's harmonica or the "clavecin magique."[88] Fi-

85 Mathon, *Collection de comptes-rendus,* 231, 126.

86 For Grimm's favorable review of Mathon's *Testament de M. Fortuné Ricard* and its similarities to Franklin's projects for Philadelphia and Boston, see *Correspondance littéraire* 14:188.

87 For brief discussions of the Physiocrats who worked on the *Ephémérides du citoyen,* see Sgard, *Dictionnaire des journalistes,* 25, 142–43, 306–8.

88 *Journal des Dames,* janvier 1765:118 and the *avis* sections of mai, juillet, août, septembre, décembre 1766, mai and juin 1767, and mars and juin 1768. See also juillet 1765:60 and juin 1766:89 for more on the importance of scientific discoveries, and juin 1766:109–12 for a wonderful description of the "clavecin magique."

nally, it may have been Franklin who interested Mathon in Free-masonry. When he returned to Lyons in 1770 he became actively involved in it, and his *Journal des Dames* already flirted openly with its tenets, publishing Masonic poems and songs, lengthy reviews of books on Masonry, and praising the late Masonic journalist Pierre Clément, former author of the periodical *Cinq Années littéraires,* whose posthumous works had just been published.[89] Wherever he found them Mathon lauded the Masonic virtues of *zèle, douceur, candeur, honnêteté,* and above all others, *bienfaisance.*

One man who seemed to embody all these characteristics for Mathon was Louis-Sébastien Mercier. Mercier, twenty-five years old and newly returned to his native Paris from a formative teaching stint in Bordeaux, had been trying along with Mathon and Sautreau for all the Académie française essay prize competitions. They always lost, and the philosophes' disciple La Harpe always won. Mathon had soured against the judgments of this institution that he had once venerated. In much the same way that Brissot would later condemn the academies' usurpation of the right to judge and crown genius, a right that properly belonged to "public opinion," Mathon much earlier denounced the literary academy, one of several designed by Colbert as official organs to bring high culture under centralized control. It seemed to Mathon now dangerously atrophied and deaf to new talent, and the *Journal des Dames* set about publishing all the worthy entries that failed to win the prize each year, so that the "public" could judge for itself.[90] Mercier's essays were particularly attractive to Mathon for their freshness and vigor. Where La Harpe seemed bent only on securing his reputation, Mercier wanted truly to improve the world. La Harpe was "feeble, prosaic, cowardly." Mercier, on the other hand, was pouring out his guts; he was zealous, intense, caring. His was precisely the kind of vital, blunt, truthful, and original voice France needed to awaken it. He had, wrote Mathon,

89 *Journal des Dames,* juillet 1765:61, octobre 1766:31–54, décembre 1766:50. For Mathon's involvement in Lyons Masonry, see his *Discours prononcé dans la loge,* discussed in Trénard, *Lyon,* 1:177–78.

90 See *Journal des Dames,* août and septembre 1765 and mars, septembre, and octobre 1767 for essays by Gaillard, Mlle Mazarelli, and others who failed to win the prize. Mathon believed that the public's judgments were sound, that "c'est aux lecteurs de décider." For echoes of this opinion nearly two decades later, see the discussion of Brissot's *De la verité* in Crowe, "Oath of the Horatii," 435, 437, 439, 442.

more natural talent than La Harpe and all the other fashionable writers put together.[91] Mercier was energetic, a true artist, committed to the benefit of humanity. Had he not just been moved to write, during a visit to Toulouse, *Calas sur l'échafaud à ses juges?* Not only his academic essays but his other writings as well were excerpted at length in the *Journal des Dames,* even though the authorities had condemned them. His *Homme sauvage,* at precisely the moment it was being pursued by the police chief, Sartine, and forbidden by the government, was lauded by Mathon as forceful, evincing "true traits of genius," and extracts of it filled twenty-five pages of one of the issues of the paper.[92] The more Grimm and the "in crowd" branded Mercier as a base and vulgar outsider, the more Mathon's *Journal des Dames* supported him. Mathon's penultimate issue, dated June 1768, devoted thirty pages to Mercier's *Songes philosophiques,* imbued with "une morale douce, pure, et bienfaisante." Here was a blatant attack on tyranny and on such social and economic abuses as the hoarding of grain, along with an outright demand that the king impose a tax on "luxury items" rather than "life's necessities." If children were starving, something in the state was rotten. The rich, not the poor, must be taxed, because "the liberty, comfort, and happiness of subjects are more important than the glory, grandeur, and power of the realm."[93] Mercier himself would become editor of the *Journal des Dames* in 1775, in part because Mathon had proven that the paper could print such *frondeur* fare and still survive.

But for how long? Mathon was becoming increasingly impatient with having to curry favor. He had long ago stopped flattering Marin, whose archroyalism made him hateful to *patriotes,* and had even quite undiplomatically criticized a poem by his protectress Mme de Maisonneuve in the *Almanach des muses.* He had turned against some of his former friends because they seemed

91 For criticisms of La Harpe, see *Journal des Dames,* décembre 1764:116, janvier 1765 passim, avril 1766:85.

92 Ibid., juillet 1767:50–75, especially 73. See BN. ms. fr. 22154, fol. 37, in which the police chief dispatched Inspector d'Hémery in pursuit of both *L'Homme sauvage* and its author.

93 Ibid., juin 1768:35–63, especially 49–51, 60–61. For more praise of Mercier, see septembre 1765:74, septembre 1766:46, octobre 1766:61–79, mars 1767:66–67. For Grimm's negative remarks on Mercier's writings of this period, see, for example, *Correspondance littéraire* 7:300, 309, 377.

too willing to dally with niceties rather than fight for reform, too preoccupied with decorum and the gentle life to say anything important. His contributor Dorat—a future editor of the *Journal des Dames*—seemed especially flippant, uncaring, indifferent. What everyone failed to understand, explained Dorat, was that he wrote only for his own enjoyment, and whether he moved his audience or not was of no consequence. Mathon, upset by this cavalier attitude, launched into a diatribe on the moral obligations of the artist to care and to affect his public. A dry heart and a frivolous spirit could produce only worthless trifles. A true artist must suffer, must give of himself, must be a committed, involved, self-sacrificing person, devoted to improving the world.[94] Mathon's interest in the impact of art on public opinion, the bond created between artist and audience in a public arena, could be seen in his fascination with the force of theater on assembled groups and with the exhibits of art at the salons, another kind of performance to which all classes had access and where Mathon found the fresh, spontaneous reactions of the unschooled crowds—"gens de toute espèce"—more interesting than the paintings.[95]

Every year brought a flare-up of some kind as Mathon grew more ornery. Bastide, whose educational ideas the *Journal des Dames* continued to attack as unpatriotic, now retaliated by plagiarizing large chunks of Mathon's journal in his own periodical, *Le Journal de Bruxelles,* also known as *Le Penseur.* Bastide's paper was being threatened by authorities in Liège and Calais, and he undoubtedly resented the fact that Mathon's was carrying on unmolested. Bastide had also once tried unsuccessfully to edit a paper for women, which may have added to his sense of competition with Mathon. The man trafficking the stolen manuscripts was another disgruntled Frenchman, a M. Fesquet, who had himself tried to start up a *Journal étranger* in Belgium but had been refused. Knowing full well that no privilege protected Mathon's *Journal des Dames,* the two men jealously sought to undermine it, and although Mathon protested vociferously, he was powerless to stop

94 *Journal des Dames,* juillet 1766:89.
95 See *Lettres à Mme ✱✱✱,* 66n. and 88. For later radicals' approval of the spontaneous reactions of the crowd, see Crowe, "Oath of the Horatii," 433–35, 437, 449–51. For more on the theater as public arena, see Chapters 6 and 7, below.

the pirating, which ended only when *Le Penseur* was finally suppressed.[96] Mathon also picked a row with the elitist *Nécrologe des hommes célèbres,* a periodical under Choiseul's protection, with which Mme de Maisonneuve had negotiated a beneficial mailing arrangement in 1768, using the new Bureau royal de la correspondance générale. A former friend and collaborator of Mathon's, Querlon, was a translator on the staff of the *Nécrologe,* but that did not stop Mathon from blasting the paper for giving literary rather than social history in its obituaries. The emotional lives and political motivations of statesmen and artists must be made known as well as their writings, and more attention should be paid to those of humble birth. The *Nécrologe* responded to this in an editorial probably by the conservative Palissot, accusing Mathon of wanting to diminish the distance between the greats and the "plus vulgaire des hommes" and of therefore being "completely mad."[97] Politically Mathon seemed to be raving; Palissot would level the same complaint when Mercier became editor of the *Journal des Dames* in 1775.

The only effort Mathon now made to soften his punches (beyond the gradual resumption of *pièces fugitives* somehow overlooked by the *Mercure*) was to pad the *Journal des Dames* with articles on music—his father was an authority on Rameau and had written some popularizations of his compositional techniques—and on curiosities. Each issue served up an entertaining potpourri of anecdotes, gleaned no doubt from reports to the Lyons academy, ranging from freaks to cataract operations to cures for migraines and chilblain. Electric shock treatments, smallpox inoculations, the passage of meteors and comets, volcanic eruptions,

96   See Mathon's protests in the *Journal des Dames,* avril 1767:80–81, and Bastide's mocking replies in the *Journal de Bruxelles* (1767) ii:374, 308, 370–72. (The copy at the Bibliothèque de l'Arsenal has terribly convoluted pagination.) For more information on Bastide and Fesquet, see Vercruysse, "Journalistes et journaux." On Bastide's own attempt at a periodical for women, see Rimbault, "Presse féminine: Production," 202.

97   Mme de Maisonneuve made the following arrangement in March 1768: "Le Bureau royal de la correspondance générale vient de se charger de recevoir des abonnements pour le *Journal des Dames.* Le meilleur moyen de concourir au succès de cet Ouvrage intéressant est sans doute de le faire connaître; c'est dans cette vue qu'on s'est déterminé à envoyer un volume *gratis* à chacun de Messieurs les Abonnés des *Deuils de Cour* et du *Nécrologe.*" See Bibliothèque Mazarine 35735, 3e pièce. Mathon's criticism of the *Nécrologe* is in *Journal des Dames,* avril 1768:78–79. The scathing response attacking Mathon is in *Nécrologe,* 1769:247–53.

newly discovered but undeciphered inscriptions on tombstones, tempests, earthquakes, quintuplets, sleeps of extraordinarily long duration, nails and hair growing to great lengths after death— these scientific phenomena and human interest stories were sprinkled liberally throughout the *Journal des Dames* of 1766, 1767, and 1768. Such *faits divers* decorated many other periodicals of the day also. The *Mercure* had many of them, as did Querlon's *Affiches de province*.[98] But the other papers printed only a small number of these and appeared to merely tickle their readers' imagination with such tidbits. The greater volume of them in Mathon's *Journal des Dames* suggests he was using them as distracting filler to dilute the impact of his *frondeur* articles. He threw in, for the same reason, an occasional diverting article on women, but this had ceased to be the central issue for Mathon and he needed to remind himself that this was to have been his paper's special focus.[99] Apart from announcing a few lecture courses and public demonstrations for ladies, Mathon mentioned one particularly pretty taxidermist who caught his interest and impressed him, a rich and lovely lady who had nonetheless bothered to acquire such an unusual talent. More amusing were the "prêteuses de têtes" who rented their heads for 6 livres a month to coiffeurs who needed practice. Then there were the women whose major contribution to society was their moral innocence, as exemplified by the crowning of a pure peasant girl at the annual Rosière de Salency. Such ceremonies, Mathon argued, should be spread throughout the realm to inspire virtue and patriotic devotion in female citizens.[100] In general, however, Mathon was not comfortable with restricting his paper to feminine topics; such a narrow focus would undermine its usefulness and both isolate and trivialize its audience. He meant his paper to be a symbol of resistance on a grand scale.

Mme de Maisonneuve had continued to lend her name to the *Journal des Dames* throughout Mathon's progressive rebelliousness.

---

98   See Marion, "Dix ans des *Affiches*." See also Favre, "Le Fait divers en 1778."

99   See, for example, *Journal des Dames,* janvier 1768:117, where in an issue devoid of feminine content we find the incongruous comment, "This journal is principally dedicated to the celebration of women whose talents have brought them distinction."

100   Ibid., juin 1764:118; juin 1765:118; mai 1766:113; juillet 1767:115; avril 1766:81–82; juin 1766. More will be said of the Rosière ceremony in later chapters.

She had watched him unabashedly declare his support for parlement's fight against "despotism," for forbidden writers like Mercier, for academic rejects, establishment outcasts in general, and all marginal groups of low social status. She had even overlooked for years his chronic lateness and chaotic handling of the business. Far from producing regular monthly issues, Mathon's were appearing as much as six months or a year behind schedule, and he had failed to pay her the agreed-upon pension. All this she put up with, apparently without embarrassment because she liked his politics and she herself favored reform. Also she could not help but admire the numerous public welfare projects he was setting up in Lyons—trade schools, water purification experiments, farming collectives to lower the prices of bread—which, he explained to his subscribers, were taking up most of his time. He apologized to them for spreading himself too thin and promised to complete their collections of the *Journal des Dames*,[101] but obviously this obligation was becoming onerous, justifiable only if he could use it to push for the *frondeur* cause.

As long as Choiseul remained powerful, the *Journal des Dames* had little to fear, but as the political climate turned hostile to him in 1768, Mme de Maisonneuve's position became untenable. Mathon was extolling Masonry when Sartine was suppressing the Grande Loge de Paris; he was siding with the parlementaires just when Maupeou, an ardent monarchist, became chancellor and began planning his royalist coup; his paper was an avant-garde of the radical anti-academicism that became rampant in the next two decades; and he fought for physiocracy although the new finance minister Terray was against free trade and supported court spending. This was infertile soil for the man whose later *Journal de Lyon* would fervently support the American Revolution, the "sons of liberty," and involvement of all citizens in *la chose commune*. When Mathon applied to the booktrade in January 1769 for continued permission to print his *Journal des Dames,* it was denied and his paper was "suspended by superior orders."[102] As much for Ma-

101 See *Journal des Dames,* novembre 1767:"Avis" and p. 61. That Mathon's issues were extremely late can be seen by comparing the official dates on their title pages with the date at the bottom when they were *achevé d'imprimer.* See also BN ms. fr. 22085, fol. 10. For descriptions of Mathon's philanthropic projects, see "Mathon de la Cour," *Archives . . . du Rhône,* and Dumas, *Histoire de l'Académie royale* 1:329–31.

102 BN ms. fr. 21993, fol. 154, no. 815; BN ms. fr. 22085, fol. 10.

thon's protection as her own, Mme de Maisonneuve never protested the paper's suspension or "exercised her right to relaunch
it."[103] And for as long as Maupeou's despotic "triumvirate"
reigned, until 1774, the dissident *Journal des Dames* remained silent. The conservative abbé Sabatier de Castres was delighted
to see the paper go. Disturbed by its *frondeur* editors and not
knowing it would have three more, he wrote a wishful but
premature obituary. "This is a doomed work, which has
finally and deservedly expired in [Mathon's] hands, after having somehow survived the murderous touch of so many other
incompetents."[104]

Mme de Maisonneuve, who seems not to have written anything other than the *Journal des Dames,* died in 1774. Mathon returned to Lyons to continue his projects and edit the reforming
Journal de Lyon, in which he urged far-reaching social change but
never violence. On 3 May 1788, the day of an important confrontation between the parlements and the Crown, documents show
that Mathon was back in Paris renting a house and disseminating
his work on finances, which he hoped would ease the mounting
tensions.[105] He supported the calling of the Estates General and
the early stages of the Revolution, objecting only when it grew
increasingly extreme. His spirit of compromise cost him his head
in November 1793 during the Terror. But this *frondeur,* whose
Journal de Lyon supported Revolutionary women's clubs and published the procès-verbaux of their meetings, had spent three decades fighting for an expansion of freedoms within the regime, and
the *Journal des Dames,* with Mme de Maisonneuve's complicity,
had served as his first weapon. Unwilling to restrict the paper to
exclusively distaff matters, Mathon's most significant contribution
to the feminist cause was his practiced faith that female and male
readers should be treated equally and in particular that newspaper
readers of both sexes should be exposed to the vigorous, transgressive ideas of writers like Mercier. His paper made clear his
belief that women should no longer be isolated as if they were not
part of the culture. Instead they should be drawn into contestation
and experience the impact of discord and provocation.

103   BN ms. fr. 22085, fol. 9.
104   Sabatier de Castres, *Trois Siècles* 2:350–51.
105   See Archives Nationales T1089 (21) and Archives de Paris, DQ[10], carton
1442, dossier 3029.

5

Marie Antoinette's Journalist Protégée

MME DE MONTANCLOS AND MAUPEOU'S DISGRACE

(1774–1775)

When Mathon's *Journal des Dames* was suspended by Sartine in 1769, it had already become associated with physiocracy, with American rebels like Franklin, with defiant women like Mme de Beaumer bent on communicating their courage and force, with subversive writers like Mercier, with anti-academicism, with the *frondeur* invocation of the public good against royal abuses, and with Jansenist *patriotes* against the Crown. Even the relatively diplomatic Mme de Maisonneuve, after the expulsion of the Jesuits, had denounced the *dévots* as "hypocrites."[1] Little wonder, then, that the paper remained suspended for the next five years, during which the royalist chancellor Maupeou reigned in a "triumvirate" with two other ministers, d'Aiguillon and Terray, under the blessing of the powerful Mme Du Barry and the archbishop of Paris, Christophe de Beaumont, supporters of the dispersed Jesuits. The political pendulum had now swung completely to the reactionary extreme.

Choiseul, who had protected the *Journal des Dames,* had lost favor in the late 1760s and was now disgraced. Mathon's paper had been severely delayed in its last years; his final issue, dated July 1768, did not squeak into print until the following year. That the last few issues of Mathon's paper appeared at all was probably due to its new, sympathetic censor, J. F. Arnoult, who had replaced

1 *Journal des Dames,* mai 1764:78.

Rousselet. Arnoult, the son of a magistrate, was a protégé of the prince de Conti, a playwright for the boulevard theaters, the author of a factious *Arbre de Cracovie* about the activities of clandestine *nouvellistes* in the Palais Royal.[2] Now, however, Sartine had silenced the *Journal des Dames,* and Maupeou had given new powers to the paper's old enemy, Marin, who during the triumvirate exercised more control than ever over the journalistic medium. In addition to his previous functions as *censeur de la police,* Marin had now become a journalist himself, invading the world of the press as editor of the official *Gazette de France.* Since the Fronde and throughout all confrontations between parlements and the Crown, the *Gazette* had always upheld the absolutist thesis that power existed only in the person of the king, calling the idea of a "general and national parlement" a "revolutionary chimera" and insisting that "the king will be served and obeyed." In 1771 d'Aiguillon hired Marin at a handsome 10,000 livres a year to push that idea even more strongly and use the privileged *Gazette* to mold public opinion in favor of the new ministry.[3]

The silencing of the *Journal des Dames* was thus symptomatic of the extremely repressive censorship of these Maupeou years. Marin and the police patrolled the printed word more vigilantly than ever. The archives of the Bastille contain special compliments from Sartine to Police Inspector d'Hémery and his zealous helper Goupil for their industrious spying, confiscation of subversive books, and routing of "troublesome authors" during these years.[4] Persecutions and arrests were not confined to writers; purveyors of suspicious texts were considered equally guilty, and there were

2   See Bibliothèque Nationale, manuscrit français (henceforth BN ms. fr.) 21993, fol. 54, no. 815, where Arnoult—sometimes spelled Arnoul—is listed as the censor for Mathon's *Journal des Dames* in 1769. For more information on his activities as a playwright, see *Biographie universelle* 2:280–81. Although he was not involved with the *Journal des Dames* when it resumed after Maupeou's fall, he did censor the liberal *Esprit des journalistes de Hollande,* and his own periodical, the *Almanach des petits spectacles de Paris,* was censored by the *frondeur* Pidansat de Mairobert until the latter's death in 1779. See BN ms. fr. 22002, p. 125, no. 855, and p. 209, no. 1329. According to the *Almanach royal* for 1767 (pp. 405–8) Arnoult lived with the Gilbert de Voisins family, famous parlementaires who fought for the civil rights of Protestants.

3   Aimé-Azam, "Ministère des affaires étrangères." See also Aubertin, *Esprit public,* 276–77.

4   See for example, Bibliothèque de l'Arsenal, Archives de la Bastille, MS 10028, nos. 361, 365, and MS 10303, no. 345.

also voluminous files kept on the detention of people who "received, lent, sold, or distributed" works against Maupeou's ministry.[5] Attempts were made to silence everything with a parlementaire bias including the *nouvelles à la main,* clandestine manuscripts against which an unusually intense campaign was launched. Sartine's men tried to ferret out and "terrorize" the *nouvellistes,* especially those in the "parish" of Mme Doublet, whose nephew Choiseul could no longer protect her.[6] In this circle was Pidansat de Mairobert, principal author of the *Mémoires secrets* after Bachaumont's death in 1771 and of the much more political *Maupeouiana* and *Journal historique, chroniques scandaleuses* of the Maupeou years. Pidansat had been branded by Police Inspector d'Hémery as early as 1750 for his dangerous tongue, "esprit frondeur," and seditious intentions.[7] Although in the liberal years after Maupeou's fall, Pidansat would become official censor of Mercier's *Journal des Dames,* his operations were entirely underground for the time being. He complained bitterly that the government had deprived journal readers of all but Marin's *Gazette* with its strictly controlled royalist propaganda. This enforced ignorance, he argued in the *Mémoires secrets* of September 1771, was designed to turn Frenchmen into docile mindless sheep, "to make us all 'happy' by bringing back the Dark Ages."[8]

A look at Jean Sgard's comprehensive list of French-language periodicals of the Old Regime bears out Pidansat's contention that journals were severely restricted during the Maupeou years. Of the forty-seven new papers launched during the triumvirate, nine were uncontroversial provincial *affiches* carrying only commercial information for local regions, and thirteen were not printed in France at all, originating outside the system of French censorship, in Cologne, Saint Petersburg, Frankfurt, Stockholm, Amster-

5 Archives de la Bastille, MS 12403.

6 Bayle and Herblay, "Journalisme clandestin," especially 402–5.

7 See the dossier on Pidansat at the Arsenal, MS 11683, and Ravaisson, *Archives de la Bastille* 12:315–16, 345, and 19:269. For the best biographical information on Pidansat (although nothing is said about his activities in the mid-1770s as an official royal censor), see Tate, *Petit de Bachaumont.* Funck-Brentano, *Figaro et ses devanciers,* 285, considered Pidansat "un des écrivains qui ont le plus contribué à frayer les voies à la Révolution." Articles by Jean Sgard on Pidansat's *Espion anglais* will appear in the *Dictionnaire des journaux* (forthcoming).

8 [Bachaumont], *Mémoires secrets* 5:326 (27 septembre 1771).

dam, Berlin, Hamburg, Dusseldorf, Luxembourg, Liège, London, Tournai, and Deux-Ponts. Of the remaining twenty-five, ten concerned politically neutral topics, for example, *Observation sur la physique* or *Lettres hebdomadaires sur les minéraux*. Ten others, more controversial, were stopped during their first year.[9] The only long-lived literary journals that were born and survived official processing during Maupeou's ministry were the *Gazette et avant coureur* and the *Journal de Genève*—whose privileges went to Panckoucke, the trusted friend of the ministers who was by now established as an official *libraire du roi*—and the *Journal des causes célèbres*—awarded to Lacombe, another government cooperator, sometimes business partner of Panckoucke, also publisher of the official *Mercure* and *Journal des savants*. Two other papers, the *Bibliographie parisienne* and the *Esprit des journaux,* were permitted as nothing more than digests of already existing papers. Finally, the *Encyclopédie militaire,* which appeared between 1770 and 1772, was the official organ of the Ministry of Foreign Affairs and printed only approved propaganda.[10] Anti-absolutist papers coming across the border were also scrutinized in Maupeou's redoubled attempt to silence all journalistic contestation. Few copies of the pro-Jansenist *Gazette de Leyde* got through during those years. The *Gazette de Deux-Ponts,* a quite *frondeur* paper edited in Germany by Mercier's friend Dubois-Fontenelle, had difficulty circulating in France; documents in the police archives show large packets of it were continually confiscated and sent to the Pilon de la Bastille.[11]

The stranglehold of Maupeou on the press and on the printed

9 Sgard, *Inventaire de la presse.* See the alphabetical list of French-language periodicals, pp. 1–29, which gives the dates for each paper. Although this list is neither complete nor entirely accurate, its contours are suggestive and support Pidansat's argument that the press was under close surveillance.

10 See Marc Martin, *Origines de la presse militaire,* 33–38. BN ms. fr. 8132, "Etat des privilèges en vigueur au 15 février 1778," shows that hardly any privileges were awarded during 1770 and 1771 except for traditional *almanachs* and *calendriers,* and very few during 1772 and 1773. Lacombe and Panckoucke stand as having received special treatment. They even got unusually long privileges, some for twenty years (see, for example, ibid., 27). After Maupeou's fall, by contrast, privileges were awarded liberally to newspapers in 1775–77 (see ibid., 35). The significance of this will be discussed in Chapters 6 and 7, below.

11 Bibliothèque de l'Arsenal, MS 10305, "Pilon de la Bastille." These unnumbered lists of books confiscated or pulped are full of works by Mercier and Pidansat and of journals that supported them. A long list called "Etat des livres à

word in general was thus not a figment of the *nouvellistes'* imagination. An unprecedented number of bookdealers went bankrupt, simply lacking enough material to make commerce viable. Terray, the new finance minister, had increased the taxes on paper, but this merely aggravated the problem caused by the paucity of permitted manuscripts. Whereas previously, *libraires* in Paris had declared bankruptcy on the average of one every five years, there were nine such declarations of financial ruin in the five years of Maupeou's reign.[12] Men of letters were thus not wide of the mark when they predicted the new chancellor would choke literature and kill art. Helvétius, for example, feared that France would soon perish of consumption.[13]

Maupeou's fierce censorship stemmed from the extreme unpopularity of his exiling of the refractory parlements in a nighttime coup during late January 1771. He had replaced the *frondeur* magistrates with yes-men, "yellow judges" drawn mostly from the Grand Conseil and traditionally loyal to the king. Maupeou wished to kill forever the notion, grown popular once again in the late 1760s, that the king was bound by laws. "His Majesty is beholden to God alone for his crown . . . is accountable only to God for his administration," declared the new chancellor. "He alone invests magistrates with their authority; they are and must be officers of His Majesty, licensed to execute his will."[14] The exiled parlements, martyrs now, came to be seen as guardians of the fundamental laws of the realm, protectors of liberty, defenders of the people and the nation, of the public good, of the community. *Patriotes* argued with Roman austerity that only the parlements could protect the "state" and the "constitution" against the arbitrary whim and extravagance of the ruling "oriental despots."[15]

la Bastille," for example, has attached to it another list showing the confiscation of the *Gazette de Deux-Ponts* beginning in 1773.

12   Zephir, "Libraires et imprimeurs," 96, provides tables with these figures, although the author makes no attempt to analyze them in their political context.

13   [Pidansat], *Journal historique* 5:115–16.

14   Maupeou, *Chancelier Maupeou,* 131. This discussion of the coup, written by a descendant of Maupeou, is interesting because in spite of its attempt to be fair, even sympathetic, it makes clear the prevailing hostility toward the man and his draconian measures.

15   Ibid., 205. On the role of the parlements in producing liberal ideology, see Richet, "Autour des origines." See also the literature summarized in Lucas, "Nobles, Bourgeois, Origins."

Louis XV was now referred to as "le Bien Aimé" only with the bitterest irony. The popularity of the ministers sank daily. Contemporary descriptions of their physiognomy were almost unanimously unflattering. All three suffered from excessive bile: d'Aiguillon with his jaundiced complexion and ruthless jaw; Terray, sinister and blotchy-faced, indulging the king while the people starved and laughing at the misfortune of others; Maupeou himself, sallow and sickly, "sometimes yellow, sometimes green," "the horror of the nation," "the most repugnant countenance on which one could spit."[16]

Maupeou would never have allowed the *Journal des Dames* to appear during these years, given its political nonconformity. What outlet did its editor and principal contributor find in the meantime? Mathon, back in Lyons, turned to writing Jansenist tracts. Mercier, more *frondeur* than ever, turned to writing plays in 1770; one of his first *drames, Olinde et Sophronie,* appeared a few days after Maupeou's coup. It was a thinly disguised attack on the triumvirate and, Grimm reluctantly reported, became wildly popular for its unflattering portrayal of the king and of his minister d'Aiguillon. It was immediately confiscated.[17] Shortly afterward another play, *Jean Hennuyer,* scathingly attacked the ruling *dévot* party and its various religious and political "fanatismes." Mercier was now regarded by Sartine as a public enemy, a fierce, bizarre man. Grimm considered his plays "revolting," "base," "disgusting," his bourgeois heros "absurd" and full of "rudeness and clumsiness," at best "impertinent," at worst "shocking," even "scandalous," but he had to admit that the works would be extremely moving if performed, that they would surely sway and inflame "the people" of Paris.[18] Only the protection of Mercier's censor Crébillon *fils,* himself in the service and circle of the *frondeurs* Orléans, saved him during these years from some "baleful consequences." "You can imagine," wrote Grimm to the august readers of his *Correspondance littéraire* in September 1772, "that

16 Maupeou, *Chancelier Maupeou,* 70, 72, 166, 192, and similar descriptions in Faure, *Disgrâce de Turgot,* 11. See also Collé, *Journal historique inédit* 3:520.

17 Grimm et al., *Correspondance littéraire* 9:273.

18 Ibid. 10:53–55, 88. For more disparaging remarks on Mercier's plays of this time, see 8:393 (reviews of performance in 12:479), 9:65–66, (performance 13:159).

Mercier's plays, such as they are, cannot be found for sale in Paris and that we have only a few copies that have escaped the vigilance of the police."[19]

Back issues of the *Journal des Dames,* which had provided thirty- and fifty-page excerpts of Mercier's works, were almost as suspect as the works themselves. The only bookdealer who would touch Mathon's paper during the Maupeou years was Edme, a fervent Jansenist and unofficial *libraire,* desperate for money, who probably felt he had nothing to lose. Edme put together and advertised complete sets of Mathon's *Journal des Dames* in 1770.[20] Restif de la Bretonne, another literary rebel and a close friend of Pidansat and Mercier, was living during these years on a bed of straw in a fifth floor garret provided by Edme. Restif described Edme as a "madman," as a Jansenist "convulsionnaire" and "cartouche des journalistes" who nearly starved to death trying to sell forbidden papers. In 1770 Edme was also pushing Mathon's newest writings, which increasingly invoked examples from English politics and continued the *patriote* campaign for the law, the public welfare, the constitution, more equitable taxation, and the involvement of citizens in affairs of state.[21] Maupeou's police did not smile upon Edme's efforts—Restif continued to harp on the "thanklessness" and "futility" of these activities—and Edme was soon forced into submission, even total capitulation, becoming the groveling "dupe" and "creature" of Christophe de Beaumont himself.[22] The *Journal des Dames* for the next four years had no one to keep its memory alive.

By 1773, however, there were signs that Maupeou was losing his grip. One of his magistrates, Goezmann, had incurred the wrath of Beaumarchais, who launched a series of devastating *mémoires* against the corrupt Maupeou parlement, the reigning ministers, and their *gazetier* Marin, "unscrupulous spy," "pusillanimous censor," henceforth to be known as "Ques-a-co" (a

19 Ibid. 10:55. A more complete discussion of Mercier's dissident literary productions will be given in Chapter 6.

20 BN ms. fr. 22085, fol. 9.

21 See, for example, Mathon's Jansenist *Discours sur le danger,* especially 4, 27, 40, on the relation between domestic virtues and civic-mindedness. This work was printed chez Edme in 1770.

22 Restif de la Bretonne, *Monsieur Nicolas* 5:2723, 2765; 6:3083, 3086, 3087–91.

Provençal idiom meaning "what's up?" symbolizing Marin's insatiable hunger for any gossip that might ingratiate him with the police). Beaumarchais described them all as snakes and toads capable of every depravity and of the foulest crimes. "The outraged public protests . . . the citizens pass sentence on the judges." Overnight, Beaumarchais created a sensation for daring to say what so many had been thinking, and he became the hero of the subculture of opposition. Pidansat's underground *Journal historique* reported that everyone had gone wild over Beaumarchais, his *mémoires* selling in record numbers as the police tried desperately to confiscate them. Marin, whose *Gazette* had no buyers, did all he could to stop the *mémoires* at the presses, but six thousand copies had managed to sell anyway, their price driven up by the wild demand. Beaumarchais's printer, it was rumored, had been forced to hire a bodyguard to protect him from the impassioned fans. Meanwhile the author of the *mémoires* basked in celebrity, even though he was soon to be censured. Impending civil disenfranchisement—or worse—only enhanced his heroic stature. When Mme Du Barry and the triumvirate repeatedly cancelled advertised performances of the *Barber of Seville,* the protestations of potential spectators became violent and Beaumarchais's writings were more clamored for than ever. Throughout he was feted by the blue-blooded opposition, the prince de Conti, former protector of Mme de Beaumer and her *Journal des Dames* "au Temple," and his nephew the duc de Chartres, future Philippe Egalité. The notion that their protégé and dinner guest was threatened with hanging made him all the more attractive to these rebel *princes du sang.*[23] And Beaumarchais, a symbol of resistance to despotism, had also won the admiration and fervent support of the teenage dauphine, Marie Antoinette. She fought for him with all her might because Mme Du Barry fought against him. For a future queen of France, the young Austrian princess seemed surprisingly eager to play with fire. And it was under Marie Antoinette's protection that the *Journal des Dames* began to appear again in January 1774, dedicated to her.

Marie Antoinette had been barred by the favorite and the min-

---

23 On Beaumarchais's popularity and Maupeou's and Marin's lack of it, see Pidansat's *Journal historique* 5:37, 64–65, 77–78, 94, 101, 122–24, 128, 138, 166–70, 173–85, 199–200, 204.

isters from any influence at court. She hated d'Aiguillon especially for having replaced her old friend Choiseul, and Maupeou for having orchestrated his disgrace. She resented her oafish husband, whose sexual insufficiency had to be kept strictly secret and had therefore led to rumors throughout Europe that she was barren. Because she was thought incapable of bearing an heir, dynastic hopes had turned to the dauphin's brothers, Provence and Artois, and there were even many at court who pushed for the sixty-four-year-old Louis XV to remarry, perhaps a Spanish princess, and sire a direct heir to the throne. Marie Antoinette had thus amounted to nothing in her three years of marriage, and there seemed some chance that she would never rule. In late 1773, when she supported Beaumarchais so fervently, she also developed a taste for Mercier's *drames* and gave her approval to the prospectus of the new *Journal des Dames*.[24] Nobody could have predicted that in just five months Louis XV would suddenly contract smallpox and die and that she and her equally inexperienced husband, respectively nineteen and twenty years old, would become France's monarchs. For now, deprived of any political power, she resolved to have some say at least in the world of culture. She failed to see that by indulging her tastes, she undermined her own future safety. "Poor queen," wrote a commentator on her penchant for revolutionary literature, "for her happy, light spirit everything was joy and pleasure: the song of the page, the speeches of the philosophical barber, the words of the *parterre*. Beaumarchais amused her, Mercier filled her with tenderness, she threw herself into their quarrels. . . . Through all . . . she walked carefree, oblivious, and blind, never suspecting the venom, hatred, and revengeful anger hidden in the comic poet's laughter and the *dramomane*'s tears."[25]

The baronne de Prinzen (or Princen or Prinzenne—all three spellings appear), nearly forty years old, widow of a German nobleman, received Marie Antoinette's blessing for the new *Journal des Dames* in late 1773. The young dauphine had already held one of the aspiring journalist's babies at its baptism, and the would-be

24   BN ms. fr. 22085, fol. 6.
25   Hallays-Dabot, *Histoire de la censure*, 140.

editor had evidently frequented the glittering entourage of foreigners with whom the lonely, homesick princess surrounded herself.[26] Marie Antoinette was probably pleased that a lively, bright woman twice her age proposed to dedicate a newspaper to singing her praises. Although the object of numerous sycophants' adulation, the dauphine had not received much positive press. This was her period of dissipation, of flirtations with Count Fersen and even with her own brother-in-law Artois. She was bored and petulant, her behavior the cause of embarrassment and despair in the private correspondence between her guardian Mercy-Argenteau and her mother Maria Theresa of Austria. Publicly too she had provoked considerable disfavor. After the initial excitement at the time of her arrival and marriage, interest in her pouting and frivolous masquerading had died down. No longer a novelty, she was either ignored or censured. But now here was someone eager to uphold her as an intelligent and virtuous model for the whole female sex. Signs of Marie Antoinette's gratitude for these overtures can still be seen at the Bibliothèque Nationale, whose gold-leafed copies of the journalist's later poems and plays carry the queen's personal arms.

And who was this baronne de Prinzen? Born Marie Emilie Mayon in 1736 in Aix-en-Provence, like Bordeaux another center of the Fronde, she described herself as "plus que bourgeoise, sans être de qualité," the daughter of "respectable parents who struck a happy medium between the idle nobility and the laborious commoners."[27] An unenthusiastic marriage to a much older German baron had forced her into a social whirl at court, a life of perfumed parties and pleasures she disliked as much as her husband adored them. His extravagance soon ruined them, however, and although, according to her story, he literally died of shame (being an "âme faible"), she welcomed the return to more modest cir-

---

26 Rabbe, *Biographie universelle* 3:647.
27 *Journal des Dames,* décembre 1774:194. This appears in the anonymous but largely autobiographical "Réflexions d'une solitaire aux îles d'Hyères." Although she never claimed these *réflexions* as her own in the newspaper, the baronne de Prinzen later included them in her two-volume *Oeuvres de Mme de Montanclos* (Paris, 1792) and published them again separately. See Delandine, *Bibliothèque de Lyon* 2:263, 313.

cumstances, the "freedom" of being unattached again, and the chance to care for her little daughters.[28] Even her detractors described the baronne de Prinzen as beautiful, and her widowhood brought forth numerous suitors, but she claimed to be uninterested in marrying again. One Charlemagne Cuvelier Grandin de Montanclos, a brigadier in the king's bodyguard, apparently prevailed upon her in the end, and the *Journal des Dames* announced in October 1774 that the ci-devant baronne de Prinzen was now Mme de Montanclos. Her second marriage seems to have been no more romantically successful than the first, for documents reveal that within months of the wedding the new husband and wife had legally separated, she living in her own house in Paris on the rue des Bernardins near the place Maubert, he retired to Troyes in Champagne.[29]

Mme de Montanclos, like Mme de Beaumer, seems to have been sufficiently independent to render her relationships with men problematical. Both quarreled with their collaborators and with their printers, the brothers Quillau, and sold the *Journal des Dames* privately for a time from home offices.[30] Both longed for marriages based on equality and mutual respect, although neither could find them. Both perceived most men as enemies, obstacles to female advancement, but both made exceptions for rebels and *frondeurs*. There were differences between the two women of course. Mme de Montanclos was less radical than Mme de Beaumer, more polished and distinctly more maternal, but even she would continue to insist on her right to a career as journalist and dramatist and would look back on her life as a feminist struggle. "O, la cruelle chose d'être auteur femelle!" she wrote in a letter in the midst of a conflict with the Comédie-Française where she was trying to get her plays performed.[31] And she later confessed in a letter to Mercier, to whom she would turn over the *Journal des*

28 *Journal des Dames,* décembre 1774:194–205. Rabbe, who does not cite any sources, appears to have based his brief notice describing Mme de Montanclos on this account.

29 See Minutier Central (henceforth M.C.), LXXXV, (652), 19 avril 1775 and attached document dated 11 avril 1775.

30 See *Journal des Dames,* novembre 1774, where subscribers are referred to the "Bureau du journal" in the editor's house.

31 Archives du Théâtre Français, dossier "Mme de Montanclos," letter dated 10 février 1783. I am indebted to Sylvie Chevalley, former archivist of the

Dames and whose close friend she remained always, that her secret of success in life had been the technique of "baring her teeth to men."[32] Familiarity with court ways had taught her how to curry favor, how to play the necessary games and secure connections, and she would now use these skills to relaunch the paper. But the fiery spirit of the new *journaliste des femmes* was never far below the surface.

The baronne de Prinzen's first issues of her *Journal des Dames* were almost entirely filled with her own writings. She seems to have stored up a fairly bursting literary portfolio without printing anything, waiting for the propitious moment to start up her paper. Journalistic privileges, as we saw, were given rarely and cautiously in these Maupeou years; not until late 1773, when police and booktrade attention was almost entirely absorbed by the Beaumarchais crisis, could the *Journal des Dames* have had a chance. Even then, it appeared only with the approval of a brand new censor, Jean Baptiste Artaud, who the baronne de Prinzen had reason to hope was a kindred spirit and would not be scared off by the journal's past.[33] Artaud had written a play that enjoyed some success at the Comédie-Française in 1773, and he had become a censor late that same year during a brief period as protégé of the duc de Duras, gentleman of the king's bedchamber, an intimate of Louis XV, and head of the Comédie's governing board.[34] The *Almanach royal* for 1774, which went to press in December 1773, listed Artaud as a new censor in belles lettres, but he disappeared from the roster in subsequent years, for he had by then left Paris to become editor of the *Courrier d'Avignon,* a paper published in the papal enclave outside direct French censorship and

---

Comédie-Française, for supplying me with additional information on Mme de Montanclos's relations with the actors, in particular their voting record on the plays she submitted.

32   BN ms. nouvelles acquisitions françaises (henceforth nouv. acq. fr.) 24030, fols. 87–88.

33   Artaud's signature appeared at the end of the *Journal des Dames* issues of early 1774. Although the paper still lacked a royal privilege, it now had a *permission de sceau* and, because of this upgrading, bore its censor's printed name for the first time since its founding in 1759. The baronne de Prinzen had first obtained a *permission tacite* (BN ms. fr. 21989, 3e registre, fol. 48), but the status of the paper was then enhanced to a *permission scellée* (BN ms. fr. 22013, 3e registre, no. 30).

34   Artaud is mentioned briefly in Grente, *Dictionnaire des lettres françaises,* 1:112. See also the chevalier de Mouhy, *Abrégé de l'histoire* 2:8.

known for its daring and contradiction of official executive policy.[35] Artaud lost favor with the duc de Duras almost immediately, for he could not hide his *frondeur* inclinations—in particular his preference for street theater, for the plebeian *spectacles de la foire*, over the royally protected Comédie. During the few months of early 1774 while he censored the *Journal des Dames*—and judging by the booktrade records he appears to have censored little else— he became a passionate fan of the drunk, destitute, but brilliantly talented boulevard actor and playwright Taconet. When Taconet died in December 1774, Artaud wrote an obituary in which he attacked as elitist the periodical *Nécrologe des hommes célèbres* for overlooking this "public loss." In terms almost identical to Mathon's earlier indictment of the *Nécrologe* published in his *Journal des Dames,* Artaud argued the importance of praising men who sacrificed their very lives for their art, in contrast to the ridiculousness of eulogizing those distinguished not by talent but only by the accident of high birth. Taconet, "disdained by high society" and "forgotten by the *Nécrologe,*" was nevertheless known and loved by "the people" whom he had amused and educated for years. Artaud denounced the aristocratic exclusivity of "les corps politiques de la littérature."[36] He approved a poem in one of the baronne de Prinzen's earliest issues of the *Journal des Dames* praising Audinot's joyful boulevard theater in contrast to the dull, stunted, antiquated Comédie.[37] He continued to write plays of his own, which Marie Antoinette enjoyed in her private *théâtre de société*. But the very month she became queen, Artaud gave up the censoring of the *Journal des Dames* and left for Avignon. Beginning in June 1774 a different censor's name appeared on the approbations. Perhaps Artaud feared that the once naughty dauphine would no longer be able to flirt with mischief now that she had the direct responsibility of statecraft.

The first order of business for the baronne de Prinzen was to secure the paper's safety. For months she was on her best behavior. Tactfully refusing to discuss the political reasons behind the *Journal des Dames*'s "successive revolutions," she said simply that she

35 See Moulinas, *Imprimerie, librairie, et presse,* and Censer and Popkin, *Press and Politics.*
36 [Artaud], *Taconet,* especially 11, 30, 42, 47, 51–52.
37 *Journal des Dames,* avril 1774:219.

meant it to be useful to "all classes of female citizens and to uphold their sex, without which the arts and sciences would still be in chaos."[38] She next proceeded to flatter and praise not only her protectress Marie Antoinette but her intimate circle, having spent enough time at court to understand the mechanisms of patronage and the importance of a network of connections. Her first issue of the new *Journal des Dames* therefore carried a purplish dedication to the dauphine, described as the "glory and example of her sex," "august," "wise," "kind," in whom "all the graces and virtues unite."[39] In this "hazardous career," wrote the new journalist, there was no chance of favorable results without the support of her beloved patroness. "To her name, so dear to France, I owe all my success."[40] The baronne de Prinzen also addressed a poem to the comtesse de Noailles, the dauphine's closest confidante—"in your heart she finds her sweetest shelter"—begging her to put in good words for the journal, to "play Maecenas to Antoinette . . . for without her continued approval I am nothing."[41] Another poem celebrated the marriage of the seventeen-year-old comte d'Artois, the dauphin's youngest brother and a close—some said too close—friend of the dauphine.[42] Fully aware of the powers of suggestion and eager to show under what influential auspices she printed, the baronne de Prinzen prematurely promoted Marie Antoinette to queen on the title page of her second issue, that of February 1774. The "mistake" was immediately rectified and switched back to dauphine in the issues of March and April; then in May, when Louis XV died, the *Journal des Dames* could legitimately read "dédié à la Reine."[43] In other ways, too, she faithfully pushed her protectress and her favorite causes, here raving about the controversial *Iphigenia* by Gluck, the dauphine's former Vi-

38 Ibid., janvier 1774:7–9.
39 Ibid., "Dédicace."
40 Ibid., 119.
41 Ibid., 106.
42 Ibid., 113.
43 See the title page of the February 1774 *Journal des Dames*, printed when Louis XV was still very much alive but referring to Marie Antoinette as "reine." The March and April issues again read "dauphine." The editor had done a similar trick when she printed in her prospectus a high price for the paper and then "lowered" it (to the 12 livres at which it had always sold) in an act of "charity" to show the bountifulness of the new dauphine. See the *Journal des Dames*, janvier 1774:"Avis" following 118.

ennese music master,[44] there praising Choiseul, still exiled in Chanteloup, whom Marie Antoinette fervently wished to restore to power, although her husband refused to consider it.[45]

But there were indications that the baronne de Prinzen found all this hustling at Versailles exhausting and soon even distasteful. Currying favor, although essential, took more energy than she had bargained for. There was something ridiculous, she seemed to think, in a middle-aged woman with small children courting idle royal teenagers. She printed a poem to a helpful babysitter, Mme Marchais, who took care of her *troupeau* of offspring at court so that she could be free for the dubious pastime of "romping" with those who "prefer pleasures and delights" to motherhood.[46] And sometimes her best intentions backfired, her most graceful overtures turned clumsy. One such incident involved the domain of art criticism, which we have already seen to be an explosive medium justifiably suspected of masking political dissidence. When she heaped praise on a portrait of Marie Antoinette by the artist de Lorge that everyone else found unflattering, the baronne de Prinzen was obliged to make a profuse public apology in the *Journal des Dames,* where it was explained that she had seen the picture at the Tuileries before it became smudged in transit to Versailles where everyone else saw it.[47]

All of this took its toll on the journalist. She was a quick-tempered, emotional woman who found criticism at once infuriating and shattering and who felt torn between her career and maternal obligations. Her sensitivity to this conflict, revealed in her private letters, could also be seen in every issue of her *Journal des Dames.* As the months went by she worried less about pleasing her protectress in order to solidify her own reputation and more about being of service to her female readers. The topic of motherhood, although a sensitive, even painful subject for the childless Marie Antoinette, nevertheless received increasing attention in the *Journal des Dames,* as did the idea that intellectually inclined women should be able to play a public role if they so chose. Once the dauphine became queen in May 1774, the journalist expected

---

44 Ibid., octobre 1774:223 and mars 1775:340–51.
45 Ibid., janvier 1775:80–81.
46 Ibid., février 1774:142.
47 Ibid., mars 1775:384–89.

her to take responsibility for social injustice and to help women reclaim their dignity. The same utopian desire to involve the queen in the feminist cause and use her sponsorship as a sign of female solidarity would motivate the Revolutionary Olympe de Gouges to dedicate her radical *Les Droits de la femme* to Marie Antoinette. The *Journal des Dames* attacked court frivolity, moral dissipation, and luxury more forcefully than ever. That the new queen was neither feminist, virtuous, nor maternal did not stop the baronne de Prinzen from calling on her to "reverse the *goût du siècle*" by making feminine modesty, seriousness, and fidelity fashionable and by restoring women's rights.[48] After the editor became Mme de Montanclos in the fall and moved to Paris, she made an even more pronounced break with prevailing court values. She was, she reminded her readers, no longer a baroness. Although the *Journal des Dames* continued to carry advertisements for cosmetics made by Maille, the *vinaigrier du roi,* for outrageous coiffures and bonnets designed by the fashionable Beaulard, and foldout pages of contredanses with music,[49] the paper was directed more and more to "mères de famille" who had turned from vain pastimes to serious parenting and had hence become solid *citoyennes.*[50]

Mme de Montanclos's feminism was more complex and nuanced than that of her two female predecessors, mostly because she so admired Rousseau's works on both the political and emotional levels. It seems paradoxical that an ambitious feminist could admire Rousseau, but Mme de Montanclos was as maternal as she was intellectual and therefore found herself open and responsive to messages in Rousseau that her predecessors had not heard. The *Nouvelle Héloïse* had just appeared when Mme de Beaumer was handing over the *Journal des Dames* to Mme de Maisonneuve in the early 1760s, and the impact of its idealization of motherhood had not yet been felt. The first two female editors thus predated the reign of domesticity and maternal tenderness. Moreover, they appear to have been childless—the first lived alone "au Temple" in a furnished room, the second mentioned no children in her will—and probably never wrestled with the problem of coordi-

---

48 Ibid., août 1774:246–47.
49 See, for example, *ibid.,* juin 1774:238; janvier 1775:135; mars 1775:393.
50 Ibid., mars 1774:36; décembre 1774:257; janvier 1775:151; février 1775:266; avril 1775:123, 128.

nating work and family, of reconciling personal and maternal ambitions. Both resented Rousseau's dim view of women's intellectual capacities and could not appreciate his arguments for their moral superiority, their unique role in forging bonds of affection and shaping character. But since then, for over a decade, Rousseau's ideas had been working a revolution in feminine psychology, and by the 1770s many women had come to see him as their champion rather than their foe. He made them feel socially useful. It was he who insisted on their special contribution of love and firm but gentle guidance to the moral regeneration of society and to public felicity. The "mère tendre" was of prime importance to the strength of the state, and motherhood gave women a strong claim on society. From breastfeeding through sensitive, relaxed, yet practical home education of their young, mothers not only cemented their families but provided the moral backbone of the *patrie*. They also passed on to future citizens attitudes toward authority and participation. Rousseau had of course argued the inequality of the sexes and denied women any public role, but he had greatly enhanced their status in the home, and his heroine Julie symbolized pride, the vision of the mother as spiritual reformer, a strong, virtuous individual.[51] Women, Rousseau stressed, must never try to be like men. They should nurture, civilize, and tame their mates and children as only the female sex could do, and they must believe this not only a useful function but one both dignified and essential. Rousseau thus validated a feminine power that men could not dispute. By emphasizing the distinction between male and female roles he denied sexual equality, but he encouraged women to take advantage of their influence in their own domain. Although not essentially innovative, Rousseau's writings gave mothers a renewed sense of social purpose. Through the home, the mother's empire, she made her invaluable civic contribution.[52]

51 See Bloch, "Women and the Reform of the Nation," and Jimack, "Paradox of Sophie and Julie." For two more discussions of motherhood, one general and the other specifically on Mme d'Epinay, see Badinter's *L'Amour en plus* and her *Emilie*.

52 For an interesting discussion of the form in which Rousseau's ideas permeated the literature of the 1760s and 1770s, see Williams (on Boudier), "Fate of French Feminism." A late edition of Boudier's work, his *Nouvel ami des femmes* (Paris, 1779), included a "notice alphabétique des femmes françaises qui se sont distinguées dans les lettres, ou autrement," in which Mme de Beaumer is listed without comment but the baronne de Prinzen's *Journal des Dames* is praised.

Mme de Montanclos's *Journal des Dames* was profoundly influenced by Rousseau. She appears to have been genuinely grateful for his boost to feminine confidence, even as she urged that confidence be expanded beyond the confines of the home. The editor, who had several small children, portrayed them as joyful, precious little beings with whom it was a pleasure, even a privilege to spend time.[53] She treated motherhood as a right that women had to reclaim and show themselves worthy of exercising. It was an awesome responsibility, but not a burden. Teaching children could even be a mutual delight. The educational theories of Fromageot and Fourcroy, both disciples of Rousseau, received extended coverage. Mothers were shown how to teach their sons and daughters themselves, at home, rather than turn them over to "mercenaries."[54] Because women, "nature's most cherished creation," could "join to the light of philosophy the warmth of feeling," they could mold their offspring with a unique blend of "wisdom, kindness, and patience."[55] Particular attention was given to the education of girls, as future mothers who would themselves need to carry on the tradition.

Mme de Montanclos, in her paper and other public statements, admitted no conflict between her own decision to pursue a career and her motherhood. She had chosen to do something entirely unconventional but never thought of abandoning her private life for her public job. Women should be able to do both, as she hoped to show by her own example. They were the natural guardians of the home, but that need not militate against their achievement of status as independent beings. Mme de Montanclos accepted Rousseau selectively and then went a step further, insisting that the "mère tendre" be also a "mère éclairée," that she be able to pursue her own interests and thus communicate to her children, especially her daughters, feelings of intrinsic worth and self-reliance. Her *Journal des Dames* held up the example of Laura Bassi, a determined bourgeoise who had earned a doctorate in physics at Bologna, and it expressed the hope that soon women everywhere would reach the summit of scholarly recognition, so that such an event would no longer be considered extraordinary.[56] She rejoiced

53 *Journal des Dames,* mars 1774:34.
54 Ibid., janvier 1774:165–75; mars 1774:34–36; janvier 1775:31.
55 Ibid., juin 1774:151; août 1774:115.
56 Ibid., mars 1775:381.

that "at last careers are open to both sexes."[57] Ultimately, however, women were to use their personal triumphs to enrich family interactions. Fanny de Beauharnais, whose lover Dorat would become the *Journal des Dames*'s last editor, contributed a feminist article called "A tous les penseurs, salut!" in which she argued that only educated, active, respected women could properly give of themselves and fulfill their roles as "wives, mothers, friends, daughters, and citizens."[58] The paper carried a long speech from a member of the Académie de Dijon, arguing that women were equally capable in science and mathematics and fighting the "unjust and destructive prejudice" that barred them from so-called virile achievements and kept them confined to the domestic sphere. If given educational opportunities and professional recognition outside the home, mothers could enlighten their children, provide examples of happiness, multiply the resources of society, and inspire patriotism, the surest guarantee of the prosperity of states.[59] Intelligent motherhood, then, was depicted as a boon, not a predicament. The *Manuel des époux* was recommended to all readers, there were stories and poems on the joys of fidelity and marriage, breastfeeding was advocated as the best guarantee for healthy, happy babies, and Charles White's *Avis aux femmes enceintes et en couches* was praised for treating childbirth as a natural, beautiful process rather than a malady and a misfortune.[60] This positive attitude toward the family expressed by female editors of the *Journal des Dames* stood in marked contrast to the unsentimental view of marriage and parental obligations held by the majority of male writers of the day.[61] It testifies to the strength of Rousseau's appeal to women, an appeal that feminists of the next generation like Mary Wollstonecraft would have to admit even as they combatted it.

Behind the scenes, however, things were not easy at all for Mme de Montanclos. Her correspondence and autobiographical stories show that she wrestled with the conflicting demands and

57 Ibid., janvier 1774:165–66.
58 Ibid., février 1774:177–89.
59 Ibid., juin 1774:127–53.
60 Ibid., mai 1774:47; juillet 1774:229; septembre 1774:7–10, 97; janvier 1775:31; mars 1775:401.
61 For a brief but very interesting discussion of male writers' matrimonial attitudes and patterns, see Darnton, "Police Inspector," 169–72.

divided loyalties of her public and private lives. Both her husbands seem to have disappointed her, for she chose to live and raise her girls alone. Her letters reveal an ambitious woman who drove herself hard, needed approval, and became ill when she lost her confidence. In a conflict with the Comédie-Française, which delayed giving her a verdict on a play she submitted, she wrote that "discouragement destroys the body as well as the mind." She wondered if her gentle, polite approach had invited the haughty *comédiens* to "victimize" her, to indulge in the "barbarous pleasure" of mistreating a woman. In a gesture of protest, of impulsive anger, she withdrew the play and threw back in the Comédie's face her special privilege of free tickets to all performances. This act would be regretted later, and when she was fifty-one years old she tried to reclaim her *entrées,* explaining that she had been so "weak from family troubles and the pains of maternity" that any obstacle thwarting her literary progress "turned my poor head." "Domestic embarrassments" combined with a "fear of cabals" led to bouts of insecurity that nearly paralyzed her. Looking back, she perceived her children as "distractions" and "emotional obstacles" to creativity, although her commitment to them had saved her ego. She genuinely loved them and enjoyed watching them develop. And they had been an excuse to hide behind. When they were grown she felt ambivalent, "sadly free, because my children have all left," but frightened at the prospect of empty time that only literary inspiration, if it came, could help her fill.[62]

There were professional as well as domestic conflicts. Mme de Montanclos had a number of faithful female contributors to the *Journal des Dames,* including the grandniece of Mme Dacier, and the marquise d'Antremont, both of whom were raising and educating their own children and enjoying the double privilege of intellectual activity and motherhood, of being "femme vraiment femme, dans toute la force du terme."[63] But there were other women who turned hostile to the journalist, feeling she was too

---

62   Archives du Théâtre Français, dossier "Mme de Montanclos." See especially letters dated 3 juillet 1782, 21 février 1783, 21 mars 1783, 15 avril 1787, 9 juillet 1787.

63   This was how the marquise d'Antremont described herself earlier in Mathon's *Journal des Dames,* avril 1768:1–4. She and "Mme d'H—, petite nièce de Mme Dacier," contributed articles and reviews to Mme de Montanclos's issues of late 1774 and early 1775.

critical, too demanding and hard on her sex. Mme de Montanclos called a spade a spade. She refused to give special dispensation to works by female authors unless they served some purpose or had some artistic merit. She strongly objected to the *Parnasse des dames,* an anthology of works by women from all periods and all nations, for it seemed to do more harm than good by resurrecting deservedly forgotten writings, adding fuel to the fire of women's detractors by "pulling from oblivion names that should have died there."[64] Her failure to defend women writers deeply wounded one Mme de Laisse, whose works Mme de Montanclos criticized in the *Journal des Dames.* The offended author wrote angry, sarcastic letters to the *Mercure* calling herself a "feeble mortal" and the journalist a "wise divinity," impeccably tasteful and "universally recognized for her fairness."[65] Although surely upset by these attacks, Mme de Montanclos was determined to spare the public the embarrassment of an ugly dispute between two women and did not strike back.[66] She would maintain her professional dignity at all costs.

Although she did not discuss political matters directly in these early issues of her *Journal des Dames,* Mme de Montanclos's rhetoric grew increasingly legalistic after Louis XVI and Marie Antoinette ascended the throne and became France's new hope in May 1774. In a bid for popularity the young king demolished the detested triumvirate. By June d'Aiguillon was out, by August Maupeou and Terray were dismissed, and the nationwide clamor for the return of the exiled parlements led to their recall by November. The *patriotes* rejoiced that law had been restored to the land, and the *Journal des Dames* reflected the juridical flavor of these months, demanding justice for the oppressed sex, featuring the work of several lawyers, and insisting that the cause of women needed legal definition and protection. Warming more and more to the role of spokeswoman, Mme de Montanclos wrote to the lawyer Jacques Vincent Delacroix claiming that she had proprietary rights to any writings by women appearing in the press. When the *Mercure* published a poem by a Mme de Courcy, the editor of the *Journal des Dames* immediately reprinted it in her own

64 *Journal des Dames,* octobre 1774:146–55.
65 *Mercure de France,* août 1774:180–85 and février 1775:152–55.
66 *Journal des Dames,* février 1775:241.

paper and felt vindicated that she had "insisted on justice being done" when these verses won a prize from the Académie de Rouen.[67] Just weeks after Maupeou's fall, and obviously encouraged by it, Mme de Montanclos called on women of all social ranks to rebel against the "tyrannical laws of silence" that had historically kept them "apathetic, tame, and mute." Her *Journal des Dames* was furthering women's advancement, and she applauded judicial *mémoires* that tried to do the same. She had high praise for one such *mémoire* by Delacroix endorsing the values of simple peasants and defending the crowning of virtuous girls from the lower classes at the ceremony of the Rosière de Salency.[68] In November, the very month the parlements were recalled amid wild rejoicing, the *Journal des Dames*'s editor printed a special letter to her readers defending "the glory of a sex nearly always undervalued" and insisting that women be justly treated from now on. "The particular purpose of this journal is to make known the virtues, intellect, and talent of the sex to which it is consecrated. It is not I who wish to shine, but I swear I want to shatter our conventions and guarantee women the justice that men refuse them as if on whim. . . . We can know everything, for our minds are flexible and thirsty, and we can do all the good of which humanity is capable."[69] All along Mme de Montanclos had linked motherhood and patriotism. The recurring image of children as "Cornelia's jewels" recalled the Roman mother of the Gracchi brothers, republican heroes. Cornelia, who despite poverty had considered herself the richest, happiest woman alive because of her fine sons, now became a feminist symbol for ambitious women.[70] And with renewed vigor, the *Journal des Dames* argued that women, for all their services to the state, deserved the protection of the law.

Mme de Montanclos's interest in the *avocat* Delacroix indicated

67   Ibid., juillet 1774:88–89; janvier 1775:32.
68   Ibid., août 1774:241–47.
69   Ibid., novembre 1774:8–9.
70   See, for example, ibid., mars 1774:34. Cornelia was also a favorite heroine of Mlle Barbier, another female journalist and playwright who wrote: "L'action de cette incomparable Romaine est si glorieuse à notre sexe que je me sentis portée d'inclination à la mettre dans le plus beau jour qu'il me serait possible" (see Chevalley, "Femmes auteurs-dramatiques," 46). For a general discussion of the resonance of republican imagery, see Parker, *The Cult of Antiquity*.

that her political tastes were becoming more daring even before she linked up with Mercier. She had at first taken on one obscure M. Rocher as a "coadjuteur littéraire" to help her with translations. Rocher was an acquaintance from her earlier life at court, an intimate of the comtesse de Bussi, who turned out to be a social conservative and a literary reactionary, waxing ecstatic over Homer but rejecting "le bel esprit moderne." In a profession of faith to the *Journal des Dames,* he declared himself on the side of the ancients against the moderns, wrote reviews belittling women's intellectual capacities, and soon lost favor with the editor.[71] Delacroix, on the other hand, a future Jacobin, was a parlementaire, a friend of Mercier, an American sympathizer, a translator of John Adams, and an admirer of "public opinion" who had attempted a periodical of his own during the Maupeou years. Six volumes of his *Spectateur français* appeared between 1772 and 1773 before being suffocated by the triumvirate, one of the many press victims referred to earlier. Delacroix had inserted among articles on mores, history, and fashion, others that were distinctly *frondeur,* in which he argued that the law must equalize conditions and protect the oppressed by providing public defenders so that "the weak will no longer be abused, because they will cease to appear weak." He praised the "économistes" and the exiled Choiseul. His call for a new tribunal that would be "pure" and "fair" was an indictment of Maupeou's parlement, as was his plea that cases be opened up to "the public, which has the right to judge magistrates, ministers, and kings." Soon Delacroix's paper was threatened and its subject matter circumscribed, but a paper devoid of serious content dismayed the "graves politiques" among his subscribers, and it also violated his own principles of what journalism should be. Invoking the example of the liberty of the press in

71 Rocher, who is not mentioned in any biographical sources, first appeared in the *Journal des Dames,* mai 1774:126. He contributed to the issues of July and August (see his antifeminist piece in July, p. 77), lamented the strains of his job in September (pp. 76–81), and had been dismissed by Mme de Montanclos by November (pp. 7–8). It was repeated in February 1775 (p. 201) that he no longer had any involvement with the paper. Rocher published five poems in the *Almanach des muses* between 1772 and 1775, long after Mathon had left the publication. One M. Rocher was awarded a *terrain* in Montreuil for his good services as *garde des plaisirs du roi* (Archives Nationales 0¹114 [768]) but because no first names appear in the *Journal des Dames,* we cannot be certain that it was the same individual.

England and bemoaning the fact that the English *Spectator* had been able to speak freely while he in France could say nothing of his government's faults or duties, he refused to "pay servile court to *les grands*." He left the corrupt ministers to their flatterers, saying they were unworthy of his truthfulness, but the stranglehold on the press made him fear for his *patrie:* "I do not know if it is possible for humanity to survive much longer in this state of degradation."[72]

In his own paper, which Delacroix intended for a socially broad audience, he had devoted considerable space to women whom he thought had great influence over "general opinion." Although he believed they could benefit from protective legislation, he felt that they had already made enormous progress in society and that they had a right to a fulfilling life outside the home.[73] Mme de Montanclos saw Delacroix as an ally, but she nevertheless admonished him for falling into the old habit of referring to women as hummingbirds and men as eagles, to which he protested that he meant the word as a compliment, for hummingbirds were the richest, most varied birds in nature. He genuinely admired the female editor's gumption in reviving the worthwhile *Journal des Dames*. His own less happy journalistic experience had taught him that such success required impeccable timing, the proper connections, and perseverance tempered by restraint, and indeed Mme de Montanclos had so far steered clear of major controversy in order to set her once moribund paper back on its feet. Delacroix's own silenced *Spectateur français,* he told her now, "could benefit from one of [her] miracles of resurrection."[74]

The critical reception of the relaunched *Journal des Dames* was mixed. Grimm, in an unusual act of mercy, mentioned its reappearance without comment, reserving judgment perhaps because

---

72 Jacques Vincent Delacroix's *Spectateur français,* now lost, can only be consulted in the form of excerpts that the editor reprinted years later. The quotations in this paragraph come from two such abridged versions of the *Spectateur:* Delacroix, *Peintures des moeurs* 1:97, 103, and 2:3–4, 41–43, 92, 209, 254, 322–330 (a blatantly *frondeur* "Discours sur les Mémoires"), 357–60; and Delacroix, *Le Spectateur français avant la Révolution* iv, 209, 481.

73 For his views on women, see Delacroix, *Peintures des moeurs* 1:89–93, 305–11 ("Sur la révolution arrivée dans l'existence des femmes"); and 2:85–87, 357–58.

74 *Journal des Dames,* juillet 1774:89–90.

the paper was now dedicated to Marie Antoinette.[75] The *Mercure,* now in the hands of La Harpe, whom Mathon had previously lambasted, stressed that the *Journal des Dames* should stay off politics, avoid all contestation and fulfill its title by concentrating on the unique characteristics of women, their "sentiment vif et délicat." Such a paper would be amusing and harmless. La Harpe, doubtless impressed that a member of the royal family had taken an interest in the new *journaliste des femmes,* found a prudent way to simultaneously restrict and flatter her by urging her to pay particular attention to female artists, since if even the Académie royale de peinture had acknowledged their talents, art must be considered a safe outlet for women's restless energy.[76] The *Journal de Verdun,* now written by H. P. Ameilhon, a secret supporter of *frondeur* causes who would soon help Mercier in many ways, was delighted that the *Journal des Dames* was "resuscitated." He had feared that its various silencings under Mme de Beaumer and Mathon, "its series of plummeting falls, had been fatal." "We must hope," he wrote of the baronne de Prinzen, "that this *savante* will finally ensure the future of this periodical."[77] Querlon, former collaborator on Mathon's *Journal des Dames* and future supporter of Mercier, also celebrated the reappearance of the paper in his *Affiches de province.* Querlon had followed carefully the political ups and downs of the *Journal des Dames.* He knew that Mme de Beaumer had meant to keep it a long time, regretted that she had not, but admired Mme de Maisonneuve's courage in placing it in Mathon's "good hands."[78] He supported its anti-establishment tendencies, although he was not free to say so outright, since his own paper, mailed with the official *Gazette,* had to maintain a conservative tone. He would become uncharacteristically bold and outspoken in his support for Mercier during the next years. For now, he welcomed the return of the *Journal des Dames* but referred only elliptically to the fact that it was much more than its title implied and would need to be delicately navigated. The baronne de Prin-

75   Grimm et al., *Correspondance littéraire* 10:373–74 (février 1774).

76   The *Mercure* review was reprinted in the *Esprit des journaux* 10, part 1, p. 42. Two women had been accepted to the Académie de peinture in 1770 but with severely restricted status. See Harris and Nochlin, *Women Artists,* 34–45.

77   *Journal (historique) de Verdun,* février 1774:132.

78   *Affiches de province,* 1764:146 and 1766:194.

zen was "a sufficiently intelligent woman to support such a work; her natural spirit will furnish her all the necessary resources."[79]

Other reviews were more peevish, but for different reasons. The *Mémoires secrets,* now written by Pidansat, seemed impatient that the *Journal des Dames* was not stating its *frondeur* position more clearly. Pidansat, perhaps distressed that the baronne de Prinzen took nearly ten months before allowing Mercier to insinuate himself into her pages, did not give her paper a positive press. He could not have known that she was making a Herculean effort by simply resisting Marie Antoinette's wish to turn the paper into a fashion magazine.[80] He mistakenly believed that the royalist Du Rozoi was influencing the new editor and was again betraying the paper, as he had done under Mme de Beaumer. In March, puzzled by the absence of parlementaire leanings in the *Journal des Dames* and evidently unable to understand that the baronne de Prinzen was merely biding her time until the paper's foundation could be secured, Pidansat announced that Du Rozoi must be collaborating, and a few months later he published an epigram wittily attacking the insipidity of the new paper.[81] The radical Le Fuel de Méricourt, close friend of Pidansat and Mercier, whose *Journal des théâtres* would scandalize high society and mobilize the police in 1776, was equally impatient with the initial timidity of the *Journal des Dames* and restless for Mercier to take over.[82] Both knew Mercier's accession to editorial duties at the paper was inevitable, but they would need to wait another few months to be satisfied. Mme Du Deffand, on the other hand, found the baronne de Prinzen plenty controversial and disliked her paper on the spot. Once the prophetess of enlightened Europe, the old lady was now blind and

---

79   Ibid., 1774:31.

80   For the dauphine's unrealized desire to address fashion in the *Journal des Dames,* see Kleinert, *Die frühen Modejournale,* 61 n. 57. For more on the influence of the royal couturière Rose Bertin, see Bernier, *Eighteenth-Century Woman,* 117–22.

81   *Mémoires secrets* 7:159 (13 mars 1774); 256 (1 novembre 1774). The editor of the *Journal des Dames* had offended the young poet Gilbert by not paying rapt attention during his poetry reading. He quipped:

> Ah Prinzen! par pitié, daignez du moins m'entendre,
> Oui, mes vers sont d'un froid et d'un lourd sans égal;
> Mais, le mal que je fais, vous pouvez me le rendre:
> Faites-moi quelque jour lire votre journal.

82   *Lettres de Mme Le Hoc,* 17–23, 63n., 195, 221–22n.

had soured on most "causes." She appeared to resent women who knew how to organize their time and ambition, for she herself felt frightened and dependent. Her hatred for Julie de Lespinasse had turned her against *Encyclopédistes* and "économistes." Her correspondence with Walpole during the mid-1770s shows that she loathed Turgot, mistrusted Beaumarchais, and did not even care much for Malesherbes, the hero of the exiled parlements. Even though she lost no love for Maupeou, she was mesmerized by his tireless devotion to his task, telling Walpole he would "die sooner than yawn; he is not a man but a demon." Thus when Mme Du Deffand found a poem dedicated to her in the *Journal des Dames* she protested loudly, both in the paper itself and in her private letters where she declared her "aversion" to this "feuille nouvelle."[83]

Although Mercier published a poem in Mme de Montanclos's *Journal des Dames* in May 1774, he only began to be featured centrally in the fall, after the editor left Versailles and took up residence in Paris near the place Maubert on the rue des Bernardins, a few short blocks from Mercier's home on rue des Noyers, facing the rue des Anglais.[84] This *quartier,* called Saint Benoît, was the "Latin Quarter," and although neither fashionable nor luxurious, it was one of the oldest and most interesting in the capital. The *Dictionnaire historique de la ville de Paris* for 1779 described its unique atmosphere of hustle and bustle combined with intellectual tradition. "This neighborhood, which is extremely populated, is principally that of book binders, book gilders, cardboardmakers, and manufacturers of gilded, marbled, and plain sheet paper. It is also [the neighborhood] of the sciences, of the colleges, of pensions for those enrolled in the university, parchment merchants, printers, engravers, *libraires,* geographers. printmakers, illustrators, illuminators [of manuscripts], and finally numerous capable artists."[85] The nearby rue du Fouarre, where the *Journal des Dames*'s printer Quillau had his workshop, had taken its name in the fourteenth century from the mats of straw on which students

83 *Journal des Dames,* février 1774:191–94, and Du Deffand, *Correspondance* 2:393.
84 These addresses can be found respectively in the *Journal des Dames,* novembre 1774 and mai 1775.
85 Hurtaut and Magny, *Dictionnaire historique* 4:195.

sat perched listening to the professors, the great scholastics, dispense wisdom. Rents here were modest; one chose this area for good, lively intellectual company, not prestige. As neighbors, Mme de Montanclos and Mercier became well acquainted after October 1774 and probably began the regular socializing that was still going on in 1789 when both had moved west a bit but were still on the Left Bank and still just a block apart, Mercier now on the rue de Seine and Mme de Montanclos on the parallel rue Mazarine.[86]

Month after month, as the political climate lightened, Mercier's works and causes received an increasingly positive press in the *Journal des Dames*. In October his play *Childeric* was praised, albeit judiciously, by the grandniece of Mme Dacier, who appreciated bourgeois *drames* and shared Mercier's love for English theater. The reviewer helped the playwright by diplomatically pointing out flattering parallels between his heroine Bazine and "our august queen Marie Antoinette," but she also underlined and endorsed his parlementaire sympathies, his hatred of despotism, his insistence that citizens have protection under the law and that the tribunals of the nation be reestablished, as rumor had it the parlements were about to be. Mercier had King Childeric say—and the quotation was repeated in the *Journal des Dames*—that "I will respect the liberty of the *patrie*. . . . [I pledge] to be the vigilant eye of the laws, to be the first to submit myself to their inviolable authority." The reviewer ended in admiration of Childeric, a king sufficiently secure not to fear admitting his faults to his assembly.[87] In December, after the parlements had been recalled, the same reviewer defended Mercier's *drames* against the criticisms of Dorat, especially his anti-war play *Le Déserteur,* which showed the inhumanity of the death sentence for runaway soldiers and was so blatantly republican that the *Journal encyclopédique* had suggested it be called *le Brutus français.*[88]

By Mme de Montanclos's second year with the *Journal des*

86 See the affectionate letter from Mme de Montanclos to Mercier about one of their frequent dinner engagements in 1789, BN ms. nouv. acq. fr. 24030, fols. 87–88.

87 *Journal des Dames,* octobre 1774:196–216.

88 Ibid., décembre 1774:230–31. See the collected reviews of *Le Déserteur* in the *Bibliographie parisienne,* 1770:87. For a discussion of Mercier's chosen subject, see Hytier, "The Decline of Military Values."

Dames, Mercier's influence could be seen everywhere. In February 1775 there was an article attacking carriages in Paris, one of Mercier's pet peeves that would appear repeatedly in his *Tableau de Paris.* These carriages, which caused filth and accidents and "infernal noise," should either be burned or taxed to benefit the poor. In a century the number of carriages careening through the crowded capital had multiplied from one hundred to fourteen hundred. They interfered with walking, thinking, working, even sleeping, and each had its insolent but useless lackey, its "dandified do-nothing" who should be cultivating rather than cluttering and encumbering the earth. Mme de Montanclos's response to this letter was that carriages were justified only if they carried mothers with small children, virtuous hardworking magistrates busy up to the last minute protecting the nation and therefore in a hurry, charitable doctors rushing to treat the poor for free, or rich widows about to give their fortune for the benefit of mankind.[89] The March 1775 issue of the *Journal des Dames* carried a passionate rave of Mercier's *Jean Hennuyer,* a play that the police had explicitly forbidden about the atrocities of the Saint Bartholomew's Day massacre of Protestants and the courage of one man who stood up against Charles IX to defend the oppressed. Readers of the journal, the reviewer cautioned, might find this criticism of society's abuses very harsh medicine, but Mercier's *drame* was one of the greatest pieces of literature in the fight against religious prejudice and fanaticism, a fight from which women should no longer shy away.[90]

The increasing boldness of Mme de Montanclos's *Journal des Dames* was made possible by her new censor, Vaquette d'Hermilly, who had taken over when the already permissive Artaud had left to work on the *Courrier d'Avignon.* Hermilly, a translator with literary ambitions of his own, came from the old military nobility as Louptière had, but he seems to have had a soft spot for unorthodox, daring writers. He had been Mathon's censor for the *Almanach des muses* in the 1760s with all its cross-references to the *Journal des Dames.*[91] A well-traveled man who had spent years in

89 *Journal des Dames,* février 1775:163–67.

90 Ibid., mars 1775:315–23.

91 The *Almanach des muses* always plugged the *Journal des Dames,* and in so doing endorsed its views and referred readers to them (for example, *Almanach,* 1765:157; 1767:159). Hermilly continued to censor Mathon's works throughout

Spain, Hermilly liked to think of himself as worldly and daring. Restif, who did not respect but humored old Hermilly, made note of the fact that he could always be bribed to approve manuscripts sent to him for judgment, that even if he found them shocking his perfunctory stamp could be bought for the proper sum.[92] That Mercier needed to keep Hermilly happy is evident; although we do not know how much money passed under the table, the *Journal des Dames* heaped praise on his translations, which were in fact so poor that Restif had needed to redo them entirely, but the review of course left out that particular detail.[93] Hermilly, whose approbation appeared on the issues between June 1774 and December 1775, changed the wording of his endorsement of the paper, making it more enthusiastic as time went on. At first, under Mme de Montanclos, he "found nothing to prevent its printing." When Mercier began to infiltrate the copy six months later, he deemed the paper "worthy." And when Mercier became its editor, Hermilly went so far as to say it was "more deserving than ever of being printed."[94] He seemed thus to be giving it more than a superficial glance. Now in his late sixties, Hermilly had been a censor for decades and seems to have appreciated the writings of anyone who would relieve his boredom, but for Mercier he had a special weakness. As editor of his own short-lived periodical, the *Bibliographie parisienne,* Hermilly had even dared to praise the writings of Mercier during the Maupeou years when they were being hunted and silenced. Hermilly also applauded the controversial writings of Linguet, who, like Mercier, wrote from the heart with "energy," "warmth," "force," and "vehemence" and used words not merely to inform but to "sway," "challenge," and "purge."[95] For Hermilly the increasingly *frondeur Journal des Dames* seems to have become more appealing with each issue.

---

the 1770s. See BN ms. fr. 22002, "Registre des privilèges et permissions simples depuis 1774," for example, p. 1, no. 3. Later he was assisted by Pidansat de Mairobert (see Chapter 6, below).

92 Restif de la Bretonne, *Monsieur Nicolas* 5:2821–22. See also Rives-Childs, *Restif de la Bretonne,* 229 and 224.

93 *Journal des Dames,* novembre 1775:148–52.

94 See Hermilly's approbations in the *Journal des Dames,* juin, août, octobre, décembre 1774 and janvier, mars, juin, septembre, décembre 1775, on the last page of these issues.

95 See the *Bibliographie parisienne* for 1769 (Paris, 1774), 27, 85, 88. For confirmation that Hermilly was the author of this periodical, see BN ms. fr. 8132, p. 8.

Mme de Montanclos, deeply involved by 1775 with additional family responsibilities resulting from her new marriage and apparently satisfied with her job of relaunching the paper, was now ready to turn it over completely to Mercier for his polemics in behalf of worthy causes. She had made enough of a stir, she believed, to have left a mark upon the public and to be remembered when she found the time and energy to stage a comeback. She even paved the way in her last issue for her return to the literary scene by promising her readers that they would hear more from her in the future, that she planned to be a *femme de lettres* all her life, that she was simply taking time out for mothering; journalistic duties had tired her and sapped her strength. Meanwhile she was turning the paper over to someone whose "energy" and "force" would give it unprecedented importance.[96] Mme de Montanclos boasted that she had prevented the paper from deteriorating into a frothy triviality and had acquired a faithful and ever-growing readership, that the number of subscribers continued to climb, and that more material was being contributed each month than could possibly be accommodated.[97] Reassured that her *Journal des Dames* had grown from shaky beginnings into a solid enterprise with a substantial following—it was now published by Lacombe, the undisputed press baron of the 1770s, who also handled the *Journal des savants, Journal encyclopédique, Mercure de France, Année littéraire,* and about ten other periodicals—Mme de Montanclos felt she had a valuable literary property to turn over to Mercier. Her paper could serve him as a mouthpiece. She could guarantee him readers. The problem was that in the eyes of the police Mercier was a marked man. They would never have approved his official takeover of the *Journal des Dames*. It would have to be negotiated privately, therefore. But first, the paper would need to be placed on a still more secure footing, so that silencing it later would be difficult and so that it could no longer be suspended for hidden reasons as it had been under Mme de Beaumer. For this purpose, Mme de Montanclos contrived to get a royal privilege for her journal, which had existed for fifteen years without one.

96 *Journal des Dames,* avril 1775:139.
97 Ibid., novembre 1774:8 and février 1775:258.

Saying nothing of her plans to sell the rights for the paper, Mme de Montanclos applied for a privilege to the new *garde des sceaux,* Miromesnil, and the new chancellor, Maurepas, and was awarded it by *brevet* from the new king, Louis XVI, her protectress's husband, on 22 March 1775.[98] For the first time the *Journal des Dames* had complete legal protection against unscrupulous counterfeiters. More important, it could be stopped now only by an official government suppression and was no longer subject to arbitrary suspensions that censors were not obliged to explain. Mme de Montanclos proudly entered her *Journal des Dames*'s new status with the booktrade guild on 29 March. Next, suspecting that her new husband, who had been unable to keep pace with her in the capital and had retreated to Troyes, would not approve her plan to let Mercier succeed her, she extracted from him a fascinating document. Although legally separated "with regard to property," he was still her spouse and would normally have had the final word on any business transactions in which she was involved. But she made him sign a statement in the presence of two notaries in Troyes and two more in Paris, permitting her to negotiate her literary property herself, to handle alone all financial affairs regarding her paper. From what we know of Mme de Montanclos's independent spirit, this document may well have been the result of an ultimatum, a precondition for any further relationship between her and her husband. In response to her insistence on this carte blanche, he had "declared . . . and irrevocably authorized Dame Marie Mayon, his wife . . . to give and hand over to whatever person she chooses, for whatever price, terms, and conditions she judges appropriate, the privilege of the *Journal des Dames*. . . . She may receive the payment, give receipts, contract whatever obligations, sign and witness whatever acts are necessary, and generally do whatever she deems correct, fair, and fitting."[99]

This enumeration of rights exceptionally granted by her husband to Mme de Montanclos shows precisely what married

98   See BN ms. fr. 21966, pp. 390–91, entry no. 559, for the full text of Mme de Montanclos's privilege and all the protections it afforded the *Journal des Dames*. See also BN ms. fr. 8132, p. 35, showing that her privilege was granted for five years, to expire on 22 March 1781.

99   M.C. LXXXV, (652), 19 avril 1775. The documents dated 11 April and signed in Troyes are attached.

women were normally *not* allowed to do. One of the foremost *jurisconsultes* of the day, Robert-Joseph Pothiers, had recently summed up their legal nonexistence in his *Traité de la puissance du mari sur la personne et les biens de la femme.*[100] Mme de Montanclos had earlier boasted that being a woman gave her a kind of freedom, for since the existing law neither acknowledged nor protected her, she was free to defy conventions.[101] Brandishing now her signed release from bondage, which flew in the face of all custom and law, Mme de Montanclos knew she had no time to lose. Having secured the notarized documents in Troyes on 11 April, she had them countersigned in Paris by her own notary, Vergne, and then in a private meeting, sold the *Journal des Dames* to Mercier on 19 April.[102]

She sold it for a song, motivated by a sense of political kinship already demonstrated by over a year of editorial support for Mercier, with no thought of making a profit. By now she had become such a staunch supporter of Mercier's that bequeathing him her paper seemed an honor. It was "henceforth his to use as he saw fit." She asked only a pittance from this man who devoted all his time, as she perceived it, to fighting for worthy causes, to shaping a better future for mankind.[103] This was no doubt a reference to his utopian and highly subversive *L'An 2440,* another of Mercier's forbidden books and police targets, about which more will be said in the next chapter. Mme de Montanclos virtually gave Mercier the *Journal des Dames,* asking only 1,500 livres, half of what Mme de Maisonneuve had paid Mme de Beaumer twelve years earlier, when the journal was in a sorry state and had no royal privilege, and only one-eighth of what Mathon had paid when buying it from Mme de Maisonneuve. Mercier gave her 900 livres and his *libraire* was to give her 100 livres of annual rente for the next six years. Mme de Montanclos had already collected 300 livres from Lacombe, her profit from the first hundred subscriptions, but all the other money that had been paid by subscribers since January

---

100 Pothiers, *Traité de la communauté.* See also his earlier *Traité des obligations* and *Traité du contrat de mariage.*

101 See, for example, *Journal des Dames,* novembre 1774.

102 M.C. LXXXV (652), 19 avril 1775, "Cession de privilège de Mme de Montanclos à M. Mercier."

103 BN ms. nouv. acq. fr. 24030, fols. 87–88.

1775 (the figure was not mentioned) was now Mercier's to claim as his own. He, anonymously, would assume full responsibility for the *Journal des Dames* as of May 1775. Meanwhile Mme de Montanclos promised to pay all expenses for the April issue currently in preparation, the last to bear her name but already marked by her successor's determination to tackle the problems of the day head on.[104]

This issue of April 1775, a joint production, contained Mme de Montanclos's last plea for loving and responsible motherhood, "for I like to think that most women these days are devoting themselves to the formation of the hearts and minds of their children."[105] Advertisements continued for dentists, lessons, free books, and whatever might help "mères de familles," and women were upheld as the artisans of family happiness and the educators of future citizens.[106] But the familiar poems and stories about maternal tenderness and the beauties of nature were now heavily message-laden, set against the background of the grain famine, about which Mercier was profoundly concerned. In one poem, a farmer's wife, with babe at her breast, was starving because her crops did not suffice to cover taxes. Turgot, the new finance minister, was lauded for giving 100,000 ecus to ease starvation in Limousin and for going personally to comfort the peasants. A letter allegedly from "the working women of the parish of Noissy near Versailles, to the queen" begged the monarchs to buy for their wardrobe only French wool and feathers to strengthen the economy and bring down the price of wheat. There was also a plea for the elimination of the hated corvée.[107]

The *Journal des Dames* had certainly come a long way from the "rien délicieux," the amusing toilette ornament, that Campigneulles had meant it to be. Mme de Montanclos, like her two female predecessors, had come to see that the problem of women's subordination was one of many social injustices and that none of them would be solved without widespread political reform.[108] For

---

104   M.C. LXXXV (652), 19 avril 1775.
105   *Journal des Dames,* avril 1775:23.
106   Ibid., 123–24.
107   Ibid., 85, 34, 37, 10–12.
108   For comments on the interrelatedness of feminism and broader social issues, see Williams, "Politics of Feminism."

that reason, all three of them supported the efforts of male *fron-deurs* in the pages of their paper and outside as well. Mme de Montanclos's journalistic experience and her friendship with Mercier reinforced her natural tendency to fight for rights and take the underdog's side in contestations. When, in 1776, Mercier's friend Le Tourneur was attacked by Voltaire and the Académie française for the "treasonous act" of translating the complete works of Shakespeare, Mme de Montanclos signed her name beside Mercier's on a list of Le Tourneur's supporters and subscribers, a gesture of protest against the elite establishment.[109] She fought fervently for fair treatment at the Comédie-Française in the 1780s when she felt the actors did not give her plays a chance, and she came to know the revolutionary Olympe de Gouges, who was suffering similar indignities at the hands of the *comédiens* and even the *comédiennes*. While de Gouges berated the female actors who she felt should demonstrate solidarity with female playwrights,[110] Mme de Montanclos attacked the men in power for their illegal procedures. "If there is a way, messieurs, to enforce my rights and see that justice is done toward me, I will find it. If you have the right to sacrifice authors to your despotic whims you must show me legal proof."[111] Her poems, printed for the next many decades in the *Journal de musique, Journal encyclopédique, Courrier de l'Europe,* and *Almanach des muses,* often starred plucky, transparently autobiographical heroines, like the plain widow who turned down a wealthy suitor because he refused her terms for an egalitarian marriage.[112] Other poems defended the Jews, the poor, and the elderly. Mme de Montanclos may have belonged to one of the female Masonic lodges that proliferated in the late 1770s and that often had parlementaire leanings. Her letters reveal that she gave frequent readings to groups composed exclusively of women; her *Journal des Dames* had preached the same virtues—fidelity, discretion, trustworthiness, charity—to which feminine Masonry was committed; and the *Journal de musique,* to which both she and

109   Le Tourneur, *Shakespeare traduit de l'anglais* 1:list of subscribers. The importance of this publication for *frondeur* politics will be discussed in Chapter 6, below.

110   See Chevalley, "Femmes auteurs-dramatiques," 44–45.

111   Archives du Théâtre Français, dossier "Mme de Montanclos," letter dated 21 février 1783.

112   See, for example, *Almanach des muses,* 1806:120.

Mathon contributed in 1777, was heavily Masonic.[113] She continued as a contributor to the *Correspondance des dames* and the *Petit Magasin des dames,* and she may have been the anonymous Mme de M. who invited women to send examples of male injustice to the *Etrennes nationales des dames,* protesting in a series of articles that appeared between 1789 and 1791 that husbands still acted like aristocrats toward their doubly oppressed wives, that men, now free, continued to treat women as a Third Estate.[114] Her plays, although panned by the mordant antifeminist Rivarol, were performed and favorably reviewed in the *Tribunal d'Apollon.* The feminist journalist Clément-Hémery thought Mme de Montanclos's literary and professional accomplishments sufficiently impressive to list her as one of the great women writers of all time, alongside Mme de Staël, Mme de Sévigné, and Mme de La Fayette.[115]

Mme de Montanclos would not have been pleased with her obituary in the *Journal des arts,* which flattered her but treated her intellectual efforts as an unfortunate deviation from the accepted feminine social course. "Author of many agreeable works, Mme de Montanclos was very beautiful. Her cast of mind was ingenious but also gentle, and although a *femme de lettres,* she managed nevertheless to be well liked."[116] It would have upset her far more, however, to know that a century later the attitude toward female journalists was still equally inhospitable. "If the advantages of modern progress are contestable on many points," wrote the author of a short sketch on the "bluestocking" Mme de Montanclos in 1913, "they are nevertheless evident in the press, where [progress] has rid us, or almost, of female journalists."[117] This was the

113   See Chevallier, *Histoire de la franc-maçonnerie* 1:200–206, especially 201. There was much overlap of theme and vocabulary. The *Journal des Dames,* mars 1775:402–3, advertised both Mathon's *Journal de musique* and his *Almanach musical.* The Rosière de Salency, a celebration of innocence and simple virtues that received much attention in the *Journal des Dames,* was also the model for female Masonry. The paper was often referred to as a "temple" (septembre 1774:112 and novembre 1774:12) and Mme de Montanclos as Minerva.

114   See Sullerot, *Histoire de la presse,* 49. See also Caroline Rimbault's notice, "Dufrenoy," in Chouillet and Moureau, *Suppléments* 2:73.

115   Rivarol, *Petit Almanach,* s.v. "Montanclos." For a more favorable view, see Clément-Hémery, *Femmes vengées,* 33.

116   Marquiset, *Bas-Bleus du Premier Empire,* 105.

117   Ibid., 93.

typical gynephobic male reaction to such militantly feminist papers as *La Fronde,* a direct descendant of the *Journal des Dames* that lasted six troubled years from 1897 to 1903 and was produced entirely by women. Even the most sympathetic male reactions to such papers were paternalistic and patronizing, marveling at the perseverance of women in a more properly "virile" profession and at their ability to produce a paper "that occasionally made one think."[118] The three women who edited the *Journal des Dames* initiated the combat against this attitude. That they found the fight lonely and exhausting, that each gave up her personal involvement with the paper very quickly, is not surprising. It was to be a bigger and longer battle than they could have imagined. But all three were impatient for the social and political changes that would improve their lot, and therefore they sympathized with men who challenged the regime, whose ideas of liberty filled them with optimism and hope. Mme de Montanclos, who greatly admired Rousseau's radical political ideas, called herself the "Jean-Jacques of the female sex"[119] and put into the hands of Mercier a chance to use his pen as a sword. Mme Roland would later consider him a "political zero" for voting against the king's execution, but in 1775 when he took over the *Journal des Dames* and used it as an instrument of combat, Mercier was regarded as a very dangerous man.

118 See Albistur, *Histoire du féminisme,* 372.
119 *Journal des Dames,* décembre 1774:191.

6

Theater Criticism and
the Journalistic Purge

M. MERCIER'S NETWORK VERSUS
THE COMÉDIE-FRANÇAISE (1775–1776)

Louis-Sébastien Mercier died with some unfinished business. In a footnote to the chapter on modern tragedy in his famous *Tableau de Paris,* Mercier vowed someday to tell the story of his "near-drastic persecution" at the hands of the authorities. The harassment he intended to describe had come in response to his attack on the Comédie-Française, first published in 1773 as *Du Théâtre, ou Nouvel essai sur l'art dramatique.* Even though he was confident (according to the footnote) that the passage of time would vindicate his critical views on French drama, their first appearance had occasioned an uproar that echoed through most of the corridors of the Old Regime bureaucracy before it finally died down. For Mercier had not merely expressed disapproval of the royally protected Théâtre Français; he had experienced its rejection of his plays as a violation of his rights and had consequently accused this entrenched institution of corruption and despotism in an outright declaration of war. In this war, Mercier's *Journal des Dames* became his major weapon, and he used it to spearhead a brief but unprecedentedly daring movement of political journalism. He never recounted his promised story of this extraordinary episode. In a sense, then, the present chapter is a posthumous fulfillment of Mercier's wish, for it is a tale he meant to tell.[1]

1 See Mercier's *Tableau de Paris* 4:99–106, especially 104n: "J'ai combattu le premier avec une extrême franchise les idées que plusieurs adoptent aujourd'hui.

Mercier was born in Paris in 1740 to bourgeois parents and spent his first two decades in the capital. What appears to have been overlooked by his biographers, yet is crucial for our story, is Mercier's earliest journalistic experience, the training he received when the Bordeaux parlement recruited him to teach in their Collège de la Magdaleine as one of the replacements for the ousted Jesuits in 1763. During the Fronde, Bordeaux had come close to declaring itself an independent republic. The city was strongly pro-English, and its people had turned out some of the most radical egalitarian tracts of that famous "révolution manquée."[2] Mercier's well-known essays and plays, written (and forbidden) upon his return to Paris, would be imbued with nostalgia for republican Rome, with calls for justice, law, constitutional government, and with denunciations of tyranny. It was surely in Bordeaux, so rich in *frondeur* tradition, that Mercier first developed this concern for the common good and public welfare and his pro-parlement sentiments. It was also there that he learned to think of the stage and the periodical press, along with the law courts, as weapons in the fight for lost liberties against arbitrary ministerial whim. And it was there that he tried his first newspaper.

Mercier and his teaching colleagues became actively involved in a journal called *L'Iris de Guienne,* which, despite its pro forma dedication to the duc de Richelieu, Bordeaux's governor, was an organ of *patriote* propaganda, designed to counteract the hegemony of the capital by enhancing the morale and strength of the provinces and by rekindling constitutionalist thought, active citizenship, and public service. The censors for *L'Iris* were local *procureurs* and *jurats,* one of its rubrics was "Causes et arrêts célèbres

---

J'ai fait imprimer, en 1773, un livre intitulé *Du Théâtre* . . . qui me valut alors de la part des journalistes (tous réunis contre moi) pas une seule raison, mais bien de grosses injures; et d'un autre côté, une persécution presque sérieuse, que je détaillerai un jour. Pour toute réponse, j'ai étendu mes idées et mes réflexions, en les frappant d'une manière plus haute et plus décidée, laissant au temps, dont je connais les effets, le soin de mettre mes opinions à leur place." For more on Mercier's role in the journalistic network, see my "*Frondeur* Journalism in the 1770s."

2   The best biography of Mercier, although it barely mentions his episode on the *Journal des Dames,* is Béclard, *Sébastien Mercier.* For brief notices on his journalistic activities, see Sgard, *Dictionnaire des journalistes,* 270–72, and my addition to that notice in Chouillet and Moureau, *Suppléments* 3:139–144. For a discussion of the popular Fronde in Bordeaux, see Keohane, *Philosophy and the State,* 217–20, and Westrich, *Ormée.*

du parlement," and its printer, Chappuis, was the official *impri-meur du parlement*. The editor of *L'Iris,* one Louis-Claude Leclerc, solicited articles highlighting such *frondeur* watchwords as "ci-toyen," "république," "liberté," "tribunal," "nation," "les lois," "le peuple." It was a heady atmosphere and inspiring company for the young and impressionable Mercier. Here the great parlementaire de Sèze contributed pieces on the social role of *auteurs dramatiques,* stressing the responsibility of the playwright to reach and teach the illiterate. Other magistrates wrote praising Diderot's contro-versial *drame Le Père de famille* for portraying loving but firm pa-rental authority as the essential building block for law, political ethics, and public felicity. One editorial glorifying Sparta and Rome defined "true politics" as "virtue itself, applied with wis-dom for the happiness of the people."

The advancement of women was a favorite cause of Leclerc's *Iris,* which carried many articles from female contributors and strongly supported a "révolution" in their education, without which the nation could never be reformed. A member of the Bor-deaux parlement named Meyniel argued that "if women had more solid learning, a generous soul and love for the public welfare would follow, and men themselves would then be more *patriote,* more virtuous, more enlightened." Sparta and Rome were only great, another article stated, because women were toughened and challenged by social and military responsibilities in those soci-eties. The *Iris* gave a passionate review to Mercier's earliest prose piece, *Discours sur le bonheur des gens de lettres,* which Leclerc called an embarrassment of riches, a "multitude of solid and brilliant thoughts" so moving that he "was transported by their beauty." Here, Mercier had written of the "rights of man and citizen," of preferring poverty to slavery, of the importance of industry, agri-culture, and commerce. What Leclerc found most admirable, however, was that Mercier "was drawn beyond his subject, as a zealous *patriote,* to deplore the lamentable education of women" and to argue that the state would prosper only "if men conquered their secret jealousy and liberated the female sex from enforced ignorance."[3]

3 See *Iris de Guienne,* 1763: août, 267–73; juillet, 183–93; janvier, 24–30; fév-rier, 99–112; mai, 27; novembre, 161–71; septembre, 35–45, especially 40. Brief

With this background it is not surprising that when Mercier returned to Paris in 1765, determined to become a writer for social causes, he linked up with Mathon's *Journal des Dames,* where he remained active in the wings for many years. Mathon, as we have seen, displayed Mercier to Paris readers as a young author of uncommon promise, a public servant whose vital and civic-minded ideas were in marked contrast to the turgid, conventional notions of La Harpe and the literary establishment. Both Mathon and Mercier had been encouraged by the academician Thomas to submit their *patriote* essays for academic prize competitions, if only to shake up the Académie française, which year after year awarded the prize to the conservative La Harpe. Thomas was a somewhat improbable academician, a foe of the *dévots* frequently reprimanded for impertinence, an admirer of republican Rome, author of a liberal *Essai sur les femmes.* But Mercier came to see the rest of the "forty immortals" as sclerotic, cliquish, small-minded men jealously guarding their reputations by blocking the upward mobility of talented newcomers. Mercier, who frequented the Café Procope, shared his frustration at discovering that the open "republic of letters" was a hoax with Thomas, Crébillon *fils,* Diderot, and Pierre Le Tourneur, all of whom remained his friends for life. When the *Journal des Dames* was suspended during the Maupeou years, Mercier looked closely at the protected papers approved by the regime to continue printing and decided that their editors, like the members of the Académie, were reactionary pedants and political conformists incapable of conceiving anything new under the sun. Only the underground newsletters of his friend Pidansat kept seditious sentiment alive. But censored journalists, he wrote to Thomas, were "condemned to impotence" in those times.[4] There was no point in even trying to revive the

---

mention is made of *L'Iris* in Bordes de Fortage, "Sébastien Mercier à Bordeaux," where it is pointed out that Mercier's *Mon Bonnet de nuit* (Paris, 1784) reprinted some of the articles he wrote for *L'Iris.* In fact *Mon Bonnet* also reproduced numerous articles from the *Journal des Dames,* for it was Mercier's habit to recycle his material for maximum exposure. I am preparing a separate study of his first journalistic experience in Bordeaux. It is of particular interest because *L'Iris* contains the earliest of Mercier's works to have survived.

4 Bibliothèque de L'Arsenal, MS 15078 (2b), fol 4, letter to Thomas dated 14 août 1770.

Journal des Dames as long as Maupeou's triumvirate reigned.

Instead, Mercier wrote a utopia, *L'An 2440, rêve s'il en fut jamais*, published anonymously in London in 1771 and smuggled into France, in which he razed to the ground the intransigent regime and restructured the world of the future to his liking. Mercier's utopia depicted an essentially republican government where a benevolent monarch and a senate together held executive powers and were both responsible to an elected legislative assembly. The preface lamented the glaring contrast between this dream and the stifling, tomblike atmosphere of the Maupeou regime. "The spirit of my century envelops and presses down on me. I see only painted corpses who walk and talk without ever having given birth to the slightest spark of life."[5] Mercier's book was meant to rouse Frenchmen from their state of torpor. Calling for a "civil war" or a "revolution," Mercier cried out that "freedom and happiness belong to those who seize them" and exhorted his readers to "choose to be either happy or wretched, if you are still capable of choice. Fear tyranny, loathe slavery, take up arms, die or live free."[6] The police were after *L'An 2440* immediately. "It is very rigorously forbidden," wrote Grimm, "and consequently wildly sought after." The chronicler went on to pan Mercier's work as a "delirious chimera," yet obviously found it threatening on all counts, "a bitter critique of everything that exists today, *les grands,* . . . the administration, government, mores, *philosophie*, habits, nothing is spared."[7] Mercier had even predicted the fall of the Bastille! The clandestine *Mémoires secrets,* written since Bachaumont's death by Pidansat, called the work "proud and sublime," "a kind of apocalypse worthy of much discussion," and the *Gazette de Deux-Ponts,* edited from across the border by another friend of Mercier's, Dubois-Fontanelle, welcomed *L'An 2440* as a message of hope. But the censored French newspapers denounced

---

5   Mercier's *L'An 2440* had numerous reprintings and several editions, and it was translated into many foreign languages. Its popularity and some of the wonders in this utopia are discussed in my "Science in French Enlightenment Utopias" and in my unpublished Ph.D. dissertation, "Science in Enlightenment Utopias." See also Mercier, *L'An 2440,* especially Trousson's introduction, 7–34. This quotation is from the preface of the 1772 London edition.

6   Mercier, *L'An 2440,* 300–301 and 300–301 nn. a and b.

7   Grimm et al., *Correspondance littéraire* 9:395–96 (décembre 1771).

it. The *Bibliothèque des sciences et des beaux arts,* for example, branded Mercier's challenge to church and state dangerously "frondeur." [8]

The confiscation of his utopia was not going to intimidate Mercier. He would win celebrity by provoking a confrontation rather than be thwarted. Viewing himself, as he said in his utopia, as a "shaper of public opinion," a protector of the nation, he realized that he needed to reach even those people who could not read with his message. And only through the theater could he encourage the illiterate to elevate themselves both morally and intellectually. So Mercier's next battle was to be with the Comédie-Française, one of the regime's most entrenched institutions, whose monopoly on the Paris stage had frustrated aspiring playwrights for decades. Mercier spent the Maupeou years churning out bourgeois and popular *drames* totally unpalatable to the monarchy. [9] There was nothing innocent about his timing. He would show the actors no more worthy to judge art than Maupeou's corrupt tribunal to judge citizens. In his long fight with the Comédie, which peaked in 1775, the revived *Journal des Dames,* purchased from Mme de Montanclos, would become his principal and for a time his sole weapon, and his journalistic (mis)adventures can only be understood in this context.

Mercier's choice of the *Journal des Dames* as the vehicle for his protest makes untenable the common opinion that he embraced Rousseau's negative view of female intellectual and political ambition. That Mercier was inconsistent in his expressed position on women cannot be denied, but he did not share Rousseau's insistence that only motherhood could validate their worth. He thought women should make the home an oasis of serenity, but also that they should cultivate their talents, and he obviously believed that those who wished to inform and involve themselves in worthy public causes should do so. His friendship with the revolutionary feminist Olympe de Gouges is well known. He would

8 *Mémoires secrets* 5:297 (16 août 1771); *Gazette de Deux-Ponts,* 1772:177–80. See also Mercier, *L'An 2440,* 63.

9 For general discussions of this new dramatic genre and its troubled relations with the Comédie, see Bonnassies, *Auteurs dramatiques;* Chauveron, *Grands Procès;* Jourdain, *Dramatic Theory and Practice;* Gaiffe, *Drame en France;* Lough, *Paris Theatre Audiences.*

help her with numerous political pamphlets and especially with her plays, one of which was called *Les Comédiens démasqués*.[10] He lamented how difficult it was for female playwrights and journalists to be taken seriously, and he wrote with great sensitivity about the threat posed to his own sex by women with literary or political ambitions.

> Man begrudges woman any superiority whatsoever. . . . He praises the modesty of woman, more accurately her humility, as the most beautiful of her traits, and since woman has more natural cleverness than man, he resents that facility of seeing, that penetration. He fears she will discover in him all his vices and especially his defects. . . . These feelings [are] hidden in the hearts of all men. . . . All men have a secret disposition to cut down [*rabaisser*] the woman who craves fame. A stunning success would be very alarming for the pride and freedom of men.

Mercier marveled that even without training, colleges, or academies, many women nonetheless accomplished great things. "Most mediocre [male] minds cannot forgive this." In spite of all the compliments man lavishes upon woman, Mercier concluded, "he wants to subjugate her completely . . . demand from her perpetual inferiority."[11] It may well have been Mercier's early experience with the *Iris de Guienne* and the *Journal des Dames* that made him appreciate women as worthy intellectual companions, shapers of opinion, and potential political actors. Certainly women were a very receptive audience for his *frondeur* protest against the aristocratic Comédie. But to understand this protest we must first cast a backward glance at Mercier's activities as a dramatist.

By 1770 Mercier was already busy writing plays, but while he would have loved the applause of the *parterre,* he wrote to Thomas that he would not submit his works to be considered for performance at the Comédie:

> I have seen the *comédiens* up close and have found them so cold, indifferent, foppish, and conceited, I vowed to myself never to be judged by their tribunal. I would hate literature as much as I now love it if I had to endure their disdain. . . . It is tragic that young playwrights are so dependent on them, but then we are

10   See Béclard, *Sébastien Mercier,* 711.
11   Mercier, *Tableau de Paris* 10:200–204, "Femmes-Auteurs."

oppressed in so many ways. . . . Drama has gone awry in
France . . . stressing always the nobility. Audiences must see
that courage, heroism, and virtue are present in the obscure
classes of society, that anyone can be a hero . . . by doing his
duty well . . . that the man is everything, and titles nothing.

Mercier went on to say that we must turn from classical themes
and artificial, rhymed dialogue and deal instead with everyday subjects in natural prose. For despite his profound admiration for the political ideals of the Roman past, Mercier believed
that literary subjects should be drawn fresh from the present,
from immediate social concerns. Writers and actors who stuck
to the traditional subjects, who dealt always with ancient kings
and queens, were turning their backs on life, "paralytics who
take their room for the universe." Instead of alienating the little
man, drama must speak to and for him. "Life is short," the letter
ended, "we must show what will be most interesting to the greatest number of fellow citizens. Anything beyond their reach is
worthless."[12]

Mercier's *drames* were designed to inspire civic spirit and responsibility by showing that dignity of purpose and purity of
character lay not with the pampered, privileged rich but with the
busy, industrious, ordinary citizen. But they were more than lessons in virtue. They were social and political lessons as well.
Olinde et Sophronie, specifically designed to infuriate Maupeou,
came out just two days after his banishing of the parlements. Mercier later gloated that "the people read into my work all manner
of unsavory allusions [to the chancellor], which pleased us tre-
mendously for it allowed us a kind of revenge."[13] *Le Déserteur*,
with its sympathetic portrayal of the runaway soldier, stressed the
brutality of war and of the death penalty for desertion. *Jean Hennuyer*, favorably reviewed in Mme de Montanclos's *Journal des
Dames*, attacked religious fanaticism, and *L'Indigent*, blatantly
democratic, starred a servant who would not allow his master to
address him in the familiar form, insisted on respect as an equal,

12   Bibliothèque de l'Arsenal, MS 15078 (2b), fol. 4, letter dated 10 juillet
1770.
13   Mercier, *Tableau de Paris* 10:25–30.

and protested, "If I am poor, it is only because too many unde-
serving are rich."[14]

That these plays got into print at all was due to Mercier's friendship with his censor, Crébillon *fils,* himself a critic of the Comédie, whose affiliation with the opposition circle of the duc
d'Orléans and the duc de Chartres—the future Philippe Egalité—
made him partial to Mercier's politics.[15] These plays were performed to wildly enthusiastic audiences in Bordeaux, as might be
expected, in Brest, in Dijon, in Mathon de la Cour's Lyons, but
Mercier meant them to be performed in Paris. The Comédie's
monopoly on the Parisian stage ultimately forced him to approach
that institution, despite the lofty disdain he had expressed in private letters to Thomas. But the Comédie, under the direct protection of the king, with four gentlemen of the king's bedchamber
for its governing board and a 12,000-livre pension for each actor
and actress, was a bastion of aristocratic taste that refused to recognize the cultural values of marginal social groups. It stuck to a
safe repertoire of Molière, Corneille, and Racine, allowing in only
an exclusive confraternity of acceptably genteel and decorous new
playwrights. Mercier was not one of them, and as he had anticipated, the manuscripts with which he bombarded the Comédie
continued to be rejected. All this fueled his fire, which exploded
in the anonymous *Du Théâtre* published by Harevelt in Amsterdam, a fierce indictment of the Comédie and through it of the
whole superannuated regime. Mercier wrote to Thomas on 21
May 1773 that he was thrilled to have finally vented his spleen and
put his festering grievances out in the open.[16]

Du Théâtre, ou Nouvel essai sur l'art dramatique was a long tract
in which Mercier's anger at the Comédie's intransigence seemed

14   Mercier, *L'Indigent* (Paris 1772), act 2, sc. 2. For a good although brief
discussion of the democratic implications of Mercier's *drames,* see Roger Mercier,
"Peuple dans le théâtre." See also Lioure, *Drame,* 30 and passim.

15   Mercier, *Tableau de Paris* 10:25–30. "Crébillon *fils* regardait la tragédie
française comme la farce la plus complète qu'ait pu inventer l'esprit humain." He
also encouraged new talent. "Il ouvrait journellement sa porte à une multitude de
versificateurs et d'auteurs débutants, . . . il aimait sincèrement les hommes de
lettres."

16   Bibliothèque de l'Arsenal, MS 15078 (2b), letter to Thomas dated 21 mai
1773. The printing of *Du Théâtre* was finished on 17 January (p. 372), so it must
have been written during 1772.

to grow fiercer as he wrote. It covered all his favorite themes—the indolence and ignorance of actors, their dissolute liaisons with noble patrons, their incompetence to judge art, their indifference to *le peuple*. A hardworking weaver, he fulminated, was more worthy than such fawning sycophants. How could these wanton, uneducated people pass judgment on great literature? Why did they refuse to accept anything new? Why did they fail to recognize the superior greatness of Shakespeare? They were incapable of weighing the moral value of anything, so affected and promiscuous had they become. Yet the system allowed them to reject plays, and their exclusive privilege prevented these plays from being shown anywhere else in Paris. This was scandalous. Plays should not merely entertain the upper classes. The stage was the proper arena for public education; theater could be powerful moral medicine. But the Comédie allowed the boulevard theaters and fairs to show only vulgar farces and freaks. With revolutionary fury, Mercier cursed the royal actors and wished that "these vile instruments of despotism be struck down dead." He went on to argue the senselessness of war and accused the author of a famous patriotic play, de Belloy, of caressing the vanity of the government just to win success. France must realize how much it has to learn from England, rather than be deluded by some myth of its own greatness. Shakespeare, Mercier continued, was a national poet who spoke to *all* his countrymen, especially the commoners. Here Mercier quoted enthusiastically from the Jansenist *frondeur* Pierre-Jean Grosley's *Londres,* where it was reported that in England ordinary people wept at the sight of Shakespeare's statue, so deeply had his message moved their souls. French writers, on the other hand, did nothing but pander to the powerful. "The poet who flatters his nation at a moment of weakness is a fainthearted briber." Mercier also attacked the establishment journalists, "folliculaires," in the fiercest terms—vermin, idiots, fools, conspirators—for supporting the corrupt Comédie. Mercier's very conception of drama was more political than literary. There was little hope for mankind unless the playwright's "lessons to men and kings" were seriously heeded, because Mercier saw the *poète dramatique* as a "legislator," a "benefactor," an "interpreter of woes and humiliations," a "public orator for the

216

oppressed."[17] The police, in a now familiar maneuver, confiscated as many copies as possible of Mercier's latest insurrectionary work; no sooner were numerous packets of *Du Théâtre* smuggled into France than they joined copies of *L'An 2440,* sent to be locked up or pulped at the Pilon de la Bastille.[18]

The Comédie, although it said nothing, must have been horrified by Mercier's exposé. On 8 August 1773 the actors actually accepted a play of Mercier's, the relatively innocuous *Natalie,* without any intention of staging it. They probably hoped to buy some time before being assaulted again. Mercier was jubilant for he believed he would finally be performed in the capital, now that he had forced the Comédie's hand. He submitted two more plays in the next few months. Then more than a year went by. Scripts submitted long after his came and went on the boards. He began to suspect foul play. In early 1775 he released his *Brouette du vinaigrier,* his most republican play so far, its extravagant, lazy, lecherous nobles unsubtly offset against the grubby but frugal vinegarmaker who labored for forty-five years from dawn to dusk, earning not only internal satisfaction but a small fortune in gold, which he carried around on stage in a wheelbarrow.[19] The critics were disgusted at Mercier's latest and most unabashed identification with "the vulgar." Fréron's *Année littéraire* sarcastically sug-

17 Mercier, *Du Théâtre,* especially chaps. 1, 8, 11, 13, 14, and pp. 137–39, 206, 207n, 212, 257–60, 308–15, 368–370 (and 370n). The flavor of Mercier's inflammatory rhetoric is worth reproducing (pp. 137–38): "Mais voir les conditions humaines les plus basses, les plus rampantes! ajoutera-t-on encore, les mettre sur la scène. Et pourquoi pas? Homme dédaigneux, approche; que je te juge à ton tour. Qui es-tu? Qui te donne le droit d'être hautain? Je vois ton habit, tes laquais, tes chevaux, ton équipage; mais toi, que fais-tu? . . . Tu souris, je t'entends; tu es homme de cour, tu consumes tes jours dans une inaction frivole, dans des intrigues puériles, dans des fatigues ambitieuses et risibles. Tu ruines tes créanciers pour paraître un homme comme il faut. . . . Verge avilissante du despotisme, un tisserand son bonnet sur la tête, me paraît plus estimable et plus utile que toi. Si je te mets sur la scène, ce sera pour la honte. Mais ces ouvriers, ces artisans peuvent y paraître avec noblesse; ce sont des hommes, que je reconnais tels à leurs moeurs, à leurs travaux. Et toi, né pour l'opprobre du genre humain, plût à Dieu que tu fusses mort à l'instant de ta naissance!"
18 Bibliothèque de l'Arsenal, Archives de la Bastille, MS 10305.
19 In the preface to the 1785 edition of the *Brouette du vinaigrier,* Mercier wrote: "Le poète dramatique est peintre universel. Je suis peintre, et tout le détail de la vie humaine m'appartient, depuis le conseil des rois jusqu'à la taverne; car après avoir soulevé la première superficie, je vois les mêmes affections régir."

gested that Mercier write a series of plays about all the *poissard* types, since nothing could be more uplifting than seeing on stage fishwives, ragpickers, chimney sweeps, washerwomen, hawkers, and pickpockets.[20] The Comédie, however, ignored Mercier's provocation and maintained its stony silence.

Finally on 4 March 1775 Mercier wrote to the Comédie demanding to know why *Natalie* had not been performed and refusing to be ignored any longer. Three days later he had his answer. The Comédie accused him of being the author of the "libelous" *Du Théâtre,* an "injurious slander," adding, "The theater would in fact deserve the odious imputations of M. Mercier if it weakened and dealt with this worm of an author." Henceforth he could consider its doors shut tight against him.[21]

Enraged by the actors' flagrant duplicity, Mercier began a many-pronged attack. He now took the first political action of his life, emerging from the literary into the judicial arena. He hired a lawyer, Henrion de Pansey, and together they drafted two *mémoires* against the Comédie. These went into circulation within two weeks. In the *mémoires* Mercier sued the actors for damages. Having accepted *Natalie,* their own rules bound them to stage it. The rights of authors, their literary property, and the sanctity of artistic creation were at issue here. Mercier claimed they had falsely accused him of libel, because everything he said in *Du Théâtre* was true. He argued that *comédiens,* trained only to act, should be forever forbidden from rendering judgments on matters far beyond their sphere of competence. The humiliation of artists by fops would have to come to an end. Fools, he stated baldly, should not judge art. He accused them of fraud and of refusing to open their accounts for authors to see. He condemned the practice of submitting scripts to actors selected to screen them, who could reject them without ever putting them to a vote. Finally he requested that his trial be handled not by the traditionally docile Grand Conseil, as the actors wished, but by the newly restored Parlement of Paris, the "citizens' tribunal of the nation" where he would be

20 *Année littéraire* (1775) vii:13.
21 These letters are in the Archives du Théâtre Français, dossier "Mercier." Parts of them are printed in Béclard, *Sébastien Mercier,* and their details were reported by Mercier's faithful friend and censor Pidansat in the *Mémoires secrets* 7:313–14 (23 mars 1775).

protected by "the law." During the Fronde, Renaudot, editor of the official *Gazette de France,* had appealed to the Grand Conseil for help in wiping out radical newspapers and silencing the opposition press. Because of the Conseil's record of unconditional royalism, Mercier was determined to deal only with the parlement. It recognized, or so he believed, the duty of the state to defend liberty and nurture genius.[22]

But Mercier did something else besides. Remembering the fate of Beaumarchais's wittily scathing *mémoires,* which had been gobbled up by police spies during the Maupeou years, he realized that his own might not reach the public. Legal *mémoires* were just political pamphlets in disguise, which because they bore the names of lawyers did not need to be censored. But once they appeared they tended to be confiscated promptly if they smacked of subversion. Mercier needed yet another way to keep his followers informed of the Comédie's abuses, or the wrongs would never be righted. His plays were being rejected; his *mémoires* he correctly anticipated would be nipped in the bud. All that remained was to acquire a legitimate newspaper with a following, a regular monthly vehicle of communication with a waiting audience, an emergency public-address system with built-in listeners. Since his journalistic enemies had always bombarded him with insults, why not beat his detractors at their own game? He personally would never have been permitted to start a new paper, but he knew where to turn for help. His friend Mme de Montanclos had been praising his plays in her *Journal des Dames.* She gladly agreed to serve as his front and, as we saw, acquired a privilege for her paper and willingly passed it to him. Now, he thought, he had all bases covered.

Why had Mercier waited until March 1775 to take on a news-

---

22 "Par l'inversion la plus bizarre, ce sont les comédiens qui régentent les auteurs, qui se croient en droit de charpenter leurs pièces au gré de leurs caprices, et qui, presque tous sans études et sans connaissances, s'imaginent que l'état de comédien leur inocule en vingt-quatre heures tout ce qui est nécessaire pour se connaître aux chefs-d'oeuvre de l'esprit humain" (*Premier mémoire pour le sieur Mercier contre la troupe des comédiens* [Paris, 1775], 8). See also *Mémoire à consulter et consultation pour le sieur Mercier contre la troupe des comédiens français, ordinaires du roi* (Paris, 1775). These *mémoires* are described in detail and with obvious relish in Metra, *Correspondance secrète* 1:414–19 (10 juin 1775), a popular clandestine newsletter. Metra was, like Pidansat, a *frondeur nouvelliste* about whom more will be said later. On Renaudot's dealings with the Grand Conseil, see Grand-Mesnil, *Mazarin,* 159.

paper of his own? It seemed to him for numerous reasons that the propitious moment had finally arrived. Maupeou was gone. France had a new, young king whose official coronation, traditionally a magnanimous moment, was but one month away and whose queen was a staunch fan of Mercier's *drames*. The progressive Physiocrat Turgot, himself a man of letters, was part of the new reforming ministry that had replaced the triumvirate. The old parlements had been recalled. Several of Mercier's *frondeur* friends had even, in the liberal euphoria of Louis XVI's first year, found their way into positions of influence. This was due mostly to the machinations of the duc de Chartres, nephew of Mme de Beaumer's former protector the prince de Conti, and a popular leader of opposition to the Crown. The improbable Chartres was an intimate friend of the new royal couple and made the most of this friendship by seizing the occasion to place his *frondeur* protégés where they could exercise some power. Pidansat, whose underground newsletters had contributed in no small measure to Maupeou's disgrace, was now actually appointed a royal censor. Crébillon *fils* was now promoted to the exalted position of *censeur de la police,* replacing the royalist Marin.[23] Le Tourneur, another close friend of Mercier's, had been *secrétaire général de la librairie* for some years, but documents show he now became an extremely involved censor in a flurry of activity before retiring to "recover his liberty."[24] Finally, rumor had it that Malesherbes, the popular former director of the booktrade, was soon to become *ministre de la maison du roi*. Malesherbes, it is true, had been no friend to Mme de Beaumer, but he was greatly loved by *men* of letters for his legendary liberalism. His imminent reappearance on the government scene delighted writers for it seemed to signal a new era of freedom, of sweeping change. Gushed the *Mémoires secrets,*

23   See the *Almanach royal,* 1775:414. Crébillon was listed as a censor in earlier volumes, but this was his first year in his new function. For more on Crébillon's takeover of this role, see Collé, *Journal historique inédit.* On Chartres's influence, see Britsch, *La Maison d'Orléans,* especially 114, 127, 155, 161, 194–99, 221–29, 234–40, 388.

24   For Le Tourneur's activity, see Bibliothèque Nationale, manuscrit français (henceforth BN ms. fr.) 22002. His abrupt withdrawal from office on 22 April 1775, just three days after Mercier's secret purchase of the *Journal des Dames,* was probably to avoid any suspicion of collusion. That holding public office represented a conflict of interests for him is suggested in Cushing, *Pierre Le Tourneur,* 9, 12, 17–18.

"Malesherbes seeks to right all the wrongs caused by the tyrannical conduct of his predecessors."[25]

With such friends in high places, Mercier felt ready to be bold and to use the press as he meant to use the stage, to reach and inform the public. His *Journal des Dames* would usher in a new era, would lead the fight for freedom of expression. For the first time legitimate, approved journalism would challenge the regime as only proscribed, clandestine *nouvellistes* had dared to do before. Mercier shared with Brissot the revolutionary idea that the press should inform the masses, lift the people out of ignorance and slavery, and thus expand human freedom.[26] He now gathered around him a network of supporters who shared his *patriote* views, many of whom had also suffered at the hands of the Comédie. In the new permissive atmosphere they too were encouraged to start up journals, and this group of self-styled *esprits frondeurs* banded together in a journalistic protest against the collective injustices of the regime. The theater of course, but also the academies, the official state-protected papers like the *Mercure* and the *Gazette,* and the king's ministers themselves all came under attack. The appearance in regularly censored periodicals of what had previously circulated only "under the cloak" was made possible by Pidansat, Crébillon, and other censors like Hermilly, Ameilhon, and Cardonne, with whom they seem to have formed a team. These protectors allowed Mercier and his cohorts to print their views in their newspapers, granted privileges to their other proposed works as well, and helped in many ways behind the scenes to save the group, as Mercier put it, from all manner of "désagréments fâcheux" and "persécutions presque sérieuses."[27] The *Journal des Dames* now became more political and more subversive than ever. Mercier would not talk down to his subscribers. Female readers would be exposed to exactly the same fare as men.

Mercier knew he had already antagonized many establishment journalists; he found both conservative and philosophe editors equally inhospitable to his cause. Because of their hostility to him

25 *Mémoires secrets* 8:168 (19 août 1775).
26 See Popkin, "Newspaper Press," especially 114–16.
27 Mercier, *Tableau de Paris* 10:29. For a fascinating record of the censorship activities of Pidansat and his team, see BN ms. fr. 22002. Pidansat is referred to as Mairobert in the document.

and to his *drames,* his *Du Théâtre* had singled out Fréron's *Année littéraire,* La Harpe's *Mercure,* and Pierre Rousseau's *Journal encyclopédique* for "vomiting the vilest insults" on worthy works, like "gnawing indestructible vermin that crop up everywhere, rendering lovely things unrecognizable."[28] The insulted journalists had fought back with predictable anger, La Harpe and Fréron in venomous diatribes, Rousseau with patronizing restraint, then claiming credit for his self-control, for not using his "infinite facilities for reprisal" despite having been "insulted without decency or measure."[29] But even before Mercier's *Journal des Dames* became a rallying point for *frondeur* journalism, a few papers had begun to support him openly. The maverick Linguet, editor since late 1774 of the *Journal de politique et de littérature,* was solidly behind authors in their fight against all privileged institutions—theaters, academies, even the Paris bar from which he had been expelled.[30] Querlon's *Affiches de province* had now begun a new category in its table of contents pointedly labeled "drames imprimés mais non-joués," emphasizing and condemning the refusal of the Comédie to perform the new genre. Querlon raved about Mercier's *drames,* defended them against the hostile journalists of the privileged papers, and now began to attack the unresponsive, self-indulgent actors. Querlon, who would later be scared off by Mercier's increasingly radical rhetoric, was enough of an ally at this point to be recognized as one of the "fearless" journalists fighting against despotism.[31] And the faithful Dubois-Fontanelle had been supporting Mercier all along.[32] Encouraged by such fellow crusaders,

---

28   *Du Théâtre,* 308 and passim. The only journalist Mercier praised in this work was the editor of the *Gazette de Deux-Ponts,* his friend Dubois-Fontanelle, "modèle d'une critique sage, ingénieuse, fine, éclairée et précise . . . cette supériorité nàturelle se fait sentir à la manière dont il analyse les ouvrages." (Ibid., 314–15n). This paper, which Mercier affectionately referred to by its nickname, the *Gazette littéraire de l'Europe,* had been faithfully supporting his *drames* during the triumvirate but experienced trouble circulating in France. See Chapter 5, above, n. 11. Mercier would continue to insult the establishment journalists in the *Journal des Dames.* See, for example, mai 1775:256; septembre 1775:280, 347, 353–54, 367–72.

29   *Année littéraire* (1774) vii:73; *Mercure de France,* décembre 1774:113; *Journal encyclopédique* (1774) vi:466–82.

30   *Journal de politique et de littérature* (1775) ii:72.

31   *Affiches de province,* 1775:108, 116, 124; 1776:103–4, 96, 148–56.

32   See, for example, *Gazette de Deux-Ponts,* 1775:45–46, 151, 365–67, 444–45. "M. Mercier a déjà publié beaucoup de *drames* et tous ont le mérite de tou-

Mercier began to warm to the role of journalistic spokesman and firebrand, fighting for nothing less than the salvation of his *patrie* through free speech.

The spring of 1775 was action packed. Just when he bought the *Journal des Dames* from Mme de Montanclos, Mercier wrote to Thomas that he needed every possible fortification, not for himself but for his cause. He had, he told Thomas, placed his soul beyond the disturbances of events, inspired and uplifted but at the same time awed by the magnitude of his undertaking, by the impact of his suit against the Comédie, and by its mushrooming into the far bigger issue of press freedom. He fought for a noble principle. "Here is the cause of all men of letters put into my feeble hands, and I will not betray them." He would "rend asunder this unbearable yoke and cry *the law* with all my force." He hoped the parlement would judge in his favor. "If the course of justice is not interrupted, I shall triumph. If it is . . . I shall tremble, more for literature than for myself."[33]

Mercier's missionary zeal permeated the *Journal des Dames* from the moment he took over. The law, the theater, and the press in concert would lift the people out of darkness and save France. His first issue, that of May 1775, even advertised itself in juridical terms, proclaiming itself the official repository of all grievances against the French theater. He welcomed articles on the subject from any interested parties, all of which would become ammunition, "evidence in the trial which the public and the authors have together launched against the Comédie."[34] Mercier announced next that he planned to break the monopoly of the Comédie-Française by fighting for the creation of a second theater, which would be more receptive to dramatic innovation and perhaps, through competition, would even jog the old theater out of its "senile conservatism." He reviewed a work by Cailhava from several years earlier, *L'Art de la comédie,* which explored the causes of decadence among actors and ways to reform them. Presenting the case of Palissot's *Les Courtisanes,* which the *comédiens* had refused

---

cher, d'attendrir, et de présenter les plus beaux exemples de vertus et de bienfaisance; ils honorent également le coeur et les talents de l'Auteur" (p. 367). See also n. 28, above.

33 See Henriet, "Trois lettres inédites."
34 *Journal des Dames,* mai 1775:208.

to put on, Mercier printed many letters in support of the wronged playwright. Neither Cailhava nor Palissot remained faithful to Mercier; both would soon turn against him, disavowing their earlier association because he became too radical. But Mercier was now gladly printing anything whatever that would strengthen his point. "The invincible laziness of the Paris *comédiens,*" Mercier summed up the May issue of the *Journal des Dames,* "can only be cured [by a second troupe]. . . . We must destroy their exclusive privilege, which will otherwise extinguish all art. So striking is the evidence presented herein that only those who applaud chaos and ignorance will disagree. The public demands that its theatrical pleasure and instruction no longer be delayed or interrupted by this capricious company."[35] Much of this repeated, in parts verbatim, the themes of Mercier's *mémoires,* to ensure maximum exposure for his cause.

The *comédiens* were furious. On 28 May they voted not even to let Mercier in as a spectator; this he discovered on 6 June when he was denied entrance.[36] Mercier provoked a row in the lobby, calling in civilians and policemen to witness the latest intolerable slight, determined to make his martyrdom a spectacle. "Mercier asked the usher if perhaps he hadn't recognized him. The guard replied that indeed he *had* and that was precisely the reason for the refusal." The *Mémoires secrets* predicted that this would be added to Mercier's already lengthy list of complaints against "les vils histrions." Mercier hammed it up for all it was worth and rallied new support for his cause. Onlookers, astonished by the magnitude and seriousness of the case, marveled that "the Mercier affair is taking an absolutely juridical turn."[37]

June's *Journal des Dames* carried a review of *Observations sur l'art du comédien et sur d'autres objets concernant cette profession* by M. d'Hennetaire, former director of the court theater in Brussels. Here, Mercier reported gleefully, "the true vanity of actors is laid bare . . . by one who knows . . . from inside . . . the abuses of which the public becomes the victim." The work ended with an

---

35 Ibid., 204–8.

36 Archives du Théâtre Français, dossier "Administration 1775," letter dated 28 mai 1775 from *les premiers gentilhommes de la chambre* to *les controlleurs de la Comédie-Française.*

37 *Mémoires secrets* 8:52 (30 mai 1775) and 69 (6 juin 1775).

indictment of the Paris theater in particular, where anarchy reigns, genius is crushed, and the actors are philistines, dissipated, tyrannical, and totally insensitive to the oppressed. Mercier insisted this book was a necessary mirror for the *comédiens* and repeated the "universal cry" for a second troupe to overthrow the "indolent despots." Also in this issue Mercier quoted from a speech the great naturalist Buffon had made at the Académie française that echoed his own impatience with the classical repertoire, "objects of sterile and antique curiosity." Buffon, who shared Mercier's belief that current events were the stuff of great literature, had talked of the bankruptcy and pedantry of the Comédie. "Why turn our backs on a vibrant and vigorous world, its muscles flexing, to resurrect instead a Greek or Roman cadaver?"[38] Buffon's remarks had been a refutation of the reception speech by the duc de Duras, maréchal de France and head of the Comédie's governing board, who exalted the classics and the actors. Mercier was overjoyed at this fleeting and unexpected alliance with the famous Buffon and would continue for years to savor and gloat over their "joint blasphemy."[39] But his *Journal des Dames* had stepped on some very sensitive toes, and there were limits to how much his censors could protect him.

Mercier was soon summoned before the new police chief, Albert, whom Pidansat described as a slow, heavy man, yet opportunistic and devoured by ambition.[40] Albert had immediately incurred the wrath of men of letters by proposing that refused manuscripts be confiscated permanently by the censors to prevent their clandestine circulation later or their being used in some other form. It seemed the new police chief meant to treat art as crime.[41] Mercier's run-in with Albert was given extensive coverage by the underground chronicler Metra, self-styled critic of "the despotism of kings, the cruelty of ministers" and another zealous parlementaire.[42] Metra reported that throughout the "inquisition" Mercier

38   *Journal des Dames,* juin 1775:342–51, 363–76.
39   See Mercier's letter to the *Journal de Paris,* 1778:639. See also his *De la Littérature,* 133.
40   *Mémoires secrets* 8:26 (10 mai 1775) and 33 (15 mai 1775).
41   Ibid. 8:82 (16 juin 1775); Metra, *Correspondance secrète* 2:16 (1 juillet 1775).
42   On Metra, see Johansson, *Sur la Correspondance littéraire,* especially 65–66.

"behaved like a Roman hero," the highest praise a republican *patriote* could bestow. What particularly impressed Metra was Mercier's refusal to admit the legitimacy of ministers or of any authority other than the law. Albert began by telling him that the court disapproved strongly of his behavior, as did the "government." "Sir," replied Mercier in a firm but modest tone, "I don't know what you mean by the government. I have a king, and I am one of his most faithful subjects. Any order I receive directly from him I will gladly obey." "Terrible things will befall you if you persist with this trial," threatened Albert. "Sir," replied Mercier evenly, "I am simply calling on the law to protect me because my citizen's rights have been wounded. I have therefore turned to the national tribunal designated to hear and judge the complaints of *all* people." [43]

This proud performance notwithstanding, Mercier's insubordination had got him into deep trouble. The June issue of his *Journal des Dames* had provoked the enormously powerful duc de Duras, for the printing by Mercier of Buffon's speech had made Duras look like a fool. He ordered dispatched a lettre de cachet for Mercier's arrest and imprisonment at four o'clock the day after his interview with Albert. Warned in the nick of time, Mercier sought refuge in the parlement, placing himself under its protection. The arrest warrant was revoked, but an *arrêt du Conseil* came in its place on 24 June, silencing Mercier's "frightful declamations" and confiscating his *mémoires* for their "scandalous rantings disrespectful of His Majesty's authority." [44]

Mercier responded immediately to the silencing of his *mémoires* in two ways. He and his lawyer filed a formal *requête au roi,* an attempt to communicate with and touch the king directly, complaining that the gentlemen of the king's bedchamber (for example, Duras) had no right to interfere in matters of legal principle and questioning the legitimacy of their authority. The parlement, and not the Grande Chambre (of the royal Conseil), was the proper arena for this battle. [45] Malesherbes, now newly

43   Metra, *Correspondance secrète* 1:421 (16 juin 1775).
44   Ibid. 1:422 (16 juin 1775) and 2:15 (1 juillet 1775). See also Béclard, *Sébastien Mercier,* 376–77.
45   *Requête au roi pour le sieur Mercier contre MM les gentilhommes de la chambre de sa majesté: Question: La Législation et la politique des spectacles, appartiennent-elles*

installed as the *ministre de la maison du roi,* took special protective charge of Mercier's case, and for a fleeting moment observers predicted this augured ill for the Comédie.[46] Even Grimm, who had mocked Mercier's pretension to speak in his newspaper and *mémoires* for the whole "republic of letters" and who had sarcastically quipped that the "very peace and glory of France" was wrapped up in this affair, now had to admit that Mercier's *requête* was "vigorous and firm" and touched upon a very important matter.[47]

The other thing Mercier did was to intensify the political arguments in his *Journal des Dames,* now the only mouthpiece he had left. In July his "Songe d'un citoyen," a response to the king's coronation at Reims, stressed the new monarch's obligations to justice and reminded him of the "code des lois." Louis XVI needed to turn his country away from decadence and flabby pleasures and toward austerity and labor. The date of "le sacre et le couronnement de sa majesté" was of negligible importance compared to 12 November 1774, the day the parlements had been recalled. It was on that date, wrote Mercier, that he and all virtuous citizens began to hope for the renewed health and prosperity of the *patrie.*[48] In the August *Journal des Dames,* after reminding the ruling powers of their obligation to resolve the grain famine "for all humanity,"[49] Mercier again dwelt on the return of the parlements for the protection of "the nation." He praised the *Discours sur les mémoires* by the lawyer Delacroix, Mme de Montanclos's republican friend, because it argued the importance of such exposés in "defending the rights of men" and "publicizing litigious facts." Mercier, whose own *mémoires* had just been suppressed, reminded his readers that they had skillfully and eloquently demonstrated "the majesty of laws, the dignity of man, the force of justice and the inevitable dominion she has over all, especially those who seek to violate her."[50] He went on that the reestablishment of the parlements had dissipated alarm, returned France to her glory, de-

---

exclusivement à MM les premiers gentilhommes de la chambre du roi? (Paris, 1775), 28. Pidansat defined *requêtes* as the next step after the silencing of *mémoires,* "une forme plus judiciaire de les répandre" (*Journal historique* 5:124).

46 *Mémoires secrets* 8:137–39 (8 août 1775).
47 Grimm et al., *Correspondance littéraire* 11:62, 106.
48 *Journal des Dames,* juillet 1775:63–75.
49 Ibid., août 1775:217–22.
50 Ibid., 233–39.

lighted all good *patriotes,* and "exposed the principles of the national constitution." Now that the "senate" was restored, the "state could breathe" and the *"patrie* had been reborn."[51] In case his readers still did not catch on, another article praised his own lawyer, Henrion de Pansey, who had delivered a brilliant speech at the opening of the reinstalled parlement the previous autumn. Only the firmness of magistrates had historically saved France from despotism. One of his nation's proudest achievements, Mercier now declared, had been the "moderating," "disinterested" role played by the parlements during the Fronde,[52] for Mercier understood the Fronde to have been a fight by "the law" and "the people" united together against tyranny.

Subsequent issues of Mercier's *Journal des Dames* continued the battle with the Comédie and the legalistic arguments for the parlements' role in resolving the matter. But Mercier dealt boldly with other related matters as well. His admiration of the English constitution went hand in hand with a love for Shakespeare, whom he now crowned the "dieu du théâtre." Mercier's good friend Le Tourneur had undertaken a translation of all the Bard's plays into French. The *Journal des Dames* now advertised it enthusiastically,[53] despite the fact that Le Tourneur's work had engendered an ugly controversy. Voltaire had been an earlier advocate of Shakespeare in France, but even though he demanded credit for this position, he had become highly critical of the excesses of the cult that now preferred the English playwright to Corneille and Racine. This, to Voltaire's mind, was a total travesty, a betrayal of the immortal French classics. Voltaire, no friend of the Fronde—which he treated in his historical writings as a reprehensible, illegal uprising—persuaded the Académie française that Le Tourneur and his coterie were unpatriotic, even treasonous.[54] Mercier countered that Shakespeare was the far superior poet, not only in his char-

---

51 Ibid., 242–43.
52 Ibid., 251–55.
53 Ibid., mai 1775:209.
54 See the two quite rabid *Lettres de Voltaire à l'Académie française lues le 25 août 1776* (Paris, 1776). See also Grimm's embarrassed defense of Voltaire, *Correspondance littéraire* 11:379–383. Voltaire had asked d'Argental on 19 July, "Avez-vous une haine assez vigoureuse contre cet impudent imbécile, et souffrirez-vous l'affront qu'il fait à la France?" There is a brief discussion of this controversy in Cushing, *Pierre Le Tourneur,* 176–94.

acter portrayal but in his high morality. Even his heroines were an inspiration. A leitmotiv of Mercier's would continue to be the debunking of Racine, perhaps because Racine's emotionally unstable heroines represented his reaction against the strong-willed, feminist *frondeuses* and cast women in a most unfavorable light.[55] On the subject of *Phèdre* Mercier wrote to a friend: "I blush for all the women who attend this hideous spectacle. Phèdre's sobs reveal nothing but shameless passion, which does not move me in the slightest, and this illicit love of hers does irreparable damage to public morality, which must always be the dramatist's chief concern."[56] By thus placing himself so squarely in the Shakespeare camp, Mercier earned the enmity of Voltaire, who refused to intervene for him with the Comédie even though he shared many of his frustrations. Voltaire's support could have helped Mercier enormously, but he withheld it. At the very moment that Mercier's *mémoires* were circulating, Voltaire wrote to La Harpe: "I have only one more wish to make, that they exile all the Paris actors to Siberia forever . . . and that they reform completely the Comédie-Française." But when Mercier challenged the government in his August *requête*, Voltaire assured Marin that he had absolutely no intention of fighting for such a renegade.[57] Le Tourneur's *Shakespeare*, not the first literary issue to become politically loaded, would soon develop into a rallying point for many *frondeur* sympathizers.

Mercier's *Journal des Dames* published poems and articles by such future revolutionaries as de Sacy, Delisle de Sales, Condorcet, and Sylvain Maréchal on the economy, freedom of the press, and the abolition of slavery.[58] He supported the brilliantly combative Beaumarchais, who had not yet become a government spy and was still a mistreated outsider, a member of the subculture of

55 See Abensour, *Histoire générale,* 157, and Lough, *Paris Theatre Audiences,* 158–159.

56 Bibliothèque de l'Arsenal, MS 15078 (2b), fols. 42–43.

57 Voltaire, *Complete Works,* letter D19430, vol. 125, p. 414, and letter D19626, vol. 126, p. 151.

58 *Journal des Dames,* issues août–decembre 1775. On Condorcet's *Du Commerce des bleds* supporting Turgot's ideas of liberty, Mercier wrote that we must have faith in "un ministre sage et éclairé qu'un coup de vent n'a pas emporté sur la route qu'il a prise, mais qui ne s'est décidé qu'après la mûre réflexion d'un jugement solide" (août 1775:219).

opposition. Mercier's paper defended Beaumarchais's controversial *Barber of Seville* and applauded his efforts to get a "cote bien taillée," a clear financial statement of what each playwright was owed, from the *comédiens*.[59] Mercier also reprinted the fiery rhetoric of his friend François de Neufchâteau's *mémoires* in behalf of yet another wronged dramatist, Lonvaye de Saussaye, describing the abuses he had suffered.[60] Mercier was cramming as much as he could into each issue of the *Journal des Dames*, using smaller and smaller type as he went along, almost as if he knew his days were numbered.

These journalistic risks had been tolerated through the good graces of Hermilly, the censor who signed the *Journal des Dames*, and Pidansat, whom the documents show to have been watching over the group.[61] Because Mercier's paper was protected by and dedicated to the queen, the duc de Duras had not been able to suppress it as he had Mercier's pamphlet *mémoires*. But Mercier's role as the ringleader of a whole network of new, like-minded journalists was by far his most dangerous, and one where his protectors' help would soon wear thin. For Mercier was determined to plug the papers of members of his coterie whose courage matched his own, several of whom were neighbors of his in the Latin Quarter near the place Maubert. The chevalier de Rutlidge, editor of *Le Babillard*, lived next door on the same street, the rue des Noyers. Le Fuel de Méricourt, editor of several papers, lived around the corner on the rue de la Harpe.[62] Mercier, who thought

---

59 *Journal des Dames,* septembre 1775:347–53 and décembre 1775:308. See also Chauveron, *Les Grands Procès,* 184–91.

60 François de Neufchâteau contributed abundantly to Mercier's *Journal des Dames*. His *mémoires* were also reprinted in Linguet's *Journal de politique* and at length in Du Coudray's *Correspondance dramatique*. See also François de Neufchâteau's poems praising the parlements, for example, *Journal des Dames,* décembre 1775:341.

61 See BN ms.fr. 22002, nos. 30, 983, 1210, 1329, 1426, where Pidansat (called Mairobert in the document) is listed as censor for works by Mercier, Mathon, and by their former censor Arnoult. He later also censored Du Rozoi's *Journal militaire* (no. 1317), of which he had said, "On ne peut en concevoir une haute idée par le nom du rédacteur." He supported the paper, although he disliked its royalist editor, because by then (February 1778) France had joined the American Revolution on the American side, and paradoxically Vergenne's official paper supported the insurgents, a cause dear to Pidansat's heart. See Marc Martin, *Origines de la presse militaire,* 39, 40, 77. Pidansat appears to have supported the cause of liberty and republicanism wherever he found it.

62 The journalists' addresses were often given in their journals.

agitation healthy and recognized public opinion as a political force, had for a while been making comments in favor of journalists who sought to shake up rather than lull their readers, who refused to spout predictable government propaganda but aimed instead to give the public enough facts to judge for itself. Linguet, for example, whose journalistic courage the young Brissot always idolized, was admiringly described in Mercier's *Journal des Dames* as "full of fire. . . . He excites in the public that commotion and extreme argument that no ordinary talent can inspire."[63] But now Mercier began to advertise new papers created by his friends with his blessing as part of his *frondeur* campaign. And from now on his fate and theirs would be inextricably intertwined.

One such paper was the *Journal anglais,* started by an obscure abbé but soon taken over by an anonymous group that included Le Tourneur. Mercier admired Le Tourneur's independent strength, his refusal to compromise his principles or capitulate to the powers, saying pointedly in a eulogy that he had achieved greatness yet "belonged to no academy."[64] Mercier advertised that the *Journal anglais* would make known to the French police the liberties that even the humblest Englishmen enjoy. England's intellectual originality and strength, argued Mercier, resulted from the fact that there "no haughty and powerful men can tyrannize others, . . . every individual is respected." Like so many Anglophiles in 1775, Mercier at first perceived the upheaval in the colonies as a civil war, an internal English matter, which would have a salubrious effect on the country by revitalizing its legal and political foundation. "The Revolution of Boston," wrote Mercier with a Machiavellian appreciation for civil strife, "is a purging fever that will reaffirm the national constitution." The colonists would reanimate a previously inactive part of the realm. Only stupor, not crisis, was fatal to states, the analysis in the *Journal des Dames* continued.[65] Had Mercier perceived the skirmishes across the ocean as a war for independence, he would surely have supported the "insurgents." His newspaper denounced the slavery of Negroes and native Americans as a violation of the "inalienable [*imprescriptibles*] rights of nature and humanity."[66] And two years

63   *Journal des Dames,* septembre 1775:227.
64   See Cushing, *Pierre Le Tourneur,* 17–18.
65   *Journal des Dames,* novembre 1775:223–28.
66   Ibid., octobre 1775:92.

later, after the Declaration of Independence, he would write that "it is perhaps in America that the human race will be recreated . . . America, the asylum of liberty . . . [proof of] what man can do when he adds to knowledge a courageous heart."[67]

Le Fuel de Méricourt, one of the most radical of Mercier's friends, had started his *Lettres sur les spectacles*—variously entitled *Lettres de Mme Le Hoc à M. Le Hic, Lettre au diable, Lettre d'une jeune actrice, Lettre d'un célibataire*—during 1775.[68] Leniently censored by Crébillon, this paper was filled with denunciations of the established order, actors, ministers, even philosophes, whom Le Fuel alternately scorned as cowardly or loathed as a "despotic cabal" blocking the channels by which outsiders might rise to literary stardom. Le Fuel's candid depiction of the Comédie's decrepitude, his revelations of personal scandals and financial irregularities in the troupe, delighted Mercier. Here was a paper in the same spirit as the *Journal des Dames*, trying to "elucidate [matters] for the public . . . so it may judge for itself, which it normally does not dare because it has no practice." Mercier admired the courage of Le Fuel, a *roturier* like himself, who was not afraid to criticize the powerful in order to salvage the nation. He exhorted him to "pursue his project indefatigably . . . to do justice to the public and *patrie* . . . to save the Parisian stage."[69]

The networking functioned reciprocally, and the other papers returned the compliments. Because these exchanges of mutual admiration were encouraged by the overlapping editors and censors, it is instructive to look in some detail at the intricacies of this journalistic support system and at the elaborate attempts made by the government to dismantle it. The *Journal anglais* was censored by H. P. Ameilhon, himself the editor of the *Journal de Verdun*, and both papers consistently supported Mercier's campaign to break the monopoly and exclusive privilege of the Comédie and to find a hospitable arena for his plebeian *drames*. Linguet's *Journal de politique* heralded Mercier as the motivating force behind "a fight that should interest all men of letters and especially the public . . . the real beneficiary of good drama." No writer, agreed Lin-

---

67   Mercier, *De la Littérature,* 19. This is quoted on p. 77 of Echeverria, *Mirage in the West* (see also pp. 19, 34).

68   On Le Fuel, see my notice "Méricourt" in Chouillet and Moureau, *Suppléments* 3:144–50.

69   *Journal des Dames,* septembre 1775:359–64.

guet, should ever surrender his literary property to the Comédie, for he risked his livelihood, his creative soul, his very life.[70] Linguet was far less of a democrat or even a demophile than Mercier, but on the issue of dramatic and journalistic freedom of expression, he and Mercier made common cause. Another new journalist, Du Coudray, whose *Correspondance dramatique* would join the group of protest papers, was praised by Linguet as a vigorous crusader: "We can only say *amen* to all the proposals of this author in this area."[71] Du Coudray called Mercier an "intrepid athlete" and later confirmed that he was the instigator of the whole "affair": "Mercier's excommunication from the theater struck every one of us as indecent. It was *his* protest that fueled the whole revolution."[72]

As all this was being written, Mercier's lawsuit against the Comédie was being obstructed by the chief legal counsel for the actors, the royalist lawyer Coqueley de Chaussepierre. Coqueley had also been a royal censor for years, and he was one of the many to refuse the *Journal des Dames* in earlier days.[73] After a youthful flirtation with daring authors led to his eleven-day confinement in the prison of Vincennes for approving something "trop libre," Coqueley had become convinced that censoring was a dangerous matter.[74] Sobered by this experience, he decided that authors and the public should no longer be told the identity of their censors, which would remain the little secret of the booktrade and the police. Coqueley became the ministers' man. He appointed himself the confidant of Sartine; in January 1770 he had written Sartine a series of suggestions for tightening censorship, arguing not only the virtues of anonymity but also the importance of seeing printed works before sale to make sure no forbidden material had been slipped back in after the censor's reading, a common practice "si contraire à la bonne police."[75] So thorough was Coqueley's con-

70 *Journal de politique et de littérature* (1775) ii:73.
71 Ibid. (1776) i:134, 509; (1775) ii:504; (1776) ii:227.
72 *Correspondance dramatique* (1777) i:33. See also Du Coudray's *Il est temps de parler*.
73 See Chapter 1, above.
74 For Coqueley's imprisonment, see Archives Nationales, "Registre des dépêches," 0¹403 (316). See also Bibliothèque de l'Arsenal, Archives de la Bastille, MS 12114, fols. 322–26.
75 BN ms. fr. 22123 fols. 108–11, "Mémoires du censeur Coqueley de Chaussepierre remis à M. de Sartine en janvier 1770." See especially fols. 109 and 110.

version to political conformity that he had been rewarded for his cooperation during the Maupeou years with an apartment in the Louvre, a sure sign that the government now considered him on its side.[76] Théophraste Renaudot had earned the same honor when the offices of his *Gazette de France* were moved to the Louvre during 1648, a reward for his staunch royalism during the Fronde.[77] Collé, another gossipy chronicler, lamented Coqueley's capitulation to the Crown and his legal and amorous involvements with the Comédie as a betrayal of his good bourgeois stock. Now the bosom buddy of the actors—they even used the informal *tu*— Coqueley lived "à pot et à rôt" with the *comédiens,* to whom he had sold out completely.[78] Metra wrote his name "cocu-et-laid" and found him altogether nefarious.[79]

As a royal censor, Coqueley was in a position to silence all the Comédie's critics. He had watched the journalistic network take shape and considered it an unholy alliance. Since he was also the Comédie's lawyer, he was now instructed by the duc de Duras to take action against Mercier's group, and the obliging Coqueley began his series of moves to wipe out the theater's negative press. Mercier's linkup with the other papers was proof positive that he had partners in crime. The apparent contagiousness of his fervor suddenly made it a far greater threat. Coqueley had already shown his hatred for Mercier, for plebeian heroes, for feminist involvement in such causes, and for the *genre dramatique* in his two satires, *Monsieur Cassandre, ou Les Effets de l'amour et du vert-de-gris,* written under the pseudonym Doucet, and *Le Roué vertueux, poème en prose en quatre chants, propre à faire, en cas de besoin, un drame à jouer deux fois par semaine.* Coqueley's lambasting of popular theater had been warmly applauded, as Mercier could have predicted, by La Harpe in the *Mercure* and by Pierre Rousseau.[80]

---

76   See Archives Nationales, "Registre des dépêches," 0¹118 (207). Coqueley was awarded his apartment in May 1772. The *Almanach royal* gave his previous address as rue des Deux Portes, Saint Sévérin (see, for example, ibid., 1767:405– 8). By 1775 he was "au vieux Louvre, arcade de la Froidmanteau" (ibid., 1775:412–15) and a few years later in a different suite "au vieux Louvre, escalier de l'Académie française, au second" (ibid., 1779:452–55).

77   See Grand-Mesnil, *Mazarin,* 50.

78   Collé, *Journal et mémoires* 3:235.

79   Metra, *Correspondance secrète* 1:422 (16 juin 1775) and 2:16 (1 juillet 1775).

80   *Mercure,* juin 1775:133–47, and *Journal encyclopédique* (1775) v:306–15.

Now Coqueley went after the *frondeur* newspapers themselves, beginning with Le Fuel's *Lettres*. This periodical eluded the police for months because its editor, as we saw, cleverly changed its title with every issue, making it a difficult target. Linguet considered such metamorphoses of the "literary Proteus" hypocritical and cowardly,[81] but they allowed Le Fuel to print eight unmolested issues raving about Mercier's *Journal des Dames* and the new role it spelled out for the periodical press. Le Fuel contrasted the fresh, uncommonly vigorous ideas in Mercier's paper with the vapid, predictable verbiage of the establishment papers, which had capitulated to pressure and were therefore a disgrace to journalism. Le Fuel agreed with Mercier that a paper should inform its readers about public affairs and teach them how, not what, to think. Mercier's was a journal "filled with singular ideas . . . of far more merit than those on the pinnacle. . . . The *comédiens* are fools who will regret their mistreatment of this man."[82] Coqueley finally confiscated Le Fuel's ninth issue of the *Lettres* by tricking Crébillon into letting him "see" it, and he then put a stop to the paper for good. Determined to ruin Le Fuel financially as well, Coqueley forced him to reimburse all subscribers to the *Lettres* because they had received only eight of the promised thirty installments. That Coqueley had prevented the appearance of the remaining complement Le Fuel was not permitted to explain.[83]

With Le Fuel snuffed out, at least temporarily, Coqueley turned to the *Journal des Dames,* a trickier case since it enjoyed the protection of Marie Antoinette and had the royal privilege secured earlier through the agency of Mme de Montanclos. Coqueley, who viewed as especially subversive the inclusion of polemics in a women's paper, appears to have stopped articles specifically against the Comédie, for in autumn 1775 Mercier's paper abandoned its frontal attack on the theater. The last issues of that year almost exclusively covered narrowly feminine subjects, which Coqueley may have reminded Mercier were ostensibly the primary business of a *Journal des Dames*. In the selection of articles, Mercier seemed suddenly to "remember" in September, "we

81   *Journal de politique* (25 octobre 1775) iii:249.
82   *Lettres de Mme Le Hoc,* 221–22n, 339.
83   See Le Fuel's later *Nouveau spectateur, ou Journal des Théâtres* 1:397 (15 juin 1776). See also Le Fuel's *Requête au roi* for the details of his copy's "mutilation."

would be hard-pressed to choose, if the nature of our journal did not force us to give preference to those dealing with women." So Mercier returned to his arguments against feminine frivolity and in favor of women's patriotic education, articles reminiscent of those in *L'Iris de Guienne*. The "Epître sur les avantages des femmes de trente ans," for example, stressed the importance of mature women as advisers and counsellors.[84]

Not only did Coqueley compel Mercier to abandon his attack on the theater; there is also some evidence that he had begun to interfere with the actual circulation of the *Journal des Dames*. Already in late 1775 La Harpe testified with perverse pleasure to the difficulty in finding copies of Mercier's issues and attempted to trivialize the threat they posed: "I don't know where in the world to find them, and I will not bother to search. . . . When one has fought such illustrious generals as Fréron and Linguet, why bother with such obscure legionnaires?"[85] In 1776 Fréron, who needed to know what Mercier was saying in his *Journal des Dames* so that he could counterattack, gleefully reported that he had "had to look high and low before finally unearthing a copy."[86] Not only was it difficult for contemporaries to find these issues; so effective was their confiscation by the authorities that today no copies of the 1776 *Journal des Dames* remain extant. That it existed we know from numerous specific references to it, but the entire year has disappeared without a trace.[87] Because it now had a privilege, Co-

84   *Journal des Dames,* septembre 1775:308 and octobre 1775:99–106. See also décembre 1775:265–70.

85   *Mercure,* novembre 1775:209.

86   *Année littéraire* (1776) iv:344.

87   The *service de cherche* of the *Bibliothèque Nationale* conducted a three-year search for me of all municipal and provincial libraries, and it was unable to turn up anything. There is, however, the following abundant proof that the issues of 1776 existed: The *Journal des théâtres* (1 avril 1776:54) gave a long extract of an article by Mercier called "Spectacles des foires et des boulevards de Paris" from the *Journal des Dames* of February 1776; the *Année littéraire* ([1776] iv:344) gave an excerpt from the *Journal des Dames,* octobre 1776:457, in which Mercier continued his attacks on Fréron, one of the most implacable foes of *le drame;* Perrin's *Almanach de l'auteur et du libraire* (Paris, 1777), which was in manuscript in late 1776, mentioned on p. 25 the *Journal des Dames* as one of the newspapers available monthly chez Lacombe; La Harpe's *Correspondance littéraire* (2:55) and the *Courrier de l'Europe* (no. 31 [1777], 248) spoke of Mercier just giving it up in early 1777, as did the *Journal encyclopédique* ([1777] ii:154) and Hurtaut and Magny, *Dictionnaire historique* 3:669. A letter to Mercier dated 24 novembre 1776 addressed him as "Auteur du *Journal des Dames*" (Bibliothèque de l'Arsenal, ms.

queley could not officially suppress it, but he could make life miserable for the author and effectively liquidate each issue by buying it up as it rolled off the press. It was one of several techniques Coqueley would soon perfect. But he had not counted on the irrepressibility of the *frondeurs,* which manifested itself in repeated journalistic reincarnations.

In February 1776 Le Fuel de Méricourt, according to documents in the Comédie's archives, had been denied entrance to the theater when he came with his friend Crébillon's free passes. He had, like Mercier the previous year, been roughed up in the lobby and bodily ejected.[88] He was now angrier than ever at Coqueley and the actors for contriving to expropriate his *Lettres* and managed with Crébillon's help to buy himself the rights to another newspaper. A journal called the *Nouveau Spectateur* had been launched twice without success, in 1770 and 1775. Its author, Le Prevost d'Exmes, had been a staunch conservative, welcomed by the *Mercure* and the *Journal encyclopédique* for his hostility to *drames.*[89] But Prevost was discouraged and bankrupt now, and Le Fuel bought his privilege, a double coup since he had acquired a protected newspaper and simultaneously disarmed a foe. He paid dearly for it, over 12,000 livres to the printer Pierre and a pension of 600 livres to Prevost.[90] But such a mighty weapon must have seemed well worth it, and Le Fuel plunged right back into the fray, using his paper for what Pidansat approvingly called "sacrilege." Prevost soon told Fréron he was horrified that his name might be associated with the "obscenities" Le Fuel was printing in the journal that had formerly been his.[91]

Le Fuel's *Nouveau Spectateur, ou Journal des théâtres* lasted from

---

15078 [2c], fols. 122–26). The yearly *Almanach des muses* listed the *Journal des Dames* among the periodicals that published *pièces fugitives* throughout that year (*Almanach des muses,* 1776:245 and 1777:277). Finally, another periodical, Du Coudray's *Correspondance dramatique* (1:84) quoted from the September 1776 issue of the *Journal des Dames.*

88   Archives du Théâtre Français, dossier "Administration 1776," letter from Albert dated 22 février 1776.

89   See the summarized reviews of Prevost's *Nouveau spectateur* in the *Bibliographie parisienne,* 1770:37. See also *Nouveau spectateur,* 1775:ix.

90   See *Mémoire à consulter pour les souscripteurs du Journal des théâtres rédigé par le sieur de Méricourt* (Liège, 1777), letters dated 17 décembre 1776 and 31 janvier 1777.

91   *Année littéraire* (1777) ii:130–38.

1 April until 15 October 1776, but after the first two issues Coqueley dismissed the faithful Crébillon and got himself assigned
instead as censor. He began immediately to sabotage Le Fuel's
efforts. Pidansat watched as Coqueley mauled and maimed the
submitted copy and delayed the appearance of issues so long that
many of Le Fuel's subscribers defected. Coqueley, the *Mémoires
secrets* reported, was "the servile lackey of the Comédie, being
indecently recompensed by them for his dirty work." Far from
the impartial judge a good censor ought to be, Coqueley was
gladly accepting bribes to silence all the actors' detractors. "Coqueley serves his clients so well," reported Pidansat, "that he has
already stopped two issues of the *Journal des théâtres*. . . . The *comédiens* are overjoyed, because this behind-the-scenes maneuver—
doubtless conspired in concert with the superiors—will cause the
demise of the newspaper without the messiness of a manifest
suppression." The chronicler, continuing to trace these developments throughout the fall of 1776, explained that Le Fuel (a "good
Roman"), after nearly being thrown in Bicêtre (the "beggar's Bastille"), had escaped finally to England, his journal given instead to
the *comédien* Préville's son-in-law, who would be sure to lavish
upon the Comédie "fawning and ridiculous praise." "Mericourt is
not dead," Pidansat concluded this sad saga, but thanks to Coqueley "his newspaper *most* definitely *is*." [92]

Pidansat probably recounted at length this story, rather than
the gory details of the *Journal des Dames*'s simultaneous asphyxia-
tion, because he was himself the censor of Mercier's paper. The
Journal des Dames's story would have been too revealing of his
direct role as a supporter of *frondeur* journalism. Instead, he got
vicarious revenge against Coqueley and the Comédie by describing Le Fuel's victimization. Pidansat admired Le Fuel; he would
later sing his praises in the *Espion anglais,* claiming that "his black
humor, his fire, the effervescent temper of a Juvenal, and his style
all show his genius, natural and correct. . . . His firmness and
austerity give force and energy to his criticism." Juvenal, great
admirer of republican Rome, had become famous for his blistering attacks on the scandals of the Roman Empire, in particular the
profligacy and depravity of high society. What Pidansat liked best

92 *Mémoires secrets* 9:121, 220, 234, 247, 289.

was that Le Fuel's *Journal des théâtres* provided the opportunity for other journalists like Mercier to attack the Comédie anonymously when their own voices were silenced. Le Fuel's paper was a celebration of misrule, "a kind of masked ball where from behind disguises one said harsh truths, tolerated with the license of a saturnalia."[93] It was not long, however, before Coqueley's machinations put an end to the festivities.

The contents of the *Journal des théâtres* show clearly the mutilations in progress. The first two issues, still under Crébillon's protection, carried articles from Mercier's now liquidated *Journal des Dames,* one of which accused the Comédie of providing for *le peuple* only a gross diet of freaks, tightrope dancers, strippers, and drunkards instead of allowing the *théâtres des boulevards* to perform instructive and inspiring plays. Given decent material, the boulevard companies of Audinot and Nicolet could surpass the acting ability of the *comédiens* in no time. Another article, signed "Le Sceptique," contained most of Mercier's other pet peeves and would reappear verbatim in his 1778 *Nouvel Examen de la tragédie française.*[94] But an ominous note, doubtless by Coqueley, warned "Le Sceptique" that his "dramatism" would soon be corrected.

The next issue, that of 1 May, contained a diatribe against Mercier's *Brouette du vinaigrier* in the exact style of Coqueley's *M. Cassandre*. What a deplorable state Racine had reduced the French stage to, and how grateful we should be for Mercier's beautiful, wise, democratic *drames!* The vinegar barrel, the torn windows, the merchant's filthy clothes—these were indeed delights to the eye. The reviewer was converted and would urge censors and police to encourage playwrights to show characters spitting, urinating, defecating right on stage. Let's have barnfuls of animals and grunting, copulating cavemen! Down with refinement and taste! Bring on the revolution, the "égalité des conditions" for which Mercier clamored. Then all theatrical productions would be as sublime as his *Brouette*.[95] For all the satire, clearly *drames* represented a severe political menace to Coqueley and to the authorities from whom he took his orders.

This issue also contained a letter from the poet Claude-Joseph

---

93 [Pidansat], *Espion anglais* 5:241–56.
94 *Journal des théâtres,* 1 avril 1776:54–55; 15 avril 1776:71–85.
95 Ibid., 1 mai 1776:129–42.

Dorat, whose youthful *Déclamation théâtrale* Le Fuel claimed as his inspiration. In this work, written six years earlier, Dorat had spelled out the abuses rampant at the Comédie and had even suggested a newspaper of theater criticism as a corrective. But times had changed. Dorat was now romantically involved with several *comédiennes,* many of his plays had been performed, he was smiled upon by the queen, and he was no longer interested in battles. He was mortified that Le Fuel had used his name in vain, and Coqueley was glad to publicize Dorat's protest in the newspaper. "My soul and my character are repulsed by your journal," Dorat wrote to Le Fuel. "I shun more than ever anything malicious. . . . I may have given you an idea, but I fail to recognize it in your indecent execution. I loathe literary quarrels and hereby make a solemn vow never to be involved in them again."[96] Little wonder, after such a promise, that Coqueley would approve Dorat to succeed Mercier as editor of the *Journal des Dames.*

The remaining issues of the *Journal des théâtres,* delayed by Coqueley and printed erratically, reflected the power struggle between author and censor, which gave them a schizophrenic quality. There were letters from Elisabetta Caminer, Mercier's Italian translator, in which she reported the popularity of his plays in her country and begged him to let her translate some new scripts as "gifts for my people."[97] There was even an extract from Restif de la Bretonne's *Paysan perverti* giving yet another view of the Comédie's dissipation, which had earlier been printed in Mercier's *Journal des Dames.* According to Metra, the police had managed to seize huge numbers of Restif's work, which Mercier had praised for the "terrifying energy" with which it portrayed common people and for a vitality and forcefulness unique to its author.[98] The permissive censor of Restif's *Paysan* was none other than Pidansat. Here, then, was Le Fuel's journal publishing an extract from Mercier's silenced paper, which had excerpted Restif's fugitive novel! It was a brave attempt, but doomed.

Interlaced with these robust articles were many others in the same issue attacking Le Fuel and everything he stood for. There

96 Ibid., 166, 168.
97 Ibid., 1 octobre:273. For more pro-Mercier articles, see 15 mai:198–206, 235, 256; 1 juin:270, 282; 15 juillet:469–476; 1 août:50.
98 See Rives-Childs, *Restif de la Bretonne,* 19, 20, 29.

were also desperate notices in which Le Fuel tried to squelch rumors that the journal was having difficulties and would be replaced by another "in genere laudativo." He claimed to have protectors and assured his subscribers, whom he did not want to lose, that the delays were due to his illness, for he had indeed developed a severe lung disease. His paper would be back on track, he promised, as soon as he recovered.[99] These inconsistent, kaleidescopic issues, in which it was not clear who had the upper hand, were reminiscent of Mme de Beaumer's *Journal des Dames* during her period of struggle with her royalist censor Marin.

But Le Fuel's *Journal des théâtres* disappeared entirely after 15 October. On 10 February 1777 his friends, in the guise of disgruntled subscribers filing a *mémoire* against him for not furnishing the newspaper they had prepaid, told the true story of Le Fuel's victimization. The *mémoire* was in fact a defamatory exposé of the villainy of ministers, censors, and all others who had conspired to extinguish the paper. Two lawyers signed the *consultation,* one of whom, Falconnet, admirer of Cicero and "avenger of the oppressed," had already been threatened with expulsion from the bar for his defense of M. Tort, a petty clerk, against the duc de Guines, French ambassador to England. Falconnet's *mémoire* was radical and licentious, according to Grimm, a "calumny deserving the most rigorous punishment,"[100] but Falconnet saw himself as a publicist fighting for the Third Estate to have a significant voice, and he therefore interpreted his mission very differently. "I defended the weak against the strong. . . . A *mémoire* makes clear a citizen's rights to judges and to the public. . . . What is a judge? The voice of the sovereign. What is a lawyer? The voice of the nation. . . . Who [else] will protest the injustice of *les grands?* Who [else] will unmask their maneuvers and intrigues?"[101] The first signer of the *mémoire* was Mercier's friend and next-door neighbor, the chevalier de Rutlidge, with whom he was frequently confused; nobody knew which of the two had written the scandalous *Bureau d'esprit,* a play attacking *précieuses* and philosophes as weak conformists. Rutlidge would soon start his own paper, *Le Babil-*

---

99   *Journal des théâtres,* 1776:397, 507, 531.

100   Grimm et al., *Correspondance littéraire* 11:90–92. See also *Mémoires secrets* 9:131 (28 mai 1776), where Pidansat likens Falconnet to Linguet.

101   Falconnet, *Barreau français moderne* 1:"Avant propos," xvi–xxxii.

lard, probably modeled on a radical underground newsletter by the same name that circulated during the Fronde and was worded so simply and priced so low that it seemed to be aimed at an audience of commoners.[102] Rutlidge saw as the task of the journalist "to criticize irreverently all received opinion," to commit the "treasonous crimes" of *lèse philosophie* and *lèse comédie.*[103] Another signer was one Hébert, quite possibly the future author of the revolutionary paper *Le Père Duchesne* and "father of popular journalism." Hébert would soon move to Paris and live on the rue des Noyers, the very street where both Mercier and Rutlidge had their lodgings. If this was the same Hébert—Rutlidge in fact became an ardent Hébertist at one point during the Revolution—it would be the first known trace of the future Père Duchesne's Parisian activities, and one altogether in character.[104]

Pidansat's *Espion anglais,* which painted a sympathetic portrait of Falconnet and all the *mémoire*'s signers, explained that the apparent reproaches against Le Fuel by the lawyers had been "inserted on purpose to avoid any suspicion of collusion between Le Fuel and his subscribers."[105] But Le Fuel's case against Coqueley and the Comédie was taken out of the parlement's hands just as Mercier's had been and shelved forever in the Grand Conseil. Coqueley censored, and doubtless wrote a good part of, a work that

102 See Grand-Mesnil, *Mazarin,* 184–85. The author postulates the existence during the Fronde of a "presse populaire à grand tirage." Roche, *Peuple de Paris,* ably shows that the lower classes could follow and perhaps even read more than has hitherto been believed.

103 See, for example, Rutlidge's *Quinzaine anglaise* (London, 1776), "Préface" and "9e lettre," vigorous attacks on Voltaire, the Académie, and the protected journals, which "usurp from the public the liberty of thinking." In his later *Mémoire au roi pour le chevalier Rutlidge* (Paris, 1790), 31, he explains that the *Quinzaine* got him thrown in jail. See also his *Essais politiques,* xiv, where he says "nous serons obligés de fronder bien des préjugés reçus . . . la discussion . . . nous exposera à parler avec liberté de quelques hommes . . . des erreurs de leur politique." See also *Le Babillard* 4:249 and 381–83. More will be said of this periodical in Chapter 7, below.

104 See Walter, *Hébert et Duchesne,* in which the biographer wonders why Hébert moved to the neighborhood near the place Maubert and tries to make sense of his interest in working for the theater and the origin of the Père Duchesne persona in the *genre poissard* (so dear to Mme de Beaumer and Mercier before him). See especially 18–21, 36–42, and appendix 8, p. 332. A youthful involvement with the *Journal des Dames* and the *Journal des théâtres* would explain away the mystery.

105 [Pidansat], *Espion anglais* 5:256.

appeared at this moment called *Les Trois Théâtres de Paris,* in whose section on jurisprudence he stated peremptorily that the king would handle in the same manner all such contestations by Mercier's entourage against his actor protégés.[106] Meanwhile the police were seizing whatever packets of the *mémoire* they could find as they came across the border from Liège, where they had been printed because no Parisian *libraire* had been willing to touch them. The confiscated packets were then sent to the Pilon de la Bastille, which filled up with cartons of the *mémoire* and of Pidansat's *Espion anglais* that told its story.[107]

How short-lived Mercier's moment of glory had been! Grimm, who mistrusted Mercier, had nevertheless grudgingly admired his sense of timing when he had first undertaken his protest against the established order. "No doubt," Grimm had written of the *frondeur* coterie in 1775, "they have decided this the propitious moment to declare war on all exclusive privilege and further their *patriote* cause."[108] But Grimm's *Correspondance littéraire* of the mid-1770s is full of denunciations of the "insolence," "barbarousness," "violent ideas," and "vulgar sympathies" of both the journalists and the scurrilous *mémoires* written in their behalf by lawyers bent on fomenting discontent, chaos, and revolution. Commoners had no right to rise up this way against their masters! Was there no decency left in the world? How could Le Fuel's scum of a paper dare to include reference to a monarch?[109] Pidansat himself, although he stayed rigorously loyal to the group, warned about a possible purge and was one of the first to predict a fearsome backlash. Even though he had taken full advantage of the "douceur du nouveau gouvernement," he feared that the "license d'écrire," the forays of men of letters into legal and political terrain previously forbidden them, had gone too far and would bring about an "inquisition" reminiscent of the Maupeou years.[110]

---

106   Des Essarts, *Trois Théâtres de Paris,* 164–68. That Coqueley was the censor is confirmed in BN ms. fr. 22002, p. 129, no. 899. This document shows that he had also delayed this work, presumably to have time to insert a section on theatrical jurisprudence.

107   Bibliothèque de l'Arsenal, Archives de la Bastille, MS 10305; *Espion anglais* 5:241–56; Metra, *Correspondance secrète* 4:244–88.

108   Grimm et al., *Correspondance littéraire* 11:62.

109   Ibid. 9:65–66, 395–96; 11:109, 226, 90–92; 12:121, 315; 13:159, 140.

110   *Mémoires secrets* 9:174 (30 juillet 1776) and 270 (24 novembre 1776).

Pidansat was correct. By the end of 1776 the liberal ministry had toppled. Malesherbes had resigned. Crébillon had been dismissed as *censeur de la police* and banished to his lands, where he would die reportedly disheartened in 1777. A new booktrade director, Le Camus de Neville, came quickly under the influence of the duc de Duras and Coqueley and bent to the task of wiping out the *frondeurs* and the "fermentation générale" they were causing. Le Fuel's *mémoire* and a *requête au roi* he wrote some months later described the systematic sabotage of his newspaper by the ministerial legerdemain of Le Camus and his "marionettes," their ruthless neglect of "law," and Le Fuel's determination to "fight injustice until extinction."[111] Describing Le Camus's "incredible atrocities," Le Fuel detailed the confiscation of six letters to his subscribers; the ransacking by police spies of his printer's shop, his hideouts, and his home; the seizing of his papers, his furniture, and even his clothing. Le Fuel directed a barrage of slander at nearly everyone in the new administration except the king himself. Le Camus, the draper's son who had flattered and bribed his way to the top, had been unanimously rejected by the Parlement of Normandy when he sought to become its *avocat général*. This "long inquisitor" had bought the post of *maître de requêtes* but needed to steal and resell Le Fuel's newspaper's privilege to repay his debts. Coqueley was false, vile, depraved, almost subhuman; he frequented "filles publiques" and tried to lure others into debauchery. The chancellor Maurepas had put forth trumped-up charges against Le Fuel, whom all knew to be innocent, and the maréchal duc de Duras "has fought more for the actresses and against me, poor devil, than for his king against France's enemies." The *requête,* written in England where Le Fuel, "destitute and half-naked," had been forced to flee for his life, ended with a long attack on the French prison system and on the bankruptcy of all her legal channels.[112]

Le Fuel was not the only one of the *Journal des Dames*'s supporters to have fled to London. Linguet had been fired in the summer of 1776 from the *Journal de politique* by the publisher Panckoucke, now the ministers' friend, and by the duc de Duras,

111 See *Mémoire à consulter,* letters of 10 novembre and 23 décembre 1776.
112 Le Fuel de Méricourt, *Requête au roi.*

because he too had dared to challenge the theater, the academies, and the regime. Linguet was no friend of the parlements, but he made common cause with the *frondeur* journalists on most other issues and had joined his voice to their chorus of protest against oppression. Linguet had told his readers that unfriendly censors were already sabotaging his paper in early 1775, interfering with his concentration, time, peace of mind [*présence d'esprit*]. In particular they had thwarted his efforts to print his "Discours sur l'état de l'Europe" and "Réflexions sur la déclamation théâtrale." He had to watch his words, he told them, more closely than a miniaturist controlled the strokes of his pen. "Observations on the theater, and on the acting ability of those pensioned by the prince to give him pleasure are not, one would think, as dangerous as political remarks. Theater secrets are perhaps slightly less redoubtable than those of the court. But do not be fooled into thinking they are without peril. The stage, like the corridors of power, can never be discussed with candor."[113] When Linguet's expected dismissal came in 1776, he ran to England, and all his fury spewed out to Vergennes, the minister of foreign affairs, in a libelous open letter that even the sympathetic Metra called a "veritable vomiting of insults" against all royal ministers. It was, like Mercier's and Le Fuel's *requêtes,* an autobiographical "case study in victimization under a despotism."[114]

La Harpe, to whom the *Journal de politique* was immediately entrusted by Panckoucke—this to add insult to injury since he was Linguet's archenemy—lost no time in turning the tables. Lest there be any confusion, he announced that since 25 July Linguet had been out of the picture entirely.[115] He next published a violent letter against Mercier's *Journal "appelé" des Dames,* whose title was merely a smokescreen for revolutionary rantings that undermined "the whole order of the well-bred."[116] A few issues later came a devastating blast at Le Fuel's *Journal des théâtres:*

> Talents of all kinds are outraged by this journal, where even [the famous actor] Le Kain and Voltaire are vilified. Above all there

113 *Journal de politique* (1775) ii:376 and (1775) iii:246–47, 251.
114 For details on this letter to Vergennes, see "Political Journalism" in Levy, *Simon-Nicolas-Henri Linguet,* 172–224.
115 *Journal de politique* (1776) iii:163.
116 Ibid. (1776) iii:260.

is a base, barbarous, vulgar style to the whole work. . . . It revolts me to stoop so low as to discuss such illiterate impudence, but we must warn readers that this fraud of a newspaper is by riffraff of the lowest classes, who write in the idiom of the populace and judge reputations in cafés. . . . How could Crébillon help but endorse a work that attacks genius, since for thirty years nobody has recognized his own?[117]

Linguet was never to forgive Panckoucke, whom he henceforth considered a man without a conscience. He, Mercier, and many other playwrights had suffered indignities that no person in a healthy society should have to bear. "The *comédiens* form a corps," Linguet wrote from London in his *Annales,* "to which dramatic authors have been sacrificed. Publishers form a corps, before which men of letters have had to grovel with no decency or justice." What this journalistic purge proved, he went on, was the "inevitable victory of everything that is 'troupe.'"[118] Always the individualist, Linguet considered this a sure sign that lawless France was crumbling. One year later, when the insatiable Panckoucke wiped out the *Journal des Dames* and the *Journal des théâtres* forever, silencing their once unique and hearty voices, Linguet would pronounce France close to death.[119]

Meanwhile Mercier was left in France to deal with the purge taking place all around him. His network of papers was disintegrating rapidly. Le Tourneur was dismissed from the *Journal anglais* by its publisher, Ruault, perhaps because the subscribers to his Shakespeare translation now included most of the *frondeur* entourage—Mercier, Mme de Montanclos, Collé, Delacroix, Dubois-Fontanelle, Falconnet, François de Neufchâteau, Henrion de Pansey, and Diderot, the one *philosophe* whom the *frondeurs* frequented, probably because he had been a principal initiator of the *drame.*[120] Ruault, clearly frightened by the government's purge, advertised that he wanted no further traffic with Mercier's troublesome writings. To avert guilt by association he printed in the establishment papers a notice that he was "selling dirt cheap the

117   Ibid. (1776) iii:389.

118   *Annales politiques, civiles, et littéraires* 3:52.

119   Ibid. 4:103–11, 189–91. See also Linguet's *Précis et consultation,* 31, 38.

120   For Ruault's hiring and firing of Le Tourneur, see the *Journal anglais* 3, no. 21:260, no. 25:512. For Le Tourneur's subscribers, see vol. 1 of his twenty-volume Shakespeare translation. I am preparing a separate piece on the political overtones of the Shakespeare controversy.

drames of M. Mercier, that is 10 sols for leather bound copies; after April there will be none in the shop at all, for by then we will have found another use for the 6,000 copies contaminating the store room." Another prominent publisher, Lacombe, who had handled the *Journal des Dames,* also found himself severely compromised by the authorities' crackdown, and he too turned against the *frondeurs.*[121] Ameilhon's *Journal de Verdun,* after supporting Linguet, Mercier, and Le Fuel and risking some "nouvelles politiques" on the parlements, was "denatured" and finally suppressed at the end of 1776.[122]

Mercier was finally sufficiently discouraged and frightened by these various persecutions and expropriations to give up the *Journal des Dames.* A newspaper that reached no readers was as ineffectual as an unperformed play. On 19 December 1776 Mercier sold the rights to his paper to his friend Chalumeau, an agronomist and republican who had contributed some ideas to *L'An 2440.*[123] A portion of Chalumeau's money, however, was advanced by Panckoucke, who having fired Linguet at the duc de Duras's orders, may well have been told to do whatever was necessary to muzzle Mercier as well. Six weeks later, in a private transaction before a notary, the *Journal des Dames* was entrusted to Dorat, who Coqueley and Panckoucke believed would be benign and placid.[124] After this sellout by Chalumeau to the enemy, Mercier was totally disillusioned and had nothing more to do with the *Journal des Dames.* He was also by this time quite exhausted. He had had high hopes, but it was clear now that his own *patrie* could not withstand a vigorous, healthy press, one "that illuminates too well the prevarications and vices of people in high places."[125] He felt that Dorat was the farthest thing from a true journalist or publicist, and he experienced Dorat's takeover of the *Journal des Dames* as an ignominious defeat for the *frondeur* cause.

121   See *L'Année littéraire* (1777) vii:209, where Fréron *fils* cooperated with Ruault's attack on Mercier. On the origin of Fréron's hatred for Mercier, see ibid. (1776) iv:344. For Lacombe's treachery, see Le Fuel's *Requête au roi,* 22–23.

122   See *Journal de Verdun* (1775) i:359, 434, 514–17; (1775) ii:102–8, 198–99; (1776) ii:132, 231, 480.

123   Archives Nationales, Minutier Central LXXXV (660), 18 décembre 1776.

124   Ibid., LVIII (480), 27 janvier 1777.

125   Mercier, *Tableau de Paris* 2:79–80. For interesting comments on the role of publicist in this period, see Baker, "French Political Thought," especially 290–91, and 298.

7

M. Dorat's Whitewashed *Mélanges littéraires* (1777–1778)

FRONDEUR JOURNALISM IN THE DIASPORA

It remains to examine the last year of the *Journal des Dames* and the scattering of *frondeur* journalists after the purge. In Claude-Joseph Dorat, Coqueley and Panckoucke felt sure they had their man, for Dorat had just promised the world and God that he would never speak ill of anyone again. To the authorities he seemed the ideal choice to replace Mercier and calm down the whole dispute with the Comédie. Where Mercier had made war, Dorat would make peace. Amorously involved with a number of *comédiennes,* addicted to the soft, elegant, aristocratic style—the "douceur de vivre," as Talleyrand called it—Dorat was eager at this moment in life to be cooperative and was not in the least interested in subversion. Had he not just publicly sworn, in an open letter repudiating Le Fuel's *Journal des théâtres,* that he shunned anything leading to unpleasantness or contention, detested literary and political quarrels, and in the future would steer clear of them?[1]

As we have seen, Mercier considered Dorat a weak and trivial man and would never have dealt with him directly. He had sold the *Journal des Dames* not to Dorat but to François-Marie Chalumeau, an agronomist whose economic liberalism and pro-American sympathies matched his own.[2] The two men had been

---

1   *Journal des théâtres,* mai 1776:166–68.
2   Archives Nationales, Minutier Central (henceforth M.C.) LXXXV (660), 18 décembre 1776. See Chalumeau's *Ma Chaumière,* in which he reminisced about

corresponding since the early 1770s, and Mercier had used some of Chalumeau's ideas in *L'An 2440*. But Chalumeau was just back from a visit to Russia and Vienna, where monarchs had granted him audiences and listened with interest to his agronomic theories. He was now eager to ingratiate himself with powerful patrons in his own country who might take seriously his writings and help transform them into practical reality. He had even landed a post in the household of the king's youngest brother, the notoriously reactionary comte d'Artois, and was far more ready to cooperate with the authorities than Mercier realized. Once having bought the *Journal des Dames* from Mercier, Chalumeau therefore readily acquiesced to Panckoucke's choice of the docile Dorat, bringing him in as the new editor six weeks later. All Mercier could do after this subterfuge was to insist before a notary that Chalumeau, in whom Mercier still evidently retained some faith, not surrender the paper entirely to Dorat for three years.[3] But the paper now fell irretrievably into Coqueley's hands, and he appears to have remained its censor until its final absorption by Panckoucke in the summer of 1778. It was Coqueley's inclination, as he had explained in his *mémoires* to Sartine, to keep secret his involvement with most of the works he censored. Not a single signature appeared in Dorat's sixteen issues of the *Journal des Dames,* even though it now boasted both "privilège" and "approbation" and had been openly signed by its other censors throughout the Montanclos and Mercier years. Pidansat's frequent comments about Dorat's "inflexible censor" who never allowed a word against the Comédie would seem to confirm that Coqueley remained in control until the end.[4]

To dissociate himself from his *frondeur* predecessors and sever the journal itself from its radical past, Dorat immediately changed

---

Mercier and the *Journal des Dames* (62, 235) and reprinted an open letter of his own from 1775 very much in favor of the American "insurgents" and predicting that their revolution would have repercussions in France (294–319).

3   M.C. LVIII (480), 27 janvier 1777.

4   [Pidansat], *Espion anglais, nouvelle édition* 2:337. Biblothèque Nationale, manuscrit français (henceforth BN ms. fr.) 22002, p. 30, no. 194, lists no censors beyond Pidansat's friend Cardonne, because Coqueley's association came later, in 1777 and 1778. Cardonne *signed* his approbations (see, for example, *Le Babillard* 3 [janvier 1779]: unnumbered page) and was far more liberal politically, allowing considerable theater criticism in Rutlidge's periodical. Had he been the *Journal des Dames*'s censor during the Dorat years, his signature would certainly have appeared.

the title of his newspaper. His first issue, in the spring of 1777, was now called *Mélanges littéraires, ou Journal des Dames dédié à la reine,* thus propitiating the authorities by emphasizing the lighter literary angle and the royal auspices under which it appeared. To make more convincing his conciliatory frame of mind, he spread it about that his interest in journalism was pecuniary and not polemical. Like Campigneulles, he hoped to produce a tasty confection that would please all and offend none. This paper was to rescue him from the sorry financial plight into which years of high living had plunged him. Pidansat, who we shall see viewed Dorat as a traitor, mocked his attempt to make a speculative venture out of a paper whose turbulent track record had been punctuated with government-enforced "languishing and vegetating." Dorat's announcement that he would raise its price from 12 to 18 livres a year and his incredibly sanguine expectation of one thousand subscribers and 6,000 livres annual profit for himself must have seemed to Pidansat altogether ridiculous. But maybe, he resentfully admitted, this seemingly glaring miscalculation would prove correct. Perhaps a light, entertaining *Journal des Dames* by a frivolous "faiseur de madrigaux" would succeed after all, in a climate increasingly hostile to serious political journalism.[5] By some inexorable logic, the Old Regime had once again reduced its only paper for women to the bagatelle it was originally intended to be.

But who was this Dorat who wished so fervently to use the *Journal des Dames* to put things right? What had he done wrong? Why were the chroniclers so embittered by his peacemaking gesture? Whom did he need to appease? What was the reason that Dorat, a veritable Lothario with women, had become one of the most disliked and ridiculed writers of his day?

Born in 1734 into a family of wealthy magistrates, Dorat had been a reluctant law student, then a musketeer for a time, until a Jansenist aunt prevailed upon him to abandon a career she considered bloodthirsty and dissipated. Wealthy enough to devote himself to poetry, his true love, Dorat turned out at a prodigious rate fables and light verse, *pièces fugitives* that became increasingly popular in the salons of the 1760s and earned him the reputation of "poète pour dames par excellence." Heady from these successes

---

5   *Mémoires secrets* 10:30–31 (6 février 1777) and 32 (9 février 1777).

and unsatisfied to remain the rage of the drawing room—
"l'homme aimable qu'on invite à souper"—Dorat decided to
court the philosophe mandarins.[6] The ineptitude with which he
did this poignantly portrays the fragile ego of a man filled with
self-doubt, at once inspired and demoralized by the constellation
of great minds all around him. Dorat sensed from the start that
he lacked what it took to be admitted into their fold, and although
dazzled by them, he deeply resented their esprit de corps. Yet he
could never resign himself to being excluded, and he harbored an
irrational hope that he would someday win a seat in the philo-
sophe-dominated Académie française. The more Dorat experienced rejection, the more perversely he coveted acceptance. His
embarrassment and frustration jaundiced his efforts to woo per-
suasively; a vicious cycle ensued. Grimm mocked Dorat's "gauch-
erie dans l'esprit," his habit of addressing great men whom he did
not know and composing awful poems that offended instead of
honoring them.[7] The abbé de Boismont, a member of the Académie, told Mme Necker that only a fool would seriously present
himself as a candidate after insulting so many of the "forty immortals."[8] Linguet, who never wavered in his own loathing for La
Harpe and for the Académie of which La Harpe seemed the quin-
tessential symbol, pitied Dorat for his indecisiveness. If he could
not grovel, he should scorn, but instead he exhausted himself in a
frenzied alternation of attacks and caresses on a door that had been
shut to him from the start.[9]

The secret of Dorat's failure was of course Voltaire, who could
make or break the fortunes of literary novices. We have already
seen how he intimidated the *Journal des Dames*'s provincial
founder, Campigneulles, and sent him reeling back to Lyons. But
Dorat, a Parisian, was much more persistent. Between 1766 and
1770 he and Voltaire exchanged over a dozen letters in which they
tried to size up each other. Dorat, even as he paid court to the

6 Grente, *Dictionnaire des lettres françaises* 1:393–94.
7 Grimm et al., *Correspondance littéraire* 8:170 (novembre 1766).
8 Desnoiresterres, *Chevalier Dorat,* 332–33. This biography, although rhetorical and frustrating for its lack of precise references, is still the only full-length
treatment of Dorat's life. See also the article on him in Sgard's *Dictionnaire des
journalistes,* 128–29.
9 Linguet, *Annales politiques, civiles et littéraires* 8 (1780), 503–12, "Mort de
M. Dorat."

great man, was already convinced he had been pegged as an intellectual lightweight and passed over by the literary powers who transformed others into stars overnight as if by magic. His *Epître de Racine à Corneille* (1765) and his *Avis aux sages du siècle* (1766) were full of such accusations, as were the prefaces of many of his works.[10] These were invariably followed by flowery apologies to Voltaire, who bounced back graciously enough for a few years. Meanwhile Dorat's suspicion that the philosophes had somehow proscribed him led him into friendship with their archenemy Fréron. Voltaire, who would rather have had the complicated young Dorat for him than against him, now tried to "rescue" him from Fréron's clutches. Playing on Dorat's vanity as he saw the unsavory friendship take shape, Voltaire urged that "literature would be less persecuted if those who cultivated letters would unite." Offering to forget Dorat's insults and support him if he would break cleanly with the "execrable" Fréron, Voltaire reminded Dorat of his "good breeding," his "natural superiority," which should prevent him from even tolerating, much less befriending, the editor of the *Année littéraire*. In 1770 Voltaire made his last plea for Dorat to do justice to his talents, to his generosity of soul, which would suffer total dishonor in Fréron's company.[11] Then their correspondence ceased. Voltaire was not about to waste more breath on a lost cause. But he would never forget the betrayal.

Dorat, for his part, seemed simply not to trust Voltaire's promises, which, had they been sincere, would already have ensured his celebrity. He had also come to enjoy very much the society of the erstwhile "abbé" Fréron, with whom he shared a taste for wine, women, song, and luxury. Fréron lived in style. He was reputed to have spent 30,000 livres for the gold decorations and furnishing of an apartment on the rue de Seine, more on a fancy carriage, yet more on a country house, all for the pleasure of entertaining friends at "les festins les plus délicieux de Paris."[12] The

10 See, for example, those cited by Linguet in ibid., 510–11.
11 See Voltaire, *Complete Works,* 132:237 for the full list of letters. See especially D14062 (115:456) and D16679 (121:11).
12 [Pidansat], *Espion anglais, nouvelle édition* 1:270–99, "Sur la mort de Fréron"; see especially 284–85, 294–95. Pidansat complained, as had Mathon and Mme de Montaclos's censor Artaud before him, that the official *Nécrologe* did not write satisfactory obituaries, "s'imprimant sous les yeux de la police." Pidansat, on the other hand, had talked to Fréron's friends, gone to his home, looked through his papers, and put together a vivid portrait.

money behind this extravagant living came from Fréron's journalism, his highly successful *Année littéraire,* which regularly lambasted the "secte des philosophes." Some years the paper brought
in as much as 40,000 livres profit for its editor, a fact that would
later inspire Dorat to think his own *Journal des Dames* could be
lucrative. Dorat now joined Fréron's staff and there received his
journalistic training, contributing poems, letters, and extracts of
his own works to the *Année littéraire.*[13] For this Voltaire could not
forgive him; sixteen times, when vacancies occurred at the Académie, Dorat was left seething with rage and pain—according to
his biographers and eulogists—as the seats were filled by others,
perhaps less talented and certainly less productive than he. But
Dorat could still not renounce his dream of academic glory and
seemed incapable of realizing how much his unpopularity with
the reigning philosophes was his own fault.

Thus ostracized by the regime's entrenched Académie, Dorat
had much in common with the *frondeur* journalists and could easily have allied himself with their coterie. Because he seemed too
cowardly to do so, he earned the enmity of that group as well.
They had held high hopes for Dorat at first. He was, after all,
from a solid Jansenist *patriote* background; his father had even
pressured him to become a magistrate in parlement. In his youth
he had displayed some definite antiroyalist tendencies, implying
in one of his plays that Louis XV resembled the indolent *rois fainéants.* Marin, the censor of this play, who had overlooked and let
pass into print the subversive lines, was sent to jail for the offense,
and as we saw took a much harder stance against Mme de Beaumer after this sobering episode.[14] Dorat had been close friends
with the fiery Linguet in the 1760s, even providing housing for
his impecunious comrade, and they had lived together and written
together on the rue de Vaugirard for years.[15] The booktrade's spies
knew that Dorat had attended a private reading by Rousseau of
his *Confessions* during one of the author's furtive stops in Paris,
and the police had started a file on Dorat as a result.[16] In 1765,
when Dorat was contributing to Mathon's *Journal des Dames,* he

---

13 Ibid. 1:293.
14 See Chapter 3, above.
15 See Desnoiresterres, *Chevalier Dorat,* 288–89. See also Sgard, *Dictionnaire
des journalistes,* 128, 242, and Levy, *Simon-Nicolas-Henri Linguet,* 14–15.
16 Pierre Manuel, *Police de Paris* 1:97.

had published his *Déclamation théâtrale,* a poem in which he criticized the Comédie-Française. Bastide's *Journal de Bruxelles* com-
mented on the "cruelty" of such a work, given the fragile egos of
the actors.[17] In 1771 Dorat put out a new edition of the *Déclamation*
with some additional letters proposing for the first time a newspaper dedicated to candid criticism of the abuses at the Comédie,
to be called *Le Spectateur des trois théâtres.* Such a paper, argued
Dorat, would bring about needed reforms as opposed to the "boring and damaging praise of even miserable players that presently
fills the timid periodicals with which Paris is inundated." Such
"truths" would be risky, for they would injure many proud and
vain actors presently "cradled in false security." Dorat feared that
his frankness would "cost him dearly," but in 1771 he appeared
ready and willing to realize the idea he had launched.[18] Finally, he
was known to have written a fierce attack on the "culte des philosophes," as yet only in manuscript, a play called *Les Prôneurs.*

But Dorat lacked both the courage and the conviction to follow
through on his *frondeur* impulses, and after several of these false
starts the promising nonconformist came to be viewed as a cow-
ard. Mathon, as we saw, grew impatient with Dorat's levity, his
lack of commitment to a political stance.[19] Dorat and Linguet had
an ugly quarrel over some stolen horses and money, and Linguet
publicly accused Dorat of besmirching his reputation and thus
causing his disbarment. He attacked him viciously in the *Journal
de politique,* casting him as the villain of the piece, the turncoat,
the government informer. The bold, outspoken rebel Linguet—
whose insolence was about to wreck his journalistic career in
France but was winning him tremendous popular support and
sympathy from his seven thousand subscribers—saw Dorat as his
enemy.[20] Linguet, according to police reports, threatened to kill
Dorat for his treachery, and because Linguet was the martyr and
hero of the moment, the entire scandal made Dorat look very
bad.[21] He had also completely abandoned his plan for a theater

17   *Journal de Bruxelles* (1767) ii:120.
18   Dorat, *Déclamation théâtrale,* letters published as "suites," pp. 192–93,
200, 204, 210–11.
19   See Chapter 4, above.
20   See Linguet's *Journal de politique* (mars 1776) i:350–51; Charavay, *Revue
des documents historiques,* 81–84; Desnoiresterres, *Chevalier Dorat,* 287–91.
21   Pierre Manuel, *Police de Paris,* 1:100–103.

journal immediately after proposing it and was embarrassed, then horrified, when Le Fuel's *Journal des théâtres* brought it to fruition and credited him with the seminal idea. Dorat had been conspicuously absent from the group rallying around Mercier during his protest against the Comédie in 1775. In fact we have seen that Fréron's *Année littéraire,* to which Dorat was a major contributor, was scathingly hostile to Mercier, denouncing his republicanism and his *drames* as threats to good taste, social stability, and political order. The *Année littéraire* vilified Mercier at every opportunity, calling him an Omar—the barbarian who burned the Alexandria library—for believing that the multitude was a better audience than the scholar, the common man a worthier dramatic subject than the king.[22]

So despite Dorat's exclusion from the Académie, which had much in common with Mercier's banishment from the Comédie and even with Linguet's disbarment, he shied away from alliance with them, from political fights, and in general from taking any dangerous action. Just when the "affaire de Mercier" erupted, Dorat wrote to one of his mistresses that he deplored the massing of journalists and dramatists against the regime. "I am not much for politics, as you know. Being far less daring than certain of our acquaintances, I let the machine go along for better or for worse, at the bidding of those who lead it."[23] Dorat's recent plays, unlike Mercier's, had been sufficiently tame and genteel to be accepted and performed by the Comédie even during the Maupeou years. The *comédiens* had been quite supportive of him, as can be seen in his correspondence with the lead actor Préville.[24] Several *comédiennes* shared his bed, and he was not about to compromise his amours or alienate the one privileged corps that granted him hospitality. Besides, he still dreamed that success as a playwright might earn him the coveted academic chair; association with Mercier's group would have jeopardized that already slim chance completely.

22 *Année littéraire* (1777) viii:198–99. See also Chapter 6, above, n. 121.
23 Dorat, *Coup d'oeil,* chap. 9, p. 61. Pages 63 and 65 show that although Dorat had numerous grievances against the Comédie, he was sufficiently loyal to it to fight against the formation of a second troupe.
24 See Archives du Théâtre Français, dossiers "Correspondance Dorat" and "Registre concernant messieurs les auteurs."

Now Dorat wasted both his energy and his fortune in a desperate attempt to buy acclaim. He paid the famous engravers Marillier and Eisen exorbitant prices to illustrate his works, but La Harpe, d'Alembert, and the other philosophes objected to this "illegitimate" means of attracting purchasers to his books. The abbé Galiani quipped to Grimm, in an untranslatable play on words mocking Dorat's dependence on pictures, that he was rapidly going under and survived only because "il se sauve de planche en planche."[25] The *frondeur* entourage objected just as much as the philosophes to Dorat's obsession with procuring fame. Pidansat's *Mémories secrets* reported that people indeed bought Dorat's books, but after cutting out the illustrations, they threw the worthless text in the trash.[26] An even greater drain on Dorat's finances was his habit of packing the theater with as many as three hundred friends and strangers paid to yell "bravo" vociferously at various points in the show. Sometimes he bought out the whole *parterre* and even some of the *loges* in an effort to drown out the claque of the philosophes trying to discredit him. Metra, who reported contemptuously that whatever success Dorat achieved had been bought dearly, described his situation and the erosion of all his support at just the moment that he took on the *Journal des Dames:* "Dorat is being attacked today from all sides. It's a free-for-all open to anyone who feels like kicking."[27] La Harpe, speaking for the philosophes, laced into Dorat in his *Journal de politique* and in his letters.[28] Dorat struck back at La Harpe in the faithful *Année*

---

25 See Desnoiresterres, *Chevalier Dorat,* 319, and Grimm et al., *Correspondance littéraire* 6:469 (janvier 1766). See Archives de la Seine, MS 6AZ 1602, which includes receipts for some of Dorat's engravings, costing as much as 300 livres each.

26 *Mémoires secrets* 14:12 (4 avril 1779).

27 Metra, *Correspondance secrète* 4:94, 334 (11 janvier 1777). See also ibid. 66–67 and 202: "A la première représentation [du *Malheureux Imaginaire* de Dorat] . . . on l'avait jugée sans appel, un des plus médiocres ouvrages. . . . D'un coup de baguette, le mercredi suivant, les esprits ont changé, on l'a applaudie avec transport. Vous qui ne croyez point aux magiciens, vous me demanderez très sérieusement la raison physique et non surnaturelle de cette révolution: or le voici . . . M. Dorat s'est avisé d'acheter tout le parterre et quelques premiers loges. Ces gens à sa dévotion ont crié à tort et à travers: *beau, admirable,* et les sots qui se sont trouvés là, et qui étaient innocents de ce complot, ont répété aux soupers de Paris, cette pièce de Dorat est charmante! . . . L'on trouva dans le parterre des cartes où étaient ces mots: 'A tel endroit, vous applaudirez; à tel vers surtout vous battrez les mains, vous trépignerez d'admiration.'"

28 See, for example, La Harpe, *Correspondance littéraire* 2:13–15, 62–63.

littéraire, where what had begun as gentle epigrammatical sparring had escalated into all-out war.[29] But when Fréron suddenly died in 1776, bequeathing his paper not to Dorat but to his own son—a hopeless imbecile by most reports—Dorat believed he had lost his sole remaining support. Discretion now seemed the better part of valor. Stranded without arms, he resolved to make peace once and for all.

At first nobody believed him. Becoming the editor of his own newspaper seemed more like an act of war than a gesture of good will. Most expected Dorat to use the *Journal des Dames,* at the very least, to continue his now familiar fight with La Harpe. La Harpe himself thought Dorat was simply adding to his arsenal of weapons, which already included the *Année littéraire,* and braced himself for a frontal assault.[30] Since La Harpe, the "fameux critique," was also the archenemy and favorite target of Linguet, Mercier, and Le Fuel, the chroniclers welcomed Dorat's entrance into the fray with a paper of his own and thought he might still redeem himself by making common cause with the *frondeurs.* Even if he would not explicitly join them, they at least hoped he would use his new paper as a battleground in which to attack their mutual foe.[31] Everyone questioned the sincerity of Dorat's pacifistic declarations. The *Courrier de l'Europe,* a French-language *frondeur* paper printed in England and reprinted in Boulogne for which Brissot was now writing, hoped that the purge of papers in France had been ineffective. Still wishing for a fight, the *Courrier* interpreted Dorat's acquisition of his own newspaper as a sign of his rapprochement with the polemical journalists. "The world of letters in France, like European politics, resembles more and more a battleground," reported the *Courrier.* "Our authors drill and fortify their respective ranks of proselytes; they retrench, they maneuver. M. Dorat, aware of his adversary La Harpe's advantage, has bought himself his own *arme périodique,* the *Journal des Dames.* Thus the warring parties protect themselves and will return shot for shot." One of Dorat's several mistresses was the countess Fanny de Beauharnais, a spirited feminist with whom Mme de

29 See Dorat's rebuttals to La Harpe in the *Année littéraire* (1776) vi:141, 261–65, 279, 339 and (1777) i:48–71. For more on the life-threatening words exchanged, see Jovicevich, *Jean-François de La Harpe,* 95–96.
30 La Harpe, *Correspondance littéraire* 2:55.
31 See, for example, Metra, *Correspondance secrète* 4:146 (8 février 1777).

Montanclos, Diderot, Restif de la Bretonne, and Mercier were also friendly. The *Courrier* printed the hunch of its editors that Mercier had actually sold the paper to the lively "Fanny," so that the *Journal des Dames* could continue in its *frondeur* and feminist vein.[32]

But the French authorities saw things differently. Coqueley and Panckoucke believed, as outsiders did not, that Dorat had no more fight in him and that he sincerely meant his newspaper to be an olive branch. He was not only destitute but sick, genuinely weary of feuding and eager to spend his remaining years in comfort and peace. Both his censor and publisher expected Dorat to be tame. They knew that he had taken on the *Journal des Dames* at a pivotal point in his life, when he was isolated, frightened, and therefore determined to be well behaved. He still coveted that seat in the Académie and would make one last effort, now that Fréron was dead, to impress the philosophes with his seriousness and convince these mandarins of his admiration for *lumières*. In his prospectus, which he called "L'Idée d'un *Journal des Dames*," he professed to model himself on Bayle and Fontenelle, to rise above insult and provocation, to be honest, impartial, objective, dignified.[33] Dorat seemed deliberately to be following to the letter the *Encyclopédie*'s prescription for good journalism, in which editors were warned against "attracting readers by malignity and the furor with which they tear and defile works by estimable authors." The *Encyclopédie*—no doubt to guard itself against the assaults of the philosophes' archfoe Fréron—had cautioned journalists to "recognize the superior talents of men of genius . . . [for] only a fool would be the enemy of a Voltaire, a Montesquieu, a Buffon."[34] Dorat now made it his business to praise this trio of luminaries. Buffon and Montesquieu were dutifully featured in his *Journal des Dames*,[35] but he mostly tried to make amends with Voltaire, since he was the darling of both the Comédie and the Académie. Dorat's second issue published a poem by the marquis de la Villette, Voltaire's close friend and soon-to-be Paris host and im-

---

32 *Courrier de l'Europe,* 14 février 1777, no. 31:249; 4 mars 1777, no. 36:289.

33 See "L'Idée d'un *Journal des Dames*," *Journal des Dames,* mars 1777:5.

34 In the *Encyclopédie,* s.vv. "Journaliste" and "Journal," both by Diderot, and "Gazette" and "Gazetier," by Voltaire.

35 *Journal des Dames,* décembre 1777:148 and mai 1778:380.

presario when the patriarch left Ferney and returned for his final
visit to the capital in the winter of 1778.[36] While Voltaire, exhausted from his transalpine trek to Paris, suffered a hemorrhage
and refused visitors during February and March, Dorat's paper
maintained a discreet silence. But when Voltaire recovered enough
to go out with his friends to the Académie and to see a performance of his *Irène* at the Comédie, Dorat wrote him a poetic overture in the *Journal des Dames*. Dorat explained that he had watched
numerous flatterers rush to Voltaire, but he had waited patiently
for the excitement to die down and sincerely wanted his attention
now, to beg his pardon.[37] This poem actually won Dorat an audience with Voltaire, but it evidently went badly, for neither Villette nor Voltaire could forgive Dorat his past sins.[38]

Dorat tried to demonstrate his good will in other ways. When
he received a satirical epigram against La Harpe from a subscriber
who assumed he would be delighted to print it, Dorat replied that
he had vowed never to use the *Journal des Dames* against La
Harpe.[39] He apologized for his own anti-philosophe play, *Les Prôneurs,* arguing that it was only cabals, systems, and affected jargon
that he had objected to, but that he had always admired the "true
philosophy" of independent thinkers. He now reminded his readers that the very motto of *Les Prôneurs* had been a quotation from
Voltaire: "Philosophy is solitary; only imposters need a sect."[40] He
plugged the *Dictionnaire universelle des sciences morales et économiques*
published by Panckoucke, a work by "true philosophers," "lovers
of mankind." He advertised a new *Journal d'éducation* endorsed by
Buffon and d'Alembert and loyally upheld Panckoucke's *Suppléments* to the *Encyclopédie,* far superior to the "mere shadow" imitations being produced by "brigands" in Geneva and Yverdon.[41]
Finally he praised the recent choices of the Académie and tried to

36 Ibid., mars 1777:81.
37 Ibid., avril 1778:269–70.
38 See Dorat's explanation of this in the *Almanach des muses,* 1779:33.
39 Charavay, *Catalogue, jeudi, 7 décembre 1865,* 54, no. 387, "Lettre de Dorat
à M. de Saint Amant (18 août 1777)."
40 *Journal des Dames,* avril 1777:352–53. See also Dorat's *Les Prôneurs,*
"Avant propos," vii:38, 45. Dorat's work was denounced, predictably, in the pro-
philosophe *Mercure* (juillet 1777) i:122–33.
41 *Journal des Dames,* septembre 1777:146–53; décembre 1777:132–41, 148;
février 1778:445–56; and avril 1778:291.

show his reverence for that august body, along with a gentle re-
minder that its founder, Cardinal Richelieu, had meant its seats to
be awarded for merit. Dorat now flattered d'Alembert, admiring
the "finesse" of his judgments in choosing occupants for the va-
cated chairs.[42]

Dorat needed also to satisfy Coqueley by making peace between the *Journal des Dames* and the Comédie. Here he obliged by
doing a complete about-face from Mercier. Only once did he allow himself to hint at certain "problems" in the theater's administration, but he pulled up short immediately, saying that "the
details of this I neither desire nor am permitted to discuss, . . .
too many would be compromised."[43] He blamed the fickle public
rather than the actors for any problems at the Comédie and came
down loud and clear against the idea of a second troupe, so dear
to Mercier and Rutledge. He also deplored their "republican fanaticism," their "bloody diatribes," against the classics. Everywhere he praised Racine, Corneille, Molière, and the royally protected actors themselves.[44] He mourned the famous *comédien* Le
Kain, who died just two days before Voltaire arrived in Paris expecting him to play the lead in his last tragedy. One man was dead,
cried Dorat, but an entire nation needed to be consoled.[45] In response to a letter from a reader asking why he had dropped theater
reviews entirely from his paper, Dorat replied that he preferred
silence to criticism. He was determined to be kind and tolerant
even though he knew, as Voltaire had lamented in his article "Gazetier" for the *Encyclopédie,* that journalistic nastiness sold better.
Dorat no longer believed in giving punches to the stomach. "I
have made a fixed resolution never to do so again." He preferred
to think of his *Journal des Dames* as a "sweet distraction" rather
than a weapon.[46] In his "Examen de conscience," marking the end
of his paper's first year, Dorat complimented himself on having
maintained his merciful neutrality in spite of the ugly quarrels
raging all around him. He had followed his "inner voice," which

42   Ibid., décembre 1777:130 and février 1778:401–10.
43   Ibid., mai 1777:419, 421.
44   Ibid., mars 1777:64–71, 157; mai 1777:372–76; septembre 1777:140; mars
1778:385.
45   Ibid., mars 1778:123.
46   Ibid., janvier 1778:277–80.

advised him to be gentle and consoling, never negative or cruel. He reiterated his hands-off policy on the Comédie, his refusal to hurt or criticize any of its members. There were indeed difficulties at the theater, but he would remain passive rather than ruffle feathers, and he would count on things righting themselves eventually. "We must let the public, time, and nature take their course."[47]

Dorat also used the *Journal de Paris,* a daily paper begun in 1777 that came out every morning, to persuade the public of his desire for peace. Since his own *Journal des Dames* appeared only monthly, it helped to clarify misunderstandings as soon as they arose by writing in the new daily that quickly became, it was said, as much a part of Paris breakfasts as the chocolate and the coffee. When the *Courrier de l'Europe,* still trying to provoke Dorat to fight, reported that he considered his own plays superior to Voltaire's *Sémiramis,* Dorat shot off a letter to the *Journal de Paris* that he would never be so "idiotic" or "presumptuous" as to compare his productions with those of the great man. He wondered by what fatality he kept being drawn into literary disputes against his will.[48] The *Journal de Paris* was then edited by a group that included Sautreau de Marsy and François de Neufchâteau, who had calmed down considerably since his 1775 *mémoires* against the Comédie. After being excluded from the Paris bar because of his "unsavory associations" with Linguet, Brissot, Beaumarchais, and Mercier and his "activities unworthy of the noble profession to which he aspires," Neufchâteau had attempted to practice law in Bordeaux, then disappeared for a few months and was rumored to have drowned himself.[49] When he resurfaced in Paris in 1777, much sobered by the reversal in his fortunes, he backed off from the *frondeur* coterie. After warning Mercier in a letter that blasting Racine and Molière was excessive and "boiled the blood" of the authorities unnecessarily, he printed articles in both the *Mercure* and the *Journal de Paris* publicly reprimanding the radical drama-

47 Ibid., février 1778:313–25.

48 *Journal de Paris,* 1777, no. 220:3; 1778, no. 24:94–95, no. 25:99, no. 27:106.

49 *Mémoires secrets* 8:115–16, 128, 10:225; Metra, *Correspondance secrète* 5:171 (23 septembre 1777): "M. François de Neufchâteau a eu le malheur de ne réussir à rien de ce qu'il a entrepris." For a taste of Neufchâteau's earlier rebelliousness, see his *mémoire* in behalf of dramatic authors reprinted in Du Coudray's *Correspondance dramatique* 1:147–58.

tists and urging "reciprocal tolerance" between authors and the Comédie."[50] In general the *Journal de Paris,* censored by Panckoucke's brother-in-law Suard, applauded the efforts of the "affable Dorat" to tone down the entire affair.[51] Querlon, editor of the *Affiches,* who had earlier criticized the Comédie strongly enough to be heralded by Du Coudray as part of a daring troika of avengers, a "fearless fighter of despots" along with Mercier and Linguet, had by 1777 been frightened into retreat, and he too praised the "polite" and "gentle" Dorat. Querlon had now reverted to Campigneulles's antifeminist and patronizing conception of the *Journal des Dames*'s audience. Female readers should be isolated from all matters of social consequence. "Those who rightly tremble at the fearsome literary feuds of our day, especially the ladies for whom [Dorat] writes, will applaud the restraint of his sentiments."[52] Mercier's friend Restif de la Bretonne described intimidated journalists like Querlon as reactionaries determined to keep people of both sexes ignorant by pretending to spare them unpleasantness and directing them away from literature treating significant issues. "O public, how they mislead you . . . on their recommendation you buy trivial books. . . . But you deserve to be duped. Why don't you judge for yourself? . . . O poor Automata!"[53] Pidansat said much the same thing for the *Journal de Paris,* which dispensed no important information and which only "frivolous and mindless readers" would even look at.[54]

Dorat's *Journal des Dames,* for all its pains, displeased almost everyone. In some ways it was a rerun of Campigneulles's unre-

50   Bibliothèque de l'Arsenal, MS. 15078 (2c), fol. 118, letter dated 27 décembre 1777. See also *Journal de Paris,* 1777, nos. 34, 85, 90, 220, 301; 1778, nos. 25 and 27, and p. 939. See also *Mercure,* janvier 1778:98.

51   See Mme Suard, *Essais de mémoires,* 135–36, in which the author explains that her husband was told by the *garde des sceaux* Miromesnil to "purge" and censor the *Journal de Paris.* BN ms. 22002, p. 285, no. 1723 lists as the paper's censor de Sancy, the very conservative bastard son of Miromesnil about whom Restif de la Bretonne wrote that he did not reproach him for his illegitimacy, but rather for the "rampomanie" and "servitudibilité" by which he tried to make up for it (*Monsieur Nicolas* 5:2839). Probably Suard and de Sancy censored the *Journal de Paris* together.

52   *Affiches de province,* 26 mars 1777:51. See also the very favorable obituary of Dorat in ibid., 1780:72, where he is referred to as the "poète des grâces" whose verse was as good as Voltaire's.

53   Restif de la Bretonne, *Monsieur Nicolas* 6:3087–89.

54   *Observateur anglais* 4:307.

warding experience on the paper. It caused extreme indignation among the philosophes. La Harpe, scandalized that Dorat would try to model himself on the great Bayle and the *Encyclopédie,* exploded that he had gone beyond the pale. "His character, fickle and false, without education, widely recognized as mediocre in all things, jealous of anything superior, is totally incompatible with journalism." And La Harpe was sure that Dorat had never heard of Bayle, much less read him or appreciated his erudition. La Harpe did not distinguish between Dorat and earlier disreputable editors of the *Journal des Dames,* all of whom filled the paper "with sarcasm, lies, and gross insults in the style of the populace."[55] La Harpe was at this point losing subscribers at the *Journal de politique,* which he had taken over after Linguet's firing by Panckoucke. Pidansat reported that nobody wanted to read this "cold, dry, boring" paper, which had once carried Linguet's fire.[56] La Harpe was therefore jealous of any new rival and did all he could to discredit Dorat's *Journal des Dames.*

But the *frondeur* coterie was even more disgusted by Dorat's total capitulation to authority. "His sphere [brain]," wrote the *Courrier de l'Europe,* "is reducible to a mathematical point." Dorat was "infantile" or, at best, "adolescent" in his failure to stand up to the regime or even the theater. He was obstructing a cause that had finally gained some momentum. "Like the Harpies, Dorat ruins everything he touches." On the Comédie he wrote only "words that signify no thoughts," "mere stuffing, filler [*remplissage*]." Would he, like his mentor Fréron, sell out to whoever bribed him and fawn all over the Comédie because the price was right? Dorat's *Journal des Dames* and its "consumptive" sidekick, the *Journal de Paris,* were worse than worthless.[57] This particular article in the *Courrier* was signed by Poultier d'Elmotte, a street actor, *frondeur* spy, and contributor to the radical *Gazette de Deux-Ponts,* who would vote for the king's beheading in the Revolution and on whom the police had already amassed a huge file.[58]

55 See La Harpe's *Journal de politique* 1 (mars 1777), 327–32, and his *Correspondance littéraire* 2:62.

56 *Mémoires secrets* 9:206 (6 septembre 1776).

57 *Courrier de l'Europe,* 1777, no. 45:393.

58 See the notice on Poultier d'Elmotte in Chouillet and Moureau, *Suppléments* 3:176–79.

But he was only one of many infuriated by the poverty of Dorat's polemics. Pidansat, always glad to publish in his *Espion anglais* any anti-Comédie material refused by the censor Coqueley, got precious little from Dorat, who he concluded was lazy, cowardly, even "flaccid."[59] Metra carried on about Dorat's "petrified mentality," Rutlidge labeled him contemptuously a "henchman of the Comédie," and Du Coudray, whose *Correspondance dramatique* tried to keep the fight alive, waited in vain to reprint something meaty from Dorat's *Journal des Dames* but was reduced to excerpting a bland article on Count Falkenstein's visit to Paris.[60] And Mercier's young rebellious friend Grimod de la Reynière, the brother-in-law of Malesherbes, who helped Le Fuel for a time with the *Journal des théâtres,* called Dorat a featherweight, a traitor, and accused him of being principally responsible for the attrition in the ranks of the fighters.[61]

Attrition there certainly had been, and Coqueley's purge of the *frondeur* papers did not stop with Dorat. Coqueley had sold the privilege of Le Fuel's *Journal des théâtres* to Le Vacher de Charnois, the son-in-law of Préville, the Comédie's most powerful actor. Le Vacher did all he could to be good in his whitewashed paper, which first appeared, with Dorat's *Journal des Dames,* in the spring of 1777. Le Vacher blamed *drames* for the sorry state of morality and literature, praised the French classics, and stated outright that he had "learned a lesson from his predecessor's downfall."[62] He published letters from former critics of the Comédie like Cailhava, who had since decided that the official French theater was worthy of his highest esteem—probably because it had performed his plays—and who now repudiated any association with the *frondeur* journalists.[63] But the Comédie and Coqueley would not even tolerate the mild and well-intentioned comments proffered by Le Vacher, and because of his divided loyalties he had to quit. This young man had himself been shocked by the actors' inordinate hostility to criticism and the frightening accusations they directed

59 [Pidansat], *Espion anglais, nouvelle édition* 1:293 and 2:337, 428, 437.

60 See *Correspondance dramatique* 1 (1777): 84, where by contrast the *Journal des Dames* under Mercier was praised for having initiated the fight.

61 *Journal des théâtres,* octobre 1777:295–99 and avril 1778:6–9.

62 Ibid., avril 1777:"Prospectus" and pp. 7, 15; août 1777:65.

63 Ibid., 113–15 (letter dated 20 juillet 1777).

at their critics; he would have fought them more vociferously if his personal ties to the troupe had not prevented it. But Le Vacher had lost his innocence. "An honest man cannot do this job without danger," he wrote to the *Journal de Paris* about theater criticism, as both an explanation of his resignation and a warning to his successor.[64]

Meanwhile, the *frondeurs* rallied to counteract Coqueley's maneuvers. Du Coudray had earlier tried to buy Le Fuel's privilege when he heard the recalcitrant editor was in trouble but had been told that "superior orders" were suppressing the *Journal des théâtres.* Du Coudray's new paper, the *Correspondance dramatique,* was thus conceived as a continuation of Le Fuel's doomed journal. Du Coudray announced that his *libraire* would give Le Fuel's former paid subscribers a one-third price reduction. He was therefore both surprised and upset to see Le Vacher in charge of a resurrected *Journal des théâtres* but figured out quickly that although Le Fuel's privilege had been nonnegotiable for an "anti-comédien" like himself, it had been given by the authorities to someone malleable. Du Coudray, blessed at first with the censor Pidansat who allowed him to print many articles in this "half-literary, half-political" war against the Comédie, correctly sensed the tide turning against the playwrights' cause. Where his first volume vigorously supported Mercier's *Journal des Dames* and the writings of Linguet and Rutlidge, the second volume of his *Correspondance dramatique* was mostly filler, long lists of the repertory of the Paris theaters since the 1720s. Reluctant to risk any more, he wrote his "dernière lettre" on 1 June 1778 and announced "enfin j'ai fini ma carrière."[65]

Rutlidge was another *frondeur,* whose *Le Babillard* had rushed in to fill the void when Mercier and Le Fuel were silenced. The censor Cardonne, part of Pidansat's team, had given permission for this paper to begin in 1777, and Rutlidge announced it as a replacement for the "*Journal des spectacles,*" which "no longer ex-

---

64 *Journal de Paris,* 1777, no. 230:3.
65 *Correspondance dramatique* 1 (1777): 144–46, 111, 254; 2 (1778): 272. For articles supportive of the *frondeurs,* see ibid. 1 (1777): 5, 25, 30, 33, 35, 55, 82, 84, 139, 147–58, 183, 188, 248. The copy at the Biblothèque de l'Arsenal has some scribbled marginalia showing that its reader was fed up with this whitewashed issue, calling the author "bien bête" (2:170).

poses the exploits of our privileged *baladins.*" After flattering his censor, an "enlightened examiner" who "does not amputate authors' limbs" as do so many of his colleagues, Rutlidge laced into any journalist who stood in the way of "freedom." He excoriated the *Journal de Paris* and the *Gazette* as totally devoid of any significant content and delivered a diatribe against La Harpe, "puffed up on the debris of the *Journal de politique,* very *philosophically* and *academically* usurped from its turbulent creator [Linguet]." He attacked Dorat's *Journal des Dames* as a worthless and hypocritical paper by a mincing, simpering fool. Such lamentable journalists were guilty of "an artificial and cowardly silence," putting their own interests and concern for their own safety before the public's needs.[66] As was typical of the *frondeurs,* Rutlidge believed that newspapers should aim to inform a wide audience and teach the public to think about important matters. He deeply resented the "cabale des philosophes" for parading as liberals when they had in fact become a "brigue littéraire" determined to keep the public ignorant and worshipful.[67] Like Mercier, Rutlidge saw the theater as a school where the people should learn, not a hotbed of immorality for the pleasure of dissipated nobles like the present Comédie.[68] The purge of all journalists trying to make that argument infuriated Rutlidge. It was he who masterminded the *mémoire* by the subscribers of the *Journal des théâtres,* likening the earthy, honest Le Fuel to the Flemish painter Teniers, whose crude scenes of peasant revelry and wild rural landscapes had so much disgusted Louis XIV. Rutlidge argued that truth and realism were necessary in politics and journalism as well as art. The censors would do everything in their power to replace *frondeur* journalists with servile lackeys, but the readers would eventually rebel and demand blunt truthfulness rather than rococo fluff. A lover of Teniers's robust work would never accept in its place a dandified portrait by the Sun King's court painter Mignard, the conventional and mannered favorite of the aristocracy. Here Rutlidge echoed

66 *Le Babillard* 3:12; 4:238, 270, 262; 3:165; 2:381. The *Almanach royal,* 1777:451–55, lists Cardonne for the first time as a new censor in belles lettres. Cardonne was the author of many "oriental tales," which Grimm considered camouflaged antiroyalist propaganda.
67 Such accusations run throughout Rutlidge's writing. See, for example, *Le Babillard* 4:140–41, 262; *Quinzaine anglaise,* vi–xv; *Oeuvres diverses* 2:40–86.
68 *Le Babillard* 4:299, 319–20.

the *frondeur* inclination, seen already in Mathon's art criticism, to direct the antirococo argument not only at pictures but also at people.[69]

Rutlidge's metaphor was perfectly apt for Dorat. He really was a courtly dandy, disdainful of the messy things in life, devastatingly charming, and although a dismal failure with his literary colleagues, a smashing success with women. Partial to the quartier du Luxembourg, Dorat entertained and kept numerous mistresses in his various residences overlooking the magnificent garden, first on the rue de Vaugirard, then on the rue de Tournon, finally on the rue d'Enfer where, Mercier explained in his *Tableau,* despite its name "one saw neither devils nor ghosts, but many wealthy humans paying dearly to inhabit its beautiful houses."[70] Dorat dressed always at the height of fashion and ran up debts of staggering proportions to tailors, jewelers, wigmakers, and coiffeurs, all of whom would turn up at his death to claim various bits of furniture in lieu of the money they could never collect.[71] His appeal was such that he could procure goods and services on credit with a smile and a prettily turned phrase. What worked on hardnosed businessmen had an even more dramatic effect on the women in Dorat's life. His extraordinary powers of seduction can be inferred from the lasting loyalty of a string of mistresses, even after they had been deceived and overthrown. Many of the *comédiennes* fell and remained under his spell. During the last years of his life he had narrowed the field down to three women. An inconspicuous wife, living on the rue de Montmartre on the opposite end of Paris from him, had borne him a son and would give birth to a daughter five months after Dorat's death. She may have been supported by Dorat's favorite mistress, the countess Fanny de Beauharnais, whose wealthy father also lived on the rue de Montmartre and to whom a Mme Dorat made at least one appeal for money.[72] Dorat never spoke of his wife. He divided his affec-

---

69 *Mémoire à consulter pour . . . le sieur de Méricourt,* 26. In *Le Babillard* 3:165, Rutlidge actually uses the adjective "mignard" to describe Dorat. On the antirococo movement, see Crowe, "The Oath of the Horatii," and Chapter 4, above.

70 Mercier, *Tableau de Paris* 2:143.

71 See BN ms. fr. 24027, fol. 127, for how Dorat coaxed ten months of grace from a tailor. See also BN ms. fr. 24005, fols. 291 and 293.

72 See Desnoiresterres, *Chevalier Dorat,* 363, and the article on Dorat in Sgard's *Dictionnaire des journalistes,* 128–29.

tions between his beloved "Fanny," who had lost interest in her own much older husband, and Mlle Fannier of the Comédie. These two women shared him amicably and did all they could to ease his last days. The 1779 *Almanach des muses* contains a love poem from him to each of them! Dorat would die on 29 April 1780 dressed up in lace, curls, powder, and all his finery, with both these women by his side. Even Grimm had to admit that the debonair Dorat died in impeccable style.[73]

A good part of Dorat's *Journal des Dames* was devoted, not surprisingly, to an appreciation of the fair sex, especially its external charms; thus it reverted to the frivolous attitude toward women already seen in conservatives like Campigneulles and Du Rozoi. This was in marked contrast to *frondeurs* like Mathon and Mercier, whose interest in women was primarily as sober, virtuous *patriotes* and *citoyennes*. Since neither Dorat nor Mme de Beauharnais took their respective marriages very seriously, the first issues of their paper veered considerably from the path of decency and austere morality it had previously preached. Dorat's advertisements, for a pension on the Champs Elysées catering to young nobles, for the expensive bonnets and coiffures of Beaulard, for cosmetics and exotic elixirs, indicate that he was aiming for a courtly rather than a family-oriented bourgeois audience.[74] Gone were the health tips and notices for tutors, lessons, and midwives. There was a fable unabashedly depicting the escapades of promiscuous women, accompanied by a justificatory footnote arguing that "it is good for the history of mores to contrast with the serious women who do honor to our century those who are distinguished instead by the looseness of their principles, the folly of their ideas, and the wildness of their caprice."[75] Again because of Dorat's commitment as a "man of the world and historian of all that goes on in it," he published a most extraordinary letter from a promiscuous woman named Mlle Arcangel, who was looking for a wealthy husband to betray. This husband would need to "learn his place," appear only twice a week, never "attend my suppers or my concerts. He will whisper endearments only in late summer, when none of my lov-

---

73 *Almanach des muses,* 1779:195–241; Grimm et al., *Correspondance littéraire* 12:421–26.
74 *Journal des Dames,* mars 1777:136–40, juin 1777:164, novembre 1777:479.
75 Ibid., juin 1777:3n.

ers are in Paris. . . . He will never attend the Comédie with me, . . . nothing casts more of a pall on the theater than a husband next to his wife in a box! He will have to go to sleep at eleven o'clock, so as not to spy on me later at night. And I will never see him in the morning, for it would ruin my entire day."[76] Dorat also filled these early issues of his *Journal des Dames* with writings by his friend and fellow reveler the marquis de Pezay. Pezay, a clever tactician in both love and war, had been military adviser to the dauphin when he became Louis XVI. This notorious rake was believed by many to have hastened Dorat's moral and financial collapse. The minister Maurepas had once been asked by the duke of Manchester to identify the dashing Pezay, dressed in a bright green suit, pink vest, and silver jewelry. Maurepas had replied "that is the king" and had gone on to explain: "He sleeps with my cousin, Mme de Montbarey, who influences Mme de Maurepas, who has me twisted around her finger. I lead the king, and so you see, it's [Pezay] there who reigns."[77] Dorat was running with a distinctly royalist crowd and had adopted in his paper the loose, promiscuous attitude of the court aristocracy.

Readers of Dorat's *Journal des Dames* seem to have been distressed both by its political conformity and by its inappropriate levity, just as Mme de Beaumer's subscribers had objected to Du Rozoi's flippant attitude. They had come to expect the paper to deal with matters of importance. They apparently protested, as Rutlidge had predicted they would, because in February 1778 Dorat apologized and promised to be "severe and chaste" in future, "more scrupulous with the too faithful portrait of our licentious ways."[78] The change in the remaining issues was quite pro-

---

76   Ibid., septembre 1777:109–16. This letter stated in no uncertain terms that "un mari étant, à tous égards, fait pour être trompé, il le sera avec toute l'adresse et la distinction possibles." It ended, "Vous allez croire que [mes offres] seront rejettées, vu la dureté et la tyrannie des clauses. Tranquillisez-vous. Je connais les hommes de mon tems, j'ai vu plus d'une fois leur âme à nud . . .[et] quelle est la portée de leur délicatesse. Il y aura foule."

77   See *Mémoires du comte Alexandre de Tilly,* 79–81. Pezay's poems and even some of his essays appear throughout the 1777 issues of the *Journal des Dames.* Pezay died at thirty-six, some said from excesses of debauchery, in December 1777. Pezay's *inventaire après décès* shows that he had in his possession numerous items once belonging to Dorat, including many of Dorat's books. See M.C. XCI (1158), 14 janvier 1778.

78   *Journal des Dames,* février 1778:323.

nounced, perhaps due to the influence of Mme de Montanclos, whose poems on marriage and family now reappeared. Even if the greater *frondeur* cause was lost because of Dorat's political coward-ice, the paper's last female editor refused to let the dignity of women be trampled as well, and as Dorat reminded Panckoucke, she still did have a share in the business.[79] A more wholesome message took over. Other poems appeared now on fidelity, par-enting, breastfeeding; some enthusiastic fathers even sent in pa-ternal rhapsodies.[80] Mme de Beauharnais, an author in her own right, wrote contributions very popular with readers.[81] Her fem-inism fluctuated between the integrative and the subversive modes; in 1776 she had published a light work called *Prose sans conséquence,* but she would later produce two feminist utopias. She pushed now for articles more directly related to the advancement of her sex. She had already sent her feminist *A tous les penseurs, salut!* to Mme de Montanclos's *Journal des Dames* and appears to have been socializing with Mercier in 1777.[82] Perhaps it was the influence of these new *frondeur* friends that inspired the aggressive tone of her articles on Amazons and another article arguing that the fathers of illegitimate children should be held responsible for supporting them.[83] Dorat's tendency in the early issues of his pa-per had been to flatter and patronize his female readers and to point out repeatedly ways in which he was sparing them technical details and prettying things up for their delicate sensibilities. He came around by the end, however, to a position much closer to Mme de Beauharnais's and said so in his penultimate issue, in some "réflexions sur les femmes et sur les avantages qu'elles retire-raient de la cultivation des lettres." It was almost surely because of his intelligent and ambitious mistress, whom Dorat now called his "model for women as they ought to be," that his parting words

79   Charavay, *Catalogue, 11 mai 1861,* 43, "Lettre de M.Dorat à M. Pan-ckoucke, 6 juin 1779, au sujet de leur traité avec Mme de Montanclos."
80   See, for example, *Journal des Dames,* mars 1778:146; avril 1778:236–45, 263–64; juin 1778:31–34.
81   Ibid., juillet 1777:233–34.
82   See Diderot, *Correspondance* 15:63–65. This letter from Diderot to Mer-cier, written in summer 1777, seems to indicate that Mercier had already been admitted into the circle of the "lovely Mme la comtesse." We know that by the 1780s Mme de Beauharnais had become fast friends with Mercier and Restif. See Turgeon, "Fanny de Beauharnais."
83   *Journal des Dames,* mai 1778:371–79; mars 1778:18.

on her sex denounced the "unjust prejudice" condemning women to a life of ignorance and boredom.[84]

Interlaced with these articles on women, Dorat's wooing of the philosophes and propitiating of the *comédiens* continued. He also courted the political powers to demonstrate his thoroughly cooperative stance. In reporting on the visit of "Count Falkenstein" to Paris, who despite his incognito everyone knew to be Marie Antoinette's brother Joseph of Austria, Dorat gushed how easy it was for subjects to love bountiful monarchs. There were poems praising Sartine, recently reassigned from police chief to minister of the navy, for his innovative buildup of France's warships. Now that Necker had replaced the Physiocrat Turgot as finance minister, Dorat printed an *éloge* of Colbert, since Necker had won a prize from the Académie française for an *éloge* of Colbert in 1773. In another article the *Journal des Dames* attacked "les Français détracteurs de la France," those who went overboard in their admiration for alternative systems of government.[85] France seemed headed once again for war with England but was understandably nervous about an alliance with "insurgent rebels," and Dorat showed his sensitivity to this embarrassing predicament by completely avoiding all mention of the American Revolution in his own paper.

Why, then, did the new police chief, Le Noir, and his men raid the offices of the *Journal des Dames* in May 1778? Their pouncing on Dorat's benign paper, which had been allowed to print and circulate unmolested throughout his tenure, appears incomprehensible. On the face of it, Dorat meant no mischief. He seemed the very picture of docility. But it was his linkup with another periodical, orchestrated by Chalumeau, that spelled doom for them both. Perhaps out of guilt or loyalty to Mercier, Chalumeau had become secretly involved with the *Journal anglais* and was printing in it all that Dorat could not in the *Journal des Dames*. When the police, who thought they had effectively dissolved the journalistic network, discovered a new connection between the two papers, they decided to liquidate both.

As we saw, the *Journal anglais* had been welcomed by Mercier's

84 Ibid., mai 1778:317–34.
85 Ibid., mai 1777:483; juin 1777:124–27, 133–63; septembre 1777:78.

Journal des Dames in 1775 when it first appeared. During 1776 it had taken a *frondeur* turn and briefly fell into the hands of Mercier's friend Le Tourneur, translator of the controversial *Shakespeare*. Ruault, the publisher, had explained in a letter to the censor Ameilhon that this paper was being watched very carefully by the minister of foreign affairs, Vergennes.[86] Such tight censorship was "bien gênant" and was doubtless the reason Ruault had decided against Le Tourneur and then ended his own involvement with the paper in the fall of 1776. The *libraire* Lacombe, who next picked it up, was already distributing a dozen other periodicals and probably did not pay much attention to their content. The anonymous staff took advantage of Lacombe's laxness throughout 1777 to slip into the *Journal anglais* French translations of Burke's "Letters to the Sheriffs of Bristol," condemning British war crimes in America. No other paper in Paris had come close to such boldness. Some extraterritorial papers like the *Courrier d'Avignon,* published in the papal enclave and operating outside Parisian censorship, had begun to lionize the parliamentary opposition in England and to portray George III as the oppressor. Papers published in Germany and Holland such as the *Courier du Bas Rhin* and the *Gazette de Leyde* were also strongly pro-American.[87] But the papers originating in the French capital had not yet printed anything so daring. The official *Gazette de France* had never even mentioned the Declaration of Independence,[88] and the *Affaires de l'Angleterre,* although it described events of the war, had been started up at Vergennes's request by the royalist Genet as an antidote to the republican *Courrier de l'Europe* and was meant to support "la politique du roi."[89] Louis XVI had certainly not yet made up his mind to support America in the summer of 1777; in fact he was trying to avoid Franklin, Adams, and Silas Deane, who had come in person to rouse Parisian opinion against Britain and rally support for American independence. The very idea of "insurgents" was profoundly frightening for absolutists. Besides, the colonists had suf-

86   Bibliothèque de l'Arsenal, MS 5313, fol. 44, "Lettre du *libraire* Ruault à Ameilhon, censeur du *Journal anglais,* 17 septembre 1775".
87   See Censer, "English Politics," and articles by D. Carroll Joynes and Jeremy Popkin on the *Gazette de Leyde,* in Censer and Popkin, *Press and Politics.*
88   Peter Ascoli, "French Press and American Revolution."
89   See "Genet," in Chouillet and Moureau, *Suppléments* 2:80–86, especially 82.

fered many sobering defeats. If December 1776 could be described by Tom Paine as "times that try men's souls," 1777 must have been ever more so, with colonial losses at Brandywine and Germantown and the rugged winter at Valley Forge.

Now, in the midst of all this uncertainty, when the Paris police had proscribed all discussion of America in cafés, the *Journal anglais* published Burke's denunciation of Britain's suspension of the right of habeas corpus and her mistreatment of American war prisoners, which the author described as a "violation of public law," "denial of human freedom," "suspension of citizens' liberties," "the most revolting injustice that has ever been seen." The closing of Boston Harbor and the destruction of the Massachusetts charter all proved, said Burke, that England and her king had become lawless, immoral, and corrupt, overturning the principles of her own constitution. The *Journal anglais* called America the "asylum of happiness and liberty." It then published "L'Art de mentir ou de faire une gazette," a harsh indictment of the protected French papers that, by suppressing all news of American victories, provided "fiction" rather than information for the public.[90] In fact the charge was accurate: the *Gazette de France* did not report a single American triumph until December 1777, when it finally printed a brief mention of Burgoyne's defeat at Saratoga.

The motivation throughout 1777 for the pro-American slant of the still anonymous *Journal anglais* probably came from Chalumeau, although his name began to be prominently featured as a contributor only in January 1778. As far back as 1775, however, Chalumeau's letters revealed a strong antipathy to "le Neptune anglais," which would be "put in its place sooner or later by the inevitable separation of its colonies."[91] Dorat too was more pro-American than he had been allowed to show in the *Journal des Dames,* and both men were acquainted with Beaumarchais, who had secretly been sending arms to the colonies. Dorat had published elsewhere a poem "Aux Insurgents," hailing the "victors for having snatched from [their] tyrants the palms of [their] hemisphere. . . . By [their] greatness a new people is added to this

---

90 *Journal anglais,* juin 1777:64–83; juillet 1777:193–94; septembre 1777:434–43.

91 Chalumeau, *Ma Chaumière,* 316–17. See also the *Journal anglais,* janvier 1778:427–32.

world."[92] The censor of the *Journal anglais,* Ameilhon, grew worried that it would soon be purged and now warned its authors not to print anything "offensive to the corps and companies that have the credit to get their complaints heard and the power to take revenge."[93]

Evidently the authorities had been getting ready to pounce on the *Journal anglais,* the paper both Chalumeau and Dorat secretly supported. In an uncharacteristically courageous act, Dorat took matters into hand. In December 1777, he signed a three-year lease for a flat on the rue de Tournon,[94] a small place clearly intended as an office since he paid nearly four times more for his second apartment on the rue d'Enfer.[95] Beginning in January 1778 Chalumeau attached his name openly to the *Journal anglais* and advertised that it was no longer chez Lacombe, but now for sale in the new "Bureau des journaux," "chez M. Deriaux, maison de M. France, au second, rue de Tournon," where the *Journal des Dames* could be bought as well.[96] The April 1778 issues of the *Journal des Dames* then announced that the two papers were on sale together. As a result of these developments, it must suddenly have occurred to the authorities that the *frondeur* connections they had severed under Mercier might be taking shape once again. Although Coqueley and Panckoucke considered Dorat tame, a certain level of ministerial mistrust toward him had never been dispelled. His own paper had a shady past, and there was no denying that in his youth he himself had frequented questionable circles—the comte de Tilly called them "sociétés fort subalternes."[97]

First the police were puzzled, then suspicious. Dorat's *Journal*

---

92 Parny, *Oeuvres,* 343–44. See a similar although more radical "Epître aux insurgents" full of Roman rhetoric in Metra, *Correspondance secrète* 5:187–89 (27 septembre 1777.)

93 BN nouvelles acquisitions françaises (henceforth nouv. acq. fr.) 23943.

94 M.C. LVIII (9), 27 décembre 1777. The *répertoire* for this *étude* describes the lease, but the actual document is missing.

95 Archives Nationales, Y11096, "Mort de M. Dorat, 29 avril 1780, procès-verbal de Formel, conseiller du roi, commissaire au Châtelet." The rue d'Enfer apartment cost 650 livres a year, whereas the quarters on the rue de Tournon cost only 187 livres 10 sols.

96 *Journal anglais,* janvier 1778:385 and janvier 1778:511. M. Deriaux was Dorat's accountant, first for his newspaper, later for his personal affairs, according to the procès-verbal.

97 *Mémoires du comte Alexandre de Tilly,* 79.

des Dames had begun to list several distributors in addition to its own office. It was for sale also from Thiboust, an *imprimeur du roi* and entirely "above suspicion," but it was being sold as well in the Palais Royal "chez Esprit," a far less reputable bookdealer who had once been a "colporteur sous le manteau" and had tried to save Le Fuel's *Journal des théâtres* from extinction.[98] The Palais Royal, the duc de Chartres's residence, was a hotbed of *frondeur* sentiment and "fermentation générale." Here, as Arthur Young reported, the bookstores filled up hourly with new, turbulent, and violent *brochures,* "nineteen out of twenty in favor of liberty."[99] To make matters worse, the *Journal anglais* was also for sale in a "bureau" on the "rue Montorgueil, près celle de Mauconseil." This just happened to be the exact location of the Comédie Italienne, fast becoming de facto the alternative theater the *frondeurs* were clamoring for, where plays by Mercier and Rutlidge were performed without the official approval of the Comédie-Française. Rutlidge joked that his plays were guilty of *lèse philosophie* and *lèse comédie,* but in fact they *were* looked upon as dangerous if not treasonous and the Théâtre Italien was known to attract a lower-class crowd.[100] All of these developments gave the police chief, Le Noir, good reason to wonder whether the *Journal des Dames* was preparing to make trouble once again. Was Dorat's "bureau" for the two papers a smokescreen of some kind? An illegal store? A political club? He decided to find out.

At eight o'clock in the morning on Saturday, 23 May 1778, Miromesnil and Le Noir authorized a raid on the "bureau du *Journal des Dames,*" claiming as their excuse that Dorat was in violation of the booktrade director Le Camus's new *arrêts* concerning the *librairie,* because his employee Deriaux was not a member of the bookdealers' guild and therefore not authorized to sell newspapers. The police seized all issues of both journals and escorted the shaken Dorat to Le Noir. The *Journal anglais* was

98 For information on Esprit and Thiboust, see Zephir, "Libraires et imprimeurs," 31, 277, 334.

99 Funck-Brentano, *Nouvellistes,* 214, 216–17, 273, 282, 298.

100 See *Le Babillard* 4:381–84, where Rutlidge describes the performance of his *Le Train de Paris, ou Les Bourgeois du temps* at the Théâtre Italien. See also Grimm's disparaging remarks about this theater, attracting riffraff no different from the crowd on the boulevards rushing to see "farceurs," *Correspondance littéraire* 13:159 and 14:61.

confiscated, for general reasons we can guess but for specific reasons we cannot know since no issues beyond January 1778 are extant.[101] In that last surviving issue Chalumeau had written flatteringly of Voltaire, the "generous humanitarian," pointing out his friendship with Mlle Pitt, sister of Lord Chatham who believed in the legitimacy of colonial grievances. The message seems to have been that if even conservative Frenchmen like Voltaire sympathized with America, France should surely join her side.[102] The issues of February through May, which are lost, may have slipped back into the paper's earlier republican vein, and probably did, since Chalumeau was later praised, along with Mercier, as a "great publicist" in a catalogue of revolutionaries written by the journalist Cousin Jacques.[103] Some sort of warning was communicated to Dorat too, perhaps because he had finally allowed himself to print in his *Journal des Dames* a poem praising La Fayette for fighting in a "just war." After putting out one last issue of the paper advertising all his own works at reduced prices, Dorat announced that he was finished with journalism and had ceded his privilege to Panckoucke.[104]

France had now entered once again a period of extremely repressive censorship. Le Camus's new booktrade laws of 30 August 1777 had been motivated by the regime's desire to better control and increase surveillance of the printed word and to restore royal finances. These new regulations on literary property upset both writers and *libraires,* who saw them as a repressive maneuver to snuff out small businesses, and in fact there were an unprecedented number of bankruptcies. "The presses . . . are dishearteningly sterile," wrote Metra. "Sellers and printers stare at each other idly waiting for . . . the reestablishment of the old laws."[105] Diderot, who regarded Le Camus as an intolerant, indeed fanatical booktrade director even before the *arrêts,* wrote to the Amsterdam publisher Marc Michel Rey that "soon, privileges will only be granted

---

101 "Saisie faite sur la demande de la communauté des libraires-imprimeurs de Paris," *L'Amateur d'autographe* 20 (février 1882):19–22.

102 *Journal anglais,* janvier 1778:427–36.

103 Beffroy de Reigny, *Dictionnaire néologique* 3:162.

104 *Journal des Dames,* mai 1778:334; juin 1778:119.

105 Metra, *Correspondance secrète* 5:343 (20 décembre 1777) and 5:318–19 (1 décembre 1777).

for *almanachs* and the Lord's Prayer, with corrections. Imagine that whole paragraphs have been deleted from a literal translation of some treatises of Plutarch! . . . Ah! If Holland wished it, she could have all our books and all our authors. I wish you all the happiness you deserve for being so daring. Without you, we would have preached in the desert."[106] Pidansat mourned the fact that Le Camus, once a good *patriote,* had been corrupted by power to the point of "despotism."[107] Le Camus's *arrêts* appeared more and more an excuse for suppressing works that made the king and ministers uneasy and allowing individuals in favor with the regime, like Panckoucke, to assume virtually monopolistic control of the entire booktrade. Panckoucke was widely suspected of being in league with the new *arrêts,* and his brother-in-law Suard's 1777 *Discours impartial sur les affaires de la librairie* strongly supported the new laws that would usher in, he claimed proudly, "an epoch of grand enterprises."[108]

As early as the fall of 1777, Metra had predicted that the *Journal des Dames* and the *Journal des théâtres* would be suppressed, mostly because of their history of theatrical and political criticism but also because the proliferation of alternative papers was causing too much competition for the *Mercure,* "which satisfies the curiosity of lackeys."[109] Like all the *frondeurs,* Metra believed it the right of the public to have news of political events and trends, and both he and Pidansat worried that if the *Mercure*'s publisher, Lacombe, went bankrupt, all the smaller independent French newspapers would be eliminated to strengthen artificially the voice of the state. Lacombe was indeed floundering, and the situation was not helped by the popularity of Linguet's *Annales politiques, civiles, et littéraires,* the *Courrier de l'Europe,* and Pidansat's previously handwritten but now printed *Mémoires secrets, Observateur anglais,* and *Espion anglais,* all coming across the border from London and satisfying the news–starved public far better than the purged French

---

106 Diderot, *Correspondance* 15:51.
107 *Mémoires secrets* 9:222 (23 septembre 1776).
108 On the suspicion of Panckoucke's collusion with Le Camus's *arrêts,* see Darnton, *Business of Enlightenment,* 68–75. See also Jean-Baptiste Antoine Suard, *Discours impartial,* 25.
109 Metra, *Correspondance secrète* 5:253–54 (8 novembre 1777).

periodicals could. "The public is shrewd," explained Metra approvingly, "[and] . . . wants to be informed."[110] Lacombe's bankruptcy, when it occurred in May 1778, had profound repercussions in the world of the press. Before a notary, Lacombe explained to his creditors that his debts totalled an overwhelming 427,600 livres but that he had tried for years "to avoid the shame of declaring his ruin." Now, because of journalistic competition, he had to announce a "general abandonment" of everything he owned; he hoped that his wife and children would be left in peace and that someone would give him a job, for he had no resources. Lacombe provided a list, including the *Journal des Dames* and *Journal des théâtres,* of the papers that had caused the demise of the *Mercure*.[111]

The state-protected *Mercure* now needed to be salvaged to reaffirm the government's control over the press, and Panckoucke, always ready to disseminate *lumières* but lacking any revolutionary inclinations, stepped in to do whatever was necessary to make the *Mercure* once again "le premier journal de la nation."[112] In exchange for rescuing the *Mercure,* which he could do only by buying out and eliminating many other troublesome papers, Panckoucke insisted on securing for himself all the privileges that had traditionally been granted to the *Mercure's* proprietor, such as free entrée to the Comédie and the Opéra, which the ministers were happy to grant. He loved wealth, success, and comfort and, as Darnton has pointed out, would continue to be fearful of radical journalists, remaining dedicated to the pre-Revolutionary power structure and to the idea of order in the world of the press.[113] In

110　On the popularity of these papers, see ibid. 5:411 (25 janvier 1778); 6:198 (4 mai 1778), 333 (juillet 1778). Metra was particularly enthusiastic about Linguet's *Annales,* "cet ouvrage qui plane glorieusement au-dessus des mille et un journaux qui nous accablent."

111　M.C. XLIII (491), 15 juin 1778, "Union des créanciers de Lacombe." The list of creditors to whom Lacombe owed a great deal of money included the journalist Pierre Rousseau (40,000 livres), Panckoucke (30,000 livres) and Lacombe's brother-in-law, the musician Gretry, who, in a less than fraternal spirit had calculated his sister's husband's exact debt to him of 26,784 livres. See also Archives Nationales Y10796, "18 mai 1778; scellé après l'absence et faillite du S. Lacombe, libraire à Paris, rue de Tournon," in which Rutlidge complained about Lacombe's interference with his *Babillard.*

112　Metra, *Correspondance secrète* 6:308 (7 juillet 1778).

113　See Darnton, *Buisness of Enlightenment,* 69–73, 499, 503–5. See also Aimé-Azam, "Ministère des affaires étrangères." The actual document showing

the summer of 1778 he began his fusion operations, buying up the *Journal des Dames* and eventually other papers and making from their "spoils" one big splendiferous *Mercure.*

Deprived of his *Journal des Dames,* Dorat became more despondent than ever, and his health deteriorated rapidly. Mme de Beauharnais wrote to the wealthy Beaumarchais, whom Dorat knew from visits to the Société des auteurs dramatiques, asking unabashedly for a loan of 20,000 livres for Dorat, "victim of a cruel reversal, an unforeseen catastrophe, the bankruptcy of a *libraire,*" and explaining that his embarrassment, worry, and shame over his journalistic failure were consuming him to the point of seriously threatening his life.[114] Beaumarchais, Panckoucke, and Chalumeau continued to lend Dorat money, but he grew completely inconsolable. By February 1780 he had needed to hire a M. Pannier, domestic and nurse, and Dorat's notary received visits from numerous bookdealers and paper merchants stating the dying journalist's exact debts to them and wanting some assurance that they could expect compensation. The notary tried to arrange things so that Dorat was "neither harassed nor pursued."[115] When he died on 29 April 1780, over thirty doctors, lawyers, notaries, tailors, wigmakers, landlords, merchants, and bookdealers, including Beaumarchais, Panckoucke, even the archbishop of Paris, came to see what goods they might collect from the debtor's estate. The inventory of Dorat's possessions listed by the police commissioner who visited the apartment on rue d'Enfer described an atmosphere of faded elegance. There were many things belonging to Mme de Beauharnais, including a fancy bed, silverware with her coat of arms, and some gilded leather volumes. In the kitchen were some copper and brass utensils but no food. There was an empty wine cellar, and a few "broken pieces of furniture of little value." The domestic explained that Dorat's last days had been miserable, that even his devoted mistresses had been unable to provide the money and special foods necessary to keep him

---

Panckoucke's takeover of the *Mercure* with ministerial blessings is in the reserve of M.C. LXXXIII (590), 12 juin 1778.

114 Loménie, *Beaumarchais* 2:579–80.

115 See, for example, M.C. XCI (1183), 18 and 22 février 1780 (visits from Thiboust and M. Larcher, paper merchant, and from Mannory, to whom Dorat owed 2,000, 2,400, and 5,500 livres respectively).

going, and that the servant himself had had to pay for the doctors' and apothecaries' last few visits.[116]

Linguet believed that the purge and usurpation of the *Journal des Dames* had killed Dorat. The obituary he wrote was for both the newspaper and the man. "In his last years, constrained by the disorder in his fortune, he took on a periodical . . . an unfortunate paper that, with a title that should have insured its success and with editors of genuine merit, experienced nothing but undeserved disasters. He was soon obliged to abandon it; since that time he languished, until his death." The villain of the piece was of course Panckoucke, Linguet's old foe from the days of his firing from the *Journal de politique.* Linguet had described with lugubrious cynicism Panckoucke's takeover of the Mercure, an "unparalleled bloodbath" in the world of the press. "The world is full of political combustion and conquest, uncertain and gory. . . . A conqueror of another kind . . . Panckoucke . . . is effecting in his field an operation without precedent." After explaining that La Harpe's and Lacombe's incompetence and political cowardice had "mortally wounded" the *Mercure* and that the government insisted on "propping up the corpse," Linguet described the devouring of the once worthy and informative *Journal des Dames* and *Journal des spectacles,* choice prey because they had been too "full of excellent observations." Here was Panckoucke, with the blessing and endorsement of the state, eliminating all free, independent voices and serving up instead a "drogue." It was a plot to force-feed the public a tranquilizer, approved pabulum, "quintessentially French." Linguet was now certain that the regime was on the brink of collapse. The only sign of life was some five hundred former subscribers of the independent journals who, as Rutlidge had predicted, refused to accept the *"Mercure* Panckoucke" as a substitute and demanded back their money. Although their own newspapers were gone forever, they could still refuse the ministers' poison.[117]

Linguet's perception of Panckoucke's 1778 journalistic takeover as an ideological purge rather than a commercial coup was shared

116 Archives Nationales, Y11096, "Mort de M. Dorat, 29 avril 1780."

117 Linguet, *Annales politiques, civiles et littéraires* 8 (1780): 503–12, "Mort de M. Dorat"; 4 (1778), 103–11, 189–91.

by many writers of the day in France as well as by observers outside her borders. It seemed to signal the death knell for the political press on French soil. Pidansat considered it proof that "grandes prétentions" had won out over truth,[118] and Mercier wrote of the depressingly predictable "*Mercure* Panckoucke" that it was "under the absolute hand of the ministers—its facts, ideas, and expressions all determined in advance. Nothing more arid than the esprit de corps of these Mercurians."[119] Newspapers in France, for men or women, would henceforth be entirely devoid of substance. Mercier wrote an open letter lamenting that journalism had now fallen irretrievably into the same state of stagnation and impotence that prevailed at the Comédie and the Académie. Pointing out that he had tried to shatter conventions and provoke healthy agitation by making the press and the theater "grand, free, strong, energetic, and full of life," he saw that as long as these media were dominated by Panckoucke, Suard, and La Harpe, they could never be vehicles for social action. The French press was doomed to sterility, turning and returning upon itself, never changing or elucidating anything. "I will leave the Academician [La Harpe] to "journalize" [*journaliser*]," concluded Mercier, "never bringing to light a single worthwhile idea."[120] It now seemed to Mercier that only in the utopian future, only in the France of 2440 would dramatists and journalists be celebrated for their social utility, "known and cherished by the entire nation."[121] Even Grimm had to admit that Panckoucke's *Mercure* had plummeted to unprecedented depths of servility to ministerial whim.[122]

Several of the *frondeurs* were already scattered outside France's borders, and others joined them now. From the relative safety of the diaspora, from England, Holland, and Switzerland, they continued to fulminate against the French regime, whose expropriation of their papers radicalized them further. As we have already seen, Linguet was in London. Le Fuel had also fled there, "pursued by death and all my other enemies."[123] In London he had started

---

118 *Mémoires secrets* 12:35 (6 juillet 1778).
119 Mercier, *Tableau de Paris* 4:10–12.
120 *Journal de Paris,* 9 juin 1778:637–38.
121 Mercier, *L'An 2440, nouvelle édition* 3:276.
122 Grimm et al., *Correspondance littéraire* 12:122–23.
123 Le Fuel, *Requête au roi,* 25–27.

up a new paper in 1777 in collaboration with the radical Italian émigré Giuseppe Baretti, a veteran journalist and author of a rabidly anti-philosophe *Discours sur Shakespeare et sur M. de Voltaire.* Mercier contributed numerous articles to this paper, which lasted until Le Fuel's death in 1778. Called *Le Journal français, italien, anglais, dramatique, lyrique, et politique,* Le Fuel's last paper was full of slander and bile. It even advertised what would have been Le Fuel's next project had his death not left it unrealized, an extravaganza of political pornography called *Histoire philosophique et politique du commerce des courtisanes, acteurs, et actrices les plus célèbres et les plus honnêtes du siècle,* starring the *comédiens,* the royal censors, and the king's ministers.[124]

The young Brissot now linked up with the émigré *frondeurs.* All along he had been sympathetic to many of the causes for which they stood, but he thought France unfertile soil for the campaign. A journalistic disciple of Linguet and himself a fervent admirer of Le Tourneur's Shakespeare translation, Brissot had decided to launch his own editorial ambitions in England instead. Linguet had congratulated him on getting out of France, calling it a "den of chicanery." It seemed to Brissot that his own country was rotting and that all hope lay with the "American insurgents." He had therefore put his energies into the *Courrier de l'Europe,* which supported them. Brissot knew both Linguet and Mercier well and agreed with them that the journalistic expropriations engineered by Panckoucke, La Harpe, and Suard were an "academic intrigue" to replace vigorous polemics with pedantry, so "cold, dull, and heavy" that it would bore its readers into torpor. "There was but one opinion on the black conduct of Panckoucke and his associates; in the world, as in the press, it was branded an infamy." Years later, Brissot would look back proudly on the *Courrier de l'Europe* as an antiroyalist explosive, a major contributor to the success of both the American and French Revolutions. It and Linguet's *Annales* were among the hottest journalistic sellers of the day. Brissot admired works written in a tone "accessible to the people," which "opened the eyes of Frenchmen to a host of prejudices and abuses." But now such works could only be printed in

124 Only a few issues of the *Journal français, italien, et anglais* are extant (see 1:4, 30, 32, 52–53, 63, 65–95; 2:3–4, 81; 6:41, 58, 67). The *Histoire philosophique* is advertised on the back flap of issue 6. See also Pidansat's sympathetic obituary of Le Fuel, *Mémoires secrets* 12:172, (27 novembre 1778).

foreign countries where liberty still thrived. Brissot lamented that the journalistic "inquisition" in France had expelled "from its own bosom" the best writers, those who understood the future. He believed it was an "absurdity and a crime on the part of the [French] government" to force such men into exile.[125] His was a bellowing voice in the choir of expatriate Frenchmen against their *patrie*. In the *Courrier de l'Europe,* as police reports put it, "Brissot cries out that France, asleep on the edge of a pit, can only be saved by a popular upheaval."[126]

For the few *frondeurs* who remained in France, the atmosphere grew increasingly stifling. Their protective and sympathetic censors were succumbing one after the next, Crébillon *fils* having died in 1777, Hermilly in 1778, Pidansat in 1779. Pidansat had arranged for the publication of his *Mémoires secrets, Observateur anglais,* and *Espion anglais* in England—Metra applauded the appearance in print of these "malicious" yet informative "defamations"[127]—but had decided that only his works, not his person, would leave French soil. Yet Pidansat suffered profound disappointment as his hopes for another Fronde faded and died. Not only the press, the academies, and the stage, but even the parlements had turned against his group. The first danger sign had been parlement's persecution of Le Fuel's lawyer, Falconnet, and its silencing of all *mémoires* defending the oppressed.[128] The magistrates seemed increasingly motivated by selfish, private interests. Parlement had retreated from its bold constitutional rhetoric when first recalled in 1774, had abandoned all interest in representing the Third Estate, and had lapsed into a period of quiescence that would last through the early 1780s. Gone were the days when Henrion de Pansey would write *mémoires* for Mercier against the Comédie. The parlement had censured or disbarred all mavericks—Beaumarchais, Linguet, François de Neufchâteau, Falconnet, Delacroix—accusing them of "writings contrary to respect for His Majesty's authority,"[129] and in the spring of 1779 Pidansat himself was ruled against in a matter of honor, his vic-

125   Brissot, *Mémoires,* 74, 64–66, 282, 266–267.
126   Pierre Manuel, *Police de Paris* 2:245.
127   Metra, *Correspondance secrète* 5:142–43.
128   [Pidansat], *Espion anglais* 5:254–55.
129   *Mémoires secrets* 9:56, 121, 131, 178, 194, 206–7, 218, 219, 221–22, 258, 274–89, 301.

torious opponent a wealthy marquis. Devastated by the parlement's betrayal, Pidansat committed suicide in 1779. The eversnide Grimm was quick to point out that Pidansat had done even this in Roman style, like Seneca, opening his veins in the public baths.[130]

Rutlidge's *Le Babillard,* in which he tried very hard to attract female readers, was the last of the French *frondeur* papers to go. It had survived Panckoucke's massive swallowing of 1778 only to perish a year later, silenced by Suard. Rutlidge's paper and all his writings were dedicated to informing his readers of matters that, even though initially shocking and painful, would ultimately make them more responsible and public-minded. It was, he knew, not fashionable to use the press for "moral amelioration," especially because the state-approved papers were so frivolous, attracting uncritical readers who "would rather give the impression of being au courant regarding chic books and the epigram of the day" than "delve deeply into themselves, a voyage from which they would return most unhappy." Like the anonymous editor of *La Spectatrice,* Rutlidge lamented the difficulty of finding readers for his severe but necessary message. "He who wishes to light the torch of truth and morality before the public . . . cannot afford to be impatient." Rutlidge objected to those "stupid pedants" who accused him of writing a "scandalous libel" simply because his paper aimed at a wide audience including both sexes and the lower classes. Like Mme de Beaumer he was compared to the radical publicist Chevrier, who had died miserably in Holland, hounded and hunted down by French spies.[131]

Rutlidge, a playwright as well as a journalist, was Mercier's next-door neighbor, and his plays *Le Bureau d'esprit* and *Les Comédiens, ou Le Foyer* had at first been thought to be the works of Mercier, filled as they were with vituperations against the aristocratic theater and the conservative philosophes. Rutlidge resented Voltaire especially for his hostility to Le Tourneur's *Shakespeare,* for his political conservatism, and for denying the public "the liberty to think for itself." Rutlidge was not beyond calling past ministers of Louis XV "vile and corrupt," "encouraging the

---

130 Grimm et al., *Correspondance littéraire* 12:338.
131 *Le Babillard* 2:369–81.

dissipations of their master and crushing, without remorse, the trembling people." Maupeou of course was high on the list of villains. For the new king, Louis XVI, to be any better, for France to avoid dissolution and ruin, "we will be obliged to oppose [*fronder*] most received opinions . . . examine abuses . . . expose . . . speak with daring . . . about the political errors of the past."[132] Rutlidge may have been helped by Pidansat behind the scenes, because *Le Babillard* broke off for a few months when Pidansat died and Rutlidge referred to the interruption as due to the death of his "father."[133] He then lost all hope and published one final issue excoriating those responsible for the purge of *frondeur* journalism and *drames*.

Rutlidge had already expressed his disgust with Panckoucke, derisively labeling the new press lord "Seigneur *Mercure,*" "le nouveau Dieu," a man who shamelessly pandered to censors and ministers, buying their approval with base adulation, lying to please them. Panckoucke's *Mercure* was a travesty, a laudanum meant to muddle the mind, "keep readers in darkness, and obstruct the habit of thought." Rutlidge's last issue of *Le Babillard,* an "article extraordinaire," blasted Panckoucke and the Comédie for discrediting his latest *drame, Le Train de Paris,* because it laid bare the vices of the nobility. Rutlidge threatened to bring Panckoucke to trial for the slanderous lies in the *Mercure.* His stupidity was bad enough, but for blatant falsification and character assassination he would now be sued.[134] Suard dealt with the threat immediately, took over as censor, and eliminated *Le Babillard.*[135] Rutlidge would later talk of his "martyrdom" during those years, when he was "reduced to poverty and ruined by my oppressors." He had been jailed for days, kept in solitary confinement, interrogated about his *frondeur* writings, his paper seized. *Le Babillard* would have been far more radical, he explained in a *mémoire* of 1790, but to get his ideas into print at all he had to "prostitute" himself to Le Noir, Sartine's "creature," and to all the other ministers. "Fero-

132 Ibid. 4:249, in which Rutlidge endorses (without admitting authorship) his own *Essais politiques.* In *Essais politiques,* see x–xv.
133 *Le Babillard* 4:257.
134 Ibid. 2:374; 4:140, 381–84.
135 BN ms. fr. 22002, p. 195. Here Suard is shown as the final censor of *Le Babillard.*

cious and unprincipled," "lying and depraved," "extravagant and uncaring," the king's men were dedicated to a politics of "coddling rich groups and powerful individuals and sacrificing to them the poor and unprotected."[136]

Suard, Panckoucke's brother-in-law, who first became a censor in 1777, fit perfectly what the government needed for the job of completing the *frondeur* purge. As his wife explained in her *mémoires,* he was a steadfast defender of monarchical principles, in whom Miromesnil and all the ministers had "perfect confidence." Always a royalist, he "never advocated the adoption of the English constitution," and he "filled the papers of that day with his feelings about the . . . respect we owe the king, and [against] the license of the press and of the theater." Suard deplored "incendiary, defamatory, and scandalous writings designed to irritate the people, lead their opinion astray, and cause insurgence against all they should love and respect." Suard declared war on such "perverse and idiotic writers," who wrongly call themselves "patriotes" but are really bent on destroying the *patrie*.[137] He wrote a revealing piece on the "censure des théâtres," arguing the dangers of free speech in a medium that "stirs up passions later expressed with extraordinary energy because of the simultaneous reaction of a multitude of assembled men." Crowds could easily get out of hand, and such "popular effervescence" must be avoided at all costs, or order would never be restored.[138]

Not only had the *frondeurs* lost their sympathetic censors; their once-powerful patrons were no longer able to protect them. Conti, who had sheltered Mme de Beaumer in the Temple, had recently died, mourned by Pidansat as one of the great *patriotes.* Conti had actually built a theater in the Temple, next to the cour de la Corderie, which was to have "ensured the independence of writers," but in his last year the Comédie "joined with the government and snuffed out the *esprit de parti*" that had developed among those who fought the monopoly of the royalist actors.[139] Conti's nephew Chartres, whose support had given the *frondeur*

136 *Mémoire au roi pour le chevalier Rutlidge,* iv, v, viii, 30–31, 38, 44.
137 Mme Suard, *Essais de mémoires,* 136, 157–58, 160, 160n, 163, 166.
138 J. B. Suard, *Mélanges de littérature* 4:312, 318.
139 *Mémoires secrets* 9:181 (6 août 1776). See also Barillet, *Recherches historiques sur le Temple,* 36 and 36 n. 1.

journalists renewed vigor after Maupeou's fall, was now in disgrace himself. Versailles frowned upon Chartres's influence in his Palais Royal enclave; he had delusions of grandeur, the pretensions of a "king of Paris," and would have to be publicly humiliated. When Chartres returned from the Battle of Ouessant, where he had in fact fought courageously, the *Gazette de France* distorted the facts, publishing stories of his cowardice and loss of nerve. He had been the leader of French Freemasonry since 1771 and had relished his role as head of a clandestine organization to which many of the *frondeur* editors belonged. For a while, Freemasonry had been tolerated by the new king, but now police and ministerial pressure were forcing the Masonic lodges to admit ladies of high society in an attempt to transform their meetings from potential political conspiracies into frivolous social gatherings.[140] Pidansat saw this as one more insidious trick by the government to obstruct liberty and truth. It was not a step forward for feminists and patriots but the reverse, because the women flocking to Masonry seemed not in the least interested in serious reform. "Gallantry has caused a prodigious degeneration of the institution of Freemasonry; nearly all lodges have been invaded by women, especially ladies of the court." Highly sensitive to the corruptions of empire, to bread-and-circuses maneuvers on the part of the authorities, Pidansat was suspicious of anything that transformed serious meetings into mindless, dazzling spectacles.[141] It seemed Chartres and his Freemasons were being undermined by the government. The ruthless thwarting of Chartres's *frondeur* plans and the monarchy's assaults on his character no doubt helped transform him into the future Philippe Egalité.

Facing the complete erosion of all his former bases of support, even Mercier, who adored Paris, was finally forced to leave. An affectionate letter from Diderot off in the country contemplating Seneca had urged Mercier to continue the "useful employment of your time and talent," to "animate" and "improve mankind," but it also pointed out that Le Camus's repressive measures made vigorous writing impossible in France.[142] Mercier's own letters from this period show that he was devastated by the cowardly betrayal

---

140 Britsch, *Maison d'Orléans*, 285, 388, 234–50.
141 *Mémoires secrets* 9:69 (18 mars 1776).
142 Diderot, *Correspondance* 15:64–65, and 51.

of his publishers.[143] He decided to follow his friend and fellow journalist Grimod de la Reynière to Switzerland. In January 1778 Mercier wrote to the Société typographique de Neuchâtel across the Swiss border, saying that he saw his literary future outside France, "and once attached to your society, I will use no other printer and will pledge to you exclusive rights to whatever flows from my pen."[144] In his own country Mercier was being labeled a "dangerous man" and a "bad subject," and with his supporters either dead, in exile, or in prison he felt increasingly vulnerable. Fréron had earlier called him "the most delirious maniac of the century" for trying to enlighten the common people, and La Harpe continually accused him of "inciting revolution" with his unrelenting emphasis on "the people," of "trying to turn the world upside down." Palissot considered Mercier an avowed enemy of the "theater and the nation," a crazy man for thinking journalists should write about *la cause publique* or inform public opinion; he was only stirring up trouble in such popular quarters as the faubourgs Saint Antoine and Saint Marcel because his "dramatic entrails were hurt and torn."[145] The only thing that kept Mercier out of jail, it seems, was the fact that the new police chief, Le Noir, liked him. Le Noir had just replaced Albert, and the catalogue of Le Noir's personal library reveals that it contained most of Mercier's works (and incidentally many other "mauvais livres" from the *frondeur* coterie). Grimm, irked by Le Noir's weakness for Mercier, found it incomprehensible, but Grimm must have had an exaggerated perception of Le Noir's protection, because Mercier himself no longer felt safe in his own country.[146] Dismayed to abandon his *patrie* but daily more aware of the precariousness of his situation, Mercier finally moved to Switzerland. He wrote some pieces for the *Journal helvétique* (also known as the *Journal de*

143 See, for example, Bibliothèque de l'Arsenal, MS 15078 (2b), fols. 29–30.

144 See Guyot, "Sébastien Mercier à Neuchâtel."

145 See La Harpe, "Réflexions sur le drame," *Oeuvres* 1:175–77, and his *Correspondance littéraire* 3:251–52, 380; *Journal français* (15 décembre 1777) iii:322–27, "Consolations à M. Mercier," and Palissot's *Mémoires* 2:157–60.

146 See *Catalogue des livres de M. Le Noir,* especially 73, 81, 87, 93, 117, 127 and the list beginning on p. 129. Le Noir's collection stands in marked contrast to that of Miromesnil, whose much bigger library had almost no forbidden books (see *Catalogue des livres de Monseigneur Hue de Miromesnil*). For Grimm's reaction to Le Noir's leniency, see Grimm et al., *Correspondance littéraire* 13:29–31.

Neuchâtel) but did not try journalism in Paris again until the Revolution, when he, Carra, Condorcet, and Brissot would launch several papers jointly.

Mercier's *Tableau de Paris,* which began to appear in the early 1780s from Neuchâtel, made it clear that his *Journal des Dames* experience was not forgotten. He singled out Coqueley as the most "sniveling" and "pusillanimous" of censors, who "risks his approbation only for insignificant things." Le Camus de Neville was blamed for emasculating and reducing French literature and journalism to drivel. Newspapers should address themselves to all people, to both sexes and to every social rank. They should be varied, independent, and critical, as interesting for the chambermaid as for the duchess, for the spice merchant and pharmacist as for the military marshal. Instead, everything was government-controlled, all attempts to speak freely immediately squelched, so that "all papers for sale in the capital say the same thing . . . none contradict each other, all are under the official thumb . . . all recite equally well their lessons." Only clandestine *nouvelles à la main,* because they "escape slavery to the protocol of minsterial ideas," have an individual character and can present a fresh point of view. Even *nouvellistes,* however, deprived of political foresight by the strict censorship practices of the regime, "have their heads in a bag" and are forced to rely on rumor. Panckoucke, who now monopolized so many newspapers, was denounced as a greedy "entrepreneur" not the least bit interested in truth.[147]

Mercier heard the strains of the regime's worsening paranoia. He wrote now that libels proliferated like so many little drums, palliatives temporarily preventing the restless from beating down the walls, their low rumble indicative nonetheless of a "volcano" ready to erupt below the surface. "The project seems to be formed . . . to suffocate the writers of Paris," Mercier reported, because they were too determined to expose vice. Mercier knew he would have been more successful had he made of his paper a *Journal des plumes et des jupes,*[148] but as a committed publicist he had wanted his *Journal des Dames* to be much more significant than that. He shared Mme de Beaumer's conviction that women should be bet-

147   Mercier, *Tableau de Paris* 2:31; 3:199; 11:182; 7:11–12; 5:14.
148   Ibid. 7:13–17; 2:79–80, 16.

ter informed in order to strengthen the moral backbone of the *patrie*. Like her, Mercier defended male and female readers' right to learn about public affairs and to see corruption unmasked. Mercier and the other *frondeurs* had tried first to work within the system, but experience had taught them that this could not succeed in France, that the government would prevail in silencing its journalistic critics. They had no choice but to join the radical emigrés or the radical underground. The failure of integrative, legitimate press channels had thus transformed the *frondeurs* from reformers into advocates of subversion. Their journalistic experience had shown conclusively that the Old Regime was too riddled with vice to be redeemed. Newspapers, beacons of truth, would not be able to shine their light until France was completely overturned, remade, and rid forever of its corrupt authorities. Bemoaning the *frondeurs'* lost fight for freedom of the press, Le Fuel concluded that government "scoundrels fear broad daylight," and Mercier, taking up the same metaphor, lamented that since brigands need the cover of night, they will shun any attempt to illuminate the true nature of their activites.[149]

149 "Les scélérats craignent le grand jour" (Le Fuel, *Requête au roi,* 21); "les brigands n'aiment pas les réverbères" (Mercier, *Tableau de Paris,* ed. Desnoires-terres, 31). In this connection it is significant that Mercier was the first historian to portray Damiens with sympathy: he believed Damiens's act had revealed a profound social resentment, unmasking a situation that needed to be confronted and that augured ill for the future of the monarchy. In his fascinating attempt to reconstruct the event from the newspapers of the day, Mercier stressed the inadequacy of the official papers and the necessity of using other, *frondeur* sources. See Rétat, *L'Attentat de Damiens,* 311–312.

Conclusion

The story of the *Journal des Dames* and other *frondeur* papers associated with it illustrates some of the intellectual, social, cultural, and even sexual tensions that had been eroding the Old Regime ever since the Fronde. These papers kept alive a dissenting journalistic spirit and fought to achieve the maximum press freedom possible under a system of censorship. The varying elasticity of that system explained both the tolerance for such alternative, marginal papers during relaxed administrations and their persecution when surveillance tightened up. Periods of leniency, such as the mid-1760s under Choiseul and the mid-1770s under Malesherbes and Turgot, encouraged the *frondeur* journalists to believe that the reform and redefinition of social values would be possible within the established order, but such periods of repression as Maupeou's ministry and Le Camus de Neville's directorship of the booktrade forced the *frondeurs* into more subversive modes of discourse.

It is suggestive that a paper explicitly for women would have been one of the first, whether elliptically or directly, to protest the elitism of the academies, to defend bourgeois and popular *drames,* to denounce foreign wars and the excessive tax burden they placed on the Third Estate, to fight for the rights of Protestants, to encourage provincial self-esteem, to uphold the law as the highest authority, and to attempt to unmask corruption in the Old Regime's most entrenched institutions. Of course this utopian campaign was interfered with at numerous junctures, forcing the paper into a much more conventional and integrative mold. But the transgressive tendencies of the *Journal des Dames* were never far below the surface, and as we have seen, they erupted at every opportunity, the paper joining together with other opposition journals whenever possible.

The *Journal des Dames*'s conservative founders unwittingly gave new legitimacy to a lower-status social group by creating for it an organ of its own. A permitted paper was not merely a genre; it was an approved institution. Its continued future relationship with its audience was assured by the fact that it was a regularly appearing medium based on a sustained, reciprocal commitment from both editors and subscribers. Books on women, even by such exceptional, true feminists as Poullain de la Barre, had nevertheless been isolated events. Their fate after their signal appearance was to be ignored, drowned out by the misogynistic torrent of writings by Molière, Boileau, La Rochefoucauld, and Saint-Evremond or at best passively absorbed by a small number of readers with a taste for novelty. Poullain's books had few echoes in the seventeenth and eighteenth centuries, as is well known. A periodical, on the other hand, was an ongoing dialogue dependent on its public for its survival and therefore necessarily responsive to it. In a very real sense, then, the medium of the *Journal des Dames* was itself a powerful message. It implicitly endorsed the worth of its designated audience, and whatever it published was sanctioned as appropriate fare for female readers. Most important, and this is what distinguished it from earlier periodical *amusements* directed at women but composed by men, the *Journal des Dames* invited the active contribution and participation of its female readers.

Over its twenty years many women shared their anxieties and hopes with the paper, delighted to finally have an arena in which to voice their grievances. As we saw, some explicitly hailed the paper as a long-awaited end to their isolation, and provincial women especially responded with gratitude to its appearance. Thus the paper was experienced by female readers as an opportunity "for avenging the insults to our sex,"[1] even though that had certainly not been the original conception of the enterprise. Very quickly audience feedback showed the "question de la femme" to be a highly charged issue. The advancement of female literary

1 *Journal des Dames,* mars 1766:63.

recognition could not remain isolated from broader social concerns. Readers' comments ranged from vague discontent to a sense of injustice and oppression, to outraged protest, but whatever their intensity, their contentious thrust could not be ignored.

The female editors of the *Journal des Dames* were the first women to direct a woman's paper, making the *Journal des Dames* the first periodical "par et pour les femmes" and, as such, a profoundly transgressive phenomenon. The political realities of absolute monarchy precluded the involvement of women in affairs of state, and because there was no male enfranchisement against which they could contrast their political nonexistence, these female editors made no precise political demands. But they saw journalism as a way of influencing their public and were determined to bring before it issues of real significance and to communicate their own courage and force. That they meant to broaden the realm of public awarness and debate can be seen in their repeated claim that they spoke to all classes of "citoyennes," that their paper was intended for "toutes femmes," "de différents états et de différents goûts." Their first wish was to galvanize women into activity, to prod the privileged from lethargy and dissipation, to encourage the lowly with examples of fine character from even the humblest social classes. By their publication of numerous and lengthy *éloges* of great women throughout history, the editors strove to counter misogynistic attitudes in women as well as men and to nurture their female readers' feelings of self-worth. Just as the seventeenth-century *frondeuses* had invoked the reign of the Amazons, the image of a gynocratic utopia was a recurrent and allusive theme in the *Journal des Dames,* underscoring the political and military talents of women and their ability to exercise public responsibilities gloriously. While the *éloges* stressed both the intellectual and moral virtues of women and their importance as a refining and civilizing force, they did not dwell on "pudeur," "douceur," and "timidité" as did panegyrics written by men to the "fair sex." The female journalists, in fact, prefigured such feminists of the Revolution as Olympe de Gouges and Mary Wollstonecraft in their suspicion that such so-called "virtues" were a patriarchal trick to keep women meek, obedient, confined, and controlled. Shyness and diffidence were no more "natural" or "good" for women than were boldness and strength. Modesty, wrote one editor, was a "contraband virtue," and another urged women to shed their self-destructive timidity.

With their claim of sexual equality, their brandishing of such new titles as *éditrice* and *autrice,* and especially their boisterous activity and pride in their journalistic careers, the female editors of the *Journal des Dames* broke down the traditional barrier between rhetoric and conduct, taking feminism out of discourse and putting it into practice. It was one thing for the founding editors to encourage blushing damsels to publish their poetry, but an altogether different matter when these damsels ceased blushing, renounced subservience, and instigated contestation. Feminism in the Enlightenment had assumed a rather tame form, as David Williams has shown, typified by the highly integrative views in Boudier de Villemert's *Ami des femmes,* a book so popular and reprinted so frequently that it can safely be supposed to have represented prevailing opinion.[2] Boudier's "scientific sexism," as another recent scholar has styled it, cast women as the very soul of society, calming the ferocity and barbarousness of men, initiating and guiding progress, using their natural grace and delicacy to inspire harmony within the family, civilizing society, but never attempting to step out of their proper sphere.[3] Yet the female editors of the *Journal des Dames* demanded equality between the sexes. They were playing no game, and their approach to their readers was bold, frontal, bossy, and provoking. They meant to "make a mark upon the world," and they practiced what they preached. The editors scorned the autocensure so common in the writings of most women, the fear inspired by their own boldness that made them retract their strong statements. Female writers of timid persuasion were of no more use than men; a faintness of heart and an acceptance of their "faiblesse intéressante" and "délicatesse charmante" inevitably reduced their bombastic rhetoric to the most meager demands. This literature of apologies for the female sex by women, which Léon Abensour has characterized as the "mountain giving birth to the mouse," was precisely what the *Journal des Dames* editors wished to avoid.[4] They meant not only

2   Williams, "Fate of French Feminism."
3   Angenot, *Champions des femmes,* 148.
4   See Abensour, *Femme et féminisme,* 355–428.

to sound belligerent but to be triumphant, to change the present, even to create their own history.

The paper's feminism was definitely ahead of its time. It did not become truly revolutionary or utopian (in Mannheim's sense), because it could not seize upon currents and collective purposes already present in society. The feminist editors certainly struck responsive chords in a number of their female readers, but the mass of women in the Old Regime were not yet aware of themselves as a group oppressed by society and did not yet identify as members of a gender. Privileged women suffered feelings of emptiness and futility, poor women protested when they were hungry, but neither group was in the habit of seeing its plight in political terms. The female editors realized quickly that their cause was part of the much broader issue of human freedom and that before there could be equality between the sexes more sweeping social and political changes would need to occur. They therefore enlisted the aid of and eventually turned their paper over to male *frondeurs,* Jansenists, Freemasons, republicans bent on social action whose sympathies went beyond feminism to include all marginal social groups. In the hands of these men, the paper became a vehicle of protest against extravagance, privilege, and all the entrenched institutions of an abusive, intransigent regime. They meant to use the press along with the parlements and the stage to win tolerance for Protestants, respect for the Third Estate, esteem for the provinces in their struggle against centralization, recognition for the rights and talents of all men and women regardless of their social station, admiration for the English, protection of all citizens by the law from arbitrary ministerial whim, and freedom of expression for themselves. It was to be a longer battle than they realized. Over a century later the feminist paper *La Fronde* still saw its mission to be much the same. Responding to a compliment from a sympathetic rival editor on its "offensive title," Marguerite Durand explained the enduring constitutional struggle that the Fronde represented for her. People might try to reduce it to a "useless war of duchesses" or a "dangerous projectile game," but in reality it was a "patient and daily subversion of the present social state that condemns to triple inferiority—human, civil, and economic—one half of the *cité.* If *La Fronde* declared a war, it is not against male antagonism but against tyrants named abuse, prejudice, decrepit social codes, [and] arbitrary laws no longer adequate for our new demands."[5]

The male *frondeurs* to whom the female editors passed on their *Journal des Dames* filled it with the same material they put in other papers and did not alter or water it down. Although they dealt less specifically with feminism than their female predecessors had, they showed considerable insight into the plight of women in all social classes and wrote about it with great sensitivity. For them feminism was a component of patriotism; society could be healthy only if all citizens, male and female, were imbued with such virtues as austerity, civic-mindedness, and respect for the laws. Mercier's *Tableau de Paris,* as John Lough has shown, was filled with admiration for industrious female workers and deplored the economic usurpation of traditionally feminine occupations by men, which forced women out of jobs and into prostitution.[6] Mercier violently disliked rich and idle women, but no more than rich and idle men, parasites on the social organism who sapped rather than contributed to its strength. Of ambitious women Mercier had much to say, for he was one of the first to articulate how threatened men felt by challenges from able, energetic members of the opposite sex. As we saw, his insights into sexual jealousy make untenable the old canard about his antifeminism. Mercier was a close friend and supporter of Olympe de Gouges, perhaps the most famous feminist of the Revolution. If women marshalled their energies and fought for the proper causes, Mercier admired them as much as his fellow men.

The academies of Paris came to be viewed by rebuffed outsiders as sclerotic, abusive bastions of privilege, and their intransigence radicalized certain marginal individuals in the years immediately preceding the Revolution; these developments have been thoroughly documented by Robert Darnton in his book on mesmerism. Decades earlier, however, from its beginning in 1759, the *Journal des Dames* had set itself up as something of an alternative academy, publishing many of the essays that had competed for academic prize competitions and lost. Even the timid founding editors had praised foreign and provincial academies for their hos-

5 *La Fronde,* no. 1, 9 décembre 1897, quoted in Albistur and Armogathe, *Historie du féminisme,* 371.
6 See Lough, "Women in Mercier's *Tableau.*"

pitality to women, an implicit criticism of the Parisian ones. The paper would dispense deserved honors to those women whom the academies refused to recognize. Mme de Maisonneuve and Mathon stated unequivocally to their readers that the judgments of the high-handed Parisian academies were not the final word; they offered examples of worthy essays whose "hardiesse" disqualified them from serious consideration for prizes but made them more socially relevant than anything written by the ubiquitously successful philosophe's darling La Harpe, "who afflicts readers but never instructs them."[7] It was for the public to judge the worthiness and utility of these essays, many of which were filled with *frondeur* fare.

The *Journal des Dames* and its associated *frondeur* papers were the only ones to support the new *genre dramatique* and to fight for the rights of playwrights to get their *drames* performed. This debate on theater, which as we saw dated back to the Fronde, concerned far more than the professional antagonisms of dramatic authors and the royal actors of the Comédie-Française. Like feminism it was a conflict between dominant, aristocratic institutions and the marginal cultural values of lower-status social groups. The official government papers fiercely opposed *drames* on both aesthetic and social grounds. Not only did they break the conventions and rules of traditional theatrical genres like tragedy and comedy; they were also dangerously democratic. Grimm's *Correspondance littéraire* attacked Beaumarchais's *drame Les Deux Amis* because it was so clearly "in honor of the Third Estate."[8] The vast majority of periodicals found *drames* scandalous for their rebellion against decency and decorum. Even the philosophes' *Journal encyclopédique* denounced the new genre as an illegitimate, detestable hybrid and its supporters as necessarily vulgar. "Bourgeois tragedy, or *drame,* which is nothing but a bastard of the street, has found very little indulgence among the enlightened public." The critic went on to explain how ridicule would be victorious over this new form, which was too sombre, too interested in small details of small lives. He denounced the popular jargon, the abuse of rules, justice, and taste, and all the other "charlatanry" of the new

7 *Journal des Dames,* janvier 1765:51.
8 *Correspondance littéraire* 8:442.

vogue.[9] That the fundamentally aristocratic *précieuses* had little use for *drames* was evident in Mlle de Lespinasse's reaction to a performance of one of them: "Oh, what a detestable play! The author is so bourgeois, and his mind is so common and limited! The public is so stupid . . . has such bad taste! . . . If only you knew how they applauded! . . . The author has courtiers and [King] Henri IV speaking in the manner of bourgeois from the rue Saint Denis!"[10]

But the authors of the *Journal des Dames,* inspired by Mercier, denounced the traditional rules of theater as "tyrannical." They objected to classical theater for depicting the lower classes only marginally and as a cause for laughter. The common people should be admitted to the theater, they argued, and plebeian characters and their daily lives should be the subject of the plays themselves. *Frondeur* journalists made it clear that they approved of *drames* as instruments of propaganda, as weapons in the fight for greater freedom. The stage, they believed, was the appropriate place to teach the illiterate civic virtue, and what better way than to show them dignified heroes from their own class to emulate. *Drames* were to be true "tableaux du siècle," illustrating all human conditions, even and especially the "vulgar," people living in obscurity, misery, and poverty but as capable of "grandeur" as any noble.

The *frondeur* papers also shared a loathing for war between nations. Their *patriotisme,* as we saw, did not mean nationalism but rather a respect for the law and a devotion to the public good. Almost all the editors of the *Journal des Dames* were admirers of the English and advocates of peace between the age-old enemies on opposite sides of the Channel. Like the editors of papers circulating during the Fronde, they believed countries should focus energy and money on their internal problems instead of imposing prohibitive taxes on starving peasants to finance costly and wasteful foreign battles. The *Journal des Dames* praised the English liberty of the press and the tradition of challenging *Spectator* journalism. It extolled Lady Wortley Montagu for her role in bringing smallpox inoculation to Europe. It drew parallels between the En-

9 *Journal encyclopédique* (1775) v:306.
10 This letter of Mlle de Lespinasse is quoted in Lough, *Paris Theatre Audiences,* 250.

Conclusion

glish parliaments and the French parlements, urging on the latter the constitutional duties of representative bodies. And the paper glorified Shakespeare for his fair portrayal of all human types and ranks, just as he was being excoriated by the establishment press for having robbed tragedy of its dignity. Mercier and his associated editors loved the English Bard, the sight of whose statue "made the common people weep," for he had touched their souls.[11]

Between 1778, when the *Journal des Dames* was finally suppressed, and the outbreak of the Revolution in 1789, no truly feminist or *frondeur* papers were printed on French soil. The climate was too inhospitable. We have seen that most of the male journalists from the *frondeur* network had scattered to other countries and that their extraterritorial French-language papers were quite radical. What meager press there was in France by or for women, however, reverted to its former integrative mode. A Mme d'Ormoy produced a *Journal de monsieur,* which Rutledge scorned for its superficiality and which was never intended, as its title makes obvious, for an audience of women. The *Cabinet des modes,* begun in 1785 by a male editor, represented a triumph for the dominant culture. By reducing women to objects of beauty and pleasure, this earliest French fashion magazine stressed frivolity and *le luxe* and discouraged women from involvement in serious matters.[12] If the fair sex had any value at all, it was as consumers whose natural fickleness and extravagance ensured an insatiable appetite and market for "costumes, decorations, embellishments, new forms of carriages, jewels, and gold." Ironically, even this paper may have communicated to women a sense of their power as an economic force, although to do so had never been the intention of its editors.[13]

What did the *frondeur* editors do during the Revolution? Some, like Mme de Beaumer and Mme de Maisonneuve, were no longer alive. Mme de Montanclos may have been the anonymous Mme

11 See, for example, the quotation from Grosley's *Londres* in Mercier's *Du théâtre,* 206, 207n.
12 See Van Dijk, "Femmes et journaux," 171, 173, 178, and Rimbault, "Presse féminine: Production," 204 and 209 n. 20. See also Chapter 2, above, n. 63.
13 See Sullerot, *Histoire de la presse,* 33.

299

de M. writing feminist articles for the *Etrennes nationales des Dames,* and Mme de Beauharnais may also have written under a pseudonym, for their friend Restif de la Bretonne mentioned both approvingly in his list of *femmes de lettres* working for worthy causes, as did the Revolutionary journalist Cousin Jacques.[14] Mathon kept constitutional and feminist thought alive in his *Journal de Lyon,* endorsing Revolutionary women's clubs and even printing their proceedings. Mercier, whom the police had always regarded as a ringleader in the fight for press freedom, returned to his *patrie,* revived the techniques and vocabulary of his *Journal des Dames,* and started up several new papers, again in an overlapping network.[15] With a group that included Carra, Brissot, Condorcet, and Tom Paine, he put out the *Annales patriotiques et littéraires de la France, La Tribune des hommes libres, La Chronique du mois, ou Les Cahiers patriotiques,* and the *Bulletin des amis de la vérité.* Until 1793, when he was forced to condemn the Jacobin excesses in the Terror, Mercier filled his papers with Roman ideas of liberty, patriotism, protection of all citizens under republican law, national tribunals, and people's rights under the constitution.[16] Familiarity with the *Journal des Dames* of the 1770s and its associated *frondeur* papers makes this rhetoric seem far less new and shocking. Linguet's acerbic journalism continued until 1792, alienating even the Revolutionary powers in the end and costing Linguet his head in 1794. His joining with the *frondeurs* in the 1770s had been only a temporary alliance. Although his writings retained their subversive thrust, he was more of a monarchist and less of a feminist than the others. Rutledge may have been part of the coterie of radical mesmerists on the eve of the Revolution. He was friendly with Marat, Brissot, and Carra, and police spies called him the "right-hand man" of d'Eprémesnil, then still considered by Le Noir an agent of sedition and by the Jansenist chronicler S. P. Hardy a "martyred patriot."[17] Rutledge appears to have practiced as well as preached his belief that women could be involved in both moth-

14   Restif de la Bretonne, *Contemporaines* 39:30, and Beffroy de Reigny, *Dictionnaire néologique* 1:460–62.

15   Pierre Manuel, *Police de Paris* 1:157.

16   Sgard, *Dictionnaire des journalistes,* 271–72.

17   See Darnton, *Mesmerism,* 104–5. See also Las Vergnas, *Chevalier Rutlidge,* and Sgard, *Dictionnaire des journalistes,* 329–31.

erhood and politics. The police reported that Rutlidge had been living for the last ten years with a woman named Maillet, by whom he had a little boy, and that she served as secretary for his political affairs, about which she was "as well-informed as he."[18]

It has always seemed somewhat puzzling that women, politically inactive since the Fronde, suddenly hurled themselves into activity during the Revolution, combining demands for bread with demands for dialogue and confrontation, as in the October March, the so-called "women's insurrection."[19] Although we cannot establish such a transgenerational influence in any rigorous way, it is possible that the aggressively feminist editors of the *Journal des Dames* and the paper's ethic of sobriety, citizenship, and participation may have helped to reawaken political attitudes, roles, and ambitions for women who then passed them on to their daughters in the pre-Revolutionary decades. The activism of *frondeur* journalism gave female editors, contributors, and subscribers a sense of awareness and involvement in the events and causes of the day and, as is well known, feminist journalism proliferated during the Revolution.[20]

From our twentieth-century perspective where domesticity and career are at opposite poles, it is easy to misconstrue the *Journal des Dames* and other *frondeur* papers' advocacy of motherhood as antifeminist. In the eighteenth century, however, the rectitude of home and family was upheld not in opposition to professional life—there were no careers for women—but in opposition to the license and dissipation of *les grands*. Women were encouraged in the *Journal des Dames* to return to mothering and educating future patriots and to thus further the cause of progress and liberty. Later during the Revolution it was still common to find radicals insisting on the crucial social significance of maternity for the propagation of freedom, as was the case with the Jacobin feminist and journalist Louise Keralio.[21] Serious motherhood was not seen to preclude an independent status for women but was essential for the transmission to future citizens of healthy attitudes toward par-

---

18 Archives Nationales, Y10506.
19 On women's activity in the Revolution, see Duhet, *Femmes et Révolution,* and Levy, Applewhite, and Johnson, *Women in Revolutionary Paris.*
20 Sullerot, *Histoire de la presse,* 42–62.
21 See Censer, *Prelude to Power,* 45, and 153–54 nn. 37–43.

ticipation and suspicion of authority. The *frondeur* editors endorsed family life, but they meant marriages to be fair and equal. We have seen that they extolled unions based on mutual respect and trust and that they condemned sexual impropriety. In 1761 the *Journal des Dames* published a message-laden tale of a young girl seduced and abandoned by a wealthy man, in 1778 a plea that the fathers of illegitimate children be held responsible for them. These same concerns later echoed in de Gouges's *Les Droits de la femme,* where she demanded the right to paternity suits so young girls would not end up in the "almshouses of shame." De Gouges also drew up a model "social contract between man and woman" establishing just the kind of conjugal equality advocated in Mme de Beaumer's articles and in Mme de Montanclos's notarized permission to transact business for herself. [22] Once healthy marriages were established, women were to see their maternal role as formative and essentially political. Mothers were in a unique position to eradicate "libertinage" from the realm and encourage civic duty. As the popular *poissard* paper *La Mère Duchêne* put it: "If infants should drink in with their milk the principles of the constitution . . . who is there beside yourselves, women, who can make the love of liberty sprout in their yet tender hearts and spirits." [23]

The *Journal des Dames* had lofty ambitions. It strove to unify princely and popular opposition, to speak to both women and men, to reach not only the capital but the provinces and even, in Mme de Beaumer's dream, the whole civilized world with its message of freedom. It was a constant struggle. As Sullerot has shown, the outspoken feminist and republican papers of the Revolution had shorter but equally troubled lives. A recent study of the modern French press has argued that the only successful and long-lasting papers for women are generally mindless publications by men, which practice a total "évacuation du réel." [24] The *Journal des Dames* was the first French paper to encourage women

22   See de Gouges, "Les Droits de la Femme."
23   "La Mère Duchêne" in Levy, Applewhite, and Johnson, *Women in Revolutionary Paris,* 100.
24   Dardigna, *Presse "féminine,"* 9–32.

to think, take a stance, and speak up. In our own century the cry "Femme, ose être!" still creates anxiety.[25] Little wonder that it did so in the unsteady last decades of the Old Regime.

In tracing the vicissitudes of this journalistic enterprise we have tried to illuminate several larger issues—the ideological, institutional, and cultural tensions of a society and regime in crisis and the role of the media and of women in sharpening and deepening those tensions. The difficulties encountered by unconventional females in this period, their "perilous visibilities," as Germaine Brée has called them,[26] have been traced within their broader social context. The *Journal des Dames* played a role in the development of a political consciousness and in the formation of public opinion in the last decades of the old order. Oddly permitted and tolerated by the booktrade authorities, it worked with many opposition papers transmitting explosive combinations of subversive principles and values that would later find their fullest expression in Revolutionary discourse.

25 Albistur, *Histoire du féminisme*, 362.
26 See Spencer, *French Women and the Age of Enlightenment*, xi. Spencer's collected volume came to my attention only after my manuscript was completed. Perhaps this story of the *Journal des Dames* at least partly satisfies the call by Elizabeth Fox-Genovese (ibid., introduction, 5) for further elucidation of the social history of eighteenth-century women through studies of the feminine press.

Appendix

The title pages of Old Regime periodicals told a tale in themselves, as shown in this small photo-essay.[1] The *Journal des Dames*'s first issue, of January 1759 (plate 1), bore no author's name and was supposedly printed in The Hague. Such anonymity and fictitious imprints were common on books printed in Paris with only a tacit permission. In this case they afforded protection for the timid founding editor, the printer, and even the censor who had secretly approved dubious material. Plate 2 shows the paper under its second male editor, a bolder man eager to have his name and academic association attached to the venture. The noble wife of the Russian ambassador had accepted the dedication of the *Journal des Dames,* and although it still bore a fictitious imprint—now the colorful Vallons de Tivoli—the filigreed border about the edge and the quality of the paper gave the journal a new look of prosperity. Mme de Beaumer, the paper's first woman editor and a feminist *frondeuse* in the bargain, was forced after a few months to acquiesce to booktrade officials and tame her fiery rhetoric. Plate 3 reveals that she called her toned-down paper the *Nouveau Journal des Dames* and was obliged to dedicate it to one of the royal princesses of the blood. Mme de Maisonneuve gave the paper yet another new look. Plate 4 shows her illustration of "impartialité" and the proper female balance of plumes and flowers with books and scrolls. This editor camouflaged her *frondeur* message so skillfully that she actually had the honor of presenting her paper at court, received a regular pension from the king, and could now

1   Photographs courtesy of the Bibliothèque de l'Arsenal, Paris.

boast openly that her *Journal des Dames* was available in Paris. Plate 5 shows a curious and deliberate "mistake" on the part of the third female editor, who promoted Marie Antoinette to queen many months before she actually took the throne and while Louis XV was still very much alive. Subsequent issues reverted to being dedicated to the dauphine, but the idea of the royal teenager's future importance had been planted in readers' minds. The paper was now distributed by the prestigious Paris *libraire* Lacombe. Mercier's *Journal des Dames,* of which I was not able to get a picture, kept the same title page but was once again anonymous because Mercier's editorship would never have been given official approval. At the bottom it stated that the paper was now for the first time printed with royal privilege and approbation. The editors had thus managed gradually to enhance the status of their enterprise even as they filled it with increasingly oppositional fare. Plate 6 depicts the *Journal des Dames* in its last form, now distributed by an official printer of the king. Dorat, the last editor, capitulated completely to the authorities and even altered the title to dissociate the paper from its *frondeur* past, making of it an innocuous *mélange littéraire.*

JOURNAL

DES DAMES,

POUR LE MOIS DE JANVIER 1759.

TOME I.

PREMIERE PARTIE.

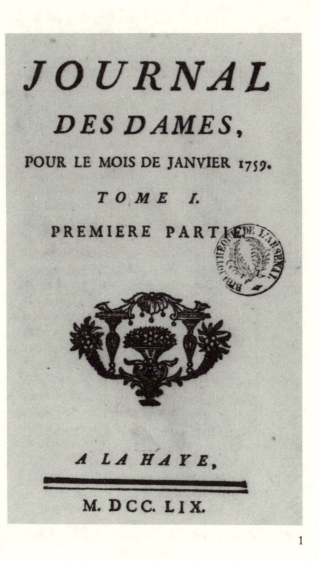

A LA HAYE,

M. DCC. LIX.

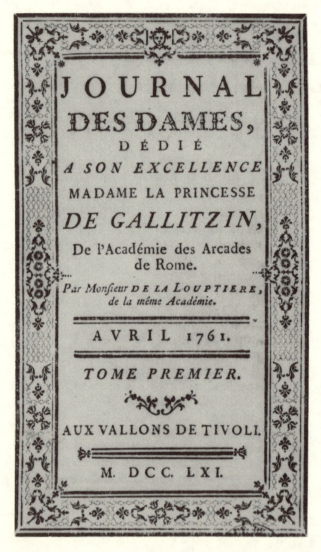

JOURNAL DES DAMES,

D É D I É

A SON EXCELLENCE

MADAME LA PRINCESSE

DE GALLITZIN,

De l'Académie des Arcades
de Rome.

*Par Monsieur DE LA LOUPTIERE,
de la même Académie.*

AVRIL 1761.

TOME PREMIER.

AUX VALLONS DE TIVOLI.

M. DCC. LXI.

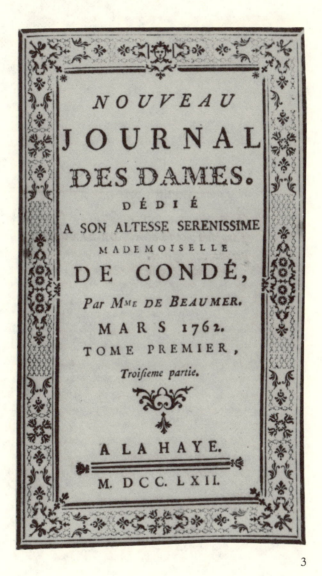

NOUVEAU
JOURNAL
DES DAMES.

DÉDIÉ

A SON ALTESSE SERENISSIME

MADEMOISELLE

DE CONDÉ,

Par Mme de Beaumer.

MARS 1762.

TOME PREMIER,

Troisieme partie.

A LA HAYE.

M. DCC. LXII.

3

JOURNAL

DES

DAMES,

Par Madame DE MAISONNEUVE,
Penſionnaire du ROI.

JANVIER *1766.*

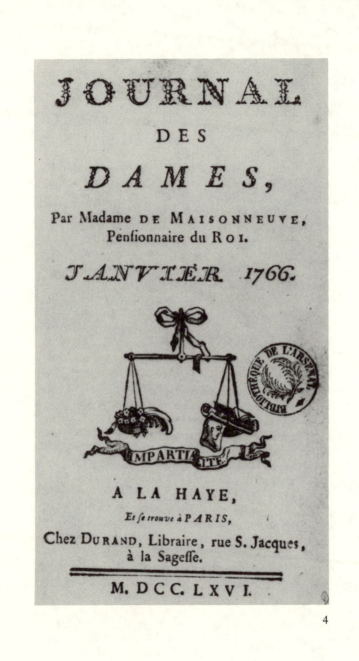

IMPARTIA LITE.

À LA HAYE,

Et ſe trouve à PARIS,

Chez DURAND, Libraire, rue S. Jacques,
à la Sageſſe.

M. DCC. LXVI.

JOURNAL

DES

DAMES,

DEDIÉ

A LA REINE,

Par Madame la Baronne DE PRINCEN.

FEVRIER 1774.

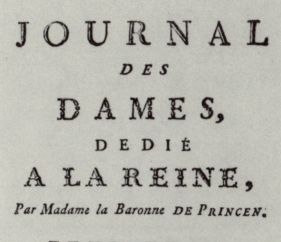

A PARIS,

Chez LACOMBE, rue Chriſtine.

M. D. CC. LXXIV.

MÉLANGES

LITTÉRAIRES,

OU

JOURNAL DES DAMES,

DÉDIÉ

A LA REINE.

JUILLET 1777. Tome II.

PAR M. DORAT.

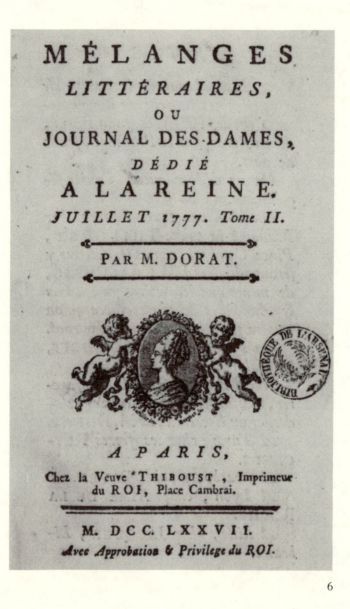

A PARIS,

Chez la Veuve THIBOUST, Imprimeur
du ROI, Place Cambrai.

M. DCC. LXXVII.

Avec Approbation & Privilege du ROI.

Bibliography

Primary Sources

MANUSCRIPTS

Archives de la Seine (Archives de Paris)
  Registre de faillite, série D4B^6, carton 20, dossier 961
  MS 6AZ 1602
  DC^{6}17, fol. 228r; DC^{6}20, fol. 95v; DC^{6}256, fol. 64v
  DC^{10}95, dossier 1305; DC^{10}422, dossier 311
  DQ^{7}3035
  DQ^{8}870
  DQ^{10}, carton 1442, dossier 3029

Archives du Théâtre-Français (Comédie-Française)
  Dossier "Administration 1775"
  Dossier "Administration 1776"
  Dossier "Correspondance Dorat"
  Dossier "Mme de Montanclos"
  Dossier "Mercier"
  Dossier "Registre concernant messieurs les auteurs"

Archives Nationales, *Minutier Central* (notarial documents)
  Etude XLIII, liasse (491), 15 juin 1778
  Etude LVIII, liasse (9), 27 décembre 1777; liasse (480), 27 janvier 1777
  Etude LXXXIII, liasse (590), 12 juin 1778 [réserve]
  Etude LXXXV, liasse (652), 11 and 19 avril 1775; liasse (660), 18 décembre 1776
  Etude XCI, liasse (1158), 14 janvier 1778; liasse (1183), 18 and 22 février 1780
  Etude XCII, liasse (847), 29 septembre 1782

———, *Section ancienne*
  Série F^4 F^{4}1940 d, F^{4}1941 g
  Série 0^1 Registre de dépêches, ordres, et correspondance du ministre de la maison du roi: 0^{1}102, 0^{1}108, 0^{1}114, 0^{1}118, 0^{1}392, 0^{1}400, 0^{1}403–6
  Série T   T1089 (21)
  Série Y   Principaux scellés: Y10506, Y10796, Y11096

307

Bibliography

Bibliothèque de l'Arsenal
  MSS 5313, 15076, 15078 (2b, 2c)

———, *Archives de la Bastille*
  MSS 10028, 10303, 10305, 11683, 11794, 11807, 12114, 12403

Bibliothèque Historique de la Ville de Paris
  Cote provisoire 4012, fol. 65 (10)

Bibliothèque Mazarine
  35735 3e pièce

Bibliothèque Nationale
  fonds français MSS 8132, 21960, 21966, 21983, 21989, 21992–94,
    22001–2, 22013, 22042, 22085, 22093, 22096, 22108, 22123, 22132,
    22134–35, 22137, 22141, 22143, 22151, 22154, 22161, 24005, 24027
  nouvelles acquisitions françaises MSS 1180, 3346, 3351, 23943, 24030

———, *Archives de la Chambre Syndicale de la Librairie et Imprimerie de Paris*
  fonds français MSS 21813–22060

———, *Collection Anisson-Duperron*
  fonds français MSS 8132, 22061–193
  nouvelles acquisitions françaises MSS 1180–83, 3344–46

PRINTED WORKS

Periodicals

Affiches de Lyon
Almanach des muses
Almanach royal
Annales politiques, civiles, et littéraires
Annales typographiques
L'Année littéraire
Annonces, affiches, et avis divers (Affiches de province)
L'Avant coureur
Le Babillard
Bibliographie parisienne, ou Catalogue d'ouvrages
*Bibliothèque des dames, ou Choix des pièces nouvelles, instructives, et amu-
  santes en prose et en vers*
Bibliothèque des femmes, ouvrage moral, critique, et philosophique
Catalogue hebdomadaire, ou Journal de la librairie
Le Censeur hebdomadaire
Correspondance des dames, ou Journal des modes et des spectacles de Paris

Bibliography

Correspondance dramatique

Courrier de l'Europe

L'Esprit des journaux

Gazette de France

Gazette et avant coureur de la littérature

Gazette universelle de littérature, ou Gazette de Deux-Ponts

L'Iris de Guienne, ouvrage périodique . . . par Louis-Claude Leclerc à Bordeaux

Journal anglais

Journal de Bruxelles, ou Le Penseur

Journal de Monsieur

Journal de musique

Journal de Paris, ou Poste du soir

Journal de politique et de littérature

Journal des savants

Journal des sciences et des beaux-arts

Journal encyclopédique

Journal étranger

Journal français

Journal français, anglais, et italien, lyrique . . . ou Nouveau journal étranger

Journal (historique) de Verdun, ou Suite de la clef

Lettres curieuses, instructives, et amusantes

Lettres de Mme Le Hoc à M. Le Hic, suivies d'autres lettres sur les spectacles et les journalistes

Mémoires pour servir à l'histoire des sciences et des beaux-arts (Mémoires de Trévoux)

Mercure de France

Nécrologe des hommes célèbres

Nouveau magasin français, ou Bibliothèque instructive et amusante

Nouveau spectateur, ou Journal des théâtres

L'Observateur anglais

L'Observateur littéraire

Recueil de toutes les feuilles de la Spectatrice qui ont paru et de celles qui n'ont point paru

La Renommée littéraire

Other Printed Works

[Artaud, J. B.] *Taconet, ou Mémoire historique pour servir à la vie de cet homme célèbre, article oublié dans le Nécrologe de 1775.* Amsterdam, 1775.

Aublet de Maubuy. *Histoire des troubles et des démêlés littéraires.* Amsterdam, 1779.

————. *La Vie des femmes illustres de la France.* 6 vols. Paris, 1762–68.

[Bachaumont, Louis Petit de.] *Mémoires secrets pour servir à l'histoire de la république des lettres en France, depuis 1762 jusqu'à nos jours.* 31 vols. London, 1777–89.

Barbier, A. A., and N. T. Des Essarts. *Nouvelle Bibliothèque d'un homme de goût.* 5 vols. Paris, 1810.

Barbier, Edmond-Jean-François. *Chronique de la Régence et du règne de Louis XV (1718–1763).* 8 vols. Paris, 1857.

————. *Journal historique et anecdotique du règne de Louis XV.* 4 vols. Paris, 1847–56.

Barillet, E. J. J. *Recherches historiques sur le Temple.* Paris, 1809.

Beaumarchais, P. A. C. de. *Compte-rendu de l'affaire des auteurs dramatiques et des comédiens français.* Paris, 1780.

————. *Le Mariage de Figaro.* Paris, 1918.

Beaumer, Mme de. *Oeuvres mêlées.* Liège and Paris, 1760, and Paris, 1761.

Beau★, Mme de. *Lettres curieuses, instructives, et amusantes, ou Correspondance historique, galante, critique, morale, philosophique, et littéraire. . . .* The Hague, 1759.

Beffroy de Reigny, Louis Abel. *Dictionnaire néologique des hommes et des choses de la Révolution, par le cousin Jacques.* 3 vols. Paris, 1800.

Boudier de Villemert, Pierre-Joseph. *Nouvel ami des femmes.* Paris, 1779.

Briquet, Mme Fortunée B. *Dictionnaire historique, littéraire, et bibliographique des françaises et des étrangères naturalisées en France.* Paris, 1804.

Brissot, J. P. *Mémoires de Brissot, avec introduction, notices, et notes par M. de Lescure.* Paris, 1877.

————. *Plan de conduite pour les députés du peuple aux Etats Généraux de mars 1789.* 1789.

Campigneulles, C. C. F. de Thorel de. *Anecdotes morales sur la fatuité.* Antwerp and Paris, 1760.

————. *Nouveaux essais en différents genres de littérature.* Geneva, 1765.

————. *Pièces fugitives de M. de Voltaire, de M. Desmahis, et de quelques autres auteurs.* Geneva and Lyons. 1761.

Catalogue des livres qui composent la bibliothèque de Monseigneur Hue de Miromesnil, garde des sceaux de France. Paris, 1781.

Catalogue des livres qui composent la bibliothèque de M. Le Noir, conseiller d'état, lieutenant général de police. Paris, 1782.

Chalumeau, Marie-F. *Ma Chaumière.* Paris, 1790.

Clément-Hémery, Albertine. *Les Femmes vengées de la sottise d'un philosophe du jour, ou Réponse au projet de loi de M. S★★ M★★★ portant défense d'apprendre à lire aux femmes.* Paris, n.d.

Collé, Charles. *Journal et mémoires*. 3 vols. Paris, 1868.

———. *Journal historique*. 3 vols. Paris, 1805–7.

———. *Journal historique inédit pour les années 1761 et 1762*. Ed. Ad van Bever. Paris, 1911.

Delacroix, Jacques Vincent. *Peintures des moeurs du siècle, ou Lettres et discours sur différents sujets*. 2 vols. Amsterdam and Paris, 1777.

———. *Le Spectateur français avant la Révolution*. Paris, L'An IV (1795).

Delisle de Sales, J. B. *Essai sur le journalisme depuis 1735 jusqu'à l'an 1800*. Paris, 1811.

Des Essarts, Nicolas-T. *Les Trois Théâtres de Paris*. Paris, 1777.

Diderot, Denis. *Correspondance*. Ed. G. Roth and J. Varloot. 16 vols. Paris, 1955–70.

———. *Oeuvres complètes*. Ed. J. Assézat and Maurice Tourneux. 20 vols. Paris, 1875–77.

Dorat, Claude-Joseph. *Coup d'oeil sur la littérature*. Paris, 1780.

———. *La Déclamation théâtrale*. Paris, 1771.

———. *Les Prôneurs*. Paris, 1777.

Doucet [Coqueley de Chaussepierre]. *Monsieur Cassandre, ou Les Effets de l'amour et du vert-de-gris*. Amsterdam and Paris, 1775.

Du Coudray, Alexandre J. *Il est temps de parler*. Paris, 1779.

Du Deffand, Mme Marie de Vichy-Chamrond. *Correspondance complète de la marquise Du Deffand par M. de Lescure*. Paris, 1865. Reprint. Geneva, 1971.

Epinay, Mme L. F. P. Tardieu d'Esclavelles d'. *Mémoires et correspondance de Mme d'Epinay*. 3 vols. Paris, 1818.

Examen fugitif des Pièces fugitives. . . . Placentia, 1761.

Falconnet, Ambroise. *Le Barreau français moderne, ou Choix de plaidoyers, mémoires, et consultations imprimés et non-imprimés*. 2 vols. Paris, 1806–9.

———. *Mémoire à consulter pour les souscripteurs du "Journal des théâtres" rédigé par le sieur de Méricourt*. Liège, 1777.

Gouges, Olympe de. *Les Droits de la femme*. Paris, 1791. Reprinted in Levy, Darline Gay, H. B. Applewhite, and M. D. Johnson, eds., *Women in Revolutionary Paris, 1789–1795* (Urbana, 1979), 87–96.

Grimm, Friedrich Melchior, baron, et al. *Correspondance littéraire, philosophique, et critique*. Ed. Maurice Tourneux. 16 vols. Paris, 1877–82.

Guibert, Mme. *Pensées détachées*. Brussels and Paris, 1771.

———. *Poésies et oeuvres diverses*. Amsterdam, 1764.

Henrion de Pansey, P. P. N. *Mémoire à consulter et consultation pour le sieur Mercier contre la troupe des comédiens français ordinaires du roi*. Paris, 1775.

————. *Premier mémoire pour le sieur Mercier contre la troupe des comédiens.* Paris, 1775.

————. *Requête au roi pour le sieur Mercier contre MM. les gentilhommes de la chambre de sa majesté.* Paris, 1775.

Hurtaut, P. T. N., and Magny. *Dictionnaire historique de la ville de Paris et de ses environs.* 4 vols. Paris, 1779.

I. K. L., *Essai dramatique: Ouvrage posthume de Léonard Gobemouche.* Paris, 1776.

Jèze. *Etat ou tableau de la ville de Paris considérée relativement au nécessaire, à l'utile, à l'agréable, et à l'administration.* Paris, 1761.

La Croix, T. F. de. *Dictionnaire portatif des femmes célèbres.* Paris, 1769. *Supplément.* Paris, 1788.

La Harpe, Jean-François de. *Correspondance littéraire depuis 1774 jusqu'à 1789.* 5 vols. Paris, 1801–7.

————. *Oeuvres.* 6 vols. Paris, 1778.

La Porte, Joseph de. *Histoire littéraire des femmes françaises, ou Lettres historiques et critiques contenant un précis de la vie et une analyse raisonnée des ouvrages des femmes qui se sont distinguées dans la littérature française.* 5 vols. Paris, 1769.

Le Fuel de Méricourt, Jean-Pierre. *Requête au roi.* London, 1777.

Lespinasse, Julie de. *Lettres.* Ed. Eugène Asse. Paris, 1876. Reprint. Geneva, 1971.

————. *Lettres inédites . . . de Julie de Lespinasse.* Ed. Charles Henry. Paris, 1887. Reprint. Geneva, 1971.

Le Tourneur, Pierre. *Shakespeare traduit de l'anglais.* 19 vols. Paris, 1776–83.

Lettres de Voltaire à l'Académie française, lues le 25 août 1776. Paris, 1776.

Linguet, S. N. H. *Précis et consultation dans la cause entre S. N. H. Linguet et C. J. Panckoucke, libraire.* Paris, 1787.

Lottin, A. M. *Catalogue alphabétique et chronologique des libraires et des imprimeurs de Paris depuis 1470 jusqu'à 1788.* Paris, 1789.

Louptière, Jean-Charles Relongue de la. *Oeuvres diverses.* 2 vols. Amsterdam, 1774.

————. *Poésies et oeuvres diverses de M. de la Louptière.* Amsterdam and Paris, 1768.

Malesherbes, C. G. Lamoignon de. *Mémoire sur la librairie et sur la liberté de la presse.* Paris, 1809.

Mannory, Louis. *Plaidoyers et mémoires.* 18 vols. Paris, 1759–66.

Manuel, Pierre. *La Police de Paris dévoilée.* 2 vols. Paris, 1792.

Marmontel, J. F. *Mémoires.* Ed. Maurice Tourneux. 3 vols. Paris, 1891.

Mathon de la Cour, Charles-Joseph. *Collection de comptes-rendus, pièces authentiques, états, et tableaux concernant les finances de France, depuis 1758 jusqu'en 1787.* Lausanne and Paris, 1788.

—————. *Discours prononcé dans la loge d'adoption du patriotisme.* Lyons, 1785.

—————. *Discours sur le danger de la lecture des livres contre la religion par rapport à la société.* Paris, 1770.

—————. *Discours sur les meilleurs moyens de faire naître et d'encourager le patriotisme dans une monarchie.* Paris, 1787.

—————. *Lettres à Mme *** sur les peintures, les sculptures, et les gravures exposées dans le Salon du Louvre cette année.* Paris, 1763.

—————. *Par quelles causes . . . les lois de Lycurgus se sont altérées.* Lyons and Paris, 1767.

Mémoires du comte Alexandre de Tilly pour servir à l'histoire des moeurs à la fin du XVIIIe siècle. Paris, 1865.

Mémoires secrets pour servir à l'histoire de la république des lettres en France, depuis 1762 jusqu'à nos jours. 31 vols. London, 1777–89.

Mercier, Louis-Sébastien. *L'An 2440: Rêve s'il en fut jamais.* Ed. Raymond Trousson. Bordeaux, 1971.

—————. *L'An 2440, nouvelle édition.* 3 vols. 1786.

—————. *La Brouette du vinaigrier.* London and Paris, 1775.

—————. *De la Littérature, et Nouvel Examen de la tragédie française.* Yverdon, 1778.

—————. *Du Théâtre, ou Nouvel Essai sur l'art dramatique.* Amsterdam, 1773.

—————. *Eloges et discours philosophiques.* Amsterdam, 1776.

—————. *L'Indigent.* Paris, 1772.

—————. *Mon Bonnet de nuit.* 3 vols. Paris, 1784.

—————. *Tableau de Paris.* Ed. Gustave Desnoiresterres. Paris, 1853.

—————. *Tableau de Paris, nouvelle édition, corrigée et augmentée.* 12 vols. Amsterdam, 1783–89.

Metra, François. *Correspondance secrète, politique, et littéraire.* 16 vols. London, 1787–89.

Montanclos, Mme de. *Oeuvres.* 2 vols. Paris, 1792.

Mouhy, Charles de Fieux. *Abrégé de l'histoire du théâtre français.* 4 vols. Paris, 1780.

Palissot de Montenoy, Charles. *Mémoires pour servir à l'histoire de notre littérature.* 2 vols. Paris, 1803.

Parny, E. *Oeuvres.* Ed. A. J. Pons. Paris, 1862.

Perrin, A. *Manuel de l'auteur et du libraire.* Paris, 1777.

[Pidansat de Mairobert, M. F.] *L'Espion anglais, ou Correspondance secrète entre Milord All'Eye et Milord All'Ear.* 10 vols. London, 1777–84.

————. *L'Espion anglais, nouvelle édition.* 2 vols. Paris, 1809.

————. *Journal historique de la révolution opérée dans la constitution de la monarchie française par M. de Maupeou, chancelier de France.* 7 vols. London and Amsterdam, 1774–76.

Piganiol de la Force, J. A. *Description historique de la ville de Paris.* 10 vols. Paris, 1765.

Pothiers, Robert-Joseph. *Traité de la communauté [et] de la puissance du mari sur la personne et les biens de la femme.* Paris, 1770.

————. *Traité des obligations, selon les règles tant du for de la conscience que du for extérieur.* 2 vols. Paris, 1761–64.

————. *Traité du contrat de mariage, par l'auteur du Traité des obligations.* 2 vols. Paris, 1768.

Le Provincial à Paris, ou Etat actuel de Paris. 4 vols. Paris, 1787.

Recueil de chansons de la très vénérable confrérie des francs-maçons. Jerusalem, 1777.

Registres des délibérations des administrateurs de la ferme générale des postes. 12 vols. Paris, 1738–91. On microfilm at the Musée de la Poste.

Restif de la Bretonne, Nicolas. *Les Contemporaines.* . . . 42 vols. Paris, 1783–85.

————. *Monsieur Nicolas, ou Le Coeur humain dévoilé.* 16 vols. Paris, 1794–97.

Rivarol, Antoine de. *Petit almanach de nos grandes femmes.* London, 1788.

Rousseau, Jean-Jacques. *Correspondance complète de Jean-Jacques Rousseau.* Ed. R. A. Leigh. 44 vols. Geneva, 1965–85.

————. *Correspondance générale de J. J. Rousseau, annotée et commentée par Théophile Dufour.* 20 vols. Paris, 1924–34.

Rutlidge, Jean-Jacques. *Essais politiques.* London, 1777.

————. *Mémoire au roi pour le chevalier Rutlidge.* Paris, 1790.

————. *Oeuvres diverses de M. le chevalier Rutlidge.* 2 vols. Yverdon, 1777.

————. *Quinzaine anglaise.* London, 1776.

————. *Le Train de Paris, ou Les Bourgeois du temps.* Yverdon, 1777.

Sabatier de Castres, Antoine. *Les Trois Siècles de la littérature française, ou Tableau de l'esprit de nos écrivains.* 4 vols. The Hague and Paris, 1781.

Saugrain, Claude. *Code de la librairie et de l'imprimerie.* Paris, 1744.

Suard, Mme Amélie Panckoucke. *Essai de mémoires sur M. Suard.* Paris, 1820.

Suard, Jean-Baptiste Antoine. *Discours impartial sur les affaires de la librairie.* Paris, 1777.

————. *Mélanges de littérature.* 5 vols. Paris, 1803–4.

Thomas, Antoine Léonard. *Essai sur les femmes*. Paris, 1772.

Voltaire, François-Marie Arouet. *The Complete Works of Voltaire*. Ed. Theodore Besterman. 135 vols. Geneva and Oxford, 1968–77.

Secondary Sources

ARTICLES AND ESSAYS

Abray, Jane. "Feminism in the French Revolution." *American Historical Review* 80 (February 1975): 43–62.

Aimé-Azam, Denise. "Le Ministère des affaires étrangères et la presse à la fin de l'ancien régime." *Cahiers de la presse,* juillet 1938:428–38.

Ascoli, Georges. "Essai sur l'histoire des idées féministes en France, du XVIe siècle à la Révolution." *Revue de synthèse historique* 13 (1906): 25–57, 99–106, 161–84.

Ascoli, Peter. "The French Press and the American Revolution." *Proceedings of the Fifth Annual Meeting of the Western Society for French History,* 1977:46–54.

Babeau, Albert. "La Louptière, le poète champenois." *Revue de Champagne et de Brie* 11 (1881): 5–15.

Baker, Keith Michael. "French Political Thought at the Accession of Louis XVI." *Journal of Modern History* 50 (1978): 279–303.

———. "On the Problem of the Ideological Origins of the French Revolution." In Dominick La Capra and Steven Kaplan, eds., *Modern European Intellectual History: Reappraisals and New Perspectives* (Ithaca, 1982), 197–219.

———. "A Script for a French Revolution: The Political Consciousness of the Abbé Mably." *Eighteenth-Century Studies* 14, no. 3 (Spring 1981): 235–63.

Balloffet, Joseph. "Monsieur Pezant, ou L'Obligeant Académicien." *Bulletin de la Société des sciences et arts du Beaujolais,* juillet–décembre 1928:180–92; janvier–juin 1929:106–28.

Barber, Gilles. "French Royal Decrees Concerning the Book Trade, 1700–1789." *Australian Journal of French Studies* 3 (1966): 312–31.

Bayle, P., and J. Herblay. "Journalisme clandestin au XVIIIe siècle." *Nouvelle Revue* 37 (1905): 213–35, 395–413.

Benhamou, Paul. "The Periodical Press in the *Encyclopédie*." *French Review* 59, no. 3 (February 1986): 410–17.

Berkowe, Christine. "L. S. Mercier et les femmes." *Romanic Review* 55 (1964): 16–29.

Birn, Raymond F. "Le *Journal des savants* sous l'ancien régime." *Journal des savants,* 1965:15–36.

Bibliography

―――. "The Profits of Ideas: *Privilège en librairie* in Eighteenth-Century France." *Eighteenth-Century Studies* 4 , no. 2 (1971): 131–68.

Bloch, Jean H. "Women and the Reform of the Nation." In Eva Jacobs et al., eds., *Women and Society in Eighteenth-Century France: Essays in Honor of J. S. Spink* (London, 1979), 3–18.

Bonno, Gabriel. "Liste chronologique des périodiques de langue française du XVIIIe siècle." *Modern Languages Quarterly* 5 (1944): 3–25.

Bordes de Fortage, L. de. "Sébastien Mercier à Bordeaux." *Revue historique de Bordeaux* 11 (1918): 193–99.

Botein, Stephen, Jack R. Censer, and Harriet Ritvo. "The Periodical Press in Eighteenth-Century English and French Society: A Cross-Cultural Approach." *Comparative Studies in Society and History* 23 (1981): 464–90.

Cahen, Léon. "La Librairie parisienne et la diffusion du livre français à la fin du XVIIIe siècle." *Revue de synthèse* 17 (1939): 159–79.

Censer, Jack R. "English Politics in the *Courrier d'Avignon.*" In Jack R. Censer and Jeremy D. Popkin, eds., *Press and Politics in Pre-Revolutionary France* (Berkeley and Los Angeles, 1987), 170–203.

Cerf, Madeleine. "La Censure royale à la fin du XVIIIe siècle." *Communications,* 1967, no. 9:7–27.

Chevalley, Sylvie. "Les Femmes auteurs-dramatiques et la Comédie-Française." *Europe,* novembre–décembre 1964:41–47.

Clancy, Patricia A. "A French Writer and Educator in England: Mme le Prince de Beaumont." *Studies on Voltaire and the Eighteenth Century* 201 (1982): 195–208.

Clinton, Katherine B. "*Femme et philosophe:* Enlightenment Origins of Feminism." *Eighteenth-Century Studies* 8, no. 3 (1975): 283–99.

Crowe, Thomas. "*The Oath of the Horatii* in 1785: Painting and Pre-Revolutionary Radicalism in France." *Art History* 1, no. 4 (December 1978): 424–71.

Darnton, Robert. "The High Enlightenment and the Low Life of Literature." In his *The Literary Underground of the Old Regime* (Cambridge, Mass., 1982), 1–41.

―――. "A Police Inspector Sorts his Files: The Anatomy of the Republic of Letters." In his *The Great Cat Massacre and Other Episodes in French Cultural History* (New York, 1984), 145–91.

―――. "Readers Respond to Rousseau: The Fabrication of Romantic Sensitivity." In his *The Great Cat Massacre and Other Episodes in French Cultural History* (New York, 1984), 215–56.

―――. "Reading, Writing, and Publishing." In his *The Literary Underground of the Old Regime* (Cambridge, Mass., 1982), 167–211.

―――. "A Spy in Grub Street." In his *The Literary Underground of the Old Regime* (Cambridge, Mass., 1982), 41–70.

Bibliography

—————. "The World of the Underground Booksellers of the Old Regime." In Ernst Hinrichs et al., eds., *Vom ancien Regime zur französischen Revolution* (Göttingen, 1978), 439–78.

Dock, Terry Smiley. "The Encyclopedists' Woman." *Proceedings of the Tenth Annual Meeting of the Western Society for French History,* 1983: 255–63.

Ehrard, J., and J. Roger. "Deux périodiques français au XVIIIe siècle: Le *Journal des savants* et les *Mémoires de Trévoux.*" In G. Bollème et al., *Livre et société dans la France du XVIIIe siècle* (Paris, 1965), 33–60.

Eisenstein, Elizabeth L. "Some Conjectures About the Impact of Printing on Western Society and Thought: A Preliminary Report." *Journal of Modern History* 40, no. 1 (1968), 1–56.

Estrée, P. d'. "Farmin de Rozoi" [*sic*]. *Revue d'histoire littéraire de la France,* 1918:211–42, 408–22, 562–79; 1922:409–32; 1928:24–29.

Favre, R. "Le Fait divers en 1778: Permanence et précarité." In Jean Varloot and Paule Jansen, eds., *L'Année 1778 à travers la presse traitée par ordinateur* (Paris, 1982), 113–46.

Furet, F. "La 'Librairie' du royaume de France au XVIIIe siècle." In G. Bollème et al., *Livre et société dans la France du XVIIIe siècle* (Paris, 1965), 3–32.

Gasc, Michèle. "La Naissance de la presse périodique locale à Lyon: *Les Affiches de Lyon—annonces et avis divers.*" *Etudes sur la presse au XVIIIe siècle* 3 (1978):61–79.

Gelbart, Nina Rattner. "*Frondeur* Journalism in the 1770s: Theatre Criticism and Radical Politics in the Pre-Revolutionary French Press." *Eighteenth-Century Studies* 17, no. 4 (Summer 1984): 493–514.

—————. "The *Journal des Dames* and its Female Editors: Politics, Feminism, and Censorship in the Old Regime Press." In Jack R. Censer and Jeremy D. Popkin, eds., *Press and Politics in Pre-Revolutionary France* (Berkeley and Los Angeles, 1987), 24–74.

—————. "Le Fuel de Méricourt" and "Mercier." In A. M. Chouillet and François Moureau, *Suppléments au Dictionnaire des journalistes* (Grenoble, 1984), 3:139–50.

—————"Organicism and the Realizability of Utopia." In Frederick Burwick, ed., *Approaches to Organic Form* (Dordrecht and Boston, forthcoming).

—————. "Science in French Enlightenment Utopias." *Proceedings of the Sixth Annual Meeting of the Western Society for French History,* 1979:120–29.

Gordon, L. S. "Le Thème de Mandrin, le 'brigand noble,' dans l'histoire des idées en France avant la Révolution." In *Au Siècle des Lumières* (Paris, 1970), 189–207.

Graham, Ruth. "Loaves and Liberty: Women in the French Revolution."

Bibliography

In Renate Bridenthal and Claudia Koonz, eds., *Becoming Visible: Women in European History* (Boston, 1977), 236–54.

Guyot, Charly. "Sébastien Mercier à Neuchâtel." In his *De Rousseau à Mirabeau: Pélérins de Môtiers et prophètes de '89* (Paris, 1936), 81–126.

Henriet, Maurice. "Trois lettres inédites de Sébastien Mercier." *Le Correspondant* 255 (1914): 383.

Hoffman, Paul. "L'Héritage des lumières: Mythes et modèles de la fémininité au XVIIIe siècle." *Romantisme: Revue du XIXe siècle,* 1976:7–23.

Hytier, Adrienne D. "The Decline of Military Values: The Theme of the Deserter in Eighteenth-Century French Literature." *Studies in Eighteenth-Century Culture* 11 (1982): 147–62.

Isherwood, Robert M. "Entertainment in the Parisian Fairs in the Eighteenth Century." *Journal of Modern History* 53 (1981): 24–48.

———. "Entertainment on the Parisian Boulevards in the Eighteenth Century." *Proceedings of the Eleventh Annual Meeting of the Western Society for French History,* 1984:142–52.

Jacob, Margaret C. "Freemasonry, Women, and the Paradox of the Enlightenment." *Women and History,* Spring 1984, no. 9:69–93.

Janes, R. M. "On the Reception of Mary Wollstonecraft's *A Vindication of the Rights of Women.*" *Journal of the History of Ideas,* April–June 1978:293–302.

Jimack, P. D. "The Paradox of Sophie and Julie: Contemporary Response to Rousseau's Ideal Wife and Ideal Mother." In Eva Jacobs et al., eds., *Women and Society in Eighteenth-Century France: Essays in Honor of J. S. Spink* (London, 1979), 152–65.

Kelly, George A. "The Political Thought of Lamoignon de Malesherbes." *Political Theory* 7, no. 4 (November 1979): 485–508.

Kleinbaum, Abby R. "Women in the Age of Light." In Renate Bridenthal and Claudia Koonz, eds., *Becoming Visible: Women in European History* (Boston, 1977), 217–35.

Lelièvre, Renée. "Un Trio de francs-maçons ignorés." *Dix-huitième Siècle* 8 (1976): 369–72.

Loche, M. "Journaux imprimés à Lyon, 1633–1794." *Le Vieux Papier,* 1968:259–84.

Lough, John. "Contemporary French Periodicals and the *Encyclopédie.*" In his *Essays on the Encyclopédie of Diderot and d'Alembert* (Oxford, 1968), 334–424.

———. "Women in Mercier's *Tableau.*" In Eva Jacobs et al., eds., *Women and Society in Eighteenth-Century France: Essays in Honor of J. S. Spink* (London, 1979), 110–22.

Lucas, Colin. "Nobles, Bourgeois, and the Origins of the French Revolution." *Past and Present* 60 (1973): 85–126.

Marion, Michel. "Dix ans des *Annonces, affiches, et avis divers* (1752–1761)." In Jacques Godechot, ed., *Regards sur l'histoire de la presse et de l'information: Mélanges offerts à Jean Prinet* (Saint-Julien-du-Sault, 1980), 23–41.

Martin, François. "L'Habitat parisien des Berthiers de Sauvigny, intendants de Paris au XVIIIe siècle." *Mémoires de la Société de l'histoire de Paris et de l'Ile de France* 101–2 (1974–75): 109–29.

Martin, Henri-Jean. "Pour une histoire de la lecture." *Revue française d'histoire du livre*, 1977:583–610.

Mason, H. T. "Women in Marivaux: Journalist to Dramatist." In Eva Jacobs et al., eds., *Women and Society in Eighteenth-Century France: Essays in Honor of J. S. Spink* (London, 1979), 42–54.

"Mathon de la Cour." *Archives historiques et statistiques du département du Rhône* 6 (1827): 295–315.

Mercier, Roger. "Le Peuple dans le théâtre de L.-S. Mercier." *Images du peuple au XVIIIe siècle: Colloque d'Aix-en-Provence, 25 et 26 octobre 1969* (Paris, 1973), 293–304.

Merland, Marie-Anne. "Tirage et vente de livres à la fin du XVIIIe siècle." *Revue française d'histoire du livre*, 1973:87–102.

Mornet, Daniel. "Sur l'intérêt historique des journaux littéraires au XVIIIe siècle et la diffusion du *Mercure de France*." *Bulletin de la Soicété d'histoire moderne*, avril 1910, no. 22:119–22.

Mylne, Vivienne. "The *Bibliotheque universelle des dames*, 1785–1797." In Eva Jacobs et al., eds., *Women and Society in Eighteenth-Century France: Essays in Honor of J. S. Spink* (London, 1979), 123–38.

Popkin, Jeremy D. "The French Revolutionary Press: New Findings and New Perspectives." *Eighteenth-Century Life* 5, no. 4 (1979): 90–104.

———"The *Gazette de Leyde* and French Politics under Louis XVI." In Jack R. Censer and Jeremy D. Popkin, eds., *Press and Politics in Pre-Revolutionary France* (Berkeley and Los Angeles, 1987), 75–132.

———. "The Newspaper Press in French Political Thought, 1789–99." *Studies in Eighteenth-Century Culture* 10 (1981): 113–35.

Ranum, Orest. "D'Alembert, Tacitus, and the Political Sociology of Despotism." *Studies on Voltaire and the Eighteenth Century* 191 (1980): 547–58.

Richet, Denis. "Autour des origines idéologiques lointaines de la Révolution française: Elites et despotisme." *Annales E.S.C.* 24 (1969): 1–23.

Rimbault, Caroline. "La Presse féminine de langue française au XVIIIe siècle: Production et diffusion." In Pierre Rétat, ed., *Le Journalisme d'ancien régime* (Lyons, 1981), 199–216.

Bibliography

Rustin, J. "Roman et destin, ou Les 'Caprices de la fortune' (Mme de Beaumer, 1760)." *Travaux de linguistique et de littérature* 4, no. 2 (1966): 59–73.

———. "Les 'Suites' de *Candide* au XVIIIe siècle." *Studies on Voltaire and the Eighteenth Century* 90 (1972): 1395–1416.

"'Saisies faites sur la demande de la communauté des libraires-imprimeurs de Paris, chez le sieur Deriaux, rue de Tournon.' Ce document conservé aux Archives nationales, Papiers du Châtelet, liasse 375." *L'Amateur d'autographes,* février 1882:19–22.

Sayous, A. "Excursions dans les journaux littéraires du XVIIIe siècle." *Bibliothèque universelle* 24 (1853): 246–69.

Smith, Peter Lester. "The Launching of the *Journal étranger* (1752–1754): The Problem of Audience." *Studies on Voltaire and the Eighteenth Century* 163 (1976): 117–27.

Starobinski, Jean. "Eloquence et liberté." *Schweizerische Zeitschrift für Geschichte* 26 (1976): 549–66.

Stewart, C. P. "The Huguenots Under Louis XV." *Proceedings of the Huguenot Society of London* 12, no. 1 (1920): 55–65.

Sullerot, Evelyne. "Lectrices et interlocutrices." *Europe,* novembre–décembre 1964:194–203.

Trénard, Louis. "La Presse française des origines à 1788." In Claude Bellanger et al., eds., *Histoire générale de la presse française* 1 (Paris, 1969): 27–402.

———. "La Presse périodique en Flandre au XVIIIe siècle." *Dix-huitième Siècle,* 1969:89–105; 1970:77–89.

Turgeon, F. K. "Fanny de Beauharnais: Biographical Notes and a Bibliography." *Modern Philology* 30 (1932–33): 61–80.

Van Dijk, Suzanne. "Femmes et journaux au XVIIIe siècle." *Australian Journal of French Studies* 18, no. 2 (1981): 164–78.

———. "*Journal des Dames* et journaux des hommes: La Notion *femme.*" In Jean Varloot and Paule Jansen, eds., *L'Année 1768 à travers la presse* (Paris, 1981), 80–101.

Vercruysse, Jéroom. "Journalistes et journaux à Bruxelles au XVIIIe siècle." In R. Mortier and H. Hasquin, eds., *Etudes sur le XVIIIe siècle* (Brussels, 1977), 4:117–27.

Watts, George. "Charles-Joseph Panckoucke: L'Atlas de la librairie française." *Studies on Voltaire and the Eighteenth Century* 68 (1969): 67–205.

Williams, David. "The Fate of French Feminism: Boudier de Villemert's *Ami des femmes.*" *Eighteenth-Century Studies* 14 (Fall 1980): 37–55.

———. "The Politics of Feminism in the French Enlightenment." In Peter Hughes and David Williams, eds., *The Varied Pattern: Studies in the Eighteenth Century* (Toronto, 1971), 333–51.

Bibliography

Zioutos, G. D. "La Presse et l'*Encyclopédie*." *Etudes de presse* 8 (1953): 318–21.

BOOKS

Abensour, Léon. *La Femme et le féminisme avant la Révolution*. Paris, 1923.
———. *Histoire générale du féminisme des origines à nos jours*. Paris, 1921.
Adburgham, Alison. *Women in Print: Writing Women and Women's Magazines from the Restoration to the Accession of Victoria*. London, 1972.
Albistur, Maïté, and Daniel Armogathe. *Histoire du féminisme français du moyen âge à nos jours*. Paris, 1977.
Angenot, Marc. *Les Champions des femmes: Examen du discours sur la supériorité des femmes, 1400–1800*. Quebec, 1977.
Ariès, Philippe. *Centuries of Childhood: A Social History of Family Life*. Trans. Robert Baldick. New York, 1962.
Ascomb, Frances. *Anglophobia in France, 1763–1789*. Durham, N.C., 1950.
Aubertin, Charles. *L'Esprit public au XVIIIe siècle*. Paris, 1889.
Badinter, Elisabeth. *L'Amour en plus: Histoire de l'amour maternel, XVIIIe–XXe siècles*. Paris, 1980.
———. *Emilie, Emilie: L'Ambition féminine au XVIIIe siècle*. Paris, 1983.
Bainville, Jacques. *Histoire de la France*. Vol. 1. Paris, 1924.
Balcou, J. *Fréron contre les philosophes*. Geneva and Paris, 1975.
Barber, Elinor G. *The Bourgeoisie in Eighteenth-Century France*. Princeton, 1955.
Barbier, A. A. *Dictionnaire des ouvrages anonymes*. 3d ed. 4 vols. Paris, 1872–79.
Bardèche, Maurice. *Histoire des femmes*. Paris, 1968.
Béclard, Léon. *Sébastien Mercier, sa vie, son oeuvre, son temps*. Paris, 1903.
Bédarida, Henri, and Paul Hazard. *L'Influence française en Italie au XVIIIe siècle*. Paris, 1934.
Belin, J. P. *Le Commerce des livres prohibés à Paris de 1750–1789*. Paris, 1913.
Bellanger, Claude, et al. *Histoire générale de la presse française*. 5 vols. Paris, 1969–74.
Belloc, Alexis. *Les Postes françaises*. Paris, 1886.
Berce, Yves-Marie. *Croquants et nu-pieds: Les Soulèvements paysans en France du XVIe au XIXe siècle*. Paris, 1974.
Bernier, Olivier. *The Eighteenth-Century Woman*. Garden City, 1981.
Bertaut, Jules. *La Vie littéraire au XVIIIe siècle*. Paris, 1954.
Biographie universelle, ancienne et moderne. Ed. M. Michaud. 45 vols. Paris, 1854.

Bibliography

Birn, Raymond F. *Pierre Rousseau and the Philosophes of Bouillon*. Studies on Voltaire and the Eighteenth Century, vol. 29. Geneva, 1964.

Blangonnet, Catherine. "Recherches sur les censeurs royaux et leur place dans la société au temps de Malesherbes (1750–1763)." Thèse de l'Ecole des Chartes, Paris, 1974.

Bollème, Geneviève, et al. *Livre et société dans la France du XVIIIe siècle*. Paris, 1965.

Bonnassies, Jules. *Les Auteurs dramatiques et la Comédie-Française aux XVIIe et XVIIIe siècles*. Paris, 1874.

———. *Les Spectacles forains et la Comédie-Française*. Paris, 1875.

Bonno, Gabriel. *La Constitution britannique devant l'opinion française de Montesquieu à Bonaparte*. New York, 1971.

Bourgin, Georges. *Essai sur la presse française: Bibliographie et archives*. Paris, 1936.

Boussy, M. T., et al. *Livre et société dans la France du XVIIIe siècle*. Paris, 1970.

Bouten, Jacob. *Mary Wollstonecraft and the Beginnings of Female Emancipation in France and England*. Amsterdam, 1922.

Brenner, Clarence. *Bibliographical List of Plays in the French Language (1700–1789)*. Berkeley, 1947.

Britsch, Amédée. *La Maison d'Orléans à la fin de l'ancien régime: La Jeunesse de Philippe Egalité (1747–1785)*. Paris, 1926.

Brun, D. "*L'Année littéraire*, 1754–1790." Thèse de l'Ecole des hautes études en sciences sociales, Paris, 1978.

Catalogue collectif des périodiques conservés dans les bibliothèques de Paris et les bibliothèques universitaires. 43 vols. Paris, 1940–62.

Censer, Jack R. *Prelude to Power: The Parisian Radical Press, 1789–1791*. Baltimore, 1976.

Censer, Jack R., and Jeremy D. Popkin, eds. *Press and Politics in Pre-Revolutionary France*. Berkeley and Los Angeles, 1987.

Charavay, Etienne. *Catalogue d'une belle collection de lettres autographes, 11 mai 1861*. Paris, 1861.

———. *Catalogue d'une belle et intéressante collection d'autographes, jeudi, 7 décembre 1865*. Paris, 1865.

———. *Revue des documents historiques, juin 1881*. 2d series, no. 30.

Chauveron, Edmond de. *Les Grands Procès de la Comédie-Française*. Paris, 1906.

Chevallier, Pierre. *Histoire de la franc-maçonnerie française*. Vol. 1, *La Maçonnerie: Ecole de l'égalité, 1725–1799*. Paris, 1974.

Chouillet, A. M., and François Moureau. *Suppléments au Dictionnaire des journalistes,* vol. 1 (Grenoble, 1980); vol. 2 (Grenoble, 1983); vol. 3 (Grenoble, 1984); vol. 4 (Grenoble, 1986).

Cioranescu, A. *Bibliographie de la littérature française du XVIIIe siècle*. 3 vols. Paris, 1969.

Correspondance du comte de Jaucourt, ministre intérimaire des affaires étrangères avec le prince de Talleyrand pendant le Congrès de Vienne, publiée par son petit-fils. Paris, 1905.

Couperus, Marianne, ed. *L'Etude des périodiques anciens: Colloque d'Utrecht*. Paris, 1971.

————. *Un Périodique français en Hollande: Le Glaneur historique (1731–1733)*. The Hague and Paris, 1971.

Couton, Georges. *Corneille et la Fronde: Théâtre et politique il y a trois siècles*. Clermont-Ferrand, 1951.

Coyecque, Ernest. *Inventaire de la collection Anisson-Duperron sur l'histoire de l'imprimerie et la librairie principalement à Paris*. 2 vols. Paris, 1900.

Cushing, Mary Gertrude. *Pierre Le Tourneur*. New York, 1908.

Dardigna, Anne-Marie. *La Presse "féminine": Fonction idéologique*. Paris, 1978.

Darnton, Robert. *The Business of Enlightenment*. Cambridge, Mass., 1979.

————. *The Great Cat Massacre and Other Episodes in French Cultural History*. New York, 1984.

————. *The Literary Underground of the Old Regime*. Cambridge, Mass., 1982.

————. *Mesmerism and the End of the Enlightenment in France*. New York, 1970.

Datz, P. *Histoire de la publicité depuis les temps les plus reculés jusqu'à nos jours*. Paris, 1894.

Decaux, Alain. *Histoire des Françaises*. Paris, 1972.

Delalain, Paul A. *Essai bibliographique de l'histoire de l'imprimerie typographique et de la librairie en France*. Paris, 1903. Reprint. Geneva, 1970.

Delandine, A. F. *Bibliothèque de Lyon: Catalogue des livres qu'elle renferme dans la classe des belles-lettres*. Paris and Lyons, n.d.

Desnoiresterres, Gustave. *Le Chevalier Dorat et les poètes légers au XVIIIe siècle*. Paris, 1887.

Dictionary of Italian Literature. Ed. Peter Dondanella et al. Westport, Conn., 1979.

Doyle, William. *Origins of the French Revolution*. New York, 1980.

————. *The Parlement of Bordeaux and the End of the Old Regime, 1771–1790*. New York, 1974.

Dufresne, Hélène. *Erudition et esprit public au XVIIIe siècle: Le Bibliothécaire Hubert-Pascal Ameilhon (1736–1811)*. Paris, 1962.

Duhet, Paule-Marie. *Les Femmes et la Révolution, 1789–1794*. Paris, 1971.

Dumas, J. B. *Histoire de l'Académie royale des sciences, belles-lettres, et arts de Lyon*. 2 vols. Lyons, 1839.

Bibliography

Durand, Yves. *Les Fermiers généraux au XVIIIe siècle*. Paris, 1971.

Echeverria, Durand. *Mirage in the West: A History of the French Image of American Society to 1815*. Princeton, 1957.

Egret, Jean. *The French Pre-Revolution*. Trans. Wesley D. Camp. Chicago, 1977.

———. *Louis XV et l'opposition parlementaire*. Paris, 1970.

Eisenstein, Elizabeth L. *The Printing Press as an Agent of Change: Communications and Cultural Transformations in Early Modern Europe*. 2 vols. Cambridge, 1979.

Faber, Frédéric. *Un Libelliste au XVIIIe siècle: J. F. Bastide en Belgique, 1766–68*. Brussels, 1880.

Falk, Henri. *Les Privilèges de libraire sous l'ancien régime: Etude historique du conflit des droits sur l'oeuvre littéraire*. Paris, 1960.

Fauchery, P. *La Destinée féminine dans le roman européen du XVIIIe siècle*. Paris, 1972.

Faure, Edgar. *La Disgrâce de Turgot*. Paris, 1961.

Faÿ, Bernard. *The Revolutionary Spirit in France and America*. Trans. Ramon Guthrie. New York, 1927.

Febvre, Lucien, and Henri-Jean Martin. *L'Apparition du livre*. Paris, 1958.

Feyel, Gilles. *La Gazette à travers ses réimpressions en province, 1631–1752*. Amsterdam, 1982.

Friedman, Leonard M. "The Nature and Role of Women as Conceived by Representative Authors of Eighteenth-Century France." Ph.D. diss., New York University, 1970.

Fritz, Paul, and Richard Morton, eds. *Woman in the Eighteenth Century and Other Essays*. Toronto and Sarasota, 1976.

Funck-Brentano, Frantz. *Figaro et ses devanciers*. Paris, 1909.

———. *Les Nouvellistes*. Paris, 1905.

Furet, François. *Penser la Révolution française*. Paris, 1978.

Furet, François, and Jacques Ozouf. *Lire et écrire*. 2 vols. Paris, 1977.

Gaiffe, Félix. *Le Drame en France au XVIIIe siècle*. Paris, 1910.

Gay, Jules. *Bibliographie des ouvrages relatifs à l'amour, aux femmes, aux mariages, etc*. 4th ed. 4 vols. Paris, 1894–1900.

Gelbart, Nina Rattner. "Science in Enlightenment Utopias: Power and Purpose in Eighteenth-Century French 'Voyages imaginaires.'" Ph.D. dissertation, University of Chicago, 1974.

Gilot, Michel, and Jean Sgard, eds. *Inventaire de la presse classique (1600–1789)*. Grenoble, 1978.

Goncourt, Edmond, et Jules Goncourt. *La Femme au XVIIIe siècle*. Paris, 1882.

Grand-Mesnil, Marie-Noëlle. *Mazarin, la Fronde, et la presse, 1647–1649*. Paris, 1967.

Bibliography

Grente, G., ed. *Dictionnaire des lettres françaises, XVIIIe siècle.* 2 vols. Paris, 1960.

Grosclaude, M. *Malesherbes, témoin et interprète de son temps.* Paris, 1962.

————. *La Vie intellectuelle à Lyon dans la deuxième moitié du XVIIIe siècle.* Paris, 1933.

Hallays-Dabot, Victor. *Histoire de la censure théâtrale en France.* Paris, 1862.

Hampson, Norman. *Will and Circumstance: Montesquieu, Rousseau, and the French Revolution.* London, 1983.

Harris, Ann Sutherland, and Linda Nochlin. *Women Artists, 1550–1950.* Los Angeles, 1976.

Hatin, Eugène. *Bibliographie historique et critique de la presse périodique française.* Paris, 1866.

————. *Les Gazettes de Hollande et la presse clandestine au XVIIe et XVIIIe siècles.* Paris, 1865.

————. *Histoire du journal en France* 2d ed. Paris, 1853.

————. *Histoire politique et littéraire de la presse en France.* 8 vols. Paris, 1859–61.

————. *Manuel historique et critique de la liberté de la presse.* Paris, 1869.

Hauvette, Henri. *Littérature italienne.* Paris, 1932.

Hazard, Paul. *The European Mind.* Cleveland and New York, 1963.

Henriot, E. *Livres et Portraits.* 3d series. Paris, 1927.

Hermann-Mascard, Nicole. *La Censure des livres à Paris à la fin de l'ancien régime (1750–1789).* Paris, 1968.

Hoffmann, Paul. *Histoire du feminisme français du moyen âge à nos jours.* Paris, 1977.

Inklar, D. *François-Thomas de Baculard d'Arnaud: Ses imitateurs en Hollande et dans d'autres pays.* Paris, 1925.

Jacob, Margaret C. *The Radical Enlightenment: Pantheists, Freemasons, and Republicans.* London, 1981.

Jacobs, Eva, et al., eds. *Women and Society in Eighteenth-Century France: Essays in Honor of J. S. Spink.* London, 1979.

Jal, Auguste. *Dictionnaire critique de biographie et d'histoire.* Paris, 1867.

Jansen, Paule, et al., eds. *L'Année 1778 à travers la presse traitée par ordinateur.* Paris, 1982.

Johansson, J. Victor. *Sur la Correspondance littéraire secrète et son éditeur.* Paris, 1960.

Jordan, David P. *The King's Trial: Louis XVI vs. the French Revolution.* Berkeley and Los Angeles, 1979.

Jourdain, Eleanor F. *Dramatic Theory and Practice in France (1690–1808).* London, 1921.

Jourdain, Isambert, Decrusy, eds. *Recueil général des anciennes lois françaises.* 29 vols. Paris, 1822–33.

Bibliography

Jovicevich, Alexander. *Jean-François de La Harpe, adepte et renégat des lumières.* South Orange, N.J., 1973.

Joynes, D. Carroll. "Jansenists and Ideologues: Opposition Theory in the Parlement of Paris." Ph.D. diss., Univ. of Chicago, 1981.

Keohane, Nannerl O. *Philosophy and the State in France.* Princeton, 1980.

Klaits, Joseph. *Printed Propaganda under Louis XVI: Absolute Monarchy and Public Opinion.* Princeton, 1976.

Kleinert, Annemarie. *Die frühen Modejournale in Frankreich.* Berlin, 1980.

Knachel, Philip A. *England and the Fronde.* Ithaca, 1967.

Krull, Edith. *Das Wirken der Frau im frühen deutschen Zeitschriftenwesen.* Berlin, 1939.

Laboulaye, Edouard de, and G. Guiffrey. *La Propriété littéraire au XVIIIe siècle.* Paris, 1859.

Lachèvre, Frédéric. *Bibliographie sommaire de l'Almanach des muses (1765–1833).* Paris, 1928.

Lacour, Leopold. *Les Origines du féminisme contemporain: Trois femmes de la Révolution: Olympe de Gouges, Théroigne de Méricourt, Rose Lacombe.* Paris, 1900.

Las Vergnas, R. *Le Chevalier Rutlidge, "gentilhomme anglais."* Paris, 1932.

Ledré, Charles. *Histoire de la presse.* Paris, 1958.

Lee, Vera. *The Reign of Women in Eighteenth-Century France.* Cambridge, Mass., 1975.

Lenardon, D. *Index du Journal encyclopédique, 1756–1793.* Geneva, 1976.

Levy, Darline Gay. *The Ideas and Careers of Simon-Nicolas-Henri Linguet: A Study in Eighteenth-Century French Politics.* Urbana, 1980.

Levy, Darline Gay, H. B. Applewhite, and M. D. Johnson. *Women in Revolutionary Paris, 1789–1795.* Urbana, 1979.

Li, Dzeh Djen. "La Presse féministe en France de 1869 à 1914." Thèse de doctorat d'Université, Paris, 1934.

Lioure, Michel. *Le Drame.* Paris, 1963.

Livois, René de. *Histoire de la presse française.* 2 vols. Lausanne, 1965.

Loménie, Louis de. *Beaumarchais et son temps.* 2 vols. Paris, 1856.

Lougee, Carolyn C. *Le Paradis des femmes: Women, Salons, and Social Stratification in Seventeenth-Century France.* Princeton, 1976.

Lough, John. *Introduction of Eighteenth-Century France.* London, 1960.

———. *Paris Theatre Audiences in the Seventeenth and Eighteenth Centuries.* London, 1965.

———. *Seventeenth-Century French Drama: The Background.* London, 1979.

———. *Writer and Public in France from the Middle Ages to the Present Day.* Oxford, 1978.

Luppe, A. de. *Les Jeunes Filles dans l'aristocratie et la bourgeoisie à la fin du XVIIIe siècle*. Paris, 1924.

Madelin, Louis. *Une Révolution manquée: La Fronde*. Paris, 1931.

Manne, E. D., and C. Ménétrier. *Galerie historique des acteurs français, mimes et paradistes*. Lyons, 1877.

―――. *Galerie historique des comédiens de la troupe de Nicolet*. Lyons, 1869.

Mannheim, Karl. *Ideology and Utopia: An Introduction to the Sociology of Knowledge*. Trans. L. Wirth and E. Shils. New York, 1936.

Manuel, Frank. *The Eighteenth Century Confronts the Gods*. Cambridge, Mass., 1959.

Marion, Marcel. *Dictionnaire des institutions de la France au XVIIe et XVIIIe siècles*. Paris, 1923.

Marquiset, A. *Les Bas-Bleus de Premier Empire*. Paris, 1913.

Martin, Angus, Vivienne Milne, and Richard Frautschi. *Bibliographie du genre romanesque français, 1751–1800*. London and Paris, 1977.

Martin, Henri-Jean. *Livre, pouvoirs, et société à Paris au XVIIIe siècle*. 2 vols. Geneva, 1969.

Martin, Henri-Jean, and Roger Chartier. *Histoire de l'édition française*. 2 vols. Paris, 1984.

Martin, Marc. *Les Origines de la presse militaire en France à la fin de l'ancien régime et sous la Révolution (1700–1799)*. Vincennes, 1975.

Maupeou, J. de. *Le Chancelier Maupeou*. Paris, 1942.

Mitton, Fernand. *La Presse française des origines à la Révolution*. 2 vols. Paris, 1943–45.

Mongrédien, Georges. *Cyrano de Bergerac*. Paris, 1964.

Moore, Alexander P. *The "Genre poissard" and the French Stage of the Eighteenth Century*. New York, 1935.

Moote, A. Lloyd. *The Revolt of the Judges: The Parlement of Paris and the Fronde, 1643–1652*. Princeton, 1971.

Mornet, Daniel. *Les Origines intellectuelles de la Révolution française*. Paris, 1933.

Morris, Madeleine F. *Le Chevalier de Jaucourt: Un Ami de la terre (1704–1780)*. Geneva, 1979.

Morton, B. N., ed. *Correspondance de Beaumarchais*. 3 vols. Paris, 1969–73.

Moulinas, René. *L'Imprimerie, la librairie, et la presse à Avignon au XVIIIe siècle*. Grenoble, 1974.

Moureau, François. *Le Mercure galant de Dufresny (1710–1714), ou Le Journalisme à la mode*. Studies on Voltaire and the Eighteenth Century, vol. 206. Oxford, 1982.

Paget, Violet [Vernon Lee, pseud.]. *Studies on the Eighteenth Century in Italy*. London, 1907.

Pappas, John N. *Berthier's Journal de Trévoux and the Philosophes*. Geneva, 1957.

Parker, Harold T. *The Cult of Antiquity and the French Revolutionaries*. Chicago, 1937.

Parny, Evariste de. *Oeuvres*. Ed. A. J. Pons. Paris, 1862.

Patouillet, Louise. *L'Emancipation des femmes et la presse en France jusqu'en 1870*. Paris, 1928.

Payer, Alice de. *Le Féminisme au temps de la Fronde*. Paris, 1922.

Payne, Harry. *The Philosophes and the People*. New Haven, 1976.

Pellisson, Maurice. *Les Hommes de lettres au XVIIIe siècle*. Paris, 1911.

Piettre, Monique A. *La Condition féminine à travers les âges*. Paris, 1974.

Pilon, Edmond. *La Vie de famille au XVIIIe siècle*. Paris, 1923.

Pollitzer, Marcel. *Les Amazones de la Fronde et le quadrille des intrigants*. Paris, 1959.

Pottinger, David T. *The French Booktrade in the Ancien Régime*. Cambridge, Mass., 1958.

Proust, Jacques. "Introduction" to Diderot's *Mémoire sur la liberté de la presse*. Paris, 1964.

Quéniart, Jean. *L'Imprimerie et la librairie à Rouen au XVIIIe siècle*. Paris, 1970.

Quérard, J. M. *La France littéraire, ou Dictionnaire bibliographique*. 12 vols. Paris, 1827–64.

———. *Les Supercheries littéraires dévoilées*. 5 vols. Paris, 1847–53.

Rabbe, Alphonse. *Biographie universelle et portative des contemporains*. 5 vols. Paris, 1834.

Ranum, Orest. *Paris in the Age of Absolutism: An Essay*. New York, 1968.

Ravaisson, F. *Archives de la Bastille, documents inédits*. 19 vols. Paris, 1866.

Rétat, Pierre. *L'Attentat de Damiens: Discours sur l'événement au XVIIIe siècle*. Lyons, 1982.

———, ed. *Le Journalisme d'ancien régime*. Lyons, 1982.

Ribbe, Charles de. *Un Journal et un journaliste à Aix avant la Révolution: Etude de moeurs sur la ville d'Aix vers la fin du XVIIIe siècle*. Aix, 1859.

Ricard, Antoine. *Une Victime de Beaumarchais: Marin*. Paris, 1885.

Rimbault, Caroline. "La Presse féminine de langue française au XVIIIe siècle: Place de la femme, système de la mode." Thèse de l'Ecole des hautes études en sciences sociales, Paris, 1981.

Rives-Childs, J. *Restif de la Bretonne: Témoignage et jugement—bibliographie*. Paris, 1949.

Robert, Paul. *Dictionnaire alphabétique et analogique de la langue française*. 6 vols. Paris, 1951.

Roche, Daniel. *Le Peuple de Paris: Essai sur la culture populaire au XVIIIe siècle*. Paris, 1981.

Bibliography

————. *Le Siècle des lumières en province: Académies et académiciens provinciaux, 1680–1789*. 2 vols. Paris, 1978.

Roth, G., ed. *Les Pseudo-Mémoires de Mme d'Epinay: Histoire de Mme de Montbrillant*. 3 vols. Paris, 1951.

Rothkrug, Lionel. *Opposition to Louis XIV: The Political and Social Origins of the French Enlightenment*. Princeton, 1965.

Rudé, George. *The Crowd in the French Revolution*. Oxford, 1967.

Sgard, Jean. *Dictionnaire des journalistes*. Grenoble, 1976.

————. *La Presse provinciale au XVIIIe siècle*. Grenoble, 1983.

Sgard, Jean, and Michel Gilot. *Inventaire de la presse classique*. Grenoble, 1978.

Sgard, Jean, and Pierre Rétat, eds. *Presse et histoire au XVIIIe siècle*. Paris, 1978.

Shaw, Edward P. *Problems and Policies of Malesherbes as Directeur de la librairie in France (1750–1763)*. Albany, 1966.

Solomon, Howard M. *Public Welfare, Science, and Propaganda in Seventeenth-Century France: The Innovations of Théophraste Renaudot*. Princeton, 1972.

Spencer, Samia I., ed. *French Women and the Age of Enlightenment*. Bloomington, 1984.

Stone, Bailey. *The Parlement of Paris, 1774–1789*. Chapel Hill, 1981.

Sullerot, Evelyne. *Histoire de la presse féminine en France des origines à 1848*. Paris, 1966.

————. *La Presse féminine*. Paris, 1963.

Tate, Robert S. *Petit de Bachaumont: His Circle and the Mémoires secrets*. Studies on Voltaire and the Eighteenth Century, vol. 65. Geneva, 1968.

Trénard, Louis. *Lyon de l'Encyclopédie au pré-romantisme*. 2 vols. Paris, 1958.

Trésor de la langue française: Dictionnaire de la langue du XIXe et XXe siècles. Ed. Paul Imbs. 11 vols. Paris, 1971–.

Tromp, E. "Organisation de l'histoire de la communauté des libraires-imprimeurs de Paris, 1618–1791." Thèse, Nîmes, 1922.

Tucoo-Chala, Suzanne. *Charles-Joseph Panckoucke et la librairie française*. Pau and Paris, 1975.

Turgeon, F. K. "Fanny de Beauharnais." Ph.D. diss., Harvard University, 1929. Typed version, Harvard University Library, 1963.

Vaillé, Eugène. *Histoire générale des postes françaises*. 6 vols. Paris, 1951–53.

Vallas, Léon. *La Musique à l'Académie de Lyon au XVIIIe siècle*. Lyons, 1908.

Van Kley, Dale. *The Damiens Affair and the Unravelling of the Old Regime*. Princeton, 1983.

Bibliography

————. *The Jansenists and the Expulsion of the Jesuits from France, 1757–1765.* New Haven and London, 1975.

Varin d'Ainvelle, Madeleine. *La Presse en France: Genèse et évolution de ses fonctions psycho-sociales.* Paris, 1965.

Varloot, Jean, and Paule Jansen, eds. *L'Année 1768 à travers la presse traitée par ordinateur.* Paris, 1981.

Villiers, Marc de. *Histoire des clubs de femmes et des légions d'amazones.* Paris, 1910.

Vingtrinier, A. *Histoire des journaux de Lyon depuis leur origine jusqu'à nos jours.* Lyons, 1852.

Walter, Gérard-Louis. *Hébert et le père Duchesne.* Paris, 1946.

Weill, Georges. *Le Journal: Origines, évolution, et rôle de la presse périodique.* Paris, 1934.

Westrich, Sal. *The Ormée of Bordeaux: A Revolution During the Fronde.* Baltimore, 1972.

White, Cynthia. *Women's Magazines, 1693–1968.* London, 1970.

Zephir, Micheline. "Les Libraires et imprimeurs parisiens à la fin du XVIIIe siècle (1750–1789)." Thèse de l'Ecole des Chartes, Paris, 1974.

Index

Unless otherwise identified (by an author's name or by type of publication), italicized titles are those of journals. Within entries, *JD* refers to the *Journal des Dames*.

331

Index

Ogier (theater critic), 20

Olinde et Sophronie (Mercier), 175, 214

Opéra, 278

Opposition press. See *Frondeur* journalism

Orangeism, 108

Orléans, Anne Marie Louis d' (*la grande mademoiselle* de Montpensier), as second Joan of Arc, 18

Orléans, duc d' (Louis Philippe d'Orléans), 215

Orléans, Philippe d' (Philippe II; regent), 21

Orléans, Philippe d' (Philippe-Egalité). *See* Chartres, duc de

Orléans princes, 24, 175. *See also* Princes of the blood

Ormée of Bordeaux, revolt of, 20

Ormoy, Mme d' (editor), 85n, 299

Ouessant, Battle of, 287

Padua, academy at, 127

Paine, Thomas, 273, 300

Painters. *See* Art criticism; Female painters

Palais royal, 171; district of, 133–34; as *frondeur* locale, 275, 287

Palissot de Montenoy, Charles: vs. Mathon, 166; and Mercier, 166, 223–24

Panckoucke, Charles Joseph, 140–41, 173, 173n, 259, 262, 278n, 286; and Dorat, 248, 249, 250, 259, 274, 276, 279; and *JD*, 140–41, 153, 156–57, 249, 258, 270, 274, 276, 280; journalistic takeover by, 277–84 passim, 289; vs. Linguet, 244, 245, 246, 263; vs. Rutledge, 285

Paris, 1, 44, 55, 61, 70, 71, 115, 119, 124, 127, 146, 180, 185, 210, 212, 215, 253, 254, 260, 261, 264, 271, 287, 289, 306; all-male academies of, 54, 296–97; "les boulevards," 123–24; carriages criticized, 198; faubourg Saint Germain, 124; *frondeur* press in, xiv, xv, 32–33; Grande Loge, 168; "Hôtel des Huguenots," 124; Hôtel de Soisson, 110; Hôtel de Soubise, 100;

inhabitants as haughty, 146, 158; journal readership in, 32–33, 42, 112–13; Loge de la Cité, 110; prices in, 33, 67, 114, 197; provincial writers in, 39–40; *quartier* of Saint Avoye, 133, 134; *quartier* of Saint Benoît ("Latin Quarter"), 196, 230; rue d'Enfer, 267; rue de Petits Champs, 87; rue du Fouare, 196–97; rue Mêlée, 123; rue Saint Antoine, 39–40; rue Saint Honoré, 133, 134; as vampire, 160. *See also* Bastille; Louvre; Palais Royal; Temple; Tuileries

Paris, archbishop of. *See* Beaumont, Christophe de

Paris, Peace of, xvi, 128

Paris parlement, as refuge for Mercier, 218–19, 226

Parlement(s), 193, 245, 247, 295, 299; conflicts with Crown, 20, 21, 24–25, 27, 28, 31, 113, 151, 158, 168, 169, 171, 174, 228; dissolved, 28, 214; *frondeurs* abandoned by, 283–84; and Jansenism, 24; and Mercier case, 228; recalled, xvii, 29, 197, 220, 227–28; revolt against, 20. *See also* Bordeaux parlement; Normandy parlement; Paris parlement

Parnasse des dames, criticized, 190

Paternity suits, 302

Patriotism, 24; ceremonies to inspire, 167; of Du Rozoi, 125; *frondeur,* 298; Mme de Beaumer quoted on, 119, 120; motherhood and, 188, 191; surge of, 151–52

Pau, academy at, 127

Payne, Harry, 32

Paysan perverti (Restif de la Bretonne), 240

Peace of Paris, xvi, 128

Peasants, extolled, 22, 191. *See also* Social classes, lower

Pellegrin, abbé, 119

Penseur, Le (also known as *Le Journal de Bruxelles*), 254; pirating of by, 165–66

Pensions: literary, 5, 26, 50, 52, 117, 136, 151, 154, 237, 305; proprietary, 156; thespian, 215

349

Index

Père de famille, Le (Diderot), 53, 92, 209
Père Duchesne, Le, 242
Petite bourgeoisie, education for, 155–56. *See also* Third Estate
Petit magasin des dames, 205
Pezant (mayor of Villefranche), 68, 68n
Pezay, marquis de (Jacques Masson), as rake, 269
Phèdre (Racine), debunked by Mercier, 229
Philosophes, 40, 246; as adversaries, 7, 12, 66, 232, 253, 282, 284, 297; alliance with royalty, 150–51; vs. Campigneulles, 40, 52, 53, 56, 61–64, 65, 66; disdain for populace, 32; and Dorat, 251, 252, 254, 256, 258–60, 263, 271; *drames* denounced by, 297–98; and feminism, 22, 30, 142; vs. *frondeurs*, 30, 31, 221–22, 232, 241; and journalism, 30–31; vs. Mathon, 159–60; vs. Mercier, 221–22; publications of, 7, 30, 31
Physiocracy, 168, 170
Physiocrats, 161, 162
Physics, for women, 108. *See also* Science
Pidansat de Mairobert, Mathieu-François, 171n, 173n, 176, 177, 218n, 221n, 225, 237, 240, 242, 243, 249, 252n, 256, 277, 286; as censor, 172, 220, 221, 230, 238, 240, 265; concern over state control of press, 277, 281; criticizes *JD*, 195; Dorat scorned by, 250, 256, 263, 264; doubles as censor and writer, 24; on Le Camus, 277; Le Fuel admired by, 238–39; on mindless journalism, 262, 263; as *nouvelliste*, 172; and Rutlidge, 285; suicide of, 283, 284, 285; warns of purge of *frondeurs*, 243–44
—quoted: on *L'An 2440*, 211; on Coqueley, 238; on Dorat's worthless books, 256n; on Du Rozoi, 230n; on harm of censorship, 172; on *Journal des théâtres*, 239; on women in Masonic lodges, 287

Pièces fugitives, in *JD*, 36, 59–60, 64, 157, 166–67
Pièces fugitives de M. de Voltaire, de M. Desmahis, et de quelques autres auteurs (anthology), 63
Piquet, Christophe, as liberal censor, 121, 122
Pitt, Mlle (sister of William Pitt), 276
Playwrights, social responsibility of, 209, 216–17. *See also* Female playwrights
Plessis-Mornay, Philippe de, 124
Poésies et oeuvres diverses (Guibert), 145, 145n
Poésies et oeuvres diverses (Louptière), 86
Poetry: honoring Louis XV, 136, 151; as suitable pursuit for women, 42, 56
Poissard types, 14, 103; plays about, 103–4, 218
Police, 41, 131, 171, 195, 198, 202, 211, 217, 244, 263, 273, 300; and *JD*, 1–2, 87, 176, 252, 274, 275; vs. Mercier, 211, 217, 225–26. *See also* Hémery, Joseph d'; Sartine, Gabriel de
Political activism: art as, 158; of women, 18, 19, 22, 35, 36, 293, 301, 302; women as unfit for, 142, 194. *See also* Fronde; *Frondeur* journalism
Pompadour, Mme de (Jeanne Antoinette Poisson), 52, 117, 125, 134, 148; as benefactress, 147–48
Popkin, Jeremy D., xv, 33
Populism, in *frondeur* press, 16
Portugal, 111
Pothiers, Robert-Joseph, 202
Pouilly, Charles, 126
Poullain de la Barre, François, 94, 292
Poultier d'Elmotte, François-Martin (actor, writer), on disgust with Dorat, 263
Praslin, duc de, 113n
Précieuses, 77, 106, 126, 241; disdain for *drames*, 298; vs. *frondeuses*, 35–36
Press: fight for freedom of, xvi, xvii, 192–93, 219, 223, 281, 289–91,

350

Index